Congressional
Procedures
and the
Policy Process

WALTER J. OLESZEK

Congressional Procedures and the Policy Process

SEVENTH EDITION

A DIVISION OF CONGRESSIONAL QUARTERLY INC.
WASHINGTON, D.C.

CQ Press
1255 22nd Street, NW, Suite 400
Washington, DC 20037

Phone: 202-729-1900; toll-free, 1-866-4CQ-PRESS (1-866-427-7737)

Web: www.cqpress.com

Cover design: Blue Bungalow Design

⊚ The paper used in this publication exceeds the requirements of the American National
Standard for Information Sciences—Permanence of Paper for Printed Library Materials, ANSI
Z39.48-1992.

Printed and bound in the United States of America

11   10   09   08   07   1   2   3   4   5

Library of Congress Cataloging-in-Publication Data

Oleszek, Walter J.
  Congressional procedures and the policy process / Walter J. Oleszek. — 7th ed.
    p. cm.
  Includes bibliographical references and index.
  ISBN-13: 978-0-87289-303-0 (alk. paper)
  ISBN-10: 0-87289-303-0 (alk. paper)
  1. United States. Congress—Rules and practice. 2. Legislation—United States.
3. Parliamentary practice—United States. I. Title.

  KF4937.O44 2007
  328.73--dc22

                                2007002110

For Janet, Mark, and Eric

Contents

Tables, Figures, and Boxes

BOXES

Preface

CONGRESS IS constantly adapting to change. New procedures, processes, and practices come about in response to developing conditions and circumstances. Some procedural innovations are incorporated formally into the rules of the House or Senate; others evolve informally. For all their variability over time, the rules of the House and Senate are constant in this sense: they establish the procedural context within which individual members and the two chambers raise issues and make—or avoid making—decisions. Members of Congress must rely on rules and procedures to expedite or delay legislation, to secure enactment of a law, or to defeat a bill.

Congressional Procedures and the Policy Process was first published in 1978, in the aftermath of major changes that affected legislative decision making and the political system. The result of many of these developments on Capitol Hill was to diffuse policymaking influence widely throughout Congress. Six years later, when the second edition appeared, the House and Senate had undergone further procedural transformations. The House, for instance, began gavel-to-gavel television coverage of its floor proceedings. The third edition was published in the late 1980s. By then, the Senate also had begun gavel-to-gavel television coverage of its floor proceedings. Furthermore, Congress had revamped its budgetary practices with the enactment of Gramm-Rudman-Hollings I and II; the House Rules Committee had crafted unique new rules for regulating floor decision making; and greater use had been made of comprehensive bills, or packages, to process much of Congress's annual workload. One effect of these and other changes was to recentralize authority in fewer legislative hands.

The fourth edition was updated during another time of momentous change on Capitol Hill. After forty years as the "permanent minority," Republicans captured control of the House in the November 1994 elections and reclaimed control of the Senate as well. The fifth edition, published in 2001, examined many of the rules and practices introduced on Capitol Hill by the Republican majority and the new fiscal environment of surpluses, not deficits. The sixth edition, published in 2004, focused on a number of significant procedural and political developments that shaped the lawmaking process, such as the return of fiscal deficits, innovative rules from the House Rules Committee, and attempts to change the Senate's cloture rule.

This new, seventh edition is published during another period of major change on Capitol Hill. For the first time in a dozen years, congressional Democrats are in charge of both chambers as a result of the November

2006 elections. What makes the 110th Congress (2007–2009) especially significant, in addition to important procedural and agenda changes, is the election of the first female in congressional history—Nancy Pelosi of California—to be Speaker of the House, the highest elective post ever held by a woman in American history. As a history-maker, Speaker Pelosi will be under intense scrutiny from her colleagues, the minority party, the president, the media, and many others as she employs the formidable procedural and political resources of her high office to address the country's pressing issues.

The fundamental objective of *Congressional Procedures and the Policy Process* is to discuss how Congress makes laws and how its rules and procedures shape domestic and foreign policy. The theme of the book is that the interplay of rules, procedures, precedents, and strategies is vital to understanding how Congress works. I emphasize the rules and procedures most significant to congressional lawmaking; I do not attempt to survey all the rules and procedures used by Congress.

Every chapter of the seventh edition has been revised to incorporate new developments and insights. Chapter 1 presents an overall view of the congressional process. Chapter 2 examines Congress's budget process, which shapes much of the legislative decision making.

Chapter 3 turns to the initial steps of the legislative process—the introduction of legislation, referral of bills to House and Senate committees, and committee action on measures. Chapter 4 explains how legislation that has emerged from committee is scheduled for floor consideration in the House. Chapter 5 then examines the main features of floor decision making in the House. Chapter 6 puts the spotlight on the Senate, with discussion of how legislation is scheduled in that chamber. Senate floor action is the subject of Chapter 7.

Chapter 8 describes how House-Senate differences are reconciled when each chamber passes a different version of the same bill and then discusses the president's veto power. Chapter 9 deals with how Congress monitors the implementation of the laws it has passed. Finally, Chapter 10 reexamines the legislative process, pulling together the major themes of the book.

Anyone who writes seven editions of a book is intellectually indebted to numerous scholars and colleagues, and I welcome the opportunity to acknowledge their generous advice and assistance. Let me start with the talented and consummate professionals associated with CQ Press. Anna Socrates, both manuscript editor and production editor for this edition, did a careful and thorough job of reviewing the manuscript and contributed greatly to the book's readability. She made the final product much better than it would have been without her skillful assistance. Charisse Kiino, the acquisitions editor, was in charge of ensuring that deadlines were met. She carried out her assignment in a helpful and effective manner. Finally, my sincere appreciation goes to Brenda Carter, director of the college division, who encouraged and helped me with this book over the years.

Much credit for whatever understanding I have of the congressional process goes to my colleagues at the Congressional Research Service (CRS). Over the years I have learned the intricacies of the House and Senate from scores of current and former CRS associates. Their research endeavors have expanded my understanding of Congress's role and responsibilities. I especially want to acknowledge Mildred Amer, Stanley Bach, Richard Beth, Colton Campbell, Christopher Davis, Paul Dwyer, Louis Fisher, William Heniff, Frederick Kaiser, Robert Keith, Michael Koempel, Elizabeth Palmer, Morton Rosenberg, Paul Rundquist, Elizabeth Rybicki, Richard Sachs, James Saturno, Judy Schneider, Stephen Stathis, and Sylvia Streeter. CRS, I should note, bears no responsibility whatsoever for the views or interpretations expressed within these pages. I must also emphasize that whatever errors remain in this book are mine alone.

I also want to gratefully acknowledge the legislative contributions and accomplishments of my late colleague, Thomas P. Carr, whose untimely passing is a major loss to CRS and to the U.S. Congress. Tom was an outstanding researcher, a colleague always willing and able to offer superb professional advice and assistance, a gifted teacher and raconteur, and someone who brought friendship, fellowship, and good humor to all fortunate to know and work with him. The legacy of his many CRS reports remains a treasure trove of valuable insight and analysis to everyone interested in the workings of the congressional process.

I am indebted also to scores of past and present House and Senate members and professional congressional aides who have shared ideas and observations and deepened my understanding of the legislative process. My deep gratitude goes to all the parliamentarians of the House and Senate for trying to improve my understanding of Congress's procedural intricacies.

In addition, I am grateful to numerous colleagues in academia who have created, with their research studies, a reservoir of knowledge about congressional activities and operations. Here I would like especially to acknowledge my longtime collaborators in various projects—Roger H. Davidson, C. Lawrence Evans, and James Thurber—who are always generous with their time and who provide excellent suggestions. My intellectual debt also extends to Donald R. Wolfensberger, director of the Congress Project at the Woodrow Wilson International Center for Scholars and former staff director of the House Rules Committee, and veteran House staffer Matt Pinkus, for their parliamentary advice over the years. I would also like to thank the reviewers of this edition: C. Lawrence Evans, College of William and Mary; Jamie Pimlott, University of Florida; and Jason Roberts, University of Minnesota.

Finally, I dedicate this seventh edition to family members—Janet, Mark, and Eric. They provided a loving and encouraging home environment, patience, and support throughout preparation of every edition.

Walter J. Oleszek
Fairfax, Virginia

CHAPTER 1

Congress and Lawmaking

ONGRESSIONAL RULES and procedures are a complex mix of intricate features that can be used to expedite, slow down, or stop action on legislation. Adroit lawmakers may influence how expeditiously legislation moves through Congress, but in doing so they must navigate around procedural obstacles. This legislative reality typically means that measures move slowly through the congressional maze, or sometimes not at all. At times members can employ procedures that will accelerate even controversial measures through the usually slow-moving Congress. Too much haste in passing major legislation can sometimes have profound and unforeseen implications, as illustrated by Senate passage in 2002 of a joint resolution authorizing a U.S.-led invasion of Iraq as the central front in the war on terror. The preemptive war against Iraq continues to divide the country, and critics argue that the Senate, which prides itself as our greatest deliberative body, fell short in thoroughly analyzing the predictions, plans, and prospects for success in Iraq. Today, with Iraq confronting sectarian violence and a host of other problems, Congress and the White House are striving to develop a workable strategy—with advice from a number of entities, such as the Iraq Study Group—that would allow our troops to disengage from that country.[1]

In the Senate, procedures are designed to emphasize extended deliberation over expedited decision making. In October 2002, however, Senate majority leader Tom Daschle, D-S.D., hastened a vote on a consequential joint resolution authorizing President George W. Bush to launch a preemptive military strike against Iraq. Daschle did so by taking procedural action to limit the possibility of any filibuster (or extended debate) on the issue. He wanted the fate of the Iraq resolution determined before the November 2002 elections, because the issues of war and terrorism were dominating the headlines and playing to the strength of the Republicans. He preferred to move the Iraq issue with dispatch and to shift the public's focus to those topics in which Democrats appeared to have the electoral advantage: the weakened state of the economy, corporate scandals, and stock market losses.

But Sen. Robert C. Byrd, D-W.Va., a master of parliamentary procedure, made it clear to the other senators that he wanted to discuss the Iraq resolution at length. He urged that no procedural attempt be made to restrict debate on such a momentous issue, arguing that the Senate should decide the matter after the impending and politically charged November 2002 midterm elections. (The elections produced GOP control of both chambers of Congress.) "I would rather that we discuss the issue after the election, when politics will be farther away from the minds of the members of the House and

Senate," he said. "It's an issue that needs more time."[2] Byrd added: "Some high-priced pollster had apparently convinced the Senate Democratic leadership that we could 'get the war behind us' and change the subject to that of the flagging economy, where the election prospects would appear to be more favorable to the Democrats."[3] (Four years later, campaigning Republicans again emphasized that they were better than Democrats in protecting the country against the terrorist threat.)

Unhappily, Byrd witnessed the majority leader use Senate rules against him. Daschle invoked a procedure called cloture, or "closure" of debate, to end any chance for lengthy discussion of the Iraq resolution. Furthermore, when word circulated that Byrd might resort to delaying tactics, such as engaging in a talkathon on the preamble to the joint resolution, the majority leader "responded by moving the preamble into the main text, preempting such a move by Byrd. And he did it after the senator and others had left for the evening."[4] The next day an irate Senator Byrd declaimed, "The wheels of legislative action ... have been greased" to restrict unfettered debate and amendment of the use-of-force resolution.[5] In the end, after five days of debate and despite complaints from some senators that cloture should not have been invoked on an issue that no one was filibustering, the Senate, by a 77-23 vote, granted President Bush on October 11, 2002, the authority to launch preemptive military action against Iraq. On March 23, 2003, the United States attacked Saddam Hussein-led Iraq.

Conflicts and disputes are commonplace when Congress debates controversial issues or party priorities. These matters arouse the partisan or ideological zeal of lawmakers on each side of the issue and make compromises hard to come by. As Rep. John D. Dingell, D-Mich., said, "Legislation is hard, pick-and-shovel work," and it often "takes a long time to do it."[6] Whether Congress can overcome the procedural and substantive wrangling regularly associated with many bills depends on numerous factors, such as backing from the public and the president. What remains constant, however, is Congress's ability to initiate ideas on its own, to refine and crystallize public debate, and to delay, block, or modify legislative proposals.

Congress is an independent policymaker as well as the nation's premier forum for addressing the economic, social, and political issues of the day—from agriculture to housing, environment to national defense, health to taxes. However, it is not impermeable to pressures from other governmental and nongovernmental forces (including the executive branch, the media, members' constituents, and lobbying groups) or from formal and informal procedural changes that affect policymaking. The lawmaking process, which can be complicated and variable, is governed by rules, procedures, precedents, and customs and is open to the use of some generally predictable strategies and tactics.

This book examines the most significant House and Senate rules and practices that influence the lawmaking process. Because no idea on Capitol Hill usually can avoid a range of parliamentary processes if it expects to become law, this book looks at some related questions: Why does Congress have rules? How do House and Senate rules differ, and what impact do those differences have on policymaking? How are rules applied strategically to accomplish partisan goals? What procedures frame budgetary debates on Capitol Hill? Can House and Senate rules be set aside to expedite consideration of legislation?

THE CONSTITUTIONAL CONTEXT

Congress's central role in policy-making can be traced to the Constitution. James Madison, Alexander Hamilton, and the other framers developed a political system in which Congress would serve as the lawmaking body and set out its relationship with the other branches of government and with the people. As a legislative scholar noted:

> [T]he Constitution has successfully provided two features of national political life that seem unassailable. The first is a Congress that is institutionally robust and capable of gathering information and seeking opinions independently of the president. The second is that Congress is still linked directly to the people through elections. The president is a stronger rival than he once was, but he is not the only game in town. It is that unbreakable electoral link that provides [Congress's] continuing legitimacy, ensuring real political power.[7]

Several familiar basic principles underlie the specific provisions of the Constitution: limited government, separation of powers, checks and balances, and federalism. Each principle continues to shape lawmaking today, despite the enormous changes that have transformed and enlarged the role of government in American society.

Limited Government

The framers of the Constitution wanted a strong and effective national government, but at the same time they wanted to avoid concentrating too much power in the central government lest it threaten personal and property rights. The Constitution is filled with implicit and explicit "auxiliary precautions" (Madison's phrase), such as checks and balances and a bill of rights. The framers believed that limits on government could be achieved by dividing power among three branches of national government and between the nation and the states. The division of power ensured both policy conflicts and cooperation, because it made officials in the several branches responsive to different constituencies, responsibilities, and perceptions of the public welfare. The framers believed that the "accumulation of all powers, legislative, executive, and judiciary, in the same hands . . . may justly be pronounced the very definition of tyranny." [8] As men of practical experience, they had witnessed firsthand the abuses of King George III and his royal governors. They also wanted to avoid the possible "elective despotism" of their own state legislatures.[9] Wary of excessive authority in either an executive or a legislative body, the framers were familiar with the works of influential political theorists, particularly John Locke and Baron de Montesquieu, who stressed the separation of powers, checks and balances, and popular control of government.

Separation of Powers

The framers combined their practical experience with a theoretical outlook and established three independent branches of national government, none having a monopoly of governing power. Their objective was twofold. First, the separation of powers was designed to restrain the power of any one branch. Second, it was meant to ensure that cooperation would be necessary for effective government. As Justice Robert Jackson wrote in a 1952 Supreme Court case, *Youngstown Sheet and Tube Co. v. Sawyer*: "While the Constitution diffuses power the better to secure liberty, it also contemplates that the practice will integrate the dispersed powers into a workable government."[10] The framers held a strong bias in favor of lawmaking by representative assemblies, and so they viewed Congress as the prime national policymaker. The Constitution names Congress the first branch of government, assigns it "all legislative power," and grants it explicit and implied responsibilities through the so-called elastic clause (Section 8 of Article I). This clause empowers Congress to make "all Laws which shall be necessary and proper for carrying into Execution" its enumerated or specific powers.

In sharp contrast, Articles II and III, creating the executive and judicial branches, respectively, describe only briefly the framework and duties of these governmental units. Although separation of powers implies that Congress "enacts" the laws, the president "executes" them, and the Supreme Court "interprets" them, the framers did not intend such a rigid division of labor. The Constitution creates a system not of separate institutions performing separate functions, but of separate institutions sharing functions (and even competing for predominant influence in exercising them). Indeed, the overlap of powers is fundamental to national decision making. The founders did, however, grant certain unique responsibilities to each branch and ensured their separateness by, for example, prohibiting any officer from serving in more than one branch simultaneously. They linked the branches through a system of checks and balances.

Checks and Balances

An essential corollary of separation of powers is checks and balances. The framers realized that members of each branch might seek to aggrandize power at the expense of the other branches. Inevitably, conflicts would develop. In particular, the Constitution provides Congress and the president with an open invitation to struggle for power.

To restrain each branch, the framers devised a system of checks and balances. Congress's own legislative power is effectively "checked" by its structure; it is a bicameral body that consists of a House of Representatives and Senate. The laws Congress passes may be vetoed in turn by the president. Treaties and the president's high-level executive, diplomatic, and judicial appointments require the approval of the Senate. Many decisions and actions of Congress and the president are subject to review by the federal judiciary.

Checks and balances have a dual effect; they encourage cooperation and accommodation among the branches—particularly between the popularly elected Congress and the president—and they introduce the potential for conflict. Since 1789 Congress and the president have cooperated with each other and protected their own powers. Each branch depends in various ways on the other. When conflicts occur, they are resolved most frequently by negotiation, bargaining, and compromise.

Federalism

Just as the three branches check each other, the state and federal governments also are countervailing forces. This division of power is another way to curb and control governing power. Although the term *federalism*—like *separation of powers* or *checks and balances*—is not mentioned in the Constitution, the framers understood that federalism was a plan of government acceptable to the thirteen original states. The Constitution's "supremacy clause" makes national laws and treaties the "supreme Law of the Land"; however, powers not granted to the national government remain with the states and the people. The inevitable clashes that occur between levels of government are often arbitrated by the Supreme Court or worked out through practical accommodations or laws.

Federalism has infused congressional proceedings with "localism." As a representative institution, Congress and its members respond to the needs and interests of states and congressional districts. The nation's diversity is given ample expression in Congress by legislators whose tenure rests on the continued support of their constituents. Federalism is a perennial issue as many lawmakers often advocate the return of federal functions to state and local governments. Conversely, lawmakers also advance legislation expanding the federal role in areas traditionally left to states and localities, such as education.

The Constitution outlines a complicated system. Power is divided among the branches and between levels of government, and popular opinion is reflected differently in each. Both Congress and the president, each with different constituencies, terms of office, and times of election, can claim to represent majority sentiment on national issues. Given each branch's independence, formidable powers, different perspectives on many issues, and intricate mix of formal and informal relationships, important national policies reflect the judgment of both the legislative and the executive branches and the views of many others—constituents, influential persons, special interests, and the like.

FUNCTIONS OF RULES AND PROCEDURES

Any decision-making body needs formal and informal rules, procedures, and conventions to function. These rules and conventions described in Box 1-1

Box 1-1 Major Sources of House and Senate Rules

U.S. Constitution. Article I, Section 5, states: "Each House may determine the Rules of Its Proceedings." In addition, other procedures of Congress are addressed, such as quorums, adjournments, and roll calls.

Standing Rules. The formal rules of the House are contained in the *Constitution, Jefferson's Manual, and Rules of the House of Representatives,* commonly called the House Manual. The Senate's rules are in the *Senate Manual Containing the Standing Rules, Orders, Laws, and Resolutions Affecting the Business of the United States Senate.* Each chamber prints its rule book biennially as a separate document.

Precedents. Each chamber has many precedents, or unwritten law, based on past rulings of the chair. The modern precedents of the Senate are compiled in one volume prepared by the Senate parliamentarian. It is revised and updated periodically, printed as a Senate document, and entitled *Senate Procedure: Precedents and Practices.* House precedents are contained in several sources. Precedents from 1789 to 1936 are found in eleven volumes: *Hinds' Precedents of the House of Representatives* (from 1789 through 1907) and *Cannon's Precedents of the House of Representatives* (from 1908 through 1936). Precedents from 1936 on can be found in the sixteen volumes that make up *Deschler's Precedents of the United States House of Representatives* and *Deschler-Brown Precedents of the United States House of Representatives.* Asher C. Hinds, Clarence A. Cannon, Lewis Deschler, William Holmes Brown, and Charles Johnson were parliamentarians of the House. A summary of important precedents through 1984 is found in *Procedure*

---

establish the procedural context for both collective and individual policy-making action and behavior.

The Constitution authorizes the House and Senate to formulate their own rules of procedure and also prescribes some basic procedures for both houses, such as overrides of presidential vetoes. Thomas Jefferson, who as vice president compiled the first parliamentary manual for the Senate, emphasized the importance of rules to any legislative body:

> It is much more material that there be a rule to go by, than what that rule is; that there may be a uniformity of proceeding in business not subject to the caprice of the Speaker or captiousness of the members. It is very material that order, decency, and regularity be preserved in a dignified public body.[11]

Rules and procedures in an organization serve many functions. Among other things, they provide stability, legitimize decisions, divide responsibilities, protect minority rights, reduce conflict, and distribute power.

Stability
Rules provide stability and predictability in personal and organizational affairs. Individuals and institutions can conduct their day-to-day business with-

in the U.S. House of Representatives. In addition, *House Practice: A Guide to the Rules, Precedents, and Procedures of the House* (2003) examines selected contemporary precedents as of the 108th Congress.

Statutory Rules. Provisions of many public laws have the force of congressional rules. These rulemaking statutes include, for example, the Legislative Reorganization Act of 1946 (PL 79-601), the Legislative Reorganization Act of 1970 (PL 91-510), and the Congressional Budget and Impoundment Control Act of 1974 (PL 93-344).

Jefferson's Manual. When Thomas Jefferson was vice president (1797–1801), he prepared a manual of parliamentary procedure for the Senate. Ironically, in 1837 the House made it a formal part of its rules, but the Senate did not grant it such status. The provisions of his manual, according to the House Manual, "govern the House in all cases to which they are applicable and in which they are not inconsistent with the standing rules and orders of the House."

Party Rules. Each of the two major political parties in each chamber has its own set of party rules. Some of these party regulations directly affect legislative procedure. The House Republican Conference, for example, has a provision that affects the Speaker's use of the suspension of the rules procedure.

Informal Practices and Customs. Each chamber develops its own informal traditions and customs. They can be uncovered by examining sources such as the *Congressional Record* (the substantially verbatim account of House and Senate floor debate), scholarly accounts, and other studies of Congress. Committees and party groups may also prepare manuals of legislative procedure and practice.

out having to debate procedure. Universities, for example, have specific requirements for bachelor's, master's, and doctorate degrees. Students know that if they are to progress from one degree to the next they must comply with rules and requirements. Daily or weekly changes in those requirements would cause chaos on any campus. Similarly, legislators need not decide each day who can speak on the floor, offer amendments, or close debate. Such matters are governed by regularized procedures that continue from one Congress to the next and generally afford similar rights and privileges to every member.

To be sure, House and Senate rules change in response to new circumstances, needs, and demands. The history of Congress is reflected in the evolution of the House and Senate rules. Increases in the size of the House in the nineteenth century, for example, produced limitations on debate for individual representatives. As veteran Democratic senator Byrd said about Senate proceedings:

> The day-to-day functioning of the Senate has given rise to a set of traditions, rules, and practices with a life and history all its own. The body of principles and procedures governing many senatorial obligations and routines ... is not so much the result of reasoned deliberations as the fruit of jousting and adjusting to circumstances in which the Senate found itself from time to time.[12]

Procedural evolution is a hallmark of Congress. The modern House and Senate differ in important ways from how each operated only a few decades ago. For example, the House today operates with more procedural and political powers centralized in the Speaker than it did in the past. In the contemporary Senate, the use or threat of dilatory procedures is a growth industry. Increasingly, the Senate depends more than ever on unanimous consent agreements as a way to avoid parliamentary stalemates.

Legitimacy

Students typically receive final course grades that are based on their classroom performance, examinations, and term papers. They accept the professors' evaluations if they believe in their fairness and legitimacy. If professors suddenly decided to use students' political opinions as the basis for final grades, a storm of protest would arise against such an arbitrary procedure. In a similar fashion, members of Congress and citizens generally accept legislative decisions when they believe the decisions have been approved according to orderly and fair procedures.

For years Congress grappled with the issue of applying to itself many of the laws it passes for the private sector and executive branch. Issues of legitimacy abound in this area. As Rep. Earl Pomeroy, D-N.D., highlighted in a story he told the House Rules Committee:

> Mr. Chairman, at one town meeting recently a constituent stood up and said, "Congressman, how are we supposed to believe the laws you guys pass are good for America, when you're telling us they're not good for Congress?" He was right. To ensure confidence in our laws we need to apply them to ourselves as well.[13]

Congress, therefore, devised a process consistent with constitutional principles to bring itself into compliance with appropriate workplace and employee protection laws (age discrimination, civil rights, and health and safety laws, for example). The landmark bill, entitled the Congressional Accountability Act of 1995, was signed into law by President Bill Clinton.

Division of Labor

Any university requires a division of labor to carry out its tasks effectively and responsibly, and rules to establish the various jurisdictions. For that reason, universities have history, chemistry, and art departments; admissions officers and bursars; and food service and physical plant managers, all with specialized assignments. For Congress, committees are the heart of the legislative process. They provide the division of labor and specialization that Congress needs to handle the roughly eight thousand measures introduced biennially and to review the administration of scores of federal programs. Like specialized bodies in many organizations, committees do not make final policy decisions but initiate recommendations that are forwarded to their respective chambers.

The jurisdiction, or policy mandate, of Congress's standing (permanent) committees is outlined in the House and Senate rules. Legislation generally is referred to the committee (or committees) having authority over the subject matter. As a result, the rules generally determine which committee, and thus which members and their staffs, will exercise significant influence over a particular issue such as defense, taxes, health, or education.

Rules also prescribe the standards that committees are expected to observe during their policy deliberations. These include quorum requirements, public notice of committee meetings and hearings, and the right to counsel for witnesses. These rules also allocate staff resources to committees and subcommittees.

Protection of Minority Rights

Colleges and universities have procedures and practices to make certain that minority ideas and beliefs are protected from suppression. Tenure for faculty members ensures that professors are free to expound unconventional views without fear of reprisal from academic administrators. Student handbooks are replete with policies and guidelines to ensure fairness and due process in the adjudication of academic grievances or violations. A fundamental purpose of the collegiate experience presumably is to encourage students to explore new areas, examine diverse ideas, and engage persons who think and believe differently than they do.

Congress provides procedural protections for individual lawmakers regardless of their party affiliation and for the minority party. However, the House and Senate differ in the extent to which they emphasize majority rule versus minority rights. The principle of majority rule is embedded in the rules, precedents, and practices of the House. Still, numerous procedural protections exist for minority members and viewpoints. For example, the minority party is represented on every standing committee; any lawmaker with contrary views can claim one-third of the debate time on conference reports if the Republican and Democratic floor managers both support it; and any committee member is entitled to have supplemental, additional, or minority views printed in committee reports on legislation. A House member declared: "This body, unlike the other, operates under the principle that a determined majority should be allowed to work its will while protecting the rights of the minority to be heard."[14] An insightful analysis of procedural change in the House by political scientist Sara Binder states that the minority party may see some of their parliamentary rights reduced "when members of the majority party believe rules changes are necessary to secure favored policy outcomes; minority parties have recouped some of those rights when cross-party coalitions emerge to demand new rights from a weakened majority party."[15]

The Senate, by contrast, operates with rules and procedures that advantage minority rights. Prime examples include the right of every senator to speak at great length—the filibuster—and to offer amendments, including nongermane amendments. If the House errs on the side of majority rule, putting decision over deliberation, the Senate tilts toward minority rights, even if that thwarts the will of the majority. As political scientist Richard F. Fenno Jr. characterized the awesome procedural prerogatives afforded each senator, "Every member of the Senate has an atomic bomb and can blow up the place. That leads to accommodation." [16]

Conflict Resolution

Rules reduce conflicts among members and units of organizations by distinguishing appropriate actions and behavior from the inappropriate. For example, universities have procedures by which students may drop or add classes. There are discussions with faculty advisers, completion of appropriate paperwork, and the approval of a dean. Students who informally try to drop or add classes may encounter conflicts with their professors as well as sanctions from the dean's office. Most of the conflicts can be avoided by observance of established procedures. Similarly, congressional rules reduce conflict by, for example, establishing procedures for the orderly consideration of floor amendments or to settle bicameral disputes on legislation. Rep. Clarence A. Cannon, D-Mo. (1923–1964), House parliamentarian and later chairman of the Appropriations Committee, explained: "The time of the House is too valuable, the scope of its enactments too far-reaching, and the constantly increasing pressure of its business too great to justify lengthy and perhaps acrimonious discussion of questions of procedure which have been authoritatively decided in former sessions." [17]

Distribution of Power

A major consequence of rules is that they generally distribute power in any organization. Rules, therefore, are often a source of conflict themselves. During the 1960s college and university campuses were the scene of struggles among students, faculty, and administrators over curricula. Unhappy students charged that their courses were irrelevant. As a result, many schools changed the rules of the game for curriculum development. Students, junior faculty, and even community groups became involved in reshaping the structure and content of educational programs. Recent years have witnessed comparable concerns as groups on various campuses have persuaded university officials to adopt rules, guidelines, or codes regarding speech that is perceived as offensive to, for example, minority groups or women (the so-called political correctness movement).

Like universities, Congress distributes power according to its rules and customs. Informal party rules establish a hierarchy of leadership positions in both chambers. House and Senate rules accord prerogatives to congressional committee chairs that are unavailable to others.

Rules are not neutral devices. They help to shore up the more powerful members and influence the attainment of member goals such as winning reelection, gaining internal influence, or winning congressional passage of legislation. Newt Gingrich, R-Ga., who served as Speaker from 1995 to 1999, once said, "The rules of the House are designed for a Speaker with a strong personality and an agenda."[18] Attempts to change the rules almost invariably are efforts to redistribute power.

RULES AND POLICYMAKING IN CONGRESS

Rules play similar roles in most complex organizations. However, Congress has its own characteristics that affect the functions of the rules. First, members owe their positions to the electorate, not to their congressional peers or to influential congressional leaders. No one in Congress has authority over the other members comparable to that of university presidents and tenured faculty over junior faculty or to that of a corporation president over lower-level executives. Members cannot be fired except by their own constituency. (Under the Constitution either chamber may expel a member by a two-thirds vote, but the authority is rarely used. The authority was last employed on July 24, 2002, when the House voted 420-1 to expel Rep. James A. Traficant Jr., D-Ohio, for corruption.) And each member has equal voting power in committees and on the floor of the House or Senate.

The rules of Congress, unlike those of many organizations, are sensitive to the rights of minorities, including the minority party, ideological minorities, and individual members. Skillful use of the rules enables the minority to check majority action by delaying, defeating, or reshaping legislation. Intensity often counts as much as numbers—an apathetic majority may find it difficult to prevail over a well-organized minority. Except in the few instances in which extraordinary majorities are needed, such as overriding presidential vetoes (requires a two-thirds vote), Senate ratification of treaties (a two-thirds vote), and ending a filibuster in the Senate (a three-fifths vote), the rules of the House and Senate require a simple majority to decide public policies.

Congress also is different from other organizations in its degree of responsiveness to external groups and pressures. The legislative branch is not as self-contained an institution as a university or a corporation. Congress is involved with every significant national and international issue. Its agenda compels members to respond to changing constituent interests and needs. Congress also is subject to numerous other influences, particularly the president, pressure groups, political parties, state and local officials, and major external events such as September 11, 2001.

Finally, Congress is a collegial, not hierarchical, body. Power flows not from the top down, as in a corporation, but in practically every direction. While presidents can say, as did Harry S Truman, "The buck stops here," responsibility in Congress is circular, with everybody and nobody appearing responsible for action or inaction. "The congressional system is not set up to have the buck stop somewhere," observed Charles E. Schumer, D-N.Y. (House, 1981–1999; Senate, 1999–).[19] Congressional policies are not produced by fiat but made commonly by shifting coalitions that vary from issue to issue. And Congress's deliberations are more accessible to the public than those of perhaps any other kind of organization. These, then, are some of the characteristics that set Congress apart from other bodies. Inevitably, these differences affect the decision-making process.

Procedure and Policy

Legislative procedures and policymaking are inextricably linked in at least four ways. First, procedures affect policy outcomes. Congress processes legislation by complex rules and procedures that permeate the institution. Some matters are only gently brushed by the rules, while others become locked in their grip. Major civil rights legislation, for example, failed for decades to win congressional approval because southern senators used their chamber's rules and procedures to kill or modify such measures.

Congressional procedures are employed to define, restrict, or expand the policy options available to members during floor debate. They may prevent consideration of certain issues or presage policy outcomes. Such structured procedures enhance the policy influence of certain members, committees, or party leaders; facilitate expeditious treatment of issues; grant priority to some policy alternatives but not others; and determine, in general, the overall character of policy decisions.

Second, policy decisions often are expressed as procedural moves. Robert H. Michel, R-Ill., who served as House minority leader from 1981 to 1995, highlighted the procedure-substance linkage: "Procedure hasn't simply become more important than substance—it has, through a strange alchemy, become the substance of our deliberations. Who rules House procedures rules the House—and to a great degree, rules the kind and scope of political debate in this country."[20] Or as Representative Dingell phrased it, "If you let me write the procedure, and I let you write the substance, I'll [beat] you every time."[21] Dingell's adage can be modified, however. With ample time, sufficient votes can overcome procedural maneuvers to produce substantive wins.

Representatives and senators on various occasions prefer not to make clear-cut decisions on certain complex and far-reaching public issues. Should a major weapons system be continued or curtailed? Should the nation's energy production needs take precedence over environmental concerns? Should financial assistance for the elderly be reduced and priority given to disadvantaged children? On questions such as these, members may be cross-pressured—the president may exert influence one way, while constituent interests dictate another approach. Legislators sometimes lack adequate information or time to make informed judgments. They may be reluctant to oppose powerful interest groups or they may feel that an issue does not lend itself to a simple "yes" or "no" vote.

As a result, legislators employ various procedural devices to handle knotty problems. A matter may be postponed on the ground of insufficient study in committee. Congress may direct an agency to prepare a detailed report before an issue is considered. The House or Senate may establish an outside commission to study a problem. Or the House or Senate may table a measure, a procedural vote that effectively defeats a proposal without rendering a clear judgment on its substance.

Third, the nature of the policy can determine the use of certain procedures. The House and Senate generally consider noncontroversial measures under expeditious procedures; controversial proposals normally involve lengthy deliberation. The House commonly passes noncontroversial or relatively noncontroversial legislation by suspending the rules, a procedure that limits debate to forty minutes, prohibits floor amendments, and requires a two-thirds vote for passage. Emergency bills or legislation with overwhelming bipartisan support can be passed quickly by way of the suspension route.

Fourth, policy outcomes are more likely to be influenced by members with procedural expertise. Members who are skilled parliamentarians are better prepared to gain approval of their proposals than those who are only vaguely familiar with the rules. Just as carpenters and lawyers must learn their trade, members of Congress need to understand the rules if they expect to perform effectively. Congressional procedures are confusing to members. "To table, to refer to committee, to amend—so many things come up," declared a junior senator. "You don't know whether you are coming or going." [22] John W. McCormack, D-Mass., who served as House Speaker from 1962 to 1971, once advised House newcomers: "Learn the rules and understand the precedents and procedures of the House. The congressman who knows how the House operates will soon be recognized for his parliamentary skills—and his prestige will rise among his colleagues, no matter what his party." [23]

Members who know the rules will always have the potential to shape legislation to their ends and to become key figures in coalitions trying to pass, modify, or defeat legislation. Those who do not understand the rules reduce their proficiency and influence as legislators. Some members even become parliamentary watchdogs or use guerrilla warfare tactics to harass the opposition or to stymie majority steamrollers.

Conventional versus Unconventional Lawmaking

A fundamental strength of Congress's lawmaking process—a principal characteristic of the legislative process apparent from Congress's earliest days—is its capacity to adjust and adapt to new circumstances. The House and Senate, not surprisingly, regularly modify, either formally or informally, their procedures and practices, making the procedures associated with lawmaking something of a moving target. What is conventional or orthodox in one era or for specific types of bills may seem unconventional or unorthodox when different patterns of congressional decision making emerge.

In recent years, some commentators and scholars have noted procedural deviations from a textbook Congress or the regular order. The "regular order" refers to what the House or Senate rulebook prescribes for the consideration of legislation. Much of the time in each chamber many of these rules are not observed because they are too cumbersome to apply in practice. Instead, each chamber creates special procedures, such as "rules" from the

Rules Committee in the House or unanimous consent agreements in the Senate. Thus, the regular order can be conceived as the default procedures in the standing rules that will be observed except when they are set aside.

Speaking of the regular order as a specifically prescribed way by which ideas become laws is somewhat misleading. Instead, this term generally refers to procedural expectations or norms for how legislation should normally be considered in the House or Senate. During the 1950s, 1960s, and early 1970s, for example, the regular order—or textbook version of lawmaking— meant introduction and referral of bills to committees; committee hearings, markups, and reports; wide amendment opportunities on the House or Senate floor; the bicameral resolution of chamber differences on legislation; and presidential consideration. This pattern, shown in Figure 1-1, still holds true for most public laws enacted by Congress, because most neither arouse much controversy nor sharply divide the two parties.

Yet the procedural expectations prevalent in certain eras have always been subject to variations and innovations, especially for priority or "must pass" legislation. During the 1990s and early 2000s, deviations from the regular order have increased, because Congress is less insular, more partisan, and more permeable to outside forces than ever before. Understandably, changes in the broader political environment—the election of activist lawmakers, the cost of congressional campaigns, the proliferation of interest groups, the rise in issue complexity, partisan polarization, breakthroughs in communications technology, clashes with presidents, crises, and more—are reflected in the procedural practices and politics of the House and Senate.

Contemporary lawmaking is a more fluid and less predictable process. Party leaders and individual members simply have more procedural room for strategic maneuvers. For example, scholars and commentators talk about obstructionism or gridlock in today's Senate. Why? The past two decades have witnessed the rise of a more polarized, individualistic, and closely divided Senate (even 50–50 during the first five months of 2001), with the result that senators now have more incentives to push their procedural prerogatives to the limit. And omnibus bills have gained prominence since the 1980s, in part because party and committee leaders can package or bury controversial provisions in one massive bill to be voted up or down. In another development, party leaders tend to bypass the standing committees more often or make adjustments in legislation after it is reported out of committee. Such leadership decisions are made to prevent major bills from getting bogged down in committee and to promote favorable action on important measures.

Procedural change is a persistent feature of the House and Senate. For example, in one of Congress's most dramatic and landmark legislative sessions, the House in early 1995 reviewed, debated, and voted on virtually everything associated with the GOP's Contract with America (a ten-point program of issues, such as tax cuts, welfare reform, and a constitutional balanced budget amendment.) The contract had served as a 1994 campaign document for Republicans—who promised to enact it within the first hundred days of the his-

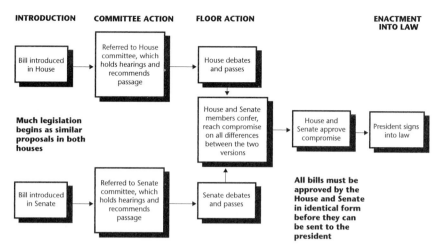

Figure 1-1 How a Bill Becomes Law

toric 104th Congress if the electorate gave them majority control—and as a governing document around which GOP House members rallied and focused on from January 4 to April 7, 1995. Reflecting the unusual accelerated pace, the House was in session 528 hours during the contract period—more than double the session hours of the first 13 weeks of the 103d Congress and almost triple those of the 102d. About twelve hundred hearings and markups were held during the hundred days—one-third more than the eight hundred held in the comparable period of the previous Congress.[24] "I'm on the [Judiciary] constitutional subcommittee," said Democratic representative Jose E. Serrano, N.Y., "and we're amending the Constitution every week. This should not be happening this way, but [Republicans] have a deadline, and we have no choice."[25] Similarly, Speaker Nancy Pelosi, D-Calif., pushed the House to enact at the start of the 110th Congress (2007–2009) the Democratic "100 legislative hours" agenda, which included such measures as ethics and lobbying reform and a hike in the minimum wage.

Several recent House Speakers, such as Thomas P. "Tip" O'Neill Jr., D-Mass. (1977–1987), employed partisan or bipartisan task forces to facilitate passage of legislation and to draft legislation. However, Speaker Gingrich accelerated the creation of task forces, most composed only of GOP lawmakers. A Capitol Hill newspaper suggested that Gingrich was "implementing a new House structure that relies heavily on task forces to carry out responsibilities handled by committees."[26] This was an overstatement, but Gingrich did create a large number of these ad hoc groups, several of which exercised important policy influence. For example, the "Design Group," composed of the principal Republican lawmakers with expertise in health issues, crafted Medicare reform legislation. "This bill, right from the start, was written in the Speaker's office," said a committee chairman.[27]

Speaker J. Dennis Hastert, R-Ill. (1999–2007), who succeeded Gingrich, de-emphasized the use of task forces; they are still created, but more selectively and for purposes beyond policy development. For example, at the start of the 109th Congress (2005–2007), House GOP leaders created a twenty-one-member "Congressional War on Terrorism Team" to bolster President Bush's views on Iraq, counter Democratic criticism of the war, and "promote an upbeat message about the war in Iraq."[28] In 2005 Senate Democratic leader Harry Reid, Nev., appointed a "High Tech Working Group" to promote, for instance, "expanded broadband deployment and enhanced health care information technology."[29]

Ideas can become law with little or no committee or floor debate in either the House or Senate. No statistics have been kept on the number of times this has occurred, but congressional insiders suggest that it is on the increase. A convenient venue for this practice is the conference stage. A major budget revision bill entirely bypassed the House and Senate committee stages; the House first considered the bill at the end of the bill-enacting process, when representatives debated the conference report. As another example, with no committee hearings or floor debate in either chamber, a one-sentence, forty-six-word, $50 billion tobacco industry tax break was quietly inserted into a budget conference report, and the president signed the resulting bill into law. When word leaked out about the tax break, it was repealed in another law.[30] An apt summary of much that characterizes contemporary lawmaking has been voiced by Sen. Bill Nelson, D-Fla.: "If you want to get anything done . . . you have to figure out how to get there. Sometimes it's not a straight line. Sometimes it's a circuitous path."[31]

Precedents and Folkways

Congress is regulated not only by formal rules but also by informal ones that influence legislative procedure and member behavior. Two types of informal rules are precedents and folkways. Precedents, the accumulated past decisions on matters of procedure, represent a blend of the formal and informal. They are the common law of Congress and govern many procedures not explicitly covered in the formal rules. As noted House parliamentarian Lewis Deschler wrote, the great majority of the "rules of all parliamentary bodies are unwritten law; they spring up by precedent and custom; these precedents and customs are this day the chief law of both Houses of Congress."[32] For example, formal rules prescribe the order of business in the House and Senate, but precedents permit variations through the unanimous consent of the members. The rulings of the Speaker of the House and presiding officer of the Senate form a large body of precedents. They are given formal status by the parliamentarians in each chamber and then become part of the accepted rules and procedures.

Folkways are unwritten norms of behavior that members are expected to observe. Like rules and precedents, folkways evolve in response to new times, demands, and lawmakers. During the 1950s, for example, scholars wrote about norms of "apprenticeship" (junior lawmakers should listen and learn from their more seasoned colleagues before actively getting involved in poli-cymaking), "courtesy" (members should be solicitous toward their col-leagues and avoid personal attacks on them), or "specialization" (a member should master a few policy areas and not try to impress colleagues by at-tempting to be a jack-of-all-trades). Today, these particular norms are "torn and frayed." [33] In both chambers, lawmakers enter a partisan and "entrepre-neurial" environment where the incentives—both inside and outside Con-gress—are to get quickly involved in lawmaking, publicity seeking, and cam-paign fund-raising. "You don't have to wait around to have influence," noted then-representative Schumer. "Entrepreneurs do very well." [34]

The "to-get-along, go-along" culture of the 1950s and 1960s Congresses is mainly a thing of the past. Newcomers who sit back quietly and defer to their elders are likely to be viewed as unusual, especially in the Senate where norms of individualism pervade the institution. According to one noted scholar, in today's Senate a member "feels minimally constrained by consen-sual codes of behavior. The relevant distinction in his life is not between the Senate and the rest of the political world but between himself (plus his staff) and everything else. . . . With the help of the Senate's formal rules, he knows he can bring the collective business to a halt. He can be a force to be reck-oned with whenever he wants to be." [35] Congressional decision making, then, is shaped by each chamber's formal and informal structure of rules, prece-dents, traditions, goals, and expectations.

CONGRESSIONAL DECISION MAKING

The congressional decision-making process is constantly evolving, but it has certain enduring features that affect consideration of all legislation. The first is the decentralized power structure of Congress, characterized by numerous specialized committees and a central party leadership that works hard to pro-mote party and policy coherence. A second feature is the existence of multi-ple decision points for most pieces of legislation. The many decision points mean that at each step of a bill's progress a majority coalition must be formed to move the measure along. This leads to the third important feature of the process: the need for bargaining and compromise to form a winning coali-tion. Finally, each Congress has only a two-year life cycle in which to pass legislation once it has been introduced. The pressure of time is an ever-present force underlying the process.

Decentralized Power Structure

Congress's decentralized character reflects both political and structural reali-ties. Politically, legislators owe their reelection to voters in widely differing states and localities; structurally, the legislative branch has an elaborate divi-sion of labor to help it manage its immense workload. Responsibility for spe-cific subject areas is dispersed among more than two hundred committees and subcommittees.

Structural decentralization means that policymaking is subject to various disintegrative processes. Broad issues are divided into smaller subissues for consideration by the committees. Overlapping and fragmented committee responsibilities can impede the development of comprehensive and coordinated national policies. Many House and Senate committees consider, for example, some aspect of health, trade, homeland security, or energy policy.[36] Jurisdictional controversies occur as committees fight to protect or expand their turf. Finally, committees develop special relationships with pressure groups, executive agencies, and scores of other interested participants. These alliances, often called *subgovernments, issue networks,* or *sloppy large hexagons,* influence numerous policy areas. Committees, then, become advocates of policies and not simply impartial instruments of the House or Senate.[37]

Political parties can sometimes provide the cohesive force needed to balance the centrifugal influences of a fragmented committee system. They serve to organize their members and elect the formal leaders of Congress. Democrats and Republicans regularly meet in policy committees and caucuses to discuss substantive and political issues. Neither party, however, commands the consistent support of all its members. Too great a spread of ideological convictions exists within each party. Too many countervailing pressures—constituency, region, individual conscience, career considerations, or committee loyalty—also influence the actions of representatives and senators. "I'll fight for my district even though it may be contrary to my national goals," once declared a House majority whip.[38] As a result, many public policies are enacted because diverse elements of both parties temporarily coalesce to achieve common goals.

Congressional party leaders, especially in the Senate, understand that attempts to dictate policy are fraught with difficulties, because they often lack the means to force agreement among competing party factions or autonomous committees and subcommittees. Box 1-2 discusses the leadership structure of Congress. "What influence I have is based upon . . . respect and reasoned persuasion and some sensitivity to the political and other concerns of individual Senators," said a Senate majority leader. "I don't have a large bag of goodies to hand out to Senators nor do I have any mechanism for disciplining Senators." [39] Because some legislators are not particularly dependent on their state or local parties for reelection, party leaders cannot count on automatic party support and so must rely heavily on their skills as bargainers and negotiators to influence legislative decisions. In addition, the power and style of any party leader depend on several factors, some outside the leader's control. Among them are personality, intellectual and political talent, the leader's view of the job, the size of the majority or minority party in the chamber, whether the White House is controlled by the opposition party, the expectations of colleagues, and the political complexion of the House or Senate during a particular historical era.

To be sure, there are eras when the leaders of the majority party exercise a large influence over committee chairs and their rank-and-file colleagues. For example, there were times during the dozen years (1995–2007) when the

House was under GOP control that it operated in a parliamentary or quasi-parliamentary manner, with rank-and-file Republicans often following the lead and direction of their top party leaders, including President George W. Bush, to approve priorities on largely party-line votes. As former GOP Rep. Mickey Edwards, Okla., said about this polarized period, House members tended "to see themselves less as members of a separate and equal institution with its own oath of office and obligations, and more as either a part of the president's team or part of the opposition to the president." [40]

Multiple Decision Points

Although Congress can on occasion act quickly, normally legislation works its way slowly through multiple decision points. One congressional report identified more than a hundred specific steps that might mark a "bill's progress through the Congress from introduction to possible enactment into law." [41]

After a bill is introduced, it usually is referred to committee and then frequently to a subcommittee. The views of executive departments and agencies also are often solicited. As a head of the Justice Department's office of legislative affairs has described it, "Almost every bill that is moving in Congress is sent to my office . . . by the committees for a reaction." [42] The full committee and subcommittee hold hearings and issue reports on the bill. The bill is then voted out of the full committee and is ready to be scheduled for consideration by the majority party leadership. After floor debate and final action in one chamber, the same steps generally are repeated in the other house. At any point in this sequential process, the bill is subject to delay, defeat, or modification. "It is very easy to defeat a bill in Congress," President John F. Kennedy once noted. "It is much more difficult to pass one." [43]

At each stage of the process, measures and procedures must receive majority (and sometimes supermajority) approval. All along the procedural route, therefore, strategically located committees, groups, or individuals can delay, block, or change proposals if they can form majority coalitions. Bargaining may be necessary at each juncture to forge the support that advances the bill to the next step in the legislative process. Thus advocates of a piece of legislation must attract not just one majority, but several successive majorities at each of the critical intersections along the legislative route. And at each legislative intersection, the strategies for constructing winning coalitions can vary to accommodate diverse issues, external circumstances, and member goals.

Bargaining and Coalition Building

Three principal forms of bargaining are used to build majority coalitions: logrolling, compromise, and nonlegislative favors. "The way you get the votes to pass anything is to ask whoever would possibly vote for something, what do they want," declared a House Ways and Means chairman. "It is an additive process." [44]

Logrolling is an exchange of voting support on different bills by different members of Congress. It is an effective means of coalition building because

Box 1-2 Leadership Structure of Congress

The party leadership in the House and Senate is crucial to the smooth functioning of the legislative process. In the House, the formal leadership consists of the Speaker, the majority and minority leaders, whips from each party, assistants to the whips, and various partisan committees. In the Senate, the vice president of the United States serves as president; in the vice president's absence, the president pro tempore or, more commonly, a temporary presiding officer of the majority party presides. The Senate also has majority and minority leaders, whips, assistant whips, and party committees.

The Speaker's fundamental power is to set the agenda of the House. Speakers achieve their influence largely through personal prestige, mastery of the art of persuasion, legislative expertise, and the support of members. Among the Speaker's formal powers are presiding over the House, deciding points of order, referring bills and resolutions to committee, scheduling legislation for floor action, and appointing House members to select, joint, and House-Senate conference committees. Speakers seldom participate in debate and usually vote only to break a tie. Their institutional prerogatives are buttressed by their role as leader of the majority party. For example, Speakers may chair their party's committee assignment panel and can expedite or delay floor action on legislation.

members rarely are equally concerned about all the measures before Congress. For example, representatives A, B, and C strongly support a bill that increases government aid to farmers. But A, B, and C are indifferent toward a second bill that increases the minimum wage, which is strongly supported by representatives D, E, and F. Because D, E, and F do not have strong feelings about the farm bill, a bargain is struck: A, B, and C agree to vote for the minimum-wage bill, and D, E, and F agree to vote for the farm bill. Thus both bills are helped on their way past the key decision points at which A, B, C, D, E, and F have influence. Logrolling may be either explicit or implicit. A, B, and C may have negotiated directly with D, E, and F. Alternatively, A, B, and C may have voted for the minimum-wage bill, letting it be known through the press or in other informal ways that they anticipate similar treatment on the farm bill from D, E, and F. The expectation is that D, E, and F will honor the tacit agreement because at a later date they may again need the support of A, B, and C.

Compromise, unlike logrolling, builds coalitions through negotiation of the content of legislation. Each side agrees to modify policy goals on a given bill in a way that is generally acceptable to the other. A middle ground is often found—particularly for those bills involving money. A, B, and C, for example, support a $50 million education bill; D, E, and F want to increase the funding to $100 million. The six meet and compromise on a $75 million bill they all can support.

Note the distinction between logrolling and compromise. In the logrolling example, the participants did not modify their objectives on the bills that mat-

The majority and minority parties of the House and Senate elect, respectively, majority and minority leaders. The House majority leader has considerable influence over the scheduling of bills and day-to-day management of the floor. He ranks just below the Speaker in importance. The minority leader heads his or her party in the House. Among other things, he or she develops policy alternatives to majority initiatives, serves as party spokesperson, and devises strategies to win back majority control of the House.

In the Senate, the majority leader is the most influential officer because neither the vice president nor the president pro tempore holds substantive powers over the chamber's proceedings. Everyday duties of the minority leader correspond to those of the majority leader, except that the minority leader has less authority over scheduling legislation. Agenda-setting is the prime prerogative of the majority leader. The minority leader speaks for his party and acts as field general for his party, promoting partisan cohesion and searching for ways to reclaim majority control of the chamber.

Each party in the House and Senate elects a whip and appoints a number of deputy, assistant, or regional whips to aid the floor leader in implementing the party's legislative program. The diversity of whips provides greater geographical, ideological, and seniority balance in the party leadership structure. At its core, the whips' job is to know where the votes are and to produce the votes on behalf of party objectives.

tered to them; each side traded voting support on a bill that meant little in return for support on a bill in which they were keenly interested. In a compromise, both sides modify their positions. "Anyone who thinks that compromise is a dirty word," remarked a House member, "should go back and read one of the fascinating accounts of all that happened in Philadelphia in 1787" (when the Constitution was drafted).[45] As one senator put it, "In politics there are no right answers, only a continuing flow of compromises between groups resulting in a changing, cloudy, and ambiguous series of public decisions where appetite and ambition compete openly with knowledge and wisdom."[46]

Nonlegislative favors are useful because policy goals are only one of the many objectives of members of Congress. Among other objectives are winning assignment to a prestigious committee, raising campaign funds, running for higher office, obtaining larger office space and more staff, or being selected to attend a conference abroad. The variety of these nonpolicy objectives creates numerous bargaining opportunities—particularly for party leaders, who can dispense many favors—from which coalitions can be built. As Senate majority leader from 1955 to 1961, Lyndon B. Johnson of Texas was especially skillful at using his powers to satisfy the personal needs of senators—all with the goal of building support for legislation he wanted.

For Johnson, each one of these assignments contained a potential opportunity for bargaining, for creating obligations, provided that he knew his fellow senators well enough to determine which invitations would matter the most to whom. If he knew that the wife of the senator from Idaho had been dreaming of a trip to Paris for ten years, or that the advisers to another senator had warned him about his slipping popularity with Italian voters, Johnson could increase the potential usefulness of assignments to the Parliamentary Conference in Paris or to the dedication of the cemeteries in Italy.[47]

In this way, Johnson made his colleagues understand that there was a debt to be repaid.

Speaker Pelosi is well-positioned to dispense nonlegislative benefits based on what party colleagues do or do not do for Democratic causes. Like her father, a former five-term House member and mayor of Baltimore who kept a "favor file" listing what he had done to help people, Speaker Pelosi keeps her own favor account. As Rep. Jim McDermott, D-Wash., explained: Some Democrats "think you just take out and take out. She understands you put in, you put in [to help the party], and then, at some point, you say, 'I need a favor.'" He added: "She won't say, 'Vote this way.' She's very realistic. She's very realistic. She'll say, 'You are free to do what you want,' but you can be sure she'll remember you if you don't do the right thing." [48]

The Congressional Cycle

Every bill introduced in Congress faces the two-year deadline of the congressional term. (The term of the 110th Congress, elected in November 2006, began at noon on January 4, 2007, and expires at noon on January 3, 2009.) Legislation introduced must be passed by both the House and the Senate in identical form within the two-year term to become law. But because Congress normally adjourns prior to the end of the two-year term, bills usually have less than two full years to germinate. Bills that have not completed the required procedural journey before final adjournment of a Congress automatically die and must be reintroduced in a new Congress to start the legislative process anew. Inaction or postponement at any stage of the process can mean the defeat of a bill.

Many measures considered by Congress come up in cycles—such as those bills required each year to continue and finance the activities of federal agencies and programs. Generally, this kind of legislation appears regularly on the congressional agenda at about the same time each year. Other legislation comes up for renewal every few years. Emergencies demand immediate attention. Other matters become timely because public interest, international events, or the president has focused on them; health care, terrorism, homeland security, Social Security, and immigration reform are examples of such issues in the early 2000s.

Complex legislation is often introduced early in the congressional term because it takes longer to process than a simple bill. A disproportionately large number of major bills are enacted during the last few weeks of a Congress. Compromises that were not possible in July can be made in December. By this time—with the two-year term about to expire—the pressures on members of the House and Senate are intense, and lawmaking can become frantic and furious. "It is a time when legislators pass dozens of bills without debate or recorded votes, a time when a canny legislator can slip in special favors for the folks back home or for special interest lobbyists roaming Capitol corridors." [49] Members plan purposefully to take advantage of the end game through deadline lawmaking.

Finally, many ideas require years or even decades of germination before they are enacted into law. Controversial proposals—reintroduced in successive Congresses—may need a four-, six-, or eight-year period before they win passage. Many of the 1960s policies of Presidents Kennedy and Johnson, for example, first were considered during the Congresses of the 1950s. Bankruptcy reform legislation required the action of four consecutive Congresses before it eventually surmounted hurdles and roadblocks to become public law in 2005. Although the House and Senate approved a major expansion of Medicare in 2003 by adding a prescription drug benefit for senior citizens, the subsequent administrative difficulties following the January 1, 2006, launching of the complex drug program prompted various lawmakers to introduce legislation to address the start-up problems, as well as gaps in coverage for the elderly under the Medicare drug benefit program. To be sure, legislative proposals to revise, refine, or revamp the nation's health-care system will occupy center stage well into the twenty-first century given America's aging society and the escalating cost of new medical technology.

THE HOUSE AND SENATE COMPARED

The "House and Senate are naturally unlike," observed Woodrow Wilson.[50] Each chamber has its own rules, precedents, and customs; different terms of office; varying constitutional responsibilities; and different constituencies. "We are constituted differently, we serve different purposes in the representative system, we operate differently, why should [the House and Senate] not have different rules," said Sen. Wayne Morse, D-Ore. (1945–1969).[51] Or as former Speaker Hastert noted, "Even though the Senate is only 30 yards away across that [Capitol] Rotunda, sometimes it's like they're 30 miles away." Table 1-1 lists some of the major differences between the chambers.

Probably the three most important structural differences are (1) the House is more than four times the size of the Senate, (2) most senators represent a broader constituency than do representatives, and (3) senators serve longer terms of office. Relatedly, the most significant procedural differences between the House and Senate are (1) the germaneness requirement for amendments in the House but not the Senate, (2) unlimited debate in the Senate but not the House, which has a motion (the previous question, see chapter 4) to cut debate off, (3) the right of recognition for senators from the presiding officer (with a few exceptions) versus the discretionary and unchallengeable recognition authority of the Speaker, and (4) a Rules Committee in the House—but not the Senate—that can determine the ground rules for debating and amending legislation on the floor. These differences affect the way the two houses operate in a number of ways.

Complexity of the Rules

Size explains much about why the two chambers differ. Because it is larger, the 435-member House is a more structured body than the 100-member Senate. Indeed, the restraints imposed on representatives by rules and precedents are far more severe than those affecting senators. House rules for the 110th Congress (2007–2009) consume over 1,300 pages. Its precedents from 1789 to 1936 are in eleven huge volumes; those from 1936 on are recorded in the sixteen large tomes of *Deschler's Precedents of the United States House of Representatives* and *Deschler-Brown Precedents of the United States House of Representatives* (see Box 1-1). By contrast, the Senate's rules, standing orders, resolutions, and laws affecting the business of the Senate are contained in over 1,000 pages and its precedents in one volume.

Whereas Senate rules maximize freedom of expression, House rules "show a constant subordination of the individual to the necessities of the whole House as the voice of the national will." [52] Furthermore, House and Senate rules differ fundamentally in their basic purpose. House rules are designed to permit a determined majority to work its will. Senate rules are intended to slow down, or even defer, action on legislation by granting inordinate parliamentary power (through the filibuster, for example) to individual members and determined minorities. "Senate rules are tilted toward not doing things," remarked Jim Wright, D-Texas, who served as Speaker from 1987 to 1989. "House rules, if you know how to use them, are tilted toward allowing the majority to get its will done." [53] Ironically, moving legislation is easier in the larger House than in the smaller Senate because of the differences in their rules. A simple majority is sufficient to pass major and controversial legislation in the House. In the Senate, at least sixty votes (necessary to break a filibuster) might be needed—sometimes more than once—to move legislation to final passage. The House acts on the basis of majority rule; the Senate stresses minority rule and often functions as a supermajoritarian institution in which sixty votes are crucial to the enactment of legislation.

The Senate, as a result, is more personal and individualistic. "The Senate is run for the convenience of one Senator, to the inconvenience of 99," said one senator. [54] It functions to a large extent by unanimous consent, in effect adjusting or disregarding its rules as it goes along. It is not uncommon for votes on a bill to be rescheduled or delayed until an interested senator can be present. Senate party leaders are careful to consult all senators who have expressed an interest in the pending legislation, because "under the rules of the Senate any one Senator can hold up the works here," said Senator Byrd, the acknowledged expert on Senate procedure. [55] In the House, the majority leadership focuses on party colleagues and usually consults only key members—often committee and factional leaders—about upcoming floor action. It is then no wonder that bills often take longer to complete in the smaller Senate than in the larger House. All senators can participate actively in shaping decisions on the floor given their unique prerogatives: unlimited debate and unlimited opportunities to offer either relevant or nonrelevant floor amend-

TABLE 1-1 Several Major Differences between the House and Senate

House	Senate
Shorter term of office (two years)	Longer term of office (six years)
Adheres closely to procedural rules on floor activity	Operates mostly by unanimous consent
Narrower constituency	Broader, more varied constituency
Originates all revenue bills	Sole power to ratify treaties and advise and consent to presidential nominations
Policy specialists	Policy generalists
Less press and media coverage	More press and media coverage
Power less evenly distributed	Power more evenly distributed
Less prestigious	More prestigious
More expeditious in floor debate	Less expeditious in floor debate
Strict germaneness requirement for floor amendments	No general germaneness rule for floor amendments
Less reliance on staff	More reliance on staff
More partisan	Somewhat less partisan
Strict limits on debate	Unlimited debate on nearly every measure
Method of operation stresses majority rule	Traditions and practices emphasize minority rights

ments to almost any bill. House members typically get involved on the floor only on measures reported from the committees on which they serve. To be sure, far-reaching issues such as major health reform or defense proposals will trigger floor participation by many representatives.

Policy Incubation

Incubation entails "keeping a proposal alive, while it picks up support, or waits for a better climate, or while the problem to which it is addressed grows."[56] Both houses fulfill this role, but policy incubation is promoted in the Senate particularly because of that body's flexible rules, more varied constituent pressures on senators, and greater press and media coverage. As the chamber with greater prestige, lesser complexity, longer term of office, and smaller size, the Senate is, news outlets find, easier to cover than the House.[57] The Senate is more involved than the House in cultivating national constituencies, formulating questions for national debate, and gaining general public support for policy proposals. The policy-generating role is particularly characteristic of senators having presidential ambitions; they need to capture headlines and national constituencies.[58]

However, when the House began televising its floor sessions in 1979 over C-SPAN (Cable-Satellite Public Affairs Network)—the Senate began gavel-to-gavel coverage in mid-1986—many activist representatives recognized the technology's bully pulpit potential. For example, when Newt Gingrich was elected to the House in 1978, he quickly saw C-SPAN as a means for mobilizing grass-roots support behind the GOP's agenda and for attacking Democrats and their decades-long control of the House. He organized floor debates and speeches, even when there was hardly anyone in the chamber, to highlight Republican ideas to the C-SPAN viewing audience and to persuade them that they ought to put the House in Republican hands. He was successful.

As Speaker of the 104th and 105th Congresses (1995–1999), Gingrich was a well-known national figure who took the public role of the Speaker to new heights.[59] For example, he went on prime-time national television after the House successfully completed action on the Contract with America, emulating presidents who address the nation. By contrast, his successor, Dennis Hastert, played a less visible public role, sharing the spotlight with other party members. As the first female Speaker (the highest elective position for a woman in American history), Nancy Pelosi cannot avoid a public role as press and media representatives seek her views on the major issues of the day and the management of the House.

Today, many Senate Republicans and Democrats who had previously served in the House emulate their former House colleagues in certain ways by conducting organized, often early morning, speeches to a largely empty chamber. These orchestrated speeches are designed to bolster their party's image and agenda. Like in the House, Senate Democrats and Republicans each have their own informal message group, which takes the floor periodically to highlight and advance party ideas and priorities to the C-SPAN viewing public. Members of each message group also challenge and critique the other party's agenda and actions.

Specialists versus Generalists

Another difference between the chambers is that representatives tend to be known as subject matter specialists while senators tend to be generalists. "If the Senate has been the nation's great forum," a representative said, then the "House has been its workshop."[60] The House's greater workforce and division of labor facilitate policy specialization. "Senators do not specialize as intensively or as exclusively in their committee work as House members do" because senators must spread their "efforts over a greater span of subjects than the average representative."[61] During the 110th Congress, for example, the average senator served on about twelve committees and subcommittees, compared with about six for the average representative.

One reason for the specialist-generalist distinction is that most senators represent a more heterogeneous constituency than House members. This difference compels the former to generalize as they attempt to be conversant on numerous national and international issues that affect their state. With their six-year term, senators are less vulnerable to immediate constituency pressures. Therefore, they can afford to be more cosmopolitan in their viewpoints than House members. Journalists tend to expect senators, more than representatives, to have an informed opinion on almost every important public issue. Senators, too, suffer from what Senator Byrd has called "fractured attention."[62] They are often away from the Senate raising campaign funds, appearing on television, giving speeches, or engaging in other activities that limit their ability to participate in floor deliberations.

One result of the generalist role is that senators must rely more than House members on knowledgeable personal and committee staff aides for advice in decision making. House members are more likely to be experts themselves on particular policy issues. If not, they often go to informed colleagues rather than staff aides for advice on legislation. "House members rely most heavily upon their colleagues for all information," one study concluded, while senators "will often turn to other sources, especially their own staffs, for their immediate information needs."[63] Consequently, Senate staff aides generally have more influence over the laws and programs of the nation than do their House counterparts. Many senators, however, certainly can hold their own with knowledgeable House members on various policy issues.

Distribution of Power

Another difference between the two chambers is that the power to influence policy is more evenly distributed in the Senate than in the House. Unlike most representatives, senators can readily exercise initiative in legislation and oversight, get floor amendments incorporated in measures reported from committees on which they are not members, influence the scheduling of bills, and, in general, participate more widely and equally in all Senate and party activities. Moreover, every senator of the majority party typically chairs at least one committee or subcommittee.

This ability to make a difference quickly is one reason the Senate is so politically attractive to House members. "I've found the Senate to be a very liberating experience," said a former representative who was elected to the Senate. "The House is so structured by its rules, and Members are so compartmentalized by ideologies or interests. Sometimes it's hard to make an impact."[64] In the 109th Congress (2005–2007), over fifty senators—a record— were former House members; by contrast, no representative served previously in the Senate. House procedures, in short, emphasize the mobilization of voting blocs to make policy; deference to individual prerogatives is the hallmark of senatorial decision making. Sen. Pat Roberts, R-Kan., a former House member, noted that a House member must legislate by coalition, but a senator has to "work with each individual senator."[65]

Similarities

The House and Senate have many similarities. Both chambers are essentially equal in power and share similar responsibilities in lawmaking, oversight, and representation. Both have heavy workloads, decentralized committee and party structures, and somewhat parallel committee jurisdictions. The roles and responsibilities of one chamber interact with those of the other. House and Senate party leaders often cooperate to coordinate action on legislation. Cooperation generally is made easier when the same party controls both houses.

Importantly, a whole range of institutional, partisan, and policy connections turns bicameralism into a force that shapes member behavior and policy outcomes. Along with traditional interchamber jealousies and rivalries, evident even when the same party controls both chambers, House members often hold negative views against what they perceive as Senate obstructionism. As House members sometimes say, "The other party is only the opposition, the Senate is the enemy!" To improve interchamber relations, the House and Senate GOP whips have attended each party's whip meetings, a practice designed "to work on what some Republicans called 'culture exchange' between the two bodies." [66] Part of the House's frustration and exasperation with the other body is the ability of any senator to block legislation through means such as filibustering, placing a "hold" on measures, or offering nonrelevant amendments. Senators have their own complaints about House procedures and policymaking. Suffice it to say that the within-chamber procedures of each body influence the policymaking activities of the other. The two houses are interlocked with national policies fundamentally shaped by the bicameral connection.

In recent years, the two chambers have become more similar in some unexpected areas. Today's House members are more dependent on staff than were their colleagues of a few decades ago, in part because issues are more complex and because more informed constituents look to Capitol Hill for assistance and information. Senators are much more involved in constituency service than ever before. Like House members, they travel frequently to their states to meet in diverse forums with their constituents. In fact, two scholars found that small-state senators "have even more contact with their constituents than the House members in those states do." [67]

Many senators, too, emulate their House colleagues by preparing to run for reelection almost immediately after being sworn into office. This situation reflects contemporary electoral developments unforeseen by the framers—the escalating costs of election races, the professionalization of campaigns (the need to hire consultants, pollsters, and the like), and the emphasis on videopolitics—that make senatorial races more competitive than most House contests.

House members enjoy more incumbent protection than senators because they attract fewer effective, well-known, or politically experienced challengers (in part by scaring off opponents with their money-raising ability), receive more favorable press and media attention, represent more homogeneous—and gerrymandered—areas, and court their constituents assiduously. Thus representatives are more likely than senators to survive periodic electoral tides that oust numerous incumbents. But not always.

The midterm election of 1994 was nationalized (instead of being a series of local elections), largely by Newt Gingrich's Contract with America, which activated segments of the attentive public dismayed with the economy, the president, the government, and the direction of the country. The result was severe losses for the Democrats, among incumbents as well as candidates in formerly Democratic open districts. An electorate angry at the party that had controlled the House for forty years and the Senate for thirty-four of those years produced a nationwide surge of votes for Republicans with only Democrats targeted for defeat. The GOP triumph shifted party control from Democrats to Republicans in both chambers—something that had not occurred since the election of 1952—and transformed Congress's policy agenda. Typically, House incumbents who stand for reelection are seldom defeated because most run in uncompetitive contests and enjoy other electoral advantages, such as high fund-raising capacity and name recognition.

This reality was much in evidence following the November 2006 elections. Like 1994, this electoral contest was nationalized because of the continuing violence and chaos that has characterized Iraq ever since the United States invaded that nation. To be sure, other local and national issues also shaped House races, such as the quality and resources of the congressional candidates, voter concern about congressional corruption, and low popular approval of the GOP-controlled Congress (in the 20s range) and President Bush (high 30s to low 40s). Democrats won back majority control of the House and Senate, but most incumbents were reelected regardless of their partisan affiliation.

PRESSURES ON MEMBERS

In making their legislative decisions, members of Congress are influenced by numerous pressures—the White House, the news media, constituents, lobbyists and interest groups, and their own party leadership and colleagues on Capitol Hill. These pressures are a central feature of the congressional environment; they affect the formal procedures and rules of Congress. All of these pressures are present in varying degrees at every step of the legislative process. The interests and influence of groups and individuals outside Congress have a considerable impact on the fate of legislation.

The President and the Executive Branch

The president and executive branch are among the most important sources of external pressure exerted on Congress. Many of the president's legislative functions and activities are not mentioned in the Constitution. The president is able to influence congressional action through techniques such as the manipulation of patronage, the allocation of federal funds and projects that may be vital to the reelection of certain members of Congress, and the handling of constituents' cases in which senators and representatives are interested. National or international crises, such as the global war on terrorism, trigger a flow of power to the president and away from Congress. The September 11,

2001 terrorist attacks clearly strengthened President Bush's assertion of executive power and some of his actions—for example, his directive to the National Security Agency to wiretap the telephone calls or e-mails of American citizens without court approval—have "invited an increasingly tense debate about his constitutional authority to unilaterally interpret the law while waging a 'global war on terrorism.' "[68]

As leader of the Democratic or Republican Party, presidents are their party's campaigner-in-chief. By most accounts, the Republicans won a historic midterm election in 2002, in which the president's party won, rather than lost, seats in both the House and Senate, something that had not occurred since 1934 for a first-term chief executive. The gains were attributed to President George W. Bush's fund-raising prowess and his extensive and aggressive electioneering for GOP candidates, especially in the closing days of the campaign (fifteen states in six days). "It was Bush's victory," declared one political analyst.[69] Four years later, despite Bush's relatively low approval ratings because of his Iraq policies, the government's inept response to Hurricane Katrina, and other matters, the president remained effective at fundraising for many (but not all) GOP candidates. On his last campaign swing, Bush blitzed ten "Red" (GOP) states during the final days of the 2006 election to boost Republican candidates in competitive races and preserve his congressional majorities.[70] His efforts were unsuccessful as both legislative chambers flipped from Republican to Democratic control.

The president also has ready access to the news media for promoting his administration's policies and commanding headlines. This bully pulpit role, as Theodore Roosevelt described it, enables presidents to mold public opinion and build popular backing for White House proposals. With advances in communications technology and the amplifying power of the media, the bully pulpit role is arguably the president's most significant resource. "Teledemocracy"—satellite press conferences, cable TV, interactive technology, talk-show formats, 800 telephone numbers, televised town-hall meetings, the Internet, and more—enables public officials to bypass traditional news outlets and communicate directly with the electorate. As a White House pollster put it, enacting the president's agenda "is not simply a matter of presenting a policy proposal, sending it to Congress and letting Congress do its work. Now you need an effort to keep the American public with you."[71]

The president's role as legislative leader derives from the Constitution. While the Constitution vests "all legislative Powers" in Congress, it also directs the president to "give to the Congress Information of the State of the Union, and recommend to their Consideration such Measures as he shall judge necessary and expedient." This function has been broadened over the years. The president presents to Congress each year, in addition to the State of the Union message, two other general statements of presidential aims: an economic report, including proposals directed at maintaining maximum employment, and a budget message outlining appropriations requests and policy proposals. During a typical session, the president transmits to Congress scores of other legislative proposals and ensures that the White House and executive agency liaison offices keep tabs on legislative activities and lobby for administration policies. The president's constitutional power to veto acts passed by Congress (a two-thirds vote in each house is needed to override a veto) often promotes legislative-executive accommodations.

The Media

Of all the pressures on Congress, none is such a two-way proposition as the relationship between legislators and the media.

Although senators and representatives must contend with the peculiarities of the news-gathering business, such as deadlines and limited space or time to describe events, and with constant media scrutiny of their actions, they also must rely on news organizations to inform the public of their legislative interests and accomplishments. At the same time, reporters must depend to some extent on inside information from members, a condition that makes many of them reluctant to displease their sources lest the pipeline of information be shut off.

But Congress is basically an open organization. Information flows freely on Capitol Hill, and secrets rarely remain secret for long. An enterprising reporter can usually find out what is newsworthy. Moreover, Congress has taken a variety of actions during the past few decades to further open its proceedings to public observation. For one thing, it has allowed nationwide, gavel-to-gavel coverage over C-SPAN of House and Senate floor proceedings. Instead of relying on press accounts of congressional actions, many citizens now have an opportunity to watch the floor sessions via the electronic gallery and make their own legislative judgments.

Recently, the Congress-media connection has undergone changes that significantly affect individual lawmakers, the two parties, and the legislative branch itself. On an individual basis, lawmakers are exploiting a large array of technologies to communicate with their constituents, generate favorable publicity, and promote their policy proposals. As Rep. David E. Price, D-N.C., described this aspect of his legislative experience:

> My staff and I also try to maintain effective contact with the news media in the district. Members of the media, especially television, are often attracted to campaign fireworks, but it takes considerably more effort to interest them in the day-to-day work of Congress. We send television feeds by satellite to local stations from Washington, offer radio commentary about matters of current interest, and arrange interviews on these topics when I am home. We provide a steady stream of press releases to newspaper, radio, and television outlets; most of these either offer news about my own initiatives or give some interpretation of major items of congressional business, often relating them to North Carolina. We also furnish copies of my statements and speeches and let stations know when they can pick up my floor appearances on C-SPAN.[72]

Lawmakers employ a variety of high-tech devices—faxes, computers, electronic mail, teleconferencing (meeting constituents in their states or districts without ever leaving Capitol Hill), and more—in addition to their traditional means—newsletters, franked mail, radio, and television—for contacting constituents or promoting issues. Members may field questions online from computer users as part of their effort "to be armed with favorable comment [on their legislation] from beyond the Beltway sent to them over the information superhighway." [73] As a sign of the times, more lawmakers are creating blogs, such as Representative Jan Schakowsky, D-Ill. "My real goal here is to . . . explore this medium for getting people to take action and be more involved," she said. Representative Mark Kirk, R-Ill., who also blogs, added that members "who rapidly update [their Web] sites are going to improve communication with [their] constituents, especially younger ones." [74]

From a party perspective, Democratic and Republican leaders devote considerable attention to ways of using the media to frame the terms of public debate on substantive and political issues so that they promote the outcome they want. In recent years, House GOP leaders, often in collaboration with the George W. Bush White House, have regularly employed sophisticated high-tech and communications strategies to highlight their goals and message to the American public. Opinion polling, televised ads, mobilization and coordination of interest groups, town meetings, think tanks, airport rallies, radio and television interviews, op-ed articles, and more are employed to muster public support. Daily and weekly "theme team" meetings are also held "to plan the message of the [day or] week for the speeches at the beginning and end of each legislative day." [75]

Similarly, Democrats employ comparable technology and message techniques to get their ideas and views out to the public, including giving their members "talking points," video materials, or other information for meetings with constituents. In the aftermath of a lobbying and ethics scandal triggered by disgraced lobbyist Jack Abramoff, who pleaded guilty to federal corruption charges, then-Minority Leader Pelosi launched an anti-corruption campaign as one part of her successful message strategy to win back Democratic control of the House in the November 2006 elections. [76]

The politics of strategic message sending are also employed by both parties in the Senate as a way to project a favorable public image and to activate and energize their core electoral supporters. For example, the Senate Republican Conference provides GOP lawmakers with various communications services, such as graphic design, Internet support, and radio and television consulting. Senate Democrats, under the leadership of Harry Reid, Nev., have their "theme team" and outreach programs designed to shape the national political debate. Senator Reid, for example, has established a "war room" communications unit, which provides, among other things, message talking points to Democratic senators. (In a jibe at Reid's war room, the Senate GOP leader informally dubbed his message unit the "peace room.") [77] An issue for Democrats in both chambers is that they have nothing comparable to the powerful megaphone of the Bush White House, and have a harder time getting their themes and ideas delivered to and heard by the general public.

From an institutional perspective, scholarly research has shown "that press coverage of Congress has declined in volume and increased sharply in negativity, while moving from coverage of what the institution does as a legislature to increased emphasis on reports, rumors, and allegations of scandal, individual and institutional."[78] The implications that flow from this finding are several, including heightened public disrespect for the legislative branch. In the judgment of Sen. Frank Lautenberg, D-N.J.:

> Democracy simply cannot function in an atmosphere of distrust. After all, when citizens view everything the Congress does in the worst possible light, they are similarly skeptical about the legislation we propose. That makes it extremely difficult to build public support. And without public support, it becomes almost impossible to address major social problems in a meaningful way.[79]

Constituent Pressures

Although many pressures compete for influence on Capitol Hill, the constituents, not the president or the party or the congressional leadership, still grant and take away a member's job.[80] A member who is popular back home can defy all three in a way unthinkable in a country such as Great Britain, where the leadership of the legislature, the executive, and the party are the same.

The extent to which members of Congress seek to follow the wishes of their constituents is determined to a considerable degree by the issue at stake. Few members would actively oppose issues deemed vital by most constituents. A farm-state legislator, for example, is unlikely to push policies designed to lower the price of foods grown by those who elect him. Likewise, few members would follow locally popular policies that would endanger the nation. Between these extremes lies a wide spectrum of different blends of pressure from constituents and from conscience. And members must make most of their decisions in this gray area. It is no coincidence that the committee assignments sought by senators and representatives are often determined by the type of constituency the legislator serves.

A fundamental change from a generation ago is that lawmakers spend more time with the people they represent. Today, most members travel weekly to their states or districts to meet with constituents. Technology, too, enables members to maintain a constant presence in their state or district even when they are not physically present. Since the advent of the cyber-Congress, lawmakers can exchange e-mails with constituents no matter where their legislative business takes them. Some lawmakers even use video e-mail. "The messages feature a 30-second to 40-second video next to a list of options that constituents can click, sending them to a lawmaker's Web site or allowing them to send a reply."[81]

Lawmakers are in close and constant touch with voter sentiments back home, but they may be too hypersensitive to constituency opinion. From a member's perspective, doing a good job on constituency service is understandably the road to electoral success. However, it tends to push lawmakers toward something more resembling an ombudsman role than a leadership role in which citizens are educated about major problems and solutions and about the unpopular decisions and difficult choices that their member of Congress may have to make to serve the national interest. As Walter Mondale (former senator, vice president, ambassador to Japan, and unsuccessful Senate candidate from Minnesota in the November 2002 elections) stated in testimony before a joint congressional reorganization panel:

> Good constituent service is, of course, necessary—and honorable—work for any member of Congress and his staff. Citizens must have somewhere to turn for help when they become victims of government bureaucracy. But constituent service can also be a bottomless pit. The danger is that a member of Congress will end up as little more than an ombudsman between citizens and government agencies. As important as this work is, it takes precious time away from Congress' central responsibilities as both a deliberative and a law-making body.[82]

Members, then, regularly confront the dilemma of how to maintain a rough balance between serving the often contradictory impulses of their constituents (provide more government services without raising taxes, for example) and the larger national interest.

Washington Lobbyists

Lobbyists and lobby groups play an active part in the legislative process. The corps of Washington lobbyists has grown markedly in number and diversity since the 1930s, in line with the expansion of federal authority and its spread into new areas. The federal government has become a tremendous force in the life of the nation, and the number of fields in which changes in federal policy may spell success or failure for special interest groups has grown enormously. Thus commercial and industrial interests; labor unions; ethnic, ideological, health, education, environmental, and racial groups; professional organizations; state and local governments; citizen groups; and representatives of foreign interests—all from time to time and some continuously—seek by one method or another to exert pressure on Congress to attain their legislative goals.

Pressure groups, whether operating at the grass-roots level to influence public opinion or through direct contacts with members of Congress, perform some important and indispensable functions. These include helping to inform both Congress and the public about problems and issues, stimulating public debate, opening a path to Congress for the wronged and needy, and making known to Congress the practical aspects of proposed legislation: whom it would help, whom it would hurt, who is for it, and who is against it.

Lobbyists also work closely with sympathetic party leaders, legislators, and their staffs drafting legislation, developing strategy, and preparing speeches. Party leaders in both chambers often work with lobbying organizations on matters such as the floor agenda, election goals, policy initiatives, or the enactment of priority legislation. As a House GOP Whip stated, "we look at the outside groups as an extension of the Whip operation" during key legislative battles.[83] In 2006 and 2007, public and legislative concern about the actions of a small number of lobbyists who gave gifts, expensive foreign trips, and campaign funds in exchange for official acts prompted each chamber to pass new lobbying restrictions.[84]

Interest groups may, in pursuing their own objectives, lead the legislature into decisions that benefit a particular pressure group but do not necessarily serve other segments of the public. A group's ability to influence legislation is based on a variety of factors: the quality of its arguments; the size, cohesion, and intensity of the organization's membership; the group's ability to augment its political power by forming ad hoc coalitions with other associations; its financial and staff resources; and the shrewdness of its leadership.

These groups understand the potency of grassroots lobbying, mobilizing constituents to pressure lawmakers by phone calls, faxes, telegrams, letters, e-mails, or personal visits. Interest groups also make efforts to build global grassroots campaigns via the Internet on behalf, for example, of the inclusion of labor and environmental standards in international trade agreements. Even if grassroots activity is manufactured, members realize they cannot simply ignore these expressions of voter opinion. Thus a crucial phase in determining whether a bill is passed, defeated, or amended on Capitol Hill is the struggle among contending interests in members' states or districts.

The proliferation of interest groups and their sophistication in using campaign funds, expert information, and technology to affect legislative decisions has, on the one hand, added to the demands on lawmakers and created difficulties in organizing winning coalitions. On the other hand, the very proliferation of these groups often enables lawmakers to play one against another. "The power of interest groups is not, of course, exercised without opposition," notes one group of scholars. "The typical issue has some interest groups on one side and some on the other, or many interest groups on many sides, not necessarily with an equal balance of power." [85] Although lawmakers must contend with more interest groups, no single one is likely to exercise dominant influence over policy formation as sometimes occurred in the past.

NOTES

1. Gail Russell Chaddock, "How Iraq Panel Went From Obscure to High Profile, *Christian Science Monitor,* November 28, 2006, 1.
2. Mary Dalrymple, "Byrd Wants to Make Case on Iraq, but Won't Filibuster," *CQ Daily Monitor,* October 3, 2002, 1, 5.
3. Sen. Robert C. Byrd, *Losing America* (New York: Norton, 2004), 173.
4. Mary Dalrymple, "Byrd's Beloved Chamber Deaf to His Pleas for Delayed Vote," *CQ Weekly,* October 12, 2002, 2674.
5. *Congressional Record,* October 9, 2002, S10167.
6. Margaret Kriz, "Still Charging," *National Journal,* December 6, 1997, 2462.
7. Charles Stewart III, "Congress and the Constitutional System," in *The Legislative Branch,* ed. Paul Quirk and Sarah Binder (New York: Oxford University Press, 2005), 30.

8. Paul L. Ford, ed., *The Federalist: A Commentary on the Constitution of the United States by Alexander Hamilton, James Madison and John Jay* (New York: Henry Holt, 1898), 319. James Madison wrote the commentary "Separation of the Departments of Power" (*Federalist* No. 47).

9. Thomas Jefferson, "Notes on Virginia," in *Free Government in the Making*, ed. Alpheus Thomas Mason (New York: Oxford University Press, 1965), 164.

10. *Youngstown Sheet and Tube Co. v. Sawyer,* 343 U.S. 579, 635.

11. *Constitution, Jefferson's Manual, and Rules of the House of Representatives,* 102d Cong., 2d sess., 1992, H. Doc. 102–405, 121–122.

12. *Congressional Record,* April 8, 1981, S3615.

13. Statement of Rep. Earl Pomeroy, D-N.D., on the application of laws to Congress, hearing before the House Rules Subcommittee on Rules, March 24, 1994, 1.

14. *Congressional Record,* September 16, 1982, H7097.

15. Sara Binder, *Minority Rights, Majority Rule* (New York: Cambridge University Press, 1997), 2.

16. Adam Clymer, "In House and Senate, 2 Kinds of G.O.P.," *New York Times,* November 15, 1994, B8.

17. Clarence Cannon, *Cannon's Procedure in the House of Representatives,* 86th Cong., 1st sess., 1959, H. Doc. 86–122, iii.

18. John M. Barry, "The Man of the House," *New York Times Magazine,* November 23, 1986, 109.

19. "Lawmakers Were Warned of Abuses at H.U.D.," *New York Times,* July 3, 1989, 9.

20. Testimony before the GOP Task Force on Congressional Reform, House Republican Research Committee, December 16, 1987, 3.

21. *National Review,* February 27, 1987, 24.

22. *Los Angeles Times,* February 7, 1977, sec. 1, 5.

23. *Congressional Record,* March 9, 1976, 5909.

24. *CQ Daily Monitor,* April 17, 1995, 1.

25. *Washington Post,* March 7, 1995, A1, A6.

26. Deborah Kalb, "Government by Task Force: The Gingrich Model," *The Hill,* February 22, 1995, 3.

27. Eric Pianin and John Yang, "House Passes Medicare Reform Bill," *Washington Post,* October 20, 1995, A4.

28. John Donnelly, "Hill Republicans Rally to Boost Iraq War Image," *CQ Today,* December 9, 2005, 1.

29. National Journal, *CongressDailyAM,* May 20, 2005, 8.

30. Edwin Chen, "$50-Billion Tobacco Tax Break Rejected by Senate, 95–3," *Los Angeles Times,* September 11, 1997, B5; the budget law was the 1985 emergency deficit reduction act sponsored by Sens. Phil Gramm, R-Texas, Warren B. Rudman, R-N.H., and Ernest F. Hollings, D-S.C., and adopted as a Senate amendment to a House-passed bill raising the national debt ceiling.

31. David Nather, "Daschle's Soft Touch Lost in Tough Senate Arena," *CQ Weekly,* July 20, 2002, 1921.

32. Quoted in *Deschler-Brown Precedents of the United States House of Representatives,* vol. 1, 94th Cong., 2d sess., 1976, H. Doc. 94–661, iv.

33. Judd Choate, *Torn and Frayed: Congressional Norms and Party Switching in an Era of Reform* (Westport, Conn.: Praeger, 2003).

34. *Wall Street Journal,* June 29, 1987, 54.

35. Richard F. Fenno Jr., "Adjusting to the Senate," in *Congress and Policy Change,* ed. Gerald C. Wright Jr., Leroy N. Rieselbach, and Lawrence C. Dodd (New York: Agathon Press, 1986), 134–136. See also Edward V. Schneier, "Norms and Folkways in Congress: How Much Has Already Changed?" *Congress and the Presidency* (Autumn 1988): 117–138; David W. Rohde, "Studying Congressional Norms: Concepts and Evidence," *Congress and the Presidency* (Autumn 1988): 139–145; and Chester W. Rogers, "New Member Socialization in the House of Representatives," *Congress and the Presidency* (Spring 1992): 47–63.

36. During the 96th Congress (1979–1981), a House reorganization panel found that eighty-three committees and subcommittees exercised some jurisdiction over energy issues in the House alone. See *Final Report of the Select Committee on Committees, U.S. House of Representatives,* 96th Cong., 2d sess., 1980, H. Rept. 96–866, 334–355.

37. Roger H. Davidson and Walter J. Oleszek, *Congress against Itself* (Bloomington: Indiana University Press, 1977); Roger H. Davidson, "Breaking Up Those 'Cozy Triangles': An Impossible Dream?" in *Legislative Reform and Public Policy,* ed. Susan Welch and John G. Peters (New York: Praeger, 1977), 30–53; Hugh Heclo, "Issue Networks and the Executive Establishment," in *The New American Political System,* ed. Anthony King (Washington, D.C.: American Enterprise Institute for Public Policy Research, 1978), 87–124; and Charles O. Jones, *The United States Congress: People, Place, and Policy* (Homewood, Ill.: Dorsey Press, 1982), 360. "Sloppy large hexagons," a phrase coined by Jones, refers to the large number of participants who shape policy issues.

38. Jeff Raimundo, "Cool Whip," *California Magazine,* April 1987, 64.

39. Richard E. Cohen, "Sen. Mitchell, A Lame Duck, Sizes Up '94," *National Journal,* March 12, 1994, 598.

40. George F. Will, "New Speaker, Old Virtues," *Newsweek,* December 4, 2006, 76.

41. Committee on House Administration, "The Bill Status System for the United States House of Representatives," July 1, 1975, 19.

42. *New York Times,* October 31, 1984, B6.

43. Donald Bruce Johnson and Jack L. Walker, "President John Kennedy Discusses the Presidency," in *The Dynamics of the American Presidency,* ed. Donald Bruce Johnson (New York: Wiley, 1964), 144.

44. *Congressional Record,* April 2, 2004, H2120.

45. *Congressional Record,* March 17, 1994, H1483.

46. *Congressional Record,* May 20, 1987, S6798.

47. Doris Kearns, *Lyndon Johnson and the American Dream* (New York: Harper and Row, 1976), 11.

48. Karen Breslau, Eleanor Clift, and Daren Briscoe, "Rolling With Pelosi," *Newsweek,* October 23, 2006, 46.

49. *Los Angeles Times,* October 6, 1982, sec. 1, 1.

50. Woodrow Wilson, *Constitutional Government in the United States* (New York: Columbia University Press, 1911), 87.

51. *Congressional Record,* February 7, 1967, 2838.

52. Asher C. Hinds, *Hinds' Precedents of the House of Representatives,* vol. 1, [U.S. Government Printing Office].

53. Janet Hook, "Speaker Jim Wright Takes Charge in the House," *Congressional Quarterly Weekly Report,* July 11, 1987, 1486.

54. *New York Times,* November 22, 1985, B8.

55. *Congressional Record*, September 10, 1987, S11944.

56. Nelson W. Polsby, "Policy Analysis and Congress," *Public Policy* (Fall 1969): 67.

57. Michael Green, "Obstacles to Reform: Nobody Covers the House," *Washington Monthly*, June 1970, 62–70.

58. See Robert L. Peabody, Norman J. Ornstein, and David W. Rohde, "The United States Senate as a Presidential Incubator: Many Are Called but Few Are Chosen," *Political Science Quarterly* (Summer 1976): 236–258.

59. See Douglas Harris, "The Rise of the Public Speakership," *Political Science Quarterly* (Summer 1998): 193–212.

60. Charles Clapp, *The Congressman* (Garden City, N.Y.: Doubleday, 1963), 39.

61. Richard F. Fenno Jr., *Congressmen in Committees* (Boston: Little, Brown, 1973), 172.

62. Robert C. Byrd, *Operations of Congress: Testimony of House and Senate Leaders*, hearing before the Joint Committee on the Organization of Congress, 103d Cong., 1st sess., February 2, 1993, 4.

63. Norman J. Ornstein, "Legislative Behavior and Legislative Structure: A Comparative Look at House and Senate Resource Utilization," in *Legislative Staffing*, ed. James J. Heaphey and Alan B. Balutis (New York: Wiley, 1975), 175.

64. Ed Henry, "The Senate's Freshman Firestorm: Torricelli 'Liberated' by His Move to Upper Chamber," *Roll Call*, June 2, 1997, 24.

65. Lindsay Sobel, "From House Chairman to Senate Freshman, Pat Roberts Rides in Smaller Farm Pasture," *The Hill*, June 11, 1997, 20.

66. Paul Kane, "Blunt, McConnell Whip Up Coordination," *Roll Call*, June 30, 2003, 1.

67. Francis Lee and Bruce Oppenheimer, *Sizing Up the Senate* (Chicago: University of Chicago Press, 1999), 56.

68. Alexis Simendinger, "King for a War," *National Journal*, January 21, 2006, 26.

69. William Schneider, "A Popularity Contest," *National Journal*, November 16, 2002, 3446.

70. Peter Baker, "The Red-State Revue, Starring G. W. Bush," *Washington Post*, November 4, 2006, A1.

71. Thomas B. Rosenstiel, "Presidents' Pollsters: Who Follows Whom?" *Los Angeles Times*, December 28, 1993, A5.

72. David E. Price, *The Congressional Experience*, 3rd ed. (Boulder, Colo.: Westview Press, 2004), 245.

73. Andrew Mollison, "Lawmakers for Balanced Budget Take Case to Computer Network," *Washington Times*, February 15, 1994, A8. See James Thurber and Colton Campbell, eds., *Congress and the Internet* (Upper Saddle River, N.J.: Prentice Hall, 2003).

74. Staci Zavattaro, "Members Seeing Advantage of Plugging Into Blogosphere," National Journal's *CongressDailyAM*, October 25, 2005, 8. See K. Daniel Glover, "The Rise of Blogs," *National Journal*, January 21, 2006, 30–39.

75. Robin Toner, "G.O.P. Mobilizes for Contract Deadline," *New York Times*, March 30, 1995, A21.

76. Stephen Dinan, "Democrats Put 'Contract on Lobbyists'," *The Washington Times*, January 19, 2006, A1.

77. John Stanton, "Frist Launches Message Shop," *Roll Call*, January 19, 2006, 1.

78. Norman J. Ornstein, "If Congress Played a Better Host to Guests, Maybe It Would Improve a Crummy Image," *Roll Call*, March 31, 1994, 15.

79. *Congressional Record*, March 25, 1994, S4025.

80. For a valuable discussion of constituent pressures, see David Mayhew, *The Electoral Connection* (New Haven, Conn.: Yale University Press, 1974).

81. Glenn Simpson, "Now Showing on an E-Mail Screen Near You: Your Congressman, Produced by Joe Taxpayer," *Wall Street Journal,* January 7, 2000, A16.

82. Walter F. Mondale, hearing before the Joint Committee on the Organization of Congress, 103d Cong., 1st sess., July 1, 1993, 33.

83. Kate Ackley, "Coalitions: Lobbyists' Holy Grail," *Roll Call,* November 8, 2005, 16.

84. See *Congressional Record,* January 4, 2007, H32–H39 for House Reforms and *Congressional Record* for the weeks starting January 8 and January 16, 2007, for debate on Senate reforms.

85. John P. Heinz, Edward O. Laumann, Robert L. Nelson, and Robert H. Salisbury, *The Hollow Core: Private Interests in National Policy Making* (Cambridge, Mass.: Harvard University Press, 1993), 391. See also Allan J. Cigler and Burdett A. Loomis, *Interest Group Politics,* 6th ed. (Washington, D.C.: CQ Press, 2002).

CHAPTER 2

The Congressional Budget Process

THE FRAMERS of the Constitution deliberately lodged the power of the purse in Congress because it is the branch of government closest to the people. "This power of the purse," wrote James Madison in *Federalist* No. 58, "may, in fact, be regarded as the most complete and effectual weapon with which any constitution can arm the immediate representatives of the people, for obtaining a redress of every grievance, and for carrying into effect every just and salutary measure." Or as Sen. Robert C. Byrd, D-W.Va., said more than two hundred years after Madison: "The greatest power of the Legislative Branch is the power of the purse." [1] Under Article I of the Constitution, only Congress is empowered to collect taxes, borrow money, and authorize expenditures. And the executive branch can spend money only for the purposes and in the amounts specified by Congress. As Section 9 of Article I proclaims: "No Money shall be drawn from the Treasury, but in Consequence of Appropriations made by Law." The Sixteenth Amendment to the Constitution also permits Congress "to lay and collect" income taxes. More specifically, the House has the constitutional authority to originate revenue measures, which the Senate can amend. If the House believes the Senate has trespassed on its revenue-initiating authority, it will subject the measure to a "blue-slip" rejection: a notification on blue paper to the Senate that it has contravened the constitutional prerogatives of the House.

The Constitution did not prescribe a budget system for the legislative branch. Instead, it evolved over time to reflect new demands and pressures, such as the huge increase in the size and cost of government from the Great Depression through today. In the U.S. system of separate institutions sharing power, the president exercises significant fiscal authority through the constitutional veto power and a wide-ranging ability to influence the lawmaking process. Congress, which also recognizes the value of the president's role in budgeting, delegated to the president in the Budget and Accounting Act of 1921 statutory responsibility for preparing an annual national budget. Using this responsibility, presidents have been able to spotlight their priorities, frame the budgetary debate, and require Congress to respond to their budgetary proposals.

If Madison and the other constitutional framers returned today, they might wonder about the overall effectiveness of the congressional purse strings. After all, about 70 percent of federal expenditures are considered to be relatively uncontrollable under existing law—that is, the government is required to spend money automatically for certain purposes because of laws previously enacted by Congress. Uncontrollables include interest on the public debt ($250 billion in fiscal 2007), entitlements (laws that require mandatory payments to all eligible individuals, such as Social Security, Medicare, and government pension programs), and contractual obligations that must be paid when due (such as the Defense Department's procurement arrangements with various businesses).

One consequence of uncontrollables is clear. If the 110th Congress adjourned immediately after convening on its opening day on January 4, 2007 without passing any laws, federal government spending for 2007 would still be more than $1 trillion. Furthermore, spending each year thereafter would continue—and increase—because many federal programs are indexed to the cost of living. Congress can convert uncontrollables into controllables by changing the basic law that establishes governmental obligations and authorizes automatic funding without regular legislative review. (There are different degrees of controllability, however. Interest on the national debt and the interest rates to finance that debt are largely beyond Congress's control.) But members who want to amend the law and subject uncontrollables—entitlement programs primarily—to annual budgetary scrutiny can incur serious political risks. Congress chooses to place programs in the uncontrollable category for a variety of reasons. Stability, certainty, and preferred status are among the values that accrue to such programs. Retirees, for example, would have "to live under a great deal of financial uncertainty" if Congress subjected Social Security to annual review.[2]

The federal budget reflects the president's and Congress's choices among competing national priorities and identifies where the nation has been, where it is now, and where the administration and legislative branch plan to make future fiscal as well as policy commitments. Thus the nation's budget is both an economic and a political document. As the ranking Democrat on the Senate Budget Committee once said: "By their nature, debates on the budget tend to be more partisan than other debates. After all, setting a broad plan for allocating resources necessarily depends on judgments based on established principles we bring with us from our views and priorities influenced by our respective partisan affiliations."[3]

In broad terms, federal budgeting is composed of four main phases:

1. preparation and submission of the budget by the president to Congress;
2. congressional review of the president's budget and action on required budgetary matters;
3. execution of budget-related laws by federal departments and agencies; and
4. audits of agency spending.

The first and third steps are controlled primarily by the executive branch; the fourth is conducted largely by the Government Accountability Office (GAO), a legislative support agency of Congress. This chapter focuses on the second stage, the basic elements and features of Congress's budgetary process.

AUTHORIZATION-APPROPRIATIONS PROCESS

Fundamental to the congressional budget process is the distinction between authorizations and appropriations. House and Senate rules created this two-step, sequential process. Authorizations establish, continue, or modify programs or policies; appropriations fund authorized programs and policies. (Congress may also "deauthorize," or eliminate, programs.) Both authorizations and appropriations bills must be approved by both houses and presented to the president for signature or veto.

In the first step, Congress passes an authorization bill that establishes or continues—a reauthorization—an agency or program and provides it with the legal authority to operate. Authorizations may be for one or more years, and such legislation typically recommends, as guidance to the appropriators, funding levels for programs and agencies. These bills also include statutory language (such as "hereby authorized to be appropriated") that permits, or authorizes, the enactment of appropriations to fund agency and program activities. The basic purposes of an authorization are highlighted in Box 2-1. Note that the example in Box 2-1 shows only one year but the act recommends funding levels for a multiyear period (FY 2006–FY 2009). Today, it is usual for most authorizations to be multiyear, with a few exceptions, such as defense and intelligence agencies that have annual authorizations. As Senate Armed Services Chairman Carl Levin, D-Mich., once stated, "every year since 1961 there has been an annual defense authorization bill enacted."[4] In 2005 and 2006, Congress encountered difficulties in passing the annual intelligence authorization bills in part because of partisan clashes. This difficulty may be eased because the House on January 9, 2007, established a select panel on the Appropriations Committee that merged the authorizing and appropriating process for the intelligence community. Select members of the Intelligence and Appropriations Committee make up this panel and are charged with both policy development and oversight of intelligence programs as well as recommending the money for the various spy agencies.

Until the 1950s most federal programs were permanently authorized. Permanent authorizations remain in effect until changed by Congress and provide continuing statutory authority for ongoing federal programs and agencies. Then, in the 1960s and 1970s authorizing committees won enactment of laws that converted many permanent authorizations into temporary authorizations. Two major factors precipitated this change. First, the authorizing committees wanted greater control of and oversight over executive and presidential activities, especially in view of the interbranch tensions that stemmed from the Vietnam War and the Watergate scandal of the Nixon administration. Second, short-term authorizations put pressure on the appropriating committees to fund programs at levels recommended by the authorizing panels.

Today, much of the federal government is funded through the annual enactment of twelve general appropriations bills. No constitutional require-

Box 2-1   Authorization of Appropriations Language

An Excerpt from Violence Against Women and Department of Justice
Reauthorization Act of 2005

SEC.1101. AUTHORIZATION OF APPROPRIATIONS FOR FISCAL YEAR 2006

* * * * *

There are authorized to be appropriated for fiscal year 2006, to carry out the activities of the Department of Justice (including any bureau, office, board, division, commission, subdivision, unit, or other component thereof), the following sums:

(1)   GENERAL ADMINISTRATION- For General Administration: $161,407,000.

(2)   ADMINISTRATIVE REVIEW AND APPEALS- For Administrative Review and Appeals: $216,286,000 for administration of clemency petitions and for immigration-related activities.

(3)   OFFICE OF INSPECTOR GENERAL- For the Office of Inspector General: $72,828,000, which shall include not to exceed $10,000 to meet unforeseen emergencies of a confidential character.

(4)   GENERAL LEGAL ACTIVITIES- For General Legal Activities: $679,661,000, which shall include—

(A) not less than $4,000,000 for the investigation and prosecution of denaturalization and deportation cases involving alleged Nazi war criminals;

(B) not less than $15,000,000 for the investigation and prosecution of violations of title 17 of the United States Code;

(C) not to exceed $20,000 to meet unforeseen emergencies of a confidential character; and

(D) $5,000,000 for the investigation and prosecution of violations of chapter 77 of title 18 of the United States Code.

(5)   ANTITRUST DIVISION- For the Antitrust Division: $144,451,000.

* * * * *

SOURCE: Public Law 109-162, *Violence Against Women and Department of Justice Reauthorization Act of 2005* (Jan. 5, 2006).

ment exists for annual appropriations, but the practice since the First Congress has been to appropriate for a single year. Another long-standing precedent is that the House originates appropriations bills based on its constitutional authority to initiate revenue-raising measures.

Appropriations bills are of three main types: (1) annual—also called regular or general; (2) supplemental—to address unexpected contingencies, such as emergency funding for natural disasters; and (3) continuing—often called continuing resolutions or CRs—to provide stop-gap or full-year funding for agencies that did not receive an annual appropriation by the start of the fiscal year, which runs from October 1 to September 30. Congress enacts about fifteen or so appropriations bills every fiscal year: the twelve regular bills, one or more supplementals, and one or more continuing appropriations. The structure of a regular appropriations act is depicted in Box 2-2.

Most activities or functions that individuals usually associate with the federal government—the Federal Bureau of Investigation (FBI), the Coast Guard, the national park system, interstate highways, defense, space exploration, foreign aid, medical research, and so on—are funded through the annual enactment of the twelve general appropriations bills. The fiscal reality is that the annual appropriations process controls only around 30 percent of all federal spending. This controllable, discretionary spending funds most domestic and defense programs. The other 70 percent or so of federal spending consists of automatic payments for either interest on the national debt or entitlements. Entitlements represent 50 percent or so of federal spending (Social Security, Medicaid, and Medicare are the largest). Money for these programs is continuously available to eligible beneficiaries under the terms of previously enacted statutes. Appropriated entitlements such as food stamps and unemployment compensation are funded through the regular appropriations process. Any shortfall in appropriated entitlement programs must be covered by supplemental appropriations.

Congressional analysts distinguish between *discretionary spending,* which is controlled through the annual appropriations process, and *direct spending,* which is used primarily to fund entitlement programs that are provided for in authorization laws. Direct spending is under the jurisdiction of the authorizing, not the appropriating, committees. Discretionary spending has borne the brunt of reductions over the years, because politicians have been eager to reduce the size and cost of government. However, the direct spending side of the budget has escalated, because Congress cannot easily control mandatory expenditure levels for the entitlement programs established by permanent law. Figure 2-1 highlights the ratio of discretionary expenditures to entitlement expenditures over time. Yes, Congress can modify those statutes, but doing so can be both difficult and an electorally risky venture. The elderly, who are well organized and who turn out to vote, are not reluctant to tell lawmakers, "Keep your hands off my Social Security!" President Bush also discovered how hard it is to overhaul Social Security when he tried unsuccessfully in 2005 to convince seniors to support the creation of individual retirement accounts so people could invest for themselves part of what they contribute to the government-run program. In 1996 Congress converted welfare—Aid to Families with Dependent Children—from an entitlement program to a fixed block-grant program.

Another budgetary distinction to bear in mind is that between *budget authority* and *budget outlays.* Appropriations approved by Congress provide budget authority, which allows government agencies to make financial commitments, up to a specified amount, that eventually result in budget outlays—that is, the spending of dollars. As one budget analyst explains it:

Box 2-2 **Excerpts from Structure of a Regular Appropriations Act**

An Act

[Title]

Making appropriations for Agriculture, Rural Development, Food and Drug Administration, and Related Agencies for the fiscal year ending September 30, 2006, and for other purposes.

[Enacting clause]

Be it enacted by the Senate and House of Representatives of the United States of America in Congress assembled, That the following sums are appropriated, out of any money in the Treasury not otherwise appropriated, for Agriculture, Rural Development, Food and Drug Administration, and Related Agencies programs for the fiscal year ending September 30, 2006, and for other purposes, namely:

[Appropriations to specified accounts]

AGRICULTURAL RESEARCH SERVICE SALARIES AND EXPENSES

For necessary expenses to enable the Agricultural Research Service to perform agricultural research and demonstration relating to production, utilization, marketing, and distribution (not otherwise provided for); home economics or nutrition and consumer use including the acquisition, preservation, and dissemination of agricultural information; and for acquisition of lands by donation, exchange, or purchase at a nominal cost not to exceed $100, and for land exchanges where the lands exchanged shall be of equal value or shall be equalized by a payment of money to the grantor which shall not exceed 25 percent of the total value of the land or interests transferred out of Federal ownership, $1,135,004,000:

* * * * *

SOURCE: Public Law 109-97, *Agriculture, Rural Development, Food and Drug Administration, and Related Agencies Act, 2006* (Nov. 10, 2005).

Congress does not directly control the level of federal spending that will occur in a particular year. Rather, it grants the executive branch authority (referred to as *budget authority*) to enter into *obligations*, which are legally binding agreements with suppliers of goods or services or with a beneficiary. When those obligations come due, the Treasury Department issues a payment. The amount of payments, called *outlays*, over an accounting period called the fiscal year (running from October 1 to September 30) equals federal expenditures for that fiscal year. Federal spending (outlays) in any given year, therefore, results from the spending authority (budget authority) granted by Congress in the current and in prior fiscal years.[5]

To state it differently, budget authority can be likened to putting money in a checking account, and budget outlays to writing a check.

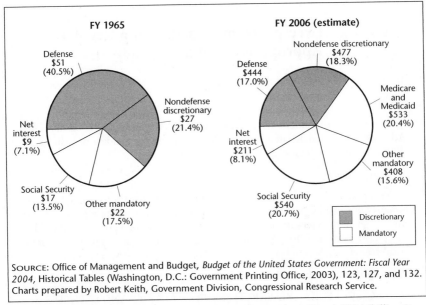

FY 1965

Defense
$51
(40.5%)

Nondefense
discretionary
$27
(21.4%)

Net
interest
$9
(7.1%)

Social Security
$17
(13.5%)

Other mandatory
$22
(17.5%)

FY 2006 (estimate)

Nondefense discretionary
$477
(18.3%)

Defense
$444
(17.0%)

Medicare
and
Medicaid
$533
(20.4%)

Net
interest
$211
(8.1%)

Other
mandatory
$408
(15.6%)

Social Security
$540
(20.7%)

Discretionary

Mandatory

SOURCE: Office of Management and Budget, *Budget of the United States Government: Fiscal Year 2004*, Historical Tables (Washington, D.C.: Government Printing Office, 2003), 123, 127, and 132. Charts prepared by Robert Keith, Government Division, Congressional Research Service.

FIGURE 2-1   Federal Spending by Major Category, Fiscal 1965 and 2006 (billions)

The conversion of budget authority to budget outlays depends on a variety of factors, including the character of the program or activity. Budget authority granted annually to pay federal salaries is typically converted to budget outlays that same year. Budget authority to build a highway is converted to budget outlays at a variable rate over several years as highway planning costs give way to construction costs. Lawmakers require both figures so they can assess the projected total cost of a multiyear program or project compared with what will be spent on it annually. Legislators are mindful that budget authority figures—instead of the outlay numbers—are the better predictors of an agency's growth or decline. Outlays, however, are reflected in each year's national deficit or surplus levels.

Authorizing and Appropriating Committees

Whether agencies receive the budget authority they request depends in part on the recommendations of the authorizing and appropriating committees. Each chamber has authorizing committees (Agriculture, Commerce, Small Business, and many others) with responsibilities that differ from those of the two appropriating committees—the House and Senate Appropriations Committees. The authorizing committees are the policy-making centers on Capitol Hill. As the substantive legislative panels, they propose solutions to public problems and advocate what they believe to be the necessary level of appropriations for new and existing federal agencies, activities, and programs, specifying either a specific amount of money or an indefinite level of funding ("such sums as may be necessary").

Each house's Appropriations Committee and their twelve parallel sub-committees recommend how much federal agencies and programs will receive in relation to available fiscal resources and economic conditions. The Appropriations subcommittee chairs are collectively known in their respective chambers as the "College of Cardinals" because of their large influence over spending issues. These chairs often include earmarks—recommendations or requirements that agencies should dedicate funds for a particular purpose—in their bills or, more commonly, in their committee reports or as part of appropriations conference reports. Tax and authorization bills also contain earmarks, such as tax breaks or transportation projects, but those in appropriation measures usually receive more public and media attention.

In general, earmarks in appropriations bills set aside specific funds for projects or programs in members' districts or states. These projects, often prejudicially called "pork," are frequently funded in response to constituents' requests for sewer grants, flood control programs, hospital or school construction, and the like. Some lawmakers enable constituents to apply for earmarks via e-mail.[6] To define an earmark can sometimes be difficult, but a former staff director of the House Appropriations Committee put it this way: "An earmark is something that flows into 434 congressional districts and not yours. When it comes to your district, it's a federal investment in jobs and education."[7]

Earmarks Under Fire. Earmarks came under critical review in 2006 for three main reasons. First, the scandals associated with the criminal indictments of lobbyist Jack Abramoff and former representative Randy "Duke" Cunningham, R-Calif., prompted increased scrutiny of earmarks. Abramoff, who referred to each chamber's appropriations panel as the "favor factory," developed ties with influential lawmakers and staff aides by, among other things, "wining and dining" and providing gifts to them. He then persuaded his Capitol Hill contacts to quietly insert earmarks into legislation for his clients who, in turn, would contribute to these lawmakers' campaigns. Cunningham, who took $2.4 million in bribes, used his position on the Defense Appropriations Subcommittee to earmark millions of dollars for favored defense contractors. In Cunningham's case, the lack of transparency—there are both "white" (public) and "black" (secret) aspects to budgeting—enabled him to slip earmarks in the secret intelligence budget without anyone's knowledge. The classified part of budgeting, said Senator John McCain, R-Ariz., a long-time champion of earmark reform, "deserves extra scrutiny now because Duke Cunningham was able to perpetrate some of his egregious crimes through exactly that vehicle."[8]

Second, there has been a dramatic increase in the number of earmarks. Senator McCain, citing data compiled by the Congressional Research Service, spotlighted the explosion.

[I]n 1994, there were 4,126 congressional earmarks added to the annual appropriations bills. In 2005, there were 15,877 earmarks, the largest number yet, that's an increase of nearly 300 percent! The level of funding associated with those earmarks has more than doubled from $23.2 billion in fiscal year 1994 to $47.4 billion in fiscal year 2005.[9]

Various factors account for the surge of earmarks. For example, with narrow partisan divisions in the House and Senate, party leaders use earmarks to attract the votes needed to pass priority legislation and to help vulnerable lawmakers "bring home the bacon" to appreciative constituents who will then return them to office. In addition, members do not want to relinquish the "power of the purse" to unelected administrators. As a House Appropriations chairman stated: "Members know the needs of their districts better than civil servants working in Washington, D.C." [10]

Third, aggressive "watchdog" groups are not reluctant to embarrass Congress by publicizing what they view as wasteful spending on bad programs or projects. An oft-cited example was the so-called "bridge to nowhere"—a "mile long, 200-foot-high span [costing $223 million] that will connect Ketchikan, [Alaska], a town with fewer than 8,000 people, to an island that has 50 residents and a small airport." [11]

Earmarks will not be eliminated entirely because many lubricate the lawmaking process and serve worthwhile and defensible purposes. Yet their proliferation led to earmark reform in the 110th Congress. The House, for example, included in its package of rules changes (H. Res. 6) at the opening of the new Congress a series of restrictions and requirements for earmarks, including limited tax and tariff benefits. Among the changes, five are important to note. Each is enforced by members raising points of order (or parlimentary objections). First, bills, joint resolutions, and certain amendments are not to be considered in the House unless all earmarks are publicly disclosed in the bill or accompanying committtee report as to their sponsors, purposes, and costs. Second, if unreported measures are brought to the floor, the appropriate committee chairman would have to include a list of earmarks in the *Congressional Record* prior to floor action on the legislation. Third, the joint explanatory statement accompanying conference reports must include a list of earmarks. Fourth, requests for earmarks must include "justifications and certification that the provisions will not benefit lawmakers or their spouses." Fifth, party leaders "cannot promise earmarks in exchange for votes on legislation." [12] The Senate also adopted comparable earmark reforms.[13]

For each authorized program and agency subject to the annual appropriations process, the Appropriations Committees have three main options: (1) provide all the funds recommended in the previously approved authorization bill, (2) propose reductions in the amounts authorized, or (3) refuse to provide any funds.[14] A newspaper headline declaring that Congress has just authorized, for example, a new $3 billion antidrug program means that the program officially exists on paper. However, it still lacks money to operate until it receives an appropriation.

Congressional rules—which are often not observed—require authorizations to precede appropriations to ensure that substantive and financial issues are subject to separate and independent analysis. This procedure also permits almost every member and committee to participate in Congress's constitutional power of the purse. Numerous exceptions are made to this two-step model, despite House and Senate rules that encourage separation of the authorization-appropriations stages.

Constitutional Underpinning

The authorization-appropriation dichotomy is not required by the Constitution. It is a process that has been institutionalized by the rules of the House and Senate and in some cases by statute. Of the two steps, the appropriations stage is on firmer legal ground because it is rooted in the Constitution. An appropriations measure, which provides departments and agencies with authority to commit funds, may be approved even if the authorization bill has not been enacted. As long as "appropriations are enacted," wrote a budget scholar, "funds may be obligated by agencies, regardless of whether . . . authorizations have been enacted." [15] Or, as one House Appropriations subcommittee chairman put it, "It's not the end of the world if we postpone the Clean Air Act or a tax measure. But the entire government will shut down if . . . appropriations" are not enacted annually.[16]

Informally, Congress has employed this division of labor since the beginning of the Republic, as did the British Parliament and the colonial legislatures. As Sen. William Plumer of New Hampshire noted in 1806: "Tis a good provision in the constitution of Maryland that prohibits their Legislature from adding any thing to an appropriation law." [17] Generally called supply bills in the early Congresses, appropriations measures had narrow purposes: to provide specific sums of money for fixed periods and stated objectives. Such bills were not to contain matters of policy.

There were exceptions to this informal rule even during the early days, but the practice of adding riders, or extraneous policy provisos, to appropriations bills mushroomed in the 1830s. This practice often provoked sharp controversy in Congress and delayed the enactment of supply bills. "By 1835," wrote a parliamentary expert, the "delays caused by injecting legislation [policy] into these [appropriations] bills had become serious, and [then representative] John Quincy Adams . . . suggested that they be stripped of everything save appropriations." [18] Two years later the House adopted a rule requiring authorization bills to precede appropriations. The Senate later followed suit.

Separate Policy and Fiscal Decisions

Several major implications flow from Congress's efforts to separate policy from fiscal decision making—matters that usually are inextricably intertwined. Among the major implications are flexibility, bicameral differences, and committee rivalries.

Flexibility. The authorization-appropriations rules, like almost all congressional rules, are not self-enforcing. Either chamber can choose to waive, ignore, or circumvent them or establish precedents and practices that obviate distinctions between the two. As one scholar has written:

> The real world of the legislative process differs considerably from the idealized model of the two-step authorization-appropriation procedure. Authorization bills contain appropriations, appropriation bills contain authorizations, and the order of their enactment is sometimes reversed. The Appropriations Committees, acting through various kinds of limitations, riders, and nonstatutory controls, are able to establish policy and act in a substantive manner. Authorization Committees have considerable power to force the hand of the Appropriations Committees and, in some cases, even to appropriate.[19]

Flexibility in the authorization-appropriations procedure allows it to accommodate stresses and strains. A failure to enact authorization bills does not bring the appropriations process (or an agency or federal program) to a halt. For example, from 1985 to 2003,Congress for various reasons was unable to enact authorization legislation for foreign relations programs, but those programs (last authorized in 2003) still received money to operate. The Congressional Budget Office (CBO) reported that the total amount of unauthorized appropriations in fiscal year 2006 was about $159 billion.[20] The must-pass annual appropriations bills often become the vehicle for extending or revamping existing laws that did not make it through the authorization process. As Rep. Obey stated:

> It seems to me what has happened in our system is that the authorization process has been jammed up many times, sometimes because of committee incompetence, sometimes because the issues are just . . . tough and we have issues that aren't resolvable over the short haul, and sometimes because the White House has chosen to simply stiff the authorizing committee because they think they can get a better deal from us on appropriations.[21]

It is not uncommon for authorizers to ask appropriators to include policy proposals or legislation in annual appropriations bills.

Bicameral Differences. Because the House and Senate are dissimilar, they have different rules governing the authorization-appropriations process. Table 2-1 compares the authorization and appropriations rules of the two houses. These differences reflect each chamber's fundamental nature: the smaller Senate permits greater procedural flexibility than the larger House.

The rules affect each chamber's legislative behavior and policy deliberations. The Senate, for example, sometimes gets off to a slower start on appropriations measures because, by tradition, it waits for the House to originate those bills. Moreover, the multistage process creates numerous opportunities to shape issues. Policy debates may be resurrected again and again in different contexts in either chamber.

An issue of some concern to the House is the committee assignment practices of the Senate. In the House, for both parties, service on the Appropria-

TABLE 2-1 Authorization-Appropriations Rules Compared

House	Senate
No unauthorized appropriations are permitted except for public works in progress. The Appropriations Committee generally cannot report a general appropriations bill unless there is an authorization law.	Unauthorized appropriations are not permitted. Exceptions are if the Senate has passed an authorization during that session; if an authorization is reported by any Senate standing committee, including Appropriations; or if an authorization is requested in the president's annual budget.
No legislation (policy) is permitted in an appropriations bill.	No legislation is permitted in an appropriations bill unless it is germane to the House-passed bill.
No appropriation is permitted in an authorization bill. Floor amendments that propose appropriations are not in order in authorization bills.	There is no equivalent rule. By custom, the House initiates appropriations bills and objects to Senate efforts aimed at circumventing this arrangement.

tions Committee is, with few exceptions, an exclusive assignment. Senators, by contrast, may serve simultaneously on both authorizing and appropriating committees. In some instances, the same senator chaired both the authorizing committee (or relevant subcommittee) and the comparable appropriations subcommittee. Fundamental bicameral imbalances are created, said a House Science chairman, when senators "are permitted to serve on both Committees. Inevitably, Members will prefer to legislate in appropriations bills (or the accompanying reports), which by their nature and by the rules of both Houses, are more protected from debate, amendment, and perfection than are corresponding authorization bills." [22] Or as another House chairman stated:

> What we have seen happening is that, because the [Senate] appropriators find that it is easy to just throw everything into the appropriation bill, very often the authorizing bills simply don't get passed, and therefore authorization bills that pass the House are left sitting in the Senate. And we will sometimes go one, two, three, four years before we get an authorization bill passed in a very important policy area.[23]

Committee Rivalries. Another consequence of the two-step system is that it breeds continuing conflict between the authorizing and appropriating committees. In the judgment of Senator McCain, "It has become standard practice around here to forgo the authorizing process and simply do everything on appropriations. That is wrong and it needs to stop." [24] As a House authorizing chairman says, "my panel plays second fiddle to the appropriators, which is where power and money is" joined.[25]

Authorizing committees generally support high levels of spending for the programs they recommend and seek ways to bypass Appropriations Committee domination. Meanwhile the appropriating panels often view themselves as guardians of the purse. It is their job, they believe, to reject or reduce many funding requests. On occasion, however, maximum funding is the preferred objective of the House and Senate Appropriations Committees.

The traditional tension between authorizers and appropriators is on view in this notable example, which involves the Transportation Committee and the Appropriations Committee in the House. The seventy-five-member Transportation Committee, now the largest committee in the history of Congress, is responsible for approving highway, mass transit, and similar projects in members' districts. The Transportation chairman rolled over opposition from the appropriators and took the highway trust fund off-budget in the Transportation Equity Act of the 21st Century (TEA-21). A trust fund is a legally created account that receives revenues from a designated source—federal gasoline taxes for the highway trust fund—to be used for a specific purpose, such as highway construction and maintenance. By taking programs off-budget, legislators place them outside the control of the appropriators and the budget-writers. (Since 1968 the federal government has used a "unified budget," which includes all of the government's financial activities. Moving a program or activity off-budget gives it a separate status.) Thus the highway trust fund became a dedicated funding stream exempt from budgetary constraints and whose funds are reserved exclusively for mandatory spending on specific projects.

The Transportation chairman even wrote a new House rule in TEA-21 that declares "out of order any attempt to lower the obligational limits for highway and transit spending spelled out in the authorizing law. If a transportation appropriations bill drops below the figures for highways and transit in the surface transportation law, a House member can raise a point of order against it." [26] The upshot was that the Transportation Committee, and not the appropriations panel, makes highway spending decisions. Not only did TEA-21 arouse the ire and tie the hands of the appropriators, it also angered the Rules Committee, which has jurisdiction over changes in the House's rulebook.

Such backdoor authorization measures—avoiding the appropriators' front door—blur the distinction between authorizations and appropriations because they permit spending by the federal government. Three common forms of backdoor authorization are (1) borrowing authority (a federal agency, for example, is authorized by law to borrow specific sums of money from the Treasury or the public, through commercial channels, to build low-cost homes or make student loans); (2) contract authority (for example, a federal agency is statutorily permitted to enter into contractual agreements with private companies for the construction of municipal sewage treatment plants, but appropriations must be provided in the future to honor these commitments); and (3) entitlement authority (federal programs such as Social Security, Medicare, and Medicaid that allow eligible recipients to be automatically entitled to federal payments). Entitlements are the fastest-growing part of the federal budget. Appropriators often suggest that various entitlement programs be taken off automatic pilot and subjected to annual appropriations review. As a House Appropriations chair stated: "Meaningful deficit reduction can only be achieved by taking a hard look at mandatory spending." [27]

Some observers suggest that another fiscal area deserves greater legislative scrutiny: "tax expenditures," which are under the jurisdiction of the tax-writing House Ways and Means and Senate Finance Committees. Tax expenditures are revenue losses to the federal treasury from various tax write-offs, credits, or deductions to encourage certain kinds of behavior, such as providing tax relief to developers so they have an incentive to build low-cost public housing units. Tax expenditures may be "viewed as spending programs channeled through the tax system." [28] In 2005, tax expenditures totaled $775 billion, more than double the amount in 1974. The Comptroller General of the United States referred to tax expenditures as a form of backdoor spending. "If you can't achieve something through a direct spending program," he noted, "there's an incentive for people to create a tax incentive to get it off the books [and] outside the budget process, but it really does have an impact on the bottom line." [29]

Exceptions to the Rules

Legislative (or policy) provisions find their way into appropriations bills notwithstanding the strictures of the rules—for example, if no member raises a point of order against the practice or if either chamber waives its rules. The House, by precedent, also permits unauthorized programs to be included in continuing resolutions that provide interim funding for agencies whose general appropriations bills have not been enacted by the start of the fiscal year.

Senate rules, unlike those for the House, grant wide leeway to appropriators to authorize projects, programs, or activities. "I'm not about to start hunkering down and running like a scared rabbit because somebody says it's got to be authorized," said Senate Appropriations chair Robert Byrd. "If this committee wants to authorize demonstration grants, it has the authority." [30] As Senate precedents state, "there is no prohibition in the Standing Rules of the Senate or the precedents against making appropriations for a project or program in the absence of an authorization." [31]

Limitation Riders. Limitation riders are the chief device used by legislators to insert policy in appropriations measures. These riders are provisions in general appropriations bills or floor amendments to those measures that prohibit the spending of funds for specific purposes. Always phrased in the negative ("None of the funds provided in this Act shall be used for . . ."), limitations are based on scores of House and Senate precedents that collectively uphold the position that because either chamber can refuse to appropriate funds for programs that have been authorized, the two bodies can also prohibit the use of funds for any part of a program or activity.

House members and staff aides, for example, devote a great deal of time to carefully drafting provisions that make policy in the guise of limitations.

For guidance they turn to the House rulebook, which is replete with precedents that have interpreted permissible from impermissible limitations. There are three basic criteria for permissible limitations. Limitations cannot (1) impose additional duties or burdens on executive branch officials, (2) interfere with their discretionary authority, or (3) require officials to make judgments or determinations not required by existing law.

Legislators sometimes add riders to appropriations bills because the riders may not survive as freestanding bills. As "must pass" vehicles headed to the White House, appropriations measures often attract extraneous policy matters. But they become difficult to pass when controversial riders trigger partisan disputes, bicameral controversies, lobbying battles, or veto threats.

The 1977 antiabortion amendment remains a classic example of the important effect a limitation can have on policy. The appropriations bill for the Department of Labor and the Department of Health, Education, and Welfare (HEW, now the Department of Health and Human Services, or HHS) contained a limitation on the use of funds "to perform abortions except where the life of the mother would be endangered if the fetus were carried to term." A point of order was raised and sustained against that amendment on the ground that it was legislation in an appropriations bill. The limitation required officials in the executive branch to determine when the life of a pregnant woman would be endangered. The language was then amended to read: "None of the funds appropriated by this Act shall be used to pay for abortions or to promote or encourage abortions, except when a physician has certified the abortion is necessary to save the life of the mother." Again, a point of order was raised that the amendment was legislation in an appropriations bill. And again the chair ruled in favor of the parliamentary objection, this time on the ground that the federal government employed many physicians and that they would be required to make life-deciding judgments. Finally, the sponsor of the proposal, Rep. Henry Hyde of Illinois, said he had no choice but to offer the following language: "None of the funds appropriated under this Act shall be used to pay for abortions or to promote or encourage abortions." There was no point of order because the amendment required no judgments by executive officials. The Hyde amendment was then adopted.[32]

When the Labor-HEW bill, containing the Hyde amendment, reached the Senate, Edward W. Brooke, R-Mass., offered an amendment that permitted abortions "where the life of the mother would be endangered if the fetus were carried to term, or where medically necessary, or for the treatment of rape or incest." Barry Goldwater, R-Ariz., said the amendment was legislation in an appropriations bill and raised a point of order. The Senate has its own procedural devices to obviate such points of order, however, and Senator Brooke used them successfully on the abortion issue. He raised what is called the "defense of germaneness" before the presiding officer had ruled on the Goldwater point of order.

Germaneness. Senate rules require that amendments—either proposed from the floor or offered by the Appropriations Committee—to general appropriations bills be germane. If a lawmaker raises a point of order against an amendment on the ground that it is legislation (or policy) in a general appropriations bill, the member who proposed the challenged amendment can raise—prior to the chair ruling on the point of order—the question, or defense, of germaneness. Under Senate rules, the issue is then submitted to the entire membership for resolution by majority vote and without debate. If the Senate decides that the proposed amendment is germane, the point of order automatically fails and the amendment may be considered. Conversely, if the Senate determines that the amendment is not germane, it also fails. In the abortion case, the Senate declared Brooke's amendment germane by a 74–21 vote. In such situations, senators typically vote on the policy issue and not on the procedural question. As Ted Stevens, R-Alaska, noted, Senate rules prohibit legislation on appropriations, but if senators raise the defense of germaneness on their amendments, "we will have a vote on germaneness, and that will be equivalent to adopting the amendment." [33] In short, technical objections can be waived to achieve preferred policy outcomes.

A 1979 precedent states that the defense of germaneness applies when the House, which originates appropriations measures, "opens the door" by including legislative language to which a Senate amendment might conceivably be germane. The Senate then has an "inherent right" to amend the House-passed provision. Since the mid-1990s the defense of germaneness, which can be raised for committee or floor amendments, has generally not been in play. Today, the Senate Appropriations Committee typically sends its own original appropriations bill to the floor for debate and amendment—that is, it no longer reports to the Senate the House-passed appropriations bill with a series of discrete Appropriations Committee amendments. Because no House language is before the Senate, the defense of germaneness is not available to senators whose amendments are challenged on the floor as being neither germane nor relevant and thus are in violation of Senate rules.

However, even when the Senate takes up a House-passed appropriations bill, the test for raising the defense of germaneness is low. Senators typically vet their proposed amendments with the Parliamentarian, who almost always states that they pass the threshold test because the House has opened the door. The defense of germaneness was last raised on October 4, 2005, when Armed Services Chairman John Warner, R-Va., attempted to add the defense authorization measure, crafted as an amendment, to the defense appropriations bill. Senator Ted Stevens, the chair of the Defense Appropriations Subcommittee, raised a point of order that the authorization violated Senate Rule XVI as non-germane legislation on an appropriations bill. Senator Warner immediately raised the defense of germaneness. The next day the Senate voted 49 yeas to 50 nays to reject the defense and the Warner amendment fell.

Reining in a Popular Device. On March 16, 1995, the Senate opened the floodgates on adding policy riders to appropriations bills. It voted to overturn the correct ruling by the presiding officer that an amendment offered by Sen. Kay Bailey Hutchison, R-Texas, dealing with the Endangered Species

Act constituted legislation on an appropriations bill and violated Senate Rule XVI. (A precedent established in this manner trumps Senate rules.) Thus was born the Hutchison precedent, and with it came a greater proliferation of riders to appropriations bills, many of them sponsored to highlight partisan agendas. As a result, it became difficult to enact appropriations bills in a timely manner. Finally, the Senate voted on July 26, 1999, to, as the Senate majority leader noted, "reinstate rule XVI which would make a point of order in order against legislation on an appropriations bill." [34]

The House experienced a rapid increase in the number of limitation riders—from forty-three in 1979 to seventy-four in 1982. Many of those dealt with social issues—particularly, school busing, school prayer, and abortion. When these controversial issues were repeatedly bottled up in the authorizing committees, members who wanted action on them turned increasingly to limitations as a vehicle for forcing House consideration. Frustrated by the sharp controversies and long delays these limitations were causing, the House changed its rules in 1983 to restrict the opportunities for members to offer limitation riders to appropriations bills.[35] The change authorized limitation amendments only if the motion to rise (or exit) from the Committee of the Whole was either rejected or not offered after the regular amendment process was completed on an appropriations bill. (The Committee of the Whole House on the state of the Union is the special forum into which the House transforms itself to consider the most important measures. It is discussed in Chapter 4. Debate and amendment may occur under the five-minute rule or as outlined by the House Rules Committee.)

When Republicans took control of the House in the mid-1990s, they again changed House rules by allowing the majority leader or a designee to have precedence in offering the motion to rise. "The intent of the rule is to permit the offering of limitation amendments at the end of the reading [for amendment], subject only to a motion to rise offered by the majority leader or a designee." [36] The effect of this change is to enhance the majority leadership's control over the offering of limitation amendments. (Democrats retained this rule when they took charge of the 110th House.)

Finally, a House rule designed to preserve committees' jurisdictional prerogatives stipulated that no committee except Ways and Means may report tax or tariff proposals. This rule was first used on October 27, 1983, when the Ways and Means chairman raised a point of order against a proposition in a general appropriations bill that concerned the duty-free entry of certain products from the Caribbean countries. The chair sustained the point of order by ruling that the provision was "a tariff measure in violation" of House rules. Just as authorizing committees may not report appropriations, appropriating and authorizing panels may not report tax and tariff proposals. Twenty years later, at the start of the 108th Congress (2003–2005), the House amended its rulebook to prohibit, for general appropriations measures, tax or tariff floor amendments that limit ("None of the funds . . .") the administration of a tax or tariff. (To date, this rule remains in effect.)

PRELUDE TO BUDGET REFORM

Congress's continuing struggle to control expenditures precipitated a comprehensive overhaul of its budgetary process. Titled the Congressional Budget and Impoundment Control Act of 1974, the law came about largely for three reasons. First, the Appropriations Committees gradually lost control of budget expenditures as the legislative, or authorizing, committees turned to backdoor financing techniques to accomplish their policy objectives. Congress thus lacked a central body to coordinate budgetary decisions, relate governmental revenue to expenditures, or calculate the effect of individual spending actions on the national economy. National fiscal policy reflected whatever emerged from Congress's excessively fragmented budget process. Second, the annual deficit had been on an upward spiral, and many lawmakers believed that a revamped budgetary process would enable Congress to gain better control of fiscal decisions. Third, presidents sometimes took advantage of Congress's piecemeal process. President Richard Nixon clashed with Congress over national spending priorities and impounded (refused to spend) monies at unprecedented levels for programs initiated by Democrats in Congress. "Far from administrative routine," wrote a budget scholar, "Nixon's impoundments in late 1972 and 1973 were designed to rewrite national policy at the expense of congressional power and intent." [37]

The combination of these three factors, along with growing public concern about the state of the national economy, led to enactment of the landmark 1974 budget law. That act established a congressional budget process that encouraged coordination and centralization. However, Congress did not institute this fiscal reorganization by abolishing the authorization, appropriations, or revenue processes. Such an attempt would have pitted the most powerful committees and members against one another and jeopardized any chance of realizing substantive budgetary changes. Instead, Congress added another budget layer to those already in place in the House and Senate. [38]

THE 1974 BUDGET ACT

Passage of the 1974 budget act had a major institutional and procedural effect on the legislative branch. Many of the act's original requirements have been modified in response to new developments. However, more than three decades later, it is still worthwhile to describe the main features of the act because they remain generally intact—the institutional entities; the timetable for budget decisions; the concurrent budget resolution (a measure that establishes Congress's framework for considering revenue, spending, and budget-related legislation); controls on backdoors and impoundments; reconciliation and the Byrd Rule; and enforcement of the concurrent budget resolution.

New Institutional Entities

The budget act created three new institutional entities: the House Budget Committee, the Senate Budget Committee, and the Congressional Budget

Office (CBO). The two Budget Committees have essentially the same functions, which include preparing annually a concurrent budget resolution, reviewing (or "scoring") the impact of existing or proposed legislation on federal expenditures, overseeing the CBO, monitoring the revenue and spending actions of the House and Senate, and, if necessary, assembling a reconciliation bill.

The two panels, however, are constituted differently. The House Budget Committee is required to have a rotating membership; most members may not serve more than eight years during a period of six consecutive Congresses. The committee must be composed of members drawn mainly from other standing committees, including five each from the Appropriations and Ways and Means Committees, one from the Rules Committee, and a leadership member from each of the two parties. Although the rotation allows many lawmakers to serve over time on this panel, it also has the effect of inhibiting cohesion (members' loyalty is to other committees), making it difficult at times for committee members to reach consensus on issues. Furthermore, the committee's fundamental task remains critical, visible, and often sharply partisan: producing a concurrent budget resolution that reflects differing Democratic and Republican views on the role and priorities of the national government.

By contrast, the Senate Budget Committee has no restrictions on tenure, and its members are not required to come from other designated committees. Indeed, the Budget Committee "has standing on a par with any other committee in the institution." [39]

The Congressional Budget Office is Congress's principal source for the information and analysis it needs to evaluate budget, tax, and spending proposals. Among other things, the 230 staff members of the CBO analyze budget, economic, and policy issues and make fiscal projections for the House and Senate Budget Committees and other congressional panels. The director of the nonpartisan CBO is appointed to a four-year term. The selection or reappointment of the director alternates between House and Senate leaders.

Because budgetary issues dominate much of the activity on Capitol Hill, the CBO's role in providing "scoring reports" and "cost estimates" to the House and Senate Budget Committees and other panels is especially significant. The small CBO scorekeeping unit measures the budgetary effects of the spending and tax plans of appropriators, authorizers, party leaders, and presidents. In doing so, it tracks pending and enacted spending and revenue measures to ensure that they are within the budgetary limits set by the concurrent budget resolution or other budget laws. CBO evaluates budget proposals against a baseline—an estimate of future spending and revenue projections for a fiscal year, assuming no change in existing budget policies. As a CBO report phrased it:

> The baseline is intended to provide a neutral, nonjudgmental foundation for assessing policy options. It is not "realistic," because tax and spending policies will change

over time. Rather, the projections . . . reflect CBO's best judgment about how the economy and other factors will affect federal revenues and spending under existing policies.[40]

Baseline estimates, like any budget plan, are only as accurate as the assumptions (inflation, unemployment, or economic growth rates) used in their formulation.

Scoring can be controversial and opens the CBO to criticism from lawmakers who do not like the results. For example, if the CBO calculates that bills of top priority to either party cost more than expected, Democrats or Republicans can be subject to partisan political attacks for sponsoring such legislation. In 2003 the House amended its rules to require the Ways and Means Committee to include in its reports accompanying tax legislation an analysis of the macroeconomic effects of the legislation. Republicans have long advocated this macroeconomic analysis, known as "dynamic scoring." Unlike "static scoring," which counts tax cuts as reductions in future revenue projections, dynamic scoring analyzes whether tax cuts create jobs and economic growth, resulting in more government revenues for the federal Treasury.

Both the CBO and the Joint Taxation Committee, which has formal responsibility for evaluating the revenue effects of tax proposals, employed dynamic scoring models to evaluate one of President George W. Bush's tax-cut plans. The results were mixed, with some models projecting larger future deficits and others demonstrating short-term economic improvements.[41] In 2006, the Bush administration created a Division of Dynamic Analysis in the Treasury Department to measure the effects of tax cuts and bolster its assertion, as Vice President Richard B. Cheney said, that "sensible tax cuts increase economic growth and add to the federal treasury." [42] Many economists cite the need for better evidence to substantiate the claim that tax cuts pay for themselves.

Timetable

To promote order and coordination in the budget process, Congress established a budgetary schedule. But the timetable, set out in Box 2-3, is changed periodically, and Congress commonly misses some of the target dates. For example, Congress is supposed to enact its concurrent budget resolution on or before April 15 of each year, but that does not always happen.

Disagreements over priorities and between the chambers, parties, and branches account, among other things, for the missed deadlines. In 1998 Congress failed for the first time to adopt a budget resolution. The House and Senate passed dramatically different resolutions, and the GOP leaders of each chamber could not agree on how to allocate funding. Four years later, also for the first time ever, the Senate could not adopt a budget resolution, in part because of partisan clashes. In 2004, for only the third time in thirty years, Congress could not adopt a budget resolution, in part because of policy disputes over tax policy. In 2006, Congress was also unable to adopt a budget

---

BOX 2-3   Congressional Budget Process Timetable

Deadline	Action to Be Completed
First Monday in February	President submits budget to Congress
February 15	Congressional Budget Office submits economic and budget outlook report to Budget Committees
Six weeks after president submits budget	Committees submit views and estimates to Budget Committees
April 1	Senate Budget Committee reports budget resolution
April 15	Congress completes action on budget resolution
May 15	Annual appropriations bills may be considered in the House, even if action on budget resolution has not been completed
June 10	House Appropriations Committee reports last regular appropriations bill
June 15	House completes action on reconciliation legislation (if required by budget resolution)
June 30	House completes action on annual appropriations bills
July 15	President submits midsession review of administration's budget to Congress
October 1	Fiscal year begins

SOURCE: Bill Heniff Jr., budget expert, Congressional Research Service.

---

resolution, in part because of bicameral conflicts. On occasion, there is debate about whether a budget resolution is even necessary, especially if it does not contain reconciliation instructions (see below). "My sense is that it's not of overwhelming importance," remarked Rep. Michael Castle, R-Del., because the significant budget battles are joined "when the appropriations bills hit the floors." [43]

When the House or Senate are late or fail to adopt a budget resolution, either chamber may adopt what is called a "deeming resolution," which is a simple House (H. Res.) or Senate (S. Res.) resolution. A deeming resolution may reflect the budget levels and enforcement procedures contained in a budget resolution adopted several months earlier by one chamber but not the other. Absent a deeming resolution, the multiyear budget levels adopted in the prior year's budget resolution remain in effect (except for discretionary spending levels for the upcoming fiscal year), but they may be "badly out of date, thereby undermining their value as a realistic basis for enforcement of present policies." [44]

The 1974 budget act prohibits the House and Senate from taking up budgetary measures before adopting the budget resolution for the upcoming fiscal year. However, the House permits appropriations bills to be taken up after May 15 even if legislators still have not agreed on a budget resolution. The House can waive the requirement by unanimous consent or majority vote; the Senate, however, requires sixty votes to waive this mandate.

When Congress is unable to complete action on one or more of the regular appropriations bills by the start of the fiscal year, it provides temporary funding for the affected federal agencies through a joint resolution called a continuing resolution or a continuing appropriation. (A record high twenty-one continuing resolutions were passed in the last year of the Clinton administration.) Traditionally, continuing resolutions have been employed to keep a few government agencies in operation for short periods, typically one to three months. Sometimes, however, they have become major policy-making instruments of massive size and scope. In 1986 and 1987, for example, Congress packaged the then thirteen regular appropriations bills into continuing resolutions.

When the GOP-controlled 109th Congress adjourned sine die in December 2006, having completed only two of the then eleven appropriations bills because of intra-party conflicts over spending levels, it passed a continuing resolution until February 15, 2007, leaving it to the incoming Democratically controlled Congress to deal with the unfinished spending bills funding most federal departments and programs. However, the two Democratic chairs of the House and Senate Appropriations Committee—Representative Obey and Senator Byrd—said they would extend the February 15 "CR" to October 1, 2007 (the start of the new fiscal year) so as not to get bogged down in old business just as the president is sending Congress his new budget for fiscal year 2008, as well as a large supplemental budget request to fund the Iraq war.[45]

Packaging a number of appropriations bills together creates what are called "megabills" or omnibus bills. These measures authorize and appropriate money to operate the federal government and make national policy in scores of diverse areas. These kinds of omnibus bills grant large powers to the small number of people who put these packages together—party and committee leaders and top executive officials. Omnibus measures usually arouse the ire of the rank and file, because typically little time is available in the final days of a session to debate these massive measures or to know what is in them.

Concurrent Budget Resolution

Congress's annual budget process centers on the adoption of a concurrent budget resolution. This measure is formulated by the Budget Committees, which consider the views and estimates of the other panels and hear the testimony of numerous witnesses. The budget resolution is composed of two basic parts. The first deals with fiscal aggregates: total federal spending (budget authority and outlays), total federal revenue, and the public debt (or surplus) for the upcoming fiscal year. The budget resolution also sets multiyear targets for these fiscal aggregates, either a five-year or ten-year projection (at least five years is required).

Various factors influence the length of the budget blueprint. One is the accuracy of the fiscal estimates. Five-year projections are likely to be more reliable than ten-year calculations. Another is avoidance of partisan criticism. If economic forecasts indicate escalating long-term deficits without any prospect of a budget coming into balance, congressional budgeteers may opt for a five- rather than ten-year projection. "If you can't show yourself in balance in 10 years, why embarrass yourself by doing a 10-year budget?" asked one senior Senate GOP budget aide.[46] Yet because the duration of the budget resolution sets the length of any reconciliation bill (described later in this chapter) that contains tax cuts, a ten-year projection may indicate a stronger economy than a five-year estimate. Conversely, a five- rather than ten-year tax-cut projection can obscure the magnitude of the long-term revenue losses while keeping the costs of the tax cuts within the limits set by the budget resolution.

The second part of the resolution subdivides the budget aggregates among twenty functional categories, such as national defense, energy, and agriculture, and establishes spending levels for each. Each functional category contains the programs that deal with a specific broad purpose regardless of the department or agency that administers them. The national defense function, for example, "is not the same as the Department of Defense; the function also includes programs administered by the Department of Energy. In addition, some DOD-administered programs are listed in other functions because their primary purpose is something other than defending the country." [47]

In effect, then, the budget resolution sets the overall level of discretionary spending for the upcoming fiscal year. That figure represents the "top line" that the appropriators cannot exceed, although emergency supplemental appropriations are exempt from the spending limit. Since 1990, when discretionary funding was about $500 billion, it has escalated primarily because of expenditures for defense, homeland security, and Gulf Coast reconstruction. For example, President Bush recommended for fiscal year 2007 that discretionary spending be fixed at $873 billion. (Both chambers agreed to deeming resolutions establishing the $873 billion number because they were unable to work out their differences on their respective concurrent budget resolutions.)[48] The bulk of that money goes to the three aforementioned program areas while non-defense and non-homeland security discretionary spending (for agriculture, environment, housing, college loans, and so on) is squeezed and on a downward trajectory.

The budget resolution may also require an optional process called reconciliation, which changes tax policy or entitlement programs. Congress develops reconciliation legislation to ensure that spending and revenue decisions comport with the policies set forth in the budget resolution.

In short, the budget resolution is a fiscal blueprint that establishes the context of congressional budgeting; guides the budgetary actions of the authorizing, appropriating, and taxing committees; and represents Congress's spending priorities. Because it is not submitted to the president, it cannot be vetoed and does not carry legal effect. As a senator explained, a budget resolution is "analogous to an architect's set of plans for constructing a building. It gives the general direction, framework, and prioritization of Federal fiscal policy each year. Those priorities then drive the individual appropriations and tax measures which will support that architectural plan." [49]

Floor Consideration of Budget Resolutions. The budget resolution is considered in the House under a rule issued by the Rules Committee. Typically, the Rules Committee permits House action on several alternative budget plans. One year the Rules Committee reported four major alternatives to the floor: three proposed by groups in the House (the "Blue Dog Coalition," the "Republican Study Committee," and the "Congressional Black Caucus and Progressive Caucus") and a "Democratic Alternative." [50] The House rejected all four and agreed to the GOP-reported budget resolution on a party-line vote. Generally, the Rules chairman points out that the order of consideration is important, "because if any one of these pass, then the debate immediately ceases and we go right to final passage." [51] (Parliamentary principles stipulate that it is not in order to re-amend something that has already been amended. A substitute budget plan, if adopted, would amend the entire text of the concurrent budget resolution leaving nothing left to further amend.) Unsurprisingly, fiscal alternatives are turned down. The majority party's budgetary blueprint prevails because that document reflects the priorities of the party in control.

Under a House rule reinstated at the start of the 108th Congress (it had been dropped from the rulebook of the 107th House), "after successful adoption of the budget [resolution] the House would automatically be 'deemed' to have passed a bill to increase the debt ceiling." [52] Called the "Gephardt Rule" after Richard Gephardt, D-Mo., who originated the rule in 1979, it underscores that votes to raise the federal debt ceiling—the statutory limit on the amount of money the government is allowed to borrow—are often controversial, in part because campaign challengers can charge lawmakers who support the hike as "big spenders." The House's "deeming" procedure avoids this problem.

The Senate, having no comparable procedure, needs to take action on the measure. Some lawmakers may use the occasion, especially in an election year, to castigate the White House or the majority party for their "borrow and spend" and fiscally irresponsible policies. They will not try to defeat the hike (from $6.2 trillion at the beginning of the 108th Congress to about $9 trillion in 2006), because that could put the government in default, unable to pay its bills. Further, partisan lawmakers could be tagged as "obstructionists" and suffer electoral consequences, as occurred in late 1995 and early 1996 when House Republicans forced two partial government shutdowns during the presidency of Bill Clinton. (From 1789 to 2000, the national debt rose to $5.6 trillion. In ten years, by 2010, the debt is expected to double in size.)

The Senate procedure for considering budget resolutions differs from that for other legislation in four major ways. First, floor action is regulated by the statutory requirements of the 1974 act as well as unanimous consent agreements negotiated by the party leadership. Second, concurrent budget resolutions are privileged, which means that they can be taken up easily either by unanimous consent or by a nondebatable motion to proceed to their consideration. (Motions to proceed for most legislation are subject to extended debate.) Third, budget resolutions carry a fifty-hour statutory debate limitation, which means that they cannot be filibustered to death. However, amendments can be taken up and voted on after the fifty hours, but without debate. This circumstance often leads to so-called "vote-a-ramas" in which senators may over several days "cast back-to-back votes on a dizzying array of dozens of amendments," many designed to provide campaign ammunition for the next election.[53] Fourth, the 1974 act imposes a germaneness requirement on amendments to budget resolutions. The act permits the germaneness standard to be set aside, but it requires at least sixty votes, instead of a simple majority, to obtain the waiver. The Senate, unlike the House, has no general germaneness rule.

The Budget Crosswalk. When the House and Senate pass budget resolutions that contain different aggregate and functional totals, which is normal practice, the disagreements usually have to be resolved by a conference committee. The conferees prepare a report that provides a bank account for the various House and Senate committees. This account distributes the total agreed-on spending for the year among the relevant committees.

This allocation procedure, called a budget crosswalk, involves two steps. First, section 302(a) of the 1974 budget act requires the joint explanatory statement that accompanies the conference report to divide the budget totals among the House and Senate committees with budgetary jurisdiction for the programs reflected in the various functional categories. The crosswalk is necessary because Congress employs the functional category designations developed by the White House's Office of Management and Budget (OMB). These designations do not correspond exactly to many House and Senate committees, with their overlapping jurisdictions.

Second, under section 302(b), the House and Senate Appropriations Committees each subdivide their spending allocations among their subcommittees. (If the concurrent budget resolution is not passed by the required April 15 date, informal allocations are made typically based on the discretionary spending amounts included in the president's budget.) The suballocations are reported by the Appropriations Committees to their respective chambers. The committee and subcommittee allocations are enforceable by members raising points of order against bills that exceed a committee's total allocation and the suballocations assigned its subcommittees. In the Senate such points of order can be overturned only by a supermajority vote of sixty.

Little is known about how the Appropriations Committees divide their spending pie among the subunits. "The allocation of the [discretionary] federal budget among the . . . Appropriations subcommittees is the most closed, the least understood, and the most consequential annual process within the

Congress," wrote one congressional budget analyst.[54] No doubt hard bargaining permeates the activities of the "College of Cardinals" as each subcommittee chair strives to maximize his or her share of spending authority.

Reconciliation

Reconciliation, as noted earlier, is an optional procedure that enables Congress to implement its comprehensive fiscal policy (as reflected in the budget resolution) by changing tax and entitlement laws. The two-step process is designed to reconcile the parts with the whole or, put differently, to bring existing law into conformity with the current budget resolution. In practice, reconciliation is used to reduce spending, primarily through entitlement savings, and to either increase revenues or cut taxes. It does not address funding that is established in annual appropriations bills. The Appropriations Committees are bound by the discretionary spending limits set forth in the budget resolution. First employed in 1980, reconciliation is used more often than not because it has proven to be an effective device for achieving budgetary savings. From 1980 to early 2006, Congress has sent twenty reconciliation bills to the White House; the president has signed seventeen and vetoed three with no override by Congress.

The first step in reconciliation calls for congressional approval of a budget resolution that instructs House and Senate committees to report legislation making cuts in spending, changes in revenue, or both on programs and agency operations by a certain date. An example of House reconciliation directives is presented in Box 2-4. The panels' recommended budget savings, which are supposed to meet or exceed the amounts designated for each committee in the resolution if multiple committees are involved, are transmitted to the respective House and Senate Budget Committees. The second step involves packaging the recommendations into an omnibus reconciliation bill, followed by floor action in each chamber. The Budget Committees cannot make substantive changes in the savings proposals received from each instructed committee. If only one committee is involved, it reports its recommendations directly to the floor.

In the first dramatic use of reconciliation, President Ronald Reagan in 1981 persuaded Congress to employ the procedure to achieve massive cuts in domestic programs (totaling about $130 billion over three years). Never before had reconciliation been employed on such a grand scale. The entire process was expedited and in a manner that short-circuited regular legislative procedures. A highly charged atmosphere produced a legislative result, wrote Howard H. Baker Jr., R-Tenn., then Senate majority leader, "that would have been impossible to achieve if each committee had reported an individual bill on subject matter solely within its jurisdiction." [55] Reconciliation forced nearly all House and Senate committees to make unwanted cuts in programs under their jurisdiction. Given their policy-making significance, these bills, not surprisingly, are shepherded through Congress by party leaders and key committee leaders.

Box 2-4   House Reconciliation Directives

This excerpt from the budget resolution for fiscal year 2006 stipulates reconciliation instructions for two House committees. (Senate reconciliation instructions are comparable.) The reconciliation directives assume that the spending reductions will be incorporated into an omnibus bill that the House Budget Committees will report (without any substantive revisions) to their chamber. The directive also establishes a deadline for the committees' submission of their recommendations.

TITLE II—RECONCILIATION AND REPORT SUBMISSIONS

SEC. 201. RECONCILIATION IN THE HOUSE OF REPRESENTATIVES.

(a) SUBMISSIONS TO SLOW THE GROWTH IN MANDATORY SPENDING- (1) Not later than September 16, 2005, the House committees named in paragraph (2) shall submit their recommendations to the House Committee on the Budget. After receiving those recommendations, the House Committee on the Budget shall report to the House a reconciliation bill carrying out all such recommendations without any substantive revision.

(2) INSTRUCTIONS-

(A) COMMITTEE ON AGRICULTURE- The House Committee on Agriculture shall report changes in laws within its jurisdiction sufficient to reduce the level of direct spending for the committee by $173,000,000 in outlays for fiscal year 2006 and $3,000,000,000 in outlays for the period of fiscal years 2006 through 2010.

(B) COMMITTEE ON EDUCATION AND LABOR- The House Committee on Education and Labor shall report changes in laws within its jurisdiction sufficient to reduce the level of direct spending for that committee by $992,000,000 in outlays for fiscal years 2005 and 2006 and $12,651,000,000 in outlays for the period of fiscal years 2005 through 2010.

* * * * *

SOURCE: House Report 109-62, Conference Report to accompany H.Con.Res. 95, *Concurrent Resolution on the Budget for Fiscal Year 2006* (April 28, 2005), 11–13.

The irony is that Congress's budget process, designed in 1974 to advance and reassert the legislative branch's power of the purse, was captured by the White House in 1981 and used to achieve President Reagan's objectives. However, reconciliation can be used by either branch or party provided it has the votes to implement its objectives. In 1995 the GOP-dominated Congress employed reconciliation to try to scale back the size of government, cut taxes, and balance the budget in seven years. "Its efforts," observed one onlooker, "led to two historic federal government shutdowns, thirteen stopgap measures, several presidential vetoes, and ultimately failed to produce a meaningful fiscal agreement with the White House." [56]

On several occasions reconciliation directives provided for more than one reconciliation bill. In 1996, for example, the directive provided for a three-stage process in which a tax cut bill would be considered in conjunction with two measures drafted to achieve savings in Medicare, welfare, and other entitlement programs. In 1999 and 2000 reconciliation involved only the tax-writing committees, and they were instructed to report tax reduction bills directly to the floor. In 2005, reconciliation instructions governed three measures, a spending bill, involving cuts in mandatory programs as part of the GOP's effort to demonstrate fiscal discipline; a tax bill, concerning $70 billion in revenue cuts; and a bill to raise the debt limit.

During the 109th Congress (2005–2007), for the first time since 1997, reconciliation was employed to slow the growth in entitlement, or mandatory, spending. The amount saved from programs such as Medicare and Medicaid was relatively small ($39.7 billion) compared to the reconciliation reduction packages of the 1990s, which averaged $350 billion. Setting aside the fact, as noted earlier, that Congress in 2006 could not adopt a concurrent resolution authorizing reconciliation, it still would have been enormously difficult to achieve even a small amount of budgetary savings using this procedure. At least six reasons explain why this was the case.

First, it is simply hard to achieve savings in popular programs in a highly polarized and closely divided Congress. Second, moderate Republicans, who run in districts with significant numbers of Democratic voters, refused to accept the deeper cuts in entitlement programs wanted by their party leaders. Third, Democrats were united in their opposition to the GOP plans (no Democrat in either chamber voted for the budget resolution) and lambasted Republicans for cutting programs that benefit the elderly and the poor while proposing additional tax cuts for the well-off. "We made the issues in that budget too hot for the Republicans to handle," declared House Democratic leader Pelosi.[57] Fourth, outside groups, such as AARP (formerly known as the American Association of Retired Persons), launched aggressive ad campaigns in the districts of moderate Republicans to pressure them to oppose the program reductions. Fifth, many Republicans had never experienced reconciliation involving mandatory programs and were wary of explaining program cuts to their constituents. Finally, as a former GOP staff director of the House Budget Committee explained, "Today is very different than the 1990s" when there was a "complete consensus that eliminating the deficit was the number one priority." [58] Efforts to reduce the deficit have not disappeared but spending on the Iraq war, homeland security, veterans benefits, Gulf Coast reconstruction, the global struggle against terrorism, or a new prescription drug bill has assumed higher priority.

Reconciliation in the House is considered under the terms of a rule from the Rules Committee. Reconciliation bills in the Senate are treated differently from other bills and amendments and under procedures outlined in the 1974 budget act. They cannot be filibustered (there is a statutory time limit of twenty hours for debate); passage requires a simple majority instead of a possible sixty votes to stop a talkathon; and amendments must be germane and deficit neutral (tax cuts or spending increases must be "offset" by equivalent revenue increases or spending reductions). It is not surprising that proposals likely to arouse controversy in the Senate, such as tax cuts, are attached to filibuster-proof reconciliation bills. To constrain lawmakers from putting issues (abortion policy, for example) extraneous to deficit reduction into reconciliation bills, the Senate adopted the so-called Byrd Rule.

The Byrd Rule

The Byrd Rule, named after Senator Byrd of West Virginia, was adopted on a temporary basis in 1985; five years later it became permanent as an amendment to the 1974 Budget Act. The rule states that reconciliation provisions must be consistent with the goals of the reconciliation instructions. Reconciliation requires committees with policy-making responsibilities—the tax-writing and authorizing committees—to either raise revenues or cut mandatory spending programs. However, these panels sometimes report policy provisions that have no effect on the budget, and may even worsen the deficit. Reconciliation has been used, for example, to expand Medicaid coverage, reinstate the broadcast fairness doctrine, and provide funds for the trade adjustment assistance program. Such provisions are inserted in reconciliation bills in part "because the budget committees are specifically prohibited from making any substantive changes in the recommendations from each committee." [59]

The objective of the Byrd Rule is to exclude extraneous—unrelated to deficit reduction—matter in reconciliation measures. Maximizing its potency, the rule can be waived only by a three-fifths vote of the Senate. Similarly, sixty votes are required to overturn a ruling of the Senate's presiding officer that a provision in a reconciliation bill (or a floor amendment to it) is extraneous. During the period from 1985 through 2004, only nine of forty-one motions to waive the Byrd rule were successful. [60]

What is extraneous, however, is not always easy to determine. The Byrd Rule itself provides six definitions of what is extraneous (and several exceptions to what is considered extraneous). The rule stipulates, for example, that a provision is extraneous if it does not produce a change in outlays or revenues or is outside the jurisdiction of the committee that recommended the provision for inclusion in the reconciliation measure. To apply such definitions in practical cases can be complex.

> The application of the [Byrd] rule can be tortuous. Take food stamps, for example. The House approved $7.3 billion in extra spending for food stamps in its reconciliation bill; the Senate did not. Conferees . . . agreed to include up to the House amount in the conference report, but [Senate] Republicans hope to strip it out, ar-

guing that it violates the Byrd rule because it would force the [Senate Agriculture] committee to miss its deficit-cutting target. The Senate Agriculture Committee's target was $3.2 billion. [Senate] Democrats argued behind the scenes that it was impossible to apply the Byrd rule to a conference report. What was the relevant "committee?" House Agriculture? Senate Agriculture? The conference committee? The House's Committee of the Whole?[61]

In the end, the Senate parliamentarian agreed that the Byrd Rule could not be applied to this case. In doing so, he cleared the way for the food stamps provision to remain in the conference report.

Because the Byrd Rule also applies to House-Senate conference reports, it has become a source of conflict between the chambers. House committee chairs charge that the Byrd Rule, "by allowing Senators to rise on points of order and strike extraneous provisions [from conference reports], gives the Senate the power to dictate House actions." [62] From 1985 through 2005, the Byrd rule has been invoked "only four times during consideration of a conference report on a reconciliation measure (twice in 1993, once in 1995, and once in 1997)." [63]

Controls on Impoundments

Title X of the 1974 budget act permits Congress to review executive impoundments of appropriated funds. The act divides impoundments into two categories—deferrals (a temporary delay in the expenditure of funds to achieve savings made possible through greater efficiencies or to provide for contingencies) and rescissions (the permanent cancellation of budget authority)—which are considered under separate procedures. Presidents are obligated to inform Congress of their proposed deferrals and rescissions and to set forth the reasons for them. The GAO is authorized to review these special messages to ensure that impoundments are not classified improperly.

To rescind budget authority, the president submits a message to Congress indicating the reasons for the rescission. Over the next forty-five days of continuous session (days when Congress is in session, not calendar days), Congress may then pass a rescission bill that cancels all, part, or none of the amount requested by the president. If both houses fail to pass a rescission bill before the expiration of the forty-five-day period, the president must make the funds available for obligation. In short, inaction produces action: the release of appropriated funds.

Enforcement of the Budget Resolution

The House and Senate enforce the goals and policies set forth in the budget resolution through devices such as scorekeeping, spending allocations to committees and subcommittees, reconciliation, budgetary information provided by the CBO, and the monitoring role of the Budget Committees, as well as through points of order such as the Byrd Rule raised on the House or Senate floor. Points of order under the budget act are either substantive or procedural in character. Substantive points of order are raised to ensure compliance with the budget resolution. For example, a lawmaker can challenge a floor amendment that would cause a standing committee to exceed its allocation of new discretionary spending authority. Procedural points of order are raised to ensure compliance with features of the 1974 budget act and companion legislation. The House and Senate permit waivers of any points of order. The House usually does this in a rule issued by the Rules Committee. The Senate, by contrast, must waive most points of order by a three-fifths vote of all senators. Senators, then, find themselves often in search of the sixty votes needed to waive some feature of the budget act so that they can accomplish a policy objective, especially when a broad consensus exists to pass a bill or amendment.

EVOLUTION OF THE BUDGET PROCESS

Congressional procedures and politics are forever changing, and the congressional budget process is no exception. In the mid-1980s and later, Congress enacted significant statutory changes in its budget process. These changes emerged from a new political climate: the politics of deficit reduction. After Ronald Reagan took office in 1981 the annual deficits soared. Reagan's objectives were clear and threefold: slash domestic spending, increase defense expenditures, and cut taxes. However, the revenue losses caused by the tax cuts, combined with rising defense expenditures and insufficient reductions in other areas, soon produced triple digit deficits in the $200 billion to $300 billion range. Never before had the nation seen such huge deficits during peacetime and during an economic expansion—that is, the one that followed the 1982 economic recession. Congress acted to stem the river of red ink through legislation.

The 1985 Balanced Budget and Emergency Deficit Control Act (Gramm-Rudman-Hollings)

As the national debt—the accumulation of annual deficits—mounted after 1981, numerous proposals were put forth to deal with the escalating deficits. One notable initiative was put forth in the mid-1980s by Senators Phil Gramm, R-Texas, Warren Rudman, R-N.H., and Ernest Hollings, D-S.C., and enacted into law. Its core feature was establishment of annual statutory deficit reduction targets that, if achieved, would over time lead to a balanced national budget. If Congress did not meet the targets, the president would have to sequester funds—that is, impose automatic across-the-board spending cuts evenly divided between defense and domestic programs. The dire prospect of a "fiscal train wreck" was supposed to create an incentive for Congress and the president to decide how best to achieve deficit reduction. But, in the end, the plan did not work, and deficits continued to climb. Congress exempted 70 percent of the budget from sequestration, and budgetary gimmicks were employed to meet the statutory targets. In response, Congress enacted another major budgetary reform—the Budget Enforcement Act (BEA) of 1990, which was amended several times before it expired on October 1, 2002.

The Budget Enforcement Act

This act once again changed the fiscal procedures of Congress. The law was intended to shift Congress's attention from deficit reduction to spending control. Thus it removed the threat of automatic, across-the-board reductions if conditions beyond Congress's control—inflation, a worsening economy, or emergency funding for crises or disasters—pushed the deficit upward.

Two enforcement mechanisms undergirded the BEA. First, it set spending caps, or limits, for discretionary spending. The spending caps could be changed, but Congress and the president would have to agree to the modification. If Congress exceeded the spending limits, the law provided for across-the-board reductions to bring spending into line with the caps. However, a loophole in the law enabled Congress and the president to escape tight spending caps and avoid a zero-sum dilemma: having to pay for spending hikes in some discretionary programs by making cuts in other programs. If Congress and the president designated expenditures above the cap as "emergency" (a flexible term that implies something unforeseen or unpredictable) spending, they were exempt from the limits imposed by the BEA. When this law was negotiated in 1990 between congressional leaders and the first President Bush, "some questioned the lack of flexibility to accommodate unforeseen natural or man-made disasters," so the safety-valve of "emergency" spending was agreed to by these decision makers. However, Congress and the president often view emergency spending as "free money" because "it is not controlled or offset vis-à-vis other federal spending." [64] For example, Congress used the emergency designation to finance the constitutionally required 2000 decennial census.

Since September 11, 2001, the "emergency" designation has been employed six times to fund the war in Iraq and Afghanistan. Lawmakers express concern about funding the terrorist war outside the regular budget process, because emergency spending can exceed the annual caps (set in the budget resolution) for discretionary expenditures. Paying for the war through "emergency" spending, which in 2006 accumulated close to $400 billion, inhibits a full-fledged legislative debate "about trade-offs between 'guns and butter,' defense spending versus other priorities—or even tradeoffs within the defense establishment." [65] A Senate budget chairman even asserted that the federal government keeps two sets of budgetary books: one for spending "within the discretionary caps" and one for emergency spending "outside the caps." He called the latter the "shadow budget." [66]

Second, the BEA subjected tax and entitlement programs to a new "pay as you go" (PAYGO) procedure. Any tax reductions or any increases in direct spending (entitlement) programs had to be offset by tax hikes or reductions in other direct spending programs. The enforcement threat was across-the-board cuts in direct spending programs not exempt under BEA. As the chief counsel of the Senate Budget Committee explained: "The 'pay-as-you-go' label implies that Congress and the President may cut taxes or create [new direct spending] programs—that is 'go'—if they also agree to provide offsetting increased revenues or spending reductions—that is 'pay.' "[67]

The onset of a surplus era in the late 1990s uncapped a pent-up desire among many lawmakers to spend money on various programs and activities and cut taxes. The requirements of the BEA were either waived or ignored as the psychology of plenty took hold in Congress. Many lawmakers viewed the budgetary restraints embedded in the BEA as an out-of-date device for dealing with fiscal surpluses. As a result, in 2002 the law was allowed to expire.

However, under a so-called "elastic clause" provision (Section 301) in the 1974 Budget Act, each chamber's budget resolution may "require such other procedures, relating to the budget, as may be appropriate to carry out the purposes of this Act." The Senate has established a PAYGO rule for itself that prohibits consideration of entitlement or tax legislation that would increase the deficit unless it is assumed in the budget resolution. Subject to a sixty-vote waiver requirement, the Senate's rule is set to expire in 2008.

The 110th House (2007–2009) amended its rules to establish a new PAYGO point of order as a way to restrain spending and impose fiscal discipliine.[68] Thus, if lawmakers propose a new tax cut or entitlement hike, they must find a way to pay for it—a so-called "offset"— so the revenue loss does not increase the budget deficit. If the House enacts a statutory "pay-go" measure and the Senate follows suit, it is unclear whether President Bush would sign the requirement into law because of his concern that "pay-go" would impede enactment of tax cuts designed to boost the economy.

A BRIEF SURPLUS ERA

Fierce battles over the budget were waged throughout most of the 1990s between congressional Republicans and President Clinton. Then, to the surprise of Democrats and Republicans, the booming economy led to surpluses starting in 1998 and a projection in 2001 of $5.6 trillion in excess revenues over ten years. The partisan battles did not end, however. Both parties competed over who could best protect Social Security. The CBO's ten-year projection of a $5.6 trillion surplus was actually made up of two surpluses. The first surplus ($2.5 trillion), generated from the payroll taxes of workers and employers, was earmarked for deposit in the Social Security trust fund. The excess in Social Security revenues is called the "off-budget" surplus. The second surplus was the "on-budget" surplus ($3.1 trillion). This was the amount of money generated from income taxes and other sources, excluding the Social Security trust fund. Normally, such funds are used to finance federal agencies and programs and day-to-day government activities.

Both parties pledged not to touch the off-budget surplus, and in 1998 President Clinton promised to "save Social Security first." No longer would Social Security be raided to pay for the general operations of the government. In fact, for the preceding two decades both parties had masked the true size of the deficit by using the extra Social Security funds to help pay for general government programs. Not to be outdone, Republicans embraced the "lockbox" concept. They promised to lock up 100 percent of the Social Security surplus.

But the terrorist attacks of September 11, 2001, and other events (Iraq and Hurricane Katrina, for instance) brought a fast end to the short-lived surplus era (1998–2002). The lockbox was picked as excess Social Security funds once more were used to fund the general government. Today, there is rather little discussion of balanced budgets; instead, record-setting deficits since September 11, 2001, have led many pundits to predict red ink as far as the eye can see. Noteworthy is the length of the first triple-digit deficit period (1981–1998) compared with the brevity of the surplus era. Simply put, deficits are easy to accumulate but hard to end; surpluses are hard to generate but easy to use up.

THE CHALLENGE AHEAD

Worrisome to many on Capitol Hill is the return of large deficits at a time when an "entitlement revolution" is under way. "Call it government by A.T.M.," remarked an analyst, "you walk up, hit the buttons and the cash to which you're entitled pops out." [69] The shift in the budget from discretionary to mandatory spending comes at a time when deficits are rising, and 76 million baby boomers (those born between 1946 and 1964) are fast approaching retirement. An aging and longer-living—thanks to medical and technological developments—population will produce an explosion of expenditures in the country's large entitlement programs, such as Social Security, Medicare, and Medicaid. In fact, in only a few decades these three programs will likely run short of cash to cover eligible beneficiaries. As a Senate Budget chair said, "If you take Medicare, Medicaid, and Social Security and combine them, we will spend more in 2030 than we spend today [$2.8 trillion] on the entire Federal Government." [70]

In addition, demographers project a smaller workforce, which will not pay enough payroll taxes to cover the retirement needs of the elderly. Higher birthrates, an influx of immigrants, or advances in worker productivity could resolve this concern. In the judgment of former CBO director Douglas Holtz-Eakin, a GOP appointee to the post, the nation cannot sustain its current fiscal course without tax hikes, a proposal that is not looked upon favorably by President Bush. "If we don't change Social Security, Medicare, or Medicaid, we're gonna raise taxes," said Holtz-Eakin. "It doesn't matter if you're a Republican, Democrat, or Martian. They're going up. You just can't avoid it" if people want to receive in the future the same type of federal services.[71]

Even with rising deficits, there is an even bleaker fiscal picture if one considers the unfunded commitments of the federal government. These commitments are largely in the retirement and health care fields, but there are other promised federal benefits in other areas, such as environmental cleanups. David Walker, the comptroller general of the United States, pointed out that at the end of fiscal year 2005 (September 30, 2005), "the U.S. government's liabilities and unfunded commitments reached over $46 trillion [excluding rebuilding the Gulf Coast or future costs associated with Iraq and Afghanistan], up from about $20 trillion just five years ago." [72] Medicare's new prescription drug program, enacted in 2003, is expected to cost "more than $1 trillion over the next decade." [73] It merits mention that the prescription drug program is the largest expansion of Medicare since President Lyndon Johnson persuaded Congress to create Medicare. And the drug program was enacted with a Republican in the White House and GOP control of Congress. As the party long known for advocating limited government and balanced budgets, many GOP lawmakers are concerned that the Republican-led government is spending far more than it is taking in. "We're growing the government at a pace that makes Democrats look thrifty," said Senator Lindsey Graham, R-S.C.[74]

Unsurprisingly, many GOP and Democratic lawmakers are advocating spending cuts, entitlement reform, budget process revisions, and economic growth as ways to set the country on a sustainable fiscal course for the future. For example, costs associated with Social Security might be accommodated by reducing the rate of spending for the program by raising the retirement age or applying means-testing to the program so that affluent retirees would have to pay taxes on their benefits. As for the government's health care programs, it is likely that these will be far harder to revamp than its retirement programs for one fundamental reason: quality medical care is what most people want for their family members, regardless of cost.

Given the government's long-term fiscal commitments and projections of rising deficits, Congress faces a serious dilemma in providing adequate funding for competing priorities (entitlements versus discretionary spending and within the discretionary category, defense and homeland security versus domestic spending) and making higher interest payments on the national debt. As an analyst for a nonpartisan think tank put it, "What we have done in the last several years is decide we can cut taxes, fight two wars, increase homeland security, expand government entitlement benefits, and leave the bill to future generations." [75] The government's overspending is funded to a large extent by borrowing from foreign nations, such as China and Japan, and there is no guarantee that this will continue indefinitely. Indeed, much of the discussion surrounding taxes, spending, or deficits is crystallized by a question posed by Rep. Barney Frank, D-Mass.: "What is the appropriate level of public activity in our society?" [76] Democrats and Republicans often provide different answers to this question.

NOTES

1. Quoted in *Roll Call*, July 29, 2002, 4.
2. House Committee on the Budget, *Congressional Control of Expenditures*, January 1977, 6. The study was prepared by Allen Schick.
3. *Congressional Record*, April 4, 2000, S2055.
4. *Congressional Record*, September 29, 2006, S10634.
5. John William Ellwood, ed., *Reductions in U.S. Domestic Spending* (New Brunswick, N.J.: Transaction Books, 1982), 21.
6. Jonathan Kaplan, "Earmarks: Apply Online," *The Hill*, February 15, 2006, 1.
7. Peter Cohn, "Moving Target," *National Journal*, February 11, 2006, 61.
8. Eamon Javers, "Dirty Secrets of the 'Black Budget,' " *Business Week*, February 27, 2006, 41.
9. *Congressional Record*, February 9, 2006, S980.
10. John Lancaster, " 'Earmark' Attack Raises Hackles," *Washington Post*, February 11, 2002, A23.
11. David Rosenbaum, "Lawmakers' Pet Projects (and Not Just for Roads) Find Home in Transportation Bill," *Washington Post*, July 30, 2005, A11.
12. The quoted material is from Steven Dennis, "House Adopts Budget, Earmark Rules," *CQ Weekly*, January 8, 2007, 125. Also see *Congressional Record*, January 4, 2007, H28. H. Res. 6 also defines "earmarks," "limited tax benefits," and "limited tariff benefits," and includes a provision designed to prevent or inhibit waivers of the earmark disclosure requirements.
13. *Congressional Record*, January 11, 2007, S415–S416, S425–S429, S435–S437; January 12, S492–S494; January 16, S567–S568.
14. Absent an authorization law, the Appropriations Committees typically base their financial recommendations on the president's budget requests.
15. Roy T. Meyers, "Biennial Budgeting," staff working paper, Congressional Budget Office, November 1987, 42.
16. Richard Munson, *The Cardinals of Capitol Hill* (New York: Grove Press, 1993), 6.
17. Everett Somerville Brown, ed., *William Plumer's Memorandum of Proceedings in the United States Senate, 1803–1807* (New York: Macmillan, 1923), 490.
18. Robert Luce, *Legislative Problems* (Boston: Houghton Mifflin, 1935), 425–426.
19. Louis Fisher, "The Authorization-Appropriation Process in Congress: Formal Rules and Informal Practices," *Catholic University Law Review* (Fall 1979): 53.
20. CBO Report, "Unauthorized Appropriations and Expiring Authorizations," January 13, 2006, 2. This report can be accessed online from the Web site of the Congressional Budget Office.
21. *Operations of the Congress: Testimony of House and Senate Leaders*, hearing before the Joint Committee on the Organization of Congress, 103d Cong., 1st sess., January 26, 1993, 75–76.
22. *Budget Process*, hearing before the Joint Committee on the Organization of Congress, 103d Cong., 1st sess., March 16, 1993, 52.
23. *Operations of the Congress*, 70.
24. *Congressional Record*, July 29, 2005, S9368.
25. Corine Hegland, "Hyde-Bound It Isn't," *National Journal*, June 28, 2003, 2106.
26. Jeff Plungis, "Shuster's Use of Budgetary 'Firewalls' Takes Other Chairman by Surprise," *CQ Weekly*, August 7, 1999, 1917.

27. Emily Pierce, "Road Map," *Roll Call,* February 8, 2005, 17.
28. *Tax Expenditures, Senate Committee on the Budget,* 108th Cong., 2d sess. (Washington, D.C.: U.S. Government Printing Office, 2004), 2.
29. Heidi Glenn, "Tax Expenditure Transparency Vital, Comptroller General Says," *Tax Notes,* March 6, 2006, 1038.
30. Jon Healey, "Lautenberg Moves to Reduce Transportation Earmarks," *Congressional Quarterly Weekly Report,* October 2, 1993, 2625.
31. Floyd M. Riddick and Alan S. Frumin, *Senate Procedure: Precedents and Practices* (Washington, D.C.: Government Printing Office, 1992), 150.
32. Fisher, "Authorization-Appropriation Process in Congress," 74–75. The House considered the issue on June 17, 1977, and the Senate on June 29, 1977. See Roger H. Davidson, "Procedures and Politics in Congress," in *The Abortion Dispute and the American System,* ed. Gilbert Y. Steiner (Washington, D.C.: Brookings, 1982), 30–46.
33. *Congressional Record,* October 20, 1993, S13966.
34. *Congressional Record,* July 26, 1999, S9171.
35. *Congressional Record,* January 3, 1983, H5–H22.
36. *Congressional Record,* January 4, 1995, H37.
37. Allen Schick, *Congress and Money* (Washington, D.C.: Urban Institute Press, 1980), 46.
38. *Ibid.,* 59.
39. Daniel P. Franklin, *Making Ends Meet: Congressional Budgeting in the Age of Deficits* (Washington, D.C.: CQ Press, 1993), 40.
40. Cited in Marc Labonte, "Baseline Budget Projections: A Discussion of Issues," CRS Report, February 3, 2006, 1.
41. See *CongressDailyAM,* March 26, 2003, 3; "What Jobs? What Growth?" (editorial), *Washington Post,* May 14, 2003, A28; Jill Barshay, "Dynamic Scoring of Tax Cuts a Work in Progress," *CQ Today,* February 28, 2003, 9–10; and Bruce Bartlett, "Upgrade at CBO," *Washington Times,* January 15, 2003, A15.
42. Nell Henderson, "Cheney Says New Unit Will Prove Tax Cuts Boost Revenue," *Washington Post,* February 11, 2006, A11.
43. David Baumann, "Does a Budget Really Matter?" *National Journal,* April 15, 2006, 39.
44. Robert Keith, "The 'Deeming Resolution': A Budget Enforcement Tool," CRS Report for Congress, November 15, 2002, 3.
45. Carl Hulse, "Democrats Decline to Take Up Unfinished Bills," *New York Times,* December 12, 2006, A25.
46. Andrew Taylor, "Republicans Split on Budget Resolution Time Element," *CQ Today,* February 27, 2003, 4.
47. Stan Collender, "Budget Battles: The Future Is Now" NationalJournal.com, January 21, 2003, 2–3.
48. *Congressional Record,* June 14, 2006, S5835. Upset with the deeming resolution, Senator Tom Harkin, D-Iowa, defined it this way: "You see, we pass a budget, but then the budget cannot get passed by the House, so, therefore, we then are going to pass a deeming resolution to deem something that we cannot pass as passed because we deem it passed."
49. *Congressional Record,* March 2, 2000, S1050.
50. *Congressional Record,* March 20, 2003, D274.
51. *Congressional Record,* May 17, 1995, H5107.

52. Andrew Taylor and Alan Ota, "GOP to Seek Budget Deal Now, Tax Cut Decision Later," *CQ Today*, April 10, 2003, 6.

53. Mark Preston, " 'Vote-a-Rama' Keeps Wearing Senate Down," *Roll Call*, March 26, 2003, 1.

54. Munson, *Cardinals of Capitol Hill*, 19.

55. Howard H. Baker Jr., "An Introduction to the Politics of Reconciliation," *Harvard Journal on Legislation* (Winter 1983): 2.

56. Anita Krishnakumar, "Reconciliation and the Fiscal Constitution: The Anatomy of the 1995–96 Budget Train Wreck," *Harvard Journal on Legislation* (Summer 1998): 489.

57. Janet Hook and Richard Simon, "Shy Votes, GOP Puts Off Budget," *Los Angeles Times*, November 11, 2005, A6.

58. David Baumann, "What Reconciliation Really Requires," NationalJournal.com, October 27, 2005, 2. Baumann is also the source for the fifth reason in this paragraph.

59. Stanley E. Collender, *The Guide to the Federal Budget, Fiscal 1995* (Washington, D.C.: Urban Institute Press, 1994), 60.

60. For a detailed study of the Byrd Rule, see Robert Keith, "The Budget Reconciliation Process: The Senate's 'Byrd Rule,' " CRS Report, April 7, 2005.

61. George Hager, "The Byrd Rule: Not an Easy Call," *Congressional Quarterly Weekly Report*, July 31, 1993, 2027.

62. Karen Foerstel, "Byrd Rule War Erupts Once Again," *Roll Call*, February 24, 1994, 13.

63. Keith, "The Budget Reconciliation Process: The Senate's 'Byrd Rule,' " 1.

64. Judd Gregg, "The Safety Valve Has Become a Fire Hose," *Wall Street Journal*, April 18, 2006, A18. The quotation in the previous sentence is also from this article by the Senate Budget Chairman.

65. Gail Russell Chaddock, "War Costs Irk the Congress," *Christian Science Monitor*, February 21, 2006, 11. See John Cranford, "The Defense Deceit," *CQ Weekly*, January 30, 2006, 262.

66. Gregg, "The Safety Valve Has Become a Fire Hose," A18.

67. William Dauster, "Budget Process Issues for 1993," *Journal of Law and Politics* 9, no. 9 (1992): 26.

68. *Congressional Record*, January 5, 2007, H69–H85.

69. Matthew Miller, "The Big Federal Freeze," *New York Times Magazine*, October 15, 2000, 5.

70. *Congressional Record*, March 13, 2006, S1990.

71. Emily Dagostino, "Tax Cuts, Increases No Cure-All for Spending Woes, Holtz-Eakin Says," *Tax Notes*, January 30, 2006, 459.

72. David M. Walker, "America's Fiscal Future," Address at the London School of Economics, March 14, 2006, 5–6. Available on the Web site of the Government Accountability Office, www.gao.gov.

73. Edmund Andrews, "80% of Budget Effectively Off Limits to Cuts," *New York Times*, April 6, 2006, A18.

74. Adam Nagourney, "Bush Troubles Weigh Heavily As Party Meets," *New York Times*, March 12, 2006, 14.

75. Gail Russell Chaddock, "GOP's Family Feud Over Spending," *Christian Science Monitor*, May 22, 2006, 10.

76. *Congressional Record*, July 16, 2002, H4749.

CHAPTER 3

Preliminary Legislative Action

I NTRODUCING A BILL in Congress is a deceptively simple procedure. House members drop their bills into the hopper, a mahogany box near the clerk's desk at the front of the chamber. Senators generally submit their proposals and accompanying statements to clerks for printing in the *Congressional Record,* or they may introduce their bills from the floor. Various assumptions are associated with the introduction of many bills, such as a problem exists and that action is required by the national government to address it rather than leaving the matter to the states or private sector to resolve. Further, lawmakers introduce legislation with different motives (policy, electoral, constituent, and so on) in mind. With gasoline prices on the increase, House and Senate members introduced hundreds of bills on energy-related issues, in part for parochial reasons. Woe to lawmakers who return to their district or state and cannot answer this question from voters: "So, what have you done about energy costs?" [1] A disarming response: "I have introduced a bill on that very topic!"

But it is one thing to introduce a bill and quite another to move it through the lawmaking process. For that reason, lawmakers contemplate a variety of pre-introductory considerations, especially for major bills, which are subject to the most scrutiny and debate. Timing is important. Should a controversial bill be introduced early or late in a legislative session? For example, a bill likely to be filibustered in the Senate might be introduced early to allow plenty of time to overcome any talkathon. Naming the legislation might also be important. An attractive title, such as the Freedom of Information Act, the American Dream Restoration Act, or an acronym like the USA-Patriot Act— "Uniting and Strengthening America by Providing Appropriate Tools Required to Intercept and Obstruct Terrorism"—could bring a bill useful media attention. "People are recognizing that interesting bill names can help bills get noticed and remembered," noted a House staffer.[2] In what might be a first for Congress, Don Young, R-Alaska, a former chair of the House Transportation and Infrastructure Committee, named a transportation bill after his wife Lula, titling the measure the Transportation and Equity Act: A Legacy for Users, or TEA-LU.[3]

Opponents, though, may play on the name in an attempt to attach an unattractive label to the measure. For example, legislation to revamp the Defense Department's personnel system was called the "civil service destruction act" by the House minority whip.[4] Disputes involving the taxation of estates led proponents of its abolishment to dub it the "death tax" while opponents of abolition called it the "Paris Hilton Benefit Act." [5] Another consideration:

should companion bills (identical legislation) be introduced concurrently in the House and Senate to expedite legislative action? How many cosponsors (members who join together to introduce a bill) should be sought, and who should they be? As Sen. Edward M. Kennedy, D-Mass., said about Sen. Strom Thurmond, R-S.C., during their service in the Senate: "Whenever Strom and I introduce a bill together, it is either an idea whose time has come or one of us has not read the bill." [6]

Considerable pre-introductory jockeying on major bills also may take the form of behind-the-scenes battles between or among committees. Because committees' jurisdictional mandates overlap, several panels may want to lay claim to bills on significant topics, such as health care or communications technology, because doing so boosts the political clout of members who serve on the winning committees and garners them campaign contributions. As one scholar explained: "Committee jurisdictions are akin to property rights [over issues], and few things in Washington are more closely guarded or as fervently pursued." [7]

The complexity and interconnectedness of many contemporary issues almost guarantee that more than one committee will share jurisdiction over legislation. Furthermore, lawmakers recently have made wider use of so-called megabills, measures that are hundreds of pages long. The average number of pages per law increased from two and a half in the 1950s to more than eighteen in the late 1990s, with some downturn evident in the 2000s. The contemporary Congress may pass fewer laws than before, but they are considerably larger.

The act of introducing a bill sets off a complex and variable chain of events that may or may not result in final passage. Although thousands of pieces of legislation are introduced in every Congress, only a small number become law. For example, of the 10,703 bills and joint resolutions introduced during the 109th Congress (2005–2007), only 417 (4 percent) became public law. Committees are the primary graveyard for most bills that die in Congress. Committees select from the vast number of bills introduced those that they feel merit further consideration.

CATEGORIES OF LEGISLATION

The winnowing process that occurs in committee suggests that the thousands of bills introduced in each Congress can be broken down into roughly three categories: bills that have so little support that they are ignored and die in committee; noncontroversial bills that are expedited through Congress; and major bills that generate so much debate that they occupy the major portion of Congress's time. Legislative proposals take four forms: bill, joint resolution, concurrent resolution, and resolution (see Glossary).

Bills Lacking Wide Support

Bills that have little support are usually introduced with no expectation that they will be enacted into law. Members introduce such bills for a variety of reasons: to go on record in support of a given proposal, to satisfy individual constituents or interest groups from the member's district or state, to convey a message to executive agencies, to publicize an issue, to attract media attention, or to fend off criticism during political campaigns. Once a member has introduced a bill, he or she can claim action on the issue and can blame the committee to which the bill has been referred for its failure to win enactment. Most of the bills introduced in each Congress fall into this category.

Noncontroversial Bills

Noncontroversial bills make up another large segment of the measures introduced. Examples are bills that authorize construction of statues of public figures, establish university programs in the memory of a senator, rename a national park, or name federal buildings after former members of Congress. Committees in both chambers have developed rapid procedures for dealing with such measures. Generally, these bills are passed on the floor rather quickly and without much debate.

Major Legislation

Bills taking up the largest percentage of a committee's time have some or all of the following characteristics: they are prepared and drafted by executive agencies or major pressure groups; they are initiated by committee chairs or other influential members of Congress; they are supported by the majority party leadership; or they deal with issues on which a significant segment of public opinion and the membership of Congress believe some sort of legislation is necessary.

Bills having such characteristics do not necessarily become law. They also are unlikely to become law in the form in which they were originally introduced. Indeed, sentiment may be so sharply divided that they do not even emerge from committee. Nevertheless, these are the major bills before Congress each year. They may affect the wage earner's paycheck (taxes and Social Security) and the consumer's pocketbook (health insurance and electricity deregulation), and they may be brought up repeatedly at presidential news conferences and covered in the electronic and print media. Overall, Congress devotes the largest portion of its committee and floor time to these bills, which account for perhaps only a hundred or so of the thousands introduced in each Congress.

Executive Branch Bills. The president's leadership in the initial stages of the congressional process is pronounced. The administration's major legislative proposals are outlined in the president's annual State of the Union address, which is televised nationally during prime time and delivered before a joint session of Congress. In the weeks and months after the address, the president sends to Congress special messages detailing his proposals in specific areas, such as defense, education, and health. Bills containing the administration's programs are drafted in the executive agencies, and members of Congress, usually committee chairs, are asked to introduce them simultaneously as companion bills in both chambers. It is customary in both chambers for the words "by request" to appear in the *Congressional Record* by the sponsor's name to flag the measure as an administration initiative. Only representatives and senators, not the president or executive officials, may introduce legislation in Congress.

Influential Members' Bills. Bills supported by influential members stand a good chance of receiving attention in committee and at the other lawmaking stages. For example, in 1999 Congress modernized a sixty-six-year-old banking law—enacted during the Great Depression to create a wall between the banking and securities industry—to reflect technological and marketplace changes. By many press accounts, it was the bulldog determination of the Senate's Banking Committee chair that enabled Congress to pass this landmark legislation after years of failed attempts by other lawmakers. As another example, Bill Thomas, R-Calif., during his chairmanship of the House Ways and Means committee, 2001–2007, shepherded to passage numerous major tax, health, and trade bills, prompting the *Wall Street Journal* to write an editorial headlined "President Thomas." [8] (After completing his six-year limit as Ways and Means chair, Thomas announced his retirement from the House at the end of the 109th Congress (2005–2007). His successor as Ways and Means chair is Democrat Charles Rangel of New York, elevated to that post as a result of the November 2006 elections.)

Must-Pass Legislation. As lawmakers, members of Congress may not want to deal with controversial, no-win public issues such as abortion or gun control. But as politicians who must answer constituent mail, respond to inquiring lobbyists and journalists, and face reelection, they may not be able to ignore them. Because members who are in basic agreement that legislation must be enacted to deal with a controversial problem often disagree sharply about the solution, they must seek a legislative compromise. Money bills also fall into the category of must-pass legislation, such as the twelve general appropriations bills.

BILL REFERRAL PROCEDURE

Once a bill is introduced it receives an identifying number. Measures introduced in the House are identified by the letters "H.R." (for House of Representatives) and an accompanying number; Senate bills are identified by the letter "S." and a number. Usually, bills are assigned numbers according to the chronological order in which they are introduced. Occasionally, however, members will ask the bill clerk to reserve a particular number. For example, H.J. Res. 51 might admit the District of Columbia as the fifty-first state. S. 25 might ban .25 caliber bullets. S. 24 might exempt people with acquired immune deficiency syndrome (AIDS) from a mandated twenty-four-month waiting period before receiving benefits under Medicare.[9] S. 1040 (after the federal tax form) might replace the current tax system with a flat tax. To be sure, bill numbers can also be used to criticize legislation. H.R. 1000, a pension security measure, "has an appropriate number," exclaimed Rep. Loretta Sanchez, D-Calif., "because it will make employees 1,000 times worse off than they are today." [10]

Bill numbers also may be assigned for political purposes. Customarily, majority party leaders of the House and Senate reserve the first several numbers for measures that reflect the majority party's priority agenda items. In the 108th Congress (2003–2005), the largest expansion of Medicare ever—providing a prescription drug benefit for the elderly—was designated by GOP leaders H.R. 1 in the House and S. 1 in the Senate to underscore the measure's political and substantive significance. Since the 106th Congress, the House has adopted an order on its opening day that states: "[T]he first ten numbers for bills (H.R. 1 through H.R. 10) shall be reserved for assignment by the Speaker to such bills as he may designate when introduced during the first session." [11] By custom, the first five or ten numbers in the Senate are reserved for the majority leader and the next five or ten for the minority leader.

Some measures are assigned the same number for several Congresses. This is often done to avoid confusion among legislators and others who have grown accustomed to referring to a proposal by its bill number. Representative John Dingell, D-Mich., regularly introduces a national health insurance plan his father first introduced in 1943 and receives "the number H.R. 15, for his district." [12] Informally, many bills also come to be known by the names of their sponsors, such as the McCain-Feingold (after Senators John McCain, R-Ariz., and Russell Feingold, D-Wis.) campaign reform act of 2002. And then there was the artfully titled "Abraham-Lincoln" bill (after Senate sponsors Spencer Abraham, R-Mich., and Blanche Lincoln, D-Ark.), intended to create a task force to recommend an appropriate way to recognize the slave laborers "who helped build the north wing of the Capitol during the 1790s." [13]

With few exceptions, bills are referred to the appropriate standing committees.[14] The job of referral is formally the responsibility of the Speaker of the House and the presiding officer of the Senate, but usually this task is carried out on their behalf by the parliamentarians of the House and Senate.[15] Precedent, public laws, turf battles, and the jurisdictional mandates of the committees as set forth in the rules of the House and Senate determine which committees receive what kinds of bills.

The vast majority of referrals are routine. Bills dealing with farm crops are sent to the House Agriculture Committee and the Senate Agriculture, Nutrition, and Forestry Committee; tax bills are sent to the House Ways and Means Committee and the Senate Finance Committee; and bills dealing with veterans benefits are sent to the Veterans' Affairs committees of each chamber.[16] Thus, referrals generally are cut-and-dried decisions. (House and Senate standing committees are listed in Box 3-1.)

Yet committees can and do clash over their jurisdictional prerogatives. Irate that the House Ways and Means Committee chairman objected on turf grounds to a provision in an appropriations bill, the Democratic leader of the

---

Box 3-1   **Standing Committees, 110th Congress (2007–2009)**

Senate

Agriculture, Nutrition, and Forestry	Environment and Public Works
Appropriations	Finance
Armed Services	Foreign Relations
Banking, Housing, and Urban Affairs	Health, Education, Labor, and Pensions
Budget	Homeland Security and Government Affairs
Commerce, Science, and Transportation	Judiciary
Energy and Natural Resources	Rules and Administration
	Small Business and Entrepreneurship
	Veterans' Affairs

House

Agriculture	Natural Resources
Appropriations	Oversight and Government Reform
Armed Services	Rules
Budget	Science and Technology
Education and Labor	Small Business
Energy and Commerce	Standards of Official Conduct
Financial Services	Transportation and Infrastructure
Foreign Affairs	Veterans' Affairs
Homeland Security	Ways and Means
House Administration	
Judiciary	

House Appropriations Committee, David R. Obey, Wis., declared: "Ways and Means is the biggest octopus not only in this Capitol, but any capital in the world. Once in a while, something ought to escape its jurisdiction." [17] A Senate Democrat on the Commerce Committee said of the Banking Committee's chair's expansionist instincts: "He does everything in the world to come in on our jurisdiction." [18] Jurisdictional border wars influence the expansion or contraction of committees' authority. Some committees even have "staffers called 'border cops,' whose jobs involve protecting turf and looking for new areas to conquer." [19]

In the House, a member is not permitted to appeal referral decisions to the entire membership except in rare instances of erroneous referral. In the Senate, the rules allow an appeal to the full Senate by majority vote, but in practice such appeals do not take place. Disputes over referral in the Senate may be resolved informally through negotiation prior to the introduction of the bill in question. Senate (and House) party leaders sometimes request that committees with overlapping responsibility work together and reach a consensus on how their respective issues should be addressed in draft legislation. Party leaders may then assume responsibility for putting the different pieces together. For example, several years ago the Senate majority whip asked the chairmen whose committees had jurisdiction over tobacco—Agriculture, Commerce, Finance, Health, and Judiciary—to "develop consensus positions in legislative form" on how to reduce teen smoking.[20]

Legislative Drafting, Referral Strategy

Bill sponsors often try to draft legislation in such a way that it will be referred to a committee likely to act favorably on it instead of one whose members are known to be less sympathetic. Lawmakers, in brief, often engage in venue-shopping during this lawmaking stage. One technique is to word the measure ambiguously so that it can fall legitimately within the jurisdiction of more than one committee. The Speaker or the presiding officer of the Senate then has some options in making the referral. (In the House and Senate, the full-time professional staff in each chamber's Office of Legislative Counsel are skilled at converting members' ideas for laws into legislative language.)[21] Or members may opt for another technique—introducing legislation that amends statutes over which their committees have jurisdiction. To lay claim to Internet legislation and avoid referral of their bill to the Commerce Committee, two House Judiciary Committee members drafted their measure to amend the Sherman Antitrust Act, which is within their panel's exclusive jurisdiction, and not the Telecommunications Act of 1996, which falls under the Commerce Committee. Artful drafting allowed the House Agriculture Committee to receive a bill dealing with eminent domain—the seizure of private land for economic development—even though the issue is typically dealt with by the House Judiciary Committee. The bill connected eminent domain with rural development. As House Parliamentarian John Sullivan stated: "The bill involved the Committee on Agriculture's jurisdiction because of the way it defined the term 'federal economic development program.' "[22] In the Senate, the Finance and the Health, Education, Labor, and Pensions (HELPS) Committees claim jurisdiction in the area of health. Finance members can obtain health legislation by addressing health care in the context of changing relevant provisions of the tax code; HELPS members could write bills that focus on employer-sponsored health plans.

Knowledge of precedents is also important in influencing the referral of legislation. Typically, references to taxes in bills mean that they will be sent to the tax-writing committee (House Ways and Means or Senate Finance). To avoid referral of his bill barring taxation of Internet commerce to the House Ways and Means Committee, a Commerce Committee member took advantage of precedents stating that "so long as the bill is limited to the taxing powers of state and local governments, it is the domain of the Judiciary or Commerce Committees."[23]

The House and Senate parliamentarians regularly provide congressional staffers with general advice on what language or terms to include in legislation so their measures will be referred to particular committees. (The parliamentarians even receive briefs from lobbyists on bill referrals.) According to the Senate parliamentarian, "A great deal of our time in the office is spent dealing with drafts of bills, the committee to which they would be referred, advising staff on what to include and what to delete if in fact they have a preference in terms of committee referral." [24]

These bill drafting techniques and others are the exceptions and not the rule. Committees guard their jurisdictional turfs closely, and the parliamentarians know and follow the precedents. Only instances of genuine jurisdictional ambiguity provide opportunities for the legislative draftsman and referral options for the Speaker and the presiding officer of the Senate to bypass one committee in favor of another.

Referral to Several Committees

When a bill cuts across the jurisdictional lines of several committees, referral may sometimes prove difficult. At the start of the 109th Congress, the House created a new standing Committee on Homeland Security, a broad issue area—as well as a large cabinet department—that overlaps the jurisdiction of several other standing committees. To insure that the legitimate interests of the existing committees were protected, a statement of legislative history was inserted in the *Congressional Record* to clarify the reference of homeland security legislation. According to the statement, for example, the new Homeland Security Committee would have primary jurisdiction over "transportation security" while the Transportation and Infrastructure Committee would retain its jurisdiction over "transportation safety." [25] As Rules Chairman David Dreier, R-Calif., one of the principal proponents of the new panel, stated: "We envision a system of purposeful redundancy. By that, we mean that more than one level of oversight and an atmosphere in which the competition of ideas is encouraged." [26]

Like homeland security, the jurisdictional mandates of other committees often are ambiguous or overlap in various policy domains. For example, House rules assign the Committee on Foreign Affairs jurisdiction over international economic policy; Commerce handles foreign commerce generally; and Ways and Means considers reciprocal trade agreements. To facilitate action, committees often share jurisdiction—formally or informally. For example, to minimize clashes on referrals the chairmen of the House Armed Services and the House Transportation and Infrastructure Committees developed a memorandum of understanding that explained how matters involving the merchant marine would be divided between them. As the chairmen wrote: "In general, matters relating to merchant marine activities will be referred to the [Armed Services] Committee if the national security aspects of the matter predominate over transportation and other merchant marine aspects." [27] This type of informal intercommittee referral agreement will be honored by the parliamentarian.

There are three types of multiple referral: joint referral of a bill concurrently to two or more committees; sequential referral to one committee, then a second, and so on; and split referral of various parts of a bill to different committees. Sometimes, multiple referrals are used in combination—after committees report a multireferred bill, another panel might obtain a sequential referral, typically for a designated time period.

The Senate makes infrequent use of multiple referrals. Measures normally are sent to a single committee based on the parliamentarian's determination as to which panel has jurisdiction over the "subject matter which predominates," the referral criterion specified for the Senate in the Legislative Reorganization Act of 1946. Multiple referrals can be implemented either by unanimous consent or upon a joint motion made by the majority and minority leaders (to date never employed). Here is an example of a multiple referral unanimous consent request:

> Mr. President, I ask unanimous consent that when the [Homeland Security] Committee reports S. 1977, the bill then be sequentially referred to the Committee on Finance for a period of up to 45 days during which the Senate is in session. I further ask unanimous consent that if the bill is not reported by the end of that period, it be discharged from the Finance Committee and placed back on the calendar.

If no senator objects, the sequential referral request is binding on the Senate. The Senate normally grants such requests because senators who offer them usually have worked out an agreement previously with all interested parties—committee chairs, party leaders, and other members concerned about the bill. By the time the bill is introduced, the appropriate bases have been touched, and so no senator is likely to object to the multiple referral. For example, on a major tobacco bill, the Senate majority leader won the unanimous consent of the Senate to permit the Finance Committee to have a one-day sequential referral of the measure, which had been reported by the Commerce Committee. Finance members wanted a brief opportunity to review tobacco-related issues that fell within their jurisdiction.[28]

Until 1975 House precedents dictated that the Speaker refer a bill to only one committee. That year, flexibility was injected into the bill referral process by two changes in the rules. First, Speakers are permitted to refer a bill to more than one committee through joint, sequential, or split referral. (Split referrals have been used infrequently because the interlocking character of bills makes them difficult to divide into parts. Table 3-1 presents a numerical comparison of multiple referrals in the House and Senate.) Multiple referrals augment the power of Speakers by enabling them to delay (by sending a bill to several panels) or expedite (by fixing committee reporting deadlines) action on legislation. Second, Speakers, subject to House approval, are permitted to create ad hoc committees to consider measures that overlap the jurisdictions of several committees.

Although Speakers seldom employ this prerogative, Speaker Thomas P. "Tip" O'Neill Jr., D-Mass., exercised this option in 1977 to create an Ad Hoc

TABLE 3-1 Multiple Referrals of Bills and Joint Resolutions

	House Referrals			Senate Referrals		
Congress	Bills and Joint Resolutions	Measures Multiply Referred	Multiple Referral Percentage	Bills and Joint Resolutions	Measures Multiply Referred	Multiple Referral Percentage
101st	6664	1308	19.63	3659	56	1.53
102d	6775	1303	19.23	3736	149	3.99
103d	5739	1100	19.17	2801	55	1.96
104th	4542	1009	22.21	2264	33	1.46
105th	5014	999	19.92	2715	39	1.44
106th	5815	1207	20.76	3343	41	1.23
107th	5892	1162	19.72	3234	20	0.62
108th	5546	1145	20.65	3077	13	0.42

SOURCE: Thomas Carr, legislative expert, Government and Finance Division, Congressional Research Service.

Energy Committee to expedite action on the Carter administration's top priority: enactment of a complex array of energy proposals. The ad hoc committee was composed of members selected from the five committees to which various parts of the energy proposal initially had been referred.[29] In 2002, the Speaker initiated the formation of the Select Committee on Homeland Security to report a comprehensive bill creating a new Department of Homeland Security after reviewing the recommendations of the dozen standing committees with some jurisdiction over homeland security issues. Every member of the nine-member select panel (five Republicans, four Democrats) held a leadership position in their party's hierarchy. Chaired by the majority leader, the select panel was modeled on the ad hoc energy panel. As House Rules Chairman Dreier stated, the process for considering the new department is "similar to the one that was used a quarter of a century ago by Speaker Tom O'Neill in addressing the energy crisis." [30]

In the Senate, the administration's 1977 energy proposals were referred to the Finance Committee and the Energy and Natural Resources Committee. The Senate has no formal rule providing for the creation of ad hoc committees by party leaders. However, Senate (and House) party leaders may create on their own authority partisan or bipartisan task forces or other ad hoc devices for considering legislation.

In 1995 the new House Republican majority abolished joint referrals (retaining sequential and split references) and added to House rules the requirement that the Speaker shall "designate a committee of primary jurisdiction upon the initial referral of a measure to a committee." [31] This change was designed to achieve greater committee accountability for legislation, while retaining significant flexibility for the Speaker in determining whether, when, and how long additional panels will receive the legislation. The House parliamentarian refers to this new form of multiple referral as an additional initial referral. Such referrals occur in this way:

> H.R. 369. A bill to require accountability for personnel performing private security functions under Federal contracts and for other purposes; to the Committee on Armed Services and in addition to the Committee on the Judiciary, for a period to be subsequently determined by the Speaker in each case for consideration of such provisions as fall within the jurisdiction of the committee concerned.[32]

For H.R. 369, the Committee on Armed Services is the primary committee of jurisdiction; the other committee obtains the measure on an additional initial basis. Secondary panels can consider measures before the primary committee, but their action does not force action on the part of the primary committee. However, once the primary committee files its report on a bill, the Speaker imposes time limits for action on the other panels. Committees jockey to be named "primary" on major bills because that designation often enhances the ability of panel members to raise campaign funds from outside groups interested in the legislation.

Jurisdictional conflict over health issues in the early 2000s between the Committees on Energy and Commerce and Ways and Means prompted the majority Republicans to again amend the multiple referral rule on the opening day, January 7, 2003, of the 108th Congress. To minimize turf disputes, they permitted the return of joint referrals without any designation of a primary committee. (Republicans disliked joint referrals when Democrats ran the House because they viewed it as a formula for stalemate.) However, Rules chairman Dreier emphasized that the change is "meant only as a minor deviation from the normal requirement under rules for the designation of one committee of primary jurisdiction and should be exercised only in extraordinary jurisdictionally deserving instances." [33] Committees may also waive their right to consider a measure, or particular sections, in the interest of expediting legislation and without their decision constituting a referral precedent when comparable measures are subsequently introduced on the topic.

Several observations may be made about multiple referral:

- Because contemporary problems tend to have repercussions in many areas, more and more of the major bills coming before Congress—particularly those in new problem areas such as homeland security—will be candidates for multiple referral.
- To the extent that multiple referral is chosen as an option, the decentralized nature of congressional decision making is reinforced.

- Every time another committee is added to the legislative process, additional opportunities arise for delay, negotiation, compromise, and bargaining.
- Multiple referrals may promote effective problem solving because several committees are bringing their expertise to bear on complex issues.
- On the one hand, when the Speaker designates a panel as primary, he knows which committee to call to get action. On the other hand, multiple referrals sometimes require the Speaker to get involved in mediating and resolving jurisdictional claims or disputes between or among committees.
- Multiple referrals are commonplace in today's House—that is, "one bill, one committee" no longer applies to the extent it once did. Many committees review legislation, including multiple subcommittees within the parent committees.
- To accommodate the interests of several panels, multiple referrals often require more complex debate and amendment arrangements on the floor and in the selection of conference committees created to resolve bicameral differences on legislation.

CONSIDERATION IN COMMITTEE

Once a bill has been referred, the receiving committee has several options. It may, for example, consider and report (approve) the bill, with or without amendments or recommendation, and send it to the full House or Senate. It may rewrite the bill entirely, reject it, or simply refuse to consider it. Failure of a committee to act on a bill is usually equivalent to killing it. When a committee does report a bill, the House or Senate often accepts its main thrust even when the chamber amends the bill on the floor.[34]

Lawmakers defer to the committees' decisions for several reasons. For one thing, committee members and their staffs have a high degree of expertise on the subjects within their jurisdiction, and a bill undergoes its sharpest congressional scrutiny at the committee stage. Therefore, a bill that has survived examination by the experts will probably be given serious consideration on the floor by the generalists of the House and Senate.

A committee's decision not to report a bill is generally respected by the chamber as a whole. After all, if the experts have decided not to approve a bill, why should their decision be second-guessed? Furthermore, the rules in both chambers—particularly those of the House—are designed to "protect the power and prerogatives of the . . . committees . . . by making it very difficult for a bill that does not have committee approval to come to the floor." [35] Formal procedures are in place for overturning committee decisions or even bypassing committees, but these procedures are employed infrequently and are seldom successful. Other ways are also available for circumventing committees.

When a committee decides to take up a major bill, the full committee may consider it immediately. But more often the chair assigns the bill to a subcommittee for study and hearings. The subcommittee usually schedules public hearings on the bill, inviting testimony from interested witnesses in both the public and private sectors. Or the subcommittee may decide not to schedule hearings if executive branch officials or interest groups strongly oppose the legislation. After the hearings, the subcommittee meets to mark up the bill—that is, to consider the bill's specific language line-by-line and section-by-section, before sending it to the full committee. The subcommittee may approve the bill unaltered, amend it, rewrite it, or block it altogether. The panel then reports its recommendations to the full committee.

When the full committee receives the bill, it may repeat the subcommittee's procedures in whole or in part, or it may simply ratify the subcommittee action. If the committee decides to send the bill to the House or Senate, it justifies its actions in a written statement called a report, which must accompany the bill.

On a major legislative proposal, the entire committee process may stretch over several Congresses, with a new bill containing identical or similar provisions introduced at the beginning of each Congress. For example, the struggle to enact controversial legislation dealing with immigration reform, clean air, gun control, or health care can take several consecutive Congresses. Decades may pass before some bills become public law. For other legislation, the process can be compressed into a very short time, especially during times of crisis such as the terrorist attacks of September 11, 2001.

THE COMMITTEE CHAIR'S ROLE

To a large extent, the options available to a committee in dealing with a bill are exercised by the chair, who has wide discretion in establishing the committee's legislative priorities. Among the chair's sources of authority are control of the committee's legislative agenda, referral of legislation to the subcommittees, management of committee funds, hiring and firing of committee staff, use of committee facilities, and designation of majority party conferees. As one House chair observed, the "real power" of the chairmen is "to set the agenda, mark the course and lead." [36]

The chair usually has had a long period of service on the committee and is likely to be better informed than most other members on the many issues coming before the committee. Moreover, the chair is often privy to the leadership's plans and policies, especially the Speaker's or the Senate majority leader's legislative objectives. Chairs can use these and other resources to delay, expedite, or modify legislation.

A chair who opposes a bill may simply refuse to schedule hearings on it or allow hearings to drag on until it is too late to finish action on the bill during the session. Or the chair could instruct the committee staff to stack the witnesses testifying against the bill; ask witnesses holding favorable views to submit statements instead of appearing in person; or try to exclude some proponents of the legislation from testifying. A staff aide for Catholic Charities described how the organization had to "fight to testify" on a welfare reform bill, and when they did "it was 8 o'clock at night after almost all the members and all the press had gone." [37]

In another tactic, chairs who oppose measures may recognize panel members who are likely to raise dilatory questions or employ obstructive tactics before others. Through control of committee funds and the power to hire and fire most staffers, the chair can block action on a bill by directing the staff to disregard it.[38]

A chair who favors a bill can give it top priority by mobilizing staff resources, compressing the time for hearings and markups, and, in general, encouraging expeditious action by committee members. Chairs sometimes bypass the public hearing stage entirely and proceed directly to full committee markup. They typically are the chief agenda-setters of committees. They employ this prerogative to powerfully influence the form in which bills are reported to the House or Senate as well as the timing of floor action on their bills. Committee chairs are also active in molding public and legislative opinion in behalf of their objectives.

The ranking minority party member on a committee also has certain prerogatives. They include hiring and firing of minority staff aides; recommending minority party conferees; acting as the minority side's spokesperson to the press and media; influencing, depending on his or her relationship with the committee leader, the panel's agenda of activities; and designating the minority floor manager for legislation reported by the committee. Like committee chairs, ranking members devise parliamentary strategy, anticipate amendments, ensure the attendance of their members, mobilize winning coalitions, and coordinate their approach to markups with the central party leadership.

Committee Chairs in Perspective

The general picture of a committee chair that had persisted during half of the twentieth century as an almost omnipotent figure underwent modification during the 1970s. Until then, committee chairs were the central figures in the legislative process, holding power equaled only by a few party leaders of great influence, such as House Speaker Sam Rayburn, D-Texas (House, 1913–1961; Speaker, 1940–1947, 1949–1953, 1955–1961), or Senate majority leader Lyndon B. Johnson, D-Texas (Senate, 1949–1961; majority leader, 1955–1961). The chairs' power was gradually trimmed under pressure from newly elected members and from some senior members who wanted to equalize the distribution of power. During the 1970s Congress approved several fundamental changes that ended the nearly absolute authority enjoyed by committee chairs.

The most significant change came when both parties modified the seniority system, specifically the practice of automatically selecting as chair the majority party member with the longest continuous service on the committee.

Seniority meant that chairs normally came from safe congressional districts, were repeatedly reelected, and served until their retirement or death. Because many safe districts during the 1950s and 1960s were in the conservative Democratic South, chairs often were sharply at odds with Democratic presidents, congressional leaders, and northern Democrats. Nevertheless, as seniority was then practiced, the chairs could not be removed. They were able to use their entrenched positions to block civil rights and social welfare legislation proposed by Democratic administrations.

Today, because of party rule and other changes made by Democrats and Republicans in each chamber, all committee chairs (and ranking minority committee members) are subject to secret ballot election within the confines of their party caucus or conference. Chairs and ranking minority committee members are now accountable for their actions to at least a majority of their party's caucus or conference. During the 1970s when Democrats were in charge of the House, they even deposed some committee and subcommittee chairs and elected other party members in their stead. With the GOP takeover of Congress in the mid-1990s, the House amended its rules to impose a six-year term limit on committee and subcommittee chairs to prevent them from accumulating too much power. Senate Republicans emulated the House's term-limit idea and imposed via a party rule, starting in 1997, a six-year term limit for their committee and subcommittee chairs. In 2002 the party rule was clarified to account for the interrupted service of the GOP chairs after Vermont senator Jim Jeffords switched from Republican to independent (but caucusing with the Democrats), giving Democrats control of the Senate.[39] One result of term limits is the loss of knowledgeable and experienced committee leaders; on the other hand, term limits infuse flexibility in the committee structure by allowing younger members a chance to head committees.

When Newt Gingrich, R-Ga., took over as Speaker (1995–1999), he ignored seniority and named several committee chairs who were ideologically in sync with the leadership's views and agenda. J. Dennis Hastert, R-Ill., who took over the Speakership in 1999, employed an unprecedented interview process to determine who would replace term-limited chairs. GOP contenders for open chairs appeared before the GOP's committee assignment panel (the Steering Committee). They were asked to respond to questions such as: How much money had they raised for the party? Did they have a communications strategy for advancing GOP priorities? What was their plan for organizing their committee? When Democrats took control of the 110th Congress (2007–2009), Speaker Nancy Pelosi's committee assignment panel (the Steering and Policy Committee) followed seniority in designating the chairs of the various standing committees.[40]

Since at least the mid-1990s, committee chairs take more direction from assertive party leaders, especially in the House. Even for rank-and-file lawmakers, there are costs if they buck their leadership. Representative Christopher Shays, R-Conn., successfully won enactment of major campaign finance reform legislation despite the strong opposition of GOP leaders. As Shays stated, "When I pushed the campaign-finance bill to the floor of the House, I was told that it was pretty much guaranteed that although I was next in line for the Government Reform Committee, I wouldn't be the next chairman." [41] Shays was not chosen to head that panel.

A variety of factors—term limits, the conferee selection process, the leadership's role in committee assignments, and more—combine to augment party power over committee power. A good example of leadership message-sending to committee chairs occurred at the start of the 109th Congress. House GOP leaders ousted Veterans' Affairs chair Christopher Smith of New Jersey, who was in the fourth year of his six-year term, as the committee's leader and also removed him from the panel. Smith's outspoken advocacy for more spending for veterans' benefits angered the Speaker and other party leaders. Democrats retained term limits for chairs when the 110th Congress opened on January 4, 2007. A question for the Pelosi-led Democrats is whether the experienced, returning "old bull" committee chairs will cooperate and follow the lead of the majority leadership or whether some will "chart their own course on certain issues." [42] In short, committee chairs remain crucial figures in the legislative process. Because Congress functions primarily through its committees, the person who heads a committee has considerable influence over the advancement or defeat of legislation.

COMMITTEE HEARINGS

The decision to hold hearings is the fundamental prerogative of committee chairs. They may be influenced by a variety of internal and external factors—requests from party leaders, colleagues, administration officials, the need to act on expiring legislation, and so on. Ultimately, however, it is the chairs who determine their committees' hearing schedule, setting the date, place, and subject matter of any hearing. Ostensibly, committee hearings are important primarily as fact-finding and educative instruments. Witnesses from the executive branch, concerned members of Congress, interest group spokespersons, academic experts, and knowledgeable citizens appear before the committee to give members their opinions about the merits or pitfalls of a given piece of legislation. From this encounter the committee members gather the information they need to act as informed lawmakers. Hearings also aid members in determining whether new laws are needed or whether changes in the administration of existing laws will be sufficient to resolve problems. "Legislation need not always be the answer," remarked a senator. "In many areas, the most important missing ingredient is attention, and an elevated awareness of the problem can be a very successful outcome of hearings." [43] Committee members are sometimes more interested in making opening statements or engaging colleagues in discussions, especially at high-profile hearings, than in listening to witnesses.

Much information is available to committee members long before the hearings take place. Major bills usually have been the subject of public debate and media coverage. The positions of the administration and the special interest groups are well known, and, in all likelihood, executive branch officials and pressure group lobbyists have already presented their views to committee members and staff aides. Because the members themselves likely have strong partisan positions on the legislation, they may have little interest in whatever additional information emerges from the hearings.[44] In general, hearings are often poorly attended by committee members, and interruptions are common because of floor votes or quorum calls.

Hearing Formats

Committees regularly utilize five hearing formats—traditional, panel, joint, field, and high-tech—when they conduct legislative (focusing on a particular bill or set of related measures), oversight, investigative, or confirmation hearings. For each type, staff research and preparatory work precede the committee hearings. Committee aides may, for example, interview witnesses in advance, compile research and documentary materials, and prepare notebooks for committee members to use at the hearings. These notebooks may list the questions—and the answers—used in probing the witnesses. A committee staff director explained:

> We write the question. Under the question we write the answer. This is the answer we expect to get on the basis of the staff research that has gone before. The Member who asks the question knows what the witness has told us in the weeks and weeks of preparation; and he knows he should get the same information. If he does not get that information, then he has the answer in front of him and he can ad lib the questions that solicit that information or refute it.[45]

Some committees even hold pre-hearings, or "listening sessions," to assess privately issues that witnesses will discuss later during the public sessions.

Sometimes hearings can be perfunctory, particularly where similar legislation has been before the committee for several years in succession. Witnesses usually read or summarize from prepared texts, while the committee members present may listen intently, feign interest, or simply look bored until the statement has been presented. Once the formal testimony is completed, each committee member, usually in order of seniority, asks the witness questions. House rules allot at least five minutes per member to question witnesses. House rules also provide that the chair or ranking minority member may designate specific committee members or staff to conduct extended questioning of up to thirty minutes per side per witness. Senate rules have no such provisions. Instead, each committee establishes its own rules governing internal procedures. For example, the rules of the Senate Energy and Natural Resources Committee give each member five minutes to question witnesses until all members have had an opportunity to ask questions. (Several comparable House and Senate rules that govern the hearings process for most committees are presented in Box 3-2.)

Box 3-2   Selected Formal Rules Governing Hearing Procedures

Although House and Senate committees have wide latitude in how they organize and conduct hearings, formal rules in each chamber regulate these proceedings. Several of the most important rules for committee hearings are described here.

Notice.   The committee chair shall publicly announce the date, place, and subject matter of a committee hearing at least one week before commencement of the hearing. House rules permit this rule to be waived either with the concurrence of the chair and ranking minority member or by majority vote of the committee. Senate rules permit the notice rule to be waived if the committee determines that good cause exists to begin a hearing at an earlier date.

Openness.   Hearings shall be open to the public and the media. Each chamber has provisions that enable committees or subcommittees to close the hearings, but only for certain enumerated reasons such as endangering national security, compromising sensitive law enforcement information, or defaming or disgracing an individual.

Quorum.   House rules stipulate that committees may fix the number of members who must be present to take testimony, but it may not be less than two. Senate rules allow committees to set any number who may be present to take testimony, including just one senator.

Witness Requirements.   Witnesses are required, unless there is good cause for noncompliance, to submit in advance copies of their written testimony to the committee. House rules also require nongovernmental witnesses to file a curriculum vitae and to disclose the amount and source of any federal grant or contract they might have received during the current and two preceding years.

Broadcasting.   House rules state that whenever any committee or subcommittee hearing is open to the public, those proceedings shall be open to coverage by radio or television or both. Senate rules provide that any public hearing of a committee or subcommittee may be broadcast under the terms specified in committee rules.

Minority Party's Right to Call Witnesses.   The minority party on a committee is entitled, upon a request made to the chairman by a majority of the minority members before the completion of the hearing, to call witnesses of its choosing to testify on the subject of the hearing for at least one day.

Committees also conduct joint hearings (with other panels or with the other body), field hearings (away from Capitol Hill), and panel sessions where two or more witnesses of similar or divergent views are arrayed at a table in front of the committee members. For example, Microsoft's Bill Gates testified before the Senate Judiciary Committee in a panel setting with other chief executive officers of computer companies who were hostile to Gates's alleged monopolistic practices. To foment some rhetorical fireworks, the committee staff deliberately placed Gates next to his chief antagonist. Congress is also increasing its use of high-tech or interactive hearings, during which witnesses located around the United States or around the world can testify before House or Senate committees via, for example, video teleconferencing. The House Agriculture Committee was "the first congressional panel to broadcast its proceedings in live audio format over the Internet." [46] In another first, an astronaut appeared before the House Science Committee and became the first person in history to testify from space. He told lawmakers "what it was like to spend months aboard the space station and how such experience could be valuable in planning missions to Mars and beyond." [47] (A House rule requires committees to "make [their] publications available in electronic form to the maximum extent feasible.")

Purposes of Hearings

Despite their limitations, hearings remain an integral part of the legislative process. They provide a permanent public record of the positions of committee members and various interest groups on a legislative proposal. In fact, the executive agencies and interest groups give high priority to preparation of congressional testimony. Above all, hearings are important because members of Congress believe them to be important. The decision to hold hearings is often a critical point in the life of a bill. Measures brought to the floor without first undergoing the scrutiny of hearings will likely receive sharp criticism. (Policies not subject to hearings often become public law, however. Offering legislative proposals as floor amendments, incorporating them into conference reports, or burying them in megabills are among the techniques for bypassing committee hearings.) The importance of the committee stage is based on the assumption that the experts—the committee members—carefully scrutinize a proposal, and hearings provide a demonstrable record of that scrutiny.

Hearings are perhaps the most orchestrated phase of policymaking and usually are part of any overall strategy to get bills enacted into law. Committee members and staff typically plan with care who should testify, when, and on what issues. Consumer advocate Ralph Nader's testimony before several congressional committees on his 1965 best-selling book, *Unsafe at Any Speed*, led to passage of the Traffic Safety Act of 1966. The testimony of celebrity witnesses, such as movie stars, television personalities, or professional athletes, is a sure-fire way to attract national attention to issues. "I haven't seen anything like this in the 30 days we have had hearings," declared a Senate subcommittee chairman about the extensive press coverage when actress Elizabeth Taylor testified on the need for more money for AIDS research.[48] Or as Sen. Arlen Specter, R-Pa., put it: "Quite candidly, when Hollywood speaks, the world listens. Sometimes when Washington speaks, the world snoozes." [49]

Witnesses who have experienced issues or problems firsthand and can tell their stories to lawmakers are especially sought after, because they put a human face on public problems.

> Speaking to a congressional committee [considering the issue of child care], a 10-year-old girl whose parents could no longer afford day care said, "Some things scare me when I'm alone—like the wind, the door creaking, and the sky getting dark fast." "This may not seem scary to you," she told the committee of adults, "but it is to young people who are alone." [50]

During Senate Finance Committee hearings about the abuses of taxpayers by the Internal Revenue Service (IRS), not only did ordinary taxpayers recount their "horror stories" of tax collection efforts by the IRS, but IRS employees "disguised behind screens, with altered voices for some witnesses," provided high drama to the proceedings.[51] Committees often want witnesses who will provide a broad coalition of endorsements for their predetermined position and promote political and public support for this course of action.

Hearings serve other functions as well. They may be used to assess the intensity of support or opposition to a bill, to gauge the capabilities of an executive agency official, to publicize the role of politically ambitious committee chairs and members, to allow citizens to express their views to their representatives, to promote new ideas or agendas, to assert the jurisdictional reach of committees, or to build public support for an issue. In carrying out its constitutional duties, the Senate holds hearings on advising and consenting to treaties and presidential nominations to the executive and judicial branches. The Judiciary Committee's televised hearings on Supreme Court nominations—such as Robert H. Bork in 1987, Clarence Thomas in 1991, and John Roberts and Samuel Alito in 2005—involve extensive preparation by both the nominee and committee chair. The nominees often participate in mock hearings called "murder boards" to get ready for the tough questions they may face. Judge Roberts "participated in some 10 mock hearings of two to three hours each at the Department of Justice, where administration lawyers and a revolving cast of Judge Roberts's colleagues and friends baited him with queries" anticipated from Democratic members of the Judiciary Committee.[52] Similarly, the Judiciary chair may prepare by participating in mock videotaped questioning of someone playing the role of the nominee.

Congress also uses oversight and investigative hearings to explore problems and issues and assess program performance. These hearings serve several purposes. They promote efficient program administration, secure the information needed to legislate, and inform public opinion. American households watched on television the unfolding drama of the 1954 Army-McCarthy hearings, the 1957 hearings into corruption of the Teamsters Union, the Senate Foreign Relations Committee's hearings during the 1960s on the Vietnam War, the Watergate hearings of the 1970s, the 1987 Iran-contra hearings, the late 1990s presidential impeachment hearings, and the 2006 hearings on the recommendations of the Iraq Study Group on how to end the chaos in Iraq and improve the prospects for security and stability in that troubled country. Investigative hearings often prompted the drafting of legislation to deal with the problems that were uncovered and subsequently led to more hearings on the legislation itself.

On occasion, individual members initiate and conduct ad hoc, or informal, investigative hearings of their own. In today's highly partisan environment on Capitol Hill, minority party members often complain that committee chairs will not schedule hearings or conduct meaningful investigations into an administration controlled by their party. During 2005 and 2006, for instance, individual House and Senate Democrats conducted their own hearings on such topics as the Iraq war, contracting abuses in Iraq, and Social Security. When several House Democrats were unable to convince a committee chair to convene a hearing about retiree pension plans at financially-troubled United Airlines, they convened what they said was the chamber's first "e-hearing." They solicited online, week-long testimony from United employees from a page on the committee's minority Web site.[53] With Democrats in charge of the 110th Congress, Senate Majority Leader Harry Reid, Nev., made it clear that "the first order of business . . . is congressional oversight." [54] His counterpart in the House, Speaker Pelosi, responded with two words—"subpoena power"—when asked what was most important in winning control of the House.[55]

House and Senate rules allow a majority of the minority members on a committee, before the completion of a hearing, to request in writing to the chair that they have a day in which to call witnesses of their choosing to testify on the measure or matter before the panel. (Usually the chair will informally accommodate the minority's requests that certain witnesses be invited to testify, unless the recommendations trigger partisan disagreement.) The formal rule, if invoked, still leaves the chair in the driver's seat, because the rule neither defines when the hearing is to occur nor the meaning of the word "day" (an hour, two, or more, for example). For instance, minority Democrats on the House Judiciary Committee invoked the minority witness rule. The chair scheduled the session for a Friday, when most lawmakers are in their district, and at "the very unusual congressional starting time of 8:30 a.m." [56] Furthermore, after listening to repeated criticisms of the Bush administration by the minority's witnesses, the chair gaveled the hearing to a close, ordered the microphones turned off, and stopped transcription of the testimony.[57]

THE MARKUP

Some time after the conclusion of the hearings, the committee or subcommittee may meet to mark up, or amend, the bill (thus the word *markup*, which refers to the committee session at which a bill is put in final form before it is reported out). At this session, committee members decide whether the legislation should be rewritten, either in whole or in part. The chair's task is to keep the committee moving, getting unanimous agreement on as many sections of the bill as possible, trying to resolve differences through compromise, sensing when to delay or speed up matters, or forcing action on issues through party-line voting. Committee chairs regularly line up leadership backing for their committee's bill, insert special provisions in legislation to win members' support, or accommodate interest groups or agency officials by soliciting their comments on a draft markup proposal or permitting them to make presentations during committee markup. Because the chair is likely to be responsible for managing the bill on the floor, he or she will try throughout markup to gather as much support within the committee as possible. A sharp split among the committee members may seriously damage chances of passing the bill in the House or Senate.

Overview

The markup is where committee members redraft portions of the bill, attempt to insert new provisions and delete others, bargain over language, and generally determine the final committee product. The different kinds of markups used by committees reflect committee traditions and customs as well as the nature of the legislation—that is, how controversial it may be. Chairs sometimes schedule informal, private pre-markup sessions for committee members, either on a partisan or bipartisan basis, to discuss possible revisions of major legislation and to develop a consensus on the bill. On an overhaul of the Clean Air Act, for example, the Senate Environment and Public Works Committee chair "scheduled several seminars prior to the formal markup, to educate the members on the major issues and to try to develop a consensus among the members on the issues." [58] In other preparatory actions, committee chairs or ranking minority members might develop markup summaries (analyses of the bill, a list of which members or outside groups are for it or against it, and so on), organize briefings for the legislative staff of individual committee members, anticipate possible amendments and develop responses to them, devise party strategy, and ascertain which members will be in attendance and where absent members can be reached.

Some committees closely adhere to formal parliamentary procedures; others conduct conceptual markups in which committee members agree generally on broad ideas or principles, and staff then draft the legal language for later review by the membership; and still other panels operate informally, largely by consensus, and in a bipartisan manner. The rules of the Senate Foreign Relations Committee even state: "Insofar as possible, [markup] proceedings of the Committee will be conducted without resort to the formalities of parliamentary procedure and with due regard for the views of all members." Overall, some markups are sedate affairs, while others are riven by partisan or substantive controversies.

Senate markups typically occur at the full committee level rather than in subcommittees. By contrast, House markups commonly occur at both the subcommittee level and full committee level. A key reason for this bicameral difference is that senators are subject to greater workload and time pressures than the average House member. For example, senators serve on about a dozen committees and subcommittees; House members sit on about a half dozen panels.

Whether in the House or Senate, markups are generally characterized by a greater degree of personal and parliamentary informality than proceedings in the chamber. As smaller entities, committees simply need less formality in their markup meetings. Moreover, in neither chamber are official parliamentarians assigned to the committees to assist in interpreting the rules. Committee and subcommittee chairs often use their own experience and judgment in enforcing the rules, or, if a particularly knotty procedural issue arises, they may request the advice of a majority committee staff aide knowledgeable in parliamentary matters or telephone the House or Senate parliamentarian and seek his or her counsel.

Rarely are points of order made on the floor against a bill's consideration on the grounds of defective committee procedure. For example, unless a committee violated an explicit House rule, House precedents stipulate that the rules or procedures of committees are for those committees to interpret. Even if a committee directly violates a House rule, the Rules Committee can obviate points of order by waiving the relevant chamber rule. The more flexible Senate has a "cleanup" rule, which states that if a committee follows proper procedure in reporting a bill to the floor—a quorum of panel members who vote in open session and in person—then challenges against consideration of the bill for violating other markup rules (holding secret sessions as a matter of convenience, for example) will not be upheld.

Committee Markup Procedures

House and Senate rules each distinguish between a quorum for markups (one-third of the committee membership) and a quorum to report legislation (a majority of the membership). Several other procedural issues suffuse House and Senate markups, such as the choice of vehicle, or document, to be used for markup purposes; the amendment process; the openness of markup sessions; and the conduct of votes. Box 3-3 summarizes selected markup procedures.

Committee and subcommittee chairs typically decide what document will be used for markup purposes. The choices include the bill as introduced and referred to the committee, a subcommittee-prepared product, the administration's proposal, a staff draft, or a legislative draft that is commonly called the "chair's mark," containing the chair's idea of what the committee members should focus on. The selection is important for both substantive and procedural reasons. Substantively, the markup vehicle frames and shapes the policy discussion among the committee members. Procedurally, keeping items in the markup document is often easier than amending it, which can arouse public debate and controversy. As Sen. Ted Stevens, R-Alaska, described the situation: "Everybody knows that . . . it is much more difficult to get something out of a committee bill than it is to put something into the committee

---

BOX 3-3   **Selected Procedures Governing Markup**

Notice.   Chamber and committee rules require public notice of markup sessions.

Quorum.   Chamber and committee rules set a quorum for markups at one-third of the membership of the panel.

Markup Vehicle.   The chair selects and lays down the vehicle to be considered for markup.

Opening Statements.   The committee chair, often in consultation with the ranking minority member, determines if all or only some panel members will make opening statements and for what length of time.

Reading for Amendment.   In the Senate, the text is considered as read and open to amendment at any point. In the House, there is a requirement that the measure must be read in its entirety, but this can be avoided by a non-debatable motion to waive the reading if printed copies of the text are available to the members. Typically, the markup vehicle is read section by section and after each section is read, the bill is open to amendment. A House committee, by unanimous consent, may agree to read the bill by title or that it be open to amendment at any point.

Amending Process.   In general, the same amending rules apply during markup as apply on the House or Senate floor. In the Senate, there are ordinarily no limits on either debate or the number of amendments that Senators may offer. In the House, amendments are considered under the five-minute rule. A member seeks recognition from the chair to speak for five minutes on the pending amendment(s).

Voting.   Proxy voting is prohibited in the House; it is permitted in the Senate under limitations stated in chamber and committee rules. In both chambers, voting is by voice, division (show of hands), or roll call.

Reporting the Measure.   Both chambers require that a majority of the panel's membership must be physically present to report, or vote out, the legislation.

---

bill." [59] Some committees make their markup document available on their panel's Internet home page.

Once the markup vehicle is before the committee and after the chair and members make brief opening statements, the committee is ready to consider amendments (proposals to change the text of the markup document) that it will recommend to either the House or Senate. (Committees merely recommend amendments because only the full House or Senate has the authority to amend the text of legislation.) In the House, the committee amendment process tracks closely the amendment process in the chamber at large. For example, the markup vehicle is commonly read (the reading is usually waived by unanimous consent) section by section, and members are recognized to offer their amendments once a section is pending before the panel. Members are accorded five minutes to discuss amendments, and the chair alternates between the majority and minority side in recognizing members to offer amendments or to debate the pending proposals. In the Senate, committee members can offer amendments to any part of the bill, and few restrictions are made on debate. Dilatory actions in Senate markups are often harder to stop than in the House, because senators in most committees can filibuster either by talking at length or by offering scores of amendments, even requiring that they be read in full. Furthermore, to stop markups from continuing, senators sometimes invoke a Senate rule, which is usually routinely waived, that forbids markups after the Senate has been in session for two hours.

Most markups are conducted in open session. House and Senate rules also require committee reports accompanying legislation to contain the names of members voting for and against any amendments and motions to report the bill. However, important measures (tax or appropriations, for example) may still be discussed in private without much protest from the media or others. Even proponents of openness admit that members can reach compromises and make tough decisions more easily when they are away from the glare of lobbyists sitting in the audience. Moreover, because of the scores of journalists and media representatives covering Capitol Hill, the results of closed sessions become quickly known once the committee opens its doors. "Closed sessions don't necessarily mean bad legislation and sunshine doesn't guarantee good laws," remarked a journalist. "Openness just makes the process and the results slightly easier to discern." [60]

During markup, House and Senate committees decide issues by voice vote, a show of hands, or a roll call vote. Senate committee chairs may collect proxy votes to win key issues—often to the chagrin of the minority committee members who are in attendance. Proxy voting permits a committee member to cast a vote for an absent colleague, but proxy voting is prohibited on the House or Senate floor. As one account of a Senate markup noted:

> [The subcommittee chairman's] preparation paid off. The committee had been in session for more than five hours and about half the members had left. But when the vote was taken, [the chair] could supplement the eight votes he had in the room with nine proxies. The vote was 17-12.[61]

In 1995 the GOP-controlled House banned proxy voting in committees and subcommittees. During their forty consecutive years in the minority, Republicans had long chafed under a system where their members attended committee markups yet were always outvoted by the handful of Democrats present because the chair voted the proxies of absent colleagues. Abolishing proxy voting was intended to promote member participation in markups. However, lawmakers with multiple committee assignments often have to sprint back and forth to cast votes in committees marking up bills simultaneously or run back and forth from committee markup sessions and the floor to cast votes. Their participation in markups is minimal. Furthermore, some

GOP chairs would discover midway through a markup that they had suddenly lost control of the proceedings. For example, twenty Republican absences in one committee "allowed Democrats to win adoption of a GOP-opposed amendment." [62]

To prevent this from happening, Republicans adopted a House rule in 2003 that permits committee chairs to postpone votes and to reschedule them when they are certain of majority support. Rep. John Dingell, D-Mich., who viewed the change as a subterfuge, pointed out that "by permitting votes to be postponed to a time certain, Members will no longer have to attend committee markups while important amendments are being debated. Instead, they will merely have to show up at a specified time to vote. It sounds an awful lot like proxy voting to me." [63] Worth noting is that the Democrats retained the ban on proxy voting when they assumed majority control of the 110th House.

Strategies During Markup

Committee chairs and members use various strategies during the markup. To accelerate action on major legislation, chairs can, for example, schedule marathon markups that go on for days or weeks and that meet daily from early morning to late at night. Or chairs might hold abbreviated markups to speed legislation to the floor. One ploy, sometimes used by opponents of a bill, is to add amendments to strengthen the measure. For example, during markup of a gun control measure by the House Judiciary Committee, the National Rifle Association (NRA), the major lobbying group opposed to gun control, told its supporters in Congress that it would be easier to defeat a strong firearms proposal. "The way we look at it," said an NRA lobbyist, "the stronger the bill that comes out of committee, the less chance it has of passing on the floor." [64] Conversely, proponents of a strong bill might try to weaken it in committee so that it stands a better chance of winning majority support on the floor. Supporters can then try to persuade the other chamber or the House-Senate conference committee to strengthen the measure.

Another approach used by a bill's opponent is to offer a flurry of amendments to make a bill complicated, confusing, and unworkable for the executive branch agencies that would have responsibility for administering the law. Moreover, offering scores of amendments, or offering one huge amendment and insisting that it be read—slowly—in full, may stall the markup and grant opponents additional time to lobby against the legislation. For example, a senator once sought to delay markup of a federal employees bill "by reading—slowly and deliberately—a lengthy statement explaining his opposition. He then offered seven amendments" and launched into a long explanation of each.[65] Sometimes minority committee members boycott markup sessions to delay or prevent these meetings from proceeding for lack of a quorum (one-third of the panel's membership is the standard requirement in both chambers).

Mobilizing grass-roots support and targeting the states or districts of key committee members are often critical to the outcome of markups. During markup by Congress's tax-writing panels, special interests work diligently to shape the thinking of these committees. As one account noted:

> For several months, the lobbyists have been working behind the scenes trying to influence the outcome by personally talking with members and aides of the tax committees in both chambers and getting members of their lobbying coalitions to write and phone their Congressmen. To bolster their arguments, the lobbyists have hired independent research firms to produce analyses that show the impact of the proposed tax changes, and they have tried to mold public opinion through press releases and advertising campaigns.[66]

To win over opponents or skeptics, chairs often willingly accept numerous amendments from their committee colleagues. In this way, these members develop a stake in the legislation and may stand united behind it on the House or Senate floor. The reverse strategy is to load down a bill with scores of costly add-ons so the legislation possibly sinks of its own weight. "We might just as well kill the president's [health reform] bill with kindness" by adding costly and untenable amendments, said a lawmaker during a markup of the House Education Committee.[67]

Another tactic of committee chairs who want to avoid votes on unfriendly or politically tailored amendments is to offer their own substitute proposal. For example, Senate Democrats on the Budget Committee wanted to force committee Republicans to vote on a tax-cut plan backed by George W. Bush that several Republicans on the panel did not support. To avoid this embarrassing vote, the Budget Committee chair offered his own substitute amendment to negate the Democratic initiative. It asked the president "to search for waste, fraud and abuse within the federal government and then apply such savings to a big tax cut." [68] The chair's parliamentary maneuver was successful.

An important factor affecting markup strategies in the Senate is the smaller size of its panels. One senator wrote that to get an amendment adopted by his Senate subcommittee he needed "only two other votes of the five-member subcommittee. In the House, subcommittees with more than 20 members are common." [69] In the House, greater effort may be needed to forge winning coalitions.

Compromise during the committee markup—or at any stage of the legislative process—is more likely when the members recognize that some sort of legislation is necessary. The outcome of markups, with their tradeoffs, compromises, and complexities, may not be perfect, but it does reflect what attracted at least a majority vote of the panel members. As a House Ways and Means chairman said after a tax markup: "We have not written perfect law. Perhaps a faculty of scholars could do a better job. A group of ideologues could have provided greater consistency. But politics is an imperfect process." [70] Rep. Barney Frank, D-Mass., emphasized this point in describing coalition building on a controversial measure: "Our goal is to find something that's 60 percent acceptable to 52 percent of the members and I think we have a 75

TABLE 3-2 Procedural Differences at Preliminary Stages of the Legislative Process

House	Senate
Bills are usually introduced before committee or floor action can proceed.	Committees may originate their own bills without first having measures sent to them.
No effective way to challenge the Speaker's (parliamentarian's) referral decisions.	Referrals are subject to appeals from the floor.
The Speaker is granted authority by House rules to refer bills to more than one committee.	Multiple referrals occur by unanimous consent, although the majority leader and minority leader can jointly offer a motion to that effect.
The Speaker is authorized, subject to House approval, to create ad hoc panels to consider legislation.	Neither the majority leader nor the presiding officer has authority under Senate rules to create ad hoc panels to process legislation.
Generally difficult to bypass committee consideration of measures.	Bypassing committee consideration of measures occurs more easily.
Floor action is sometimes less important for shaping policies than committee action.	Floor action is as important as committee action in decision making.

percent chance of doing that." [71] Once committees conclude their markups, members often mobilize to achieve their objectives, such as lobbying colleagues and organizing pep rallies on Capitol Hill. Table 3-2 lists several major differences between the House and the Senate in the introduction, referral, and committee consideration of legislation.

THE REPORT

Assuming that major differences have been ironed out in the markup, the committee then meets to vote on reporting the bill out of committee. House and Senate rules require a committee majority to be present for this purpose; otherwise, a point of order may be made on the floor that will force the bill to be returned to committee. Bills voted out of committee unanimously stand a good chance on the floor. A sharply divided committee vote presages an equally sharp dispute on the floor. A bill is rejected if the committee vote is a tie.

Committees have several options when they vote to report, or approve, a bill. They may report the bill without any changes, with various discrete amendments, or with a complete substitute amendment that is the functional equivalent of a new bill. Or a committee that is proposing to amend a bill extensively may instruct the chairman to incorporate the modifications in a new measure, known as a clean bill. This bill will be reintroduced, assigned a new bill number, referred back to the committee, and reported by the panel.

The clean bill procedure is employed for various reasons, such as expediting floor consideration of legislation. Another factor for the House is the germaneness rule. Provisions already in a bill are *ipso facto* considered to be germane and, therefore, are protected in the House against points of order. (Germaneness rules apply to proposed amendments and not to provisions in the bill itself.) In the Senate, committees may report a clean bill to avoid running afoul of Senate Rule XV. The thrust of this rule states that it is not in order for the Senate to consider any proposed committee amendment "which contains any significant matter not within the jurisdiction of the committee proposing such amendment." Finally, a clean bill may reflect negotiated agreements between key committee members and executive officials.

Committees may take other actions besides favorably reporting a bill. They may report out a bill adversely (unfavorably), recommending that the bill not be passed by the full chamber, or they may report legislation without a formal recommendation, allowing the chamber to decide the bill's merits. In either case, the bill may be sent to the full chamber and scheduled for floor action. Committees adamantly opposed to a measure may decide not to take any action at all, thereby blocking further consideration except through special procedures.

After the bill is reported, the committee chair instructs the staff to prepare a written report. (House rules require a written report to accompany legislation; Senate rules do not impose that requirement, but it is informally observed in most cases.) The report describes the purposes and scope of the bill, explains the committee revisions, notes proposed changes in existing law, and usually includes the views of the executive branch agencies consulted. Committee members opposing the bill often submit dissenting, or minority, views. Any committee member may file minority, supplemental, or additional views, which are printed in the committee report. House and Senate rules also require committee reports to contain certain information, such as five-year cost estimates, oversight findings, and regulatory impact statements. Measures are open to points of order on the floor if their committee report fails to contain this material. On an omnibus measure, a report may be more than a thousand pages long.

Reports are directed primarily at House and Senate members and seek to persuade them to endorse the committee's recommendations when the bill comes up for a floor vote. The reports are the principal official means of communicating a committee decision to the entire chamber. Committee reports are also used by executive officials to fathom legislative intent when they are interpreting ambiguous statutory phrases. Federal judges too, examine committee reports and other aspects of legislative history (hearings, floor debates, and conference reports) when laws are challenged in court. Some federal justices, most notably Supreme Court Justice Antonin Scalia, argue that legislative history should be minimized in the interpretation of ambiguous statutes. Instead of examining staff-written committee reports to determine what Congress intended, Justice Scalia argues, judges should consider only the exact text of the statute, because lawmakers vote on that and not on legislative history. Supreme Court Justice Stephen G. Breyer, by contrast, answers "that no one claims that legislative history is in any strong sense 'the law,' but rather that it is useful in ascertaining the meaning of words in the statute." [72]

Reports are numbered, by Congress and chamber, in the order in which they are filed with the clerk of the House or Senate. Thus in the 109th Congress the first House report was designated as H. Rept. 109–1 and the first Senate report as S. Rept. 109–1. The first page of a report is shown in Figure 3-1 on page 108. Both the committee-reported bill and its accompanying report are then assigned to the appropriate House or Senate calendar to await scheduling for floor action.

BYPASSING COMMITTEES

Party leaders are not reluctant to employ techniques to circumvent committee consideration of priority legislation, such as the use of partisan task forces to craft legislation or to propose changes in legislation after committees report their handiwork. Committees in the House or Senate may be bypassed in other ways as well, such as attaching legislative riders to appropriations bills, having the House Rules Committee bring bills to the floor without committee hearings or markups, offering to pending legislation on the Senate floor nonrelevant amendments that embody bills pigeonholed in committee, or adding new propositions to conference reports during bicameral negotiations on legislation.

Various overlapping reasons account for the tendency to circumvent committees, but five are among the most important. The first is time. Two classic examples are the 1995 House Republican Contract with America and the 2007 Democratic "100-hour" legislative agenda. In both cases party leaders believed that committees had insufficient time to conduct hearings and markups and issue reports on their agenda items before the promised time period of one hundred days or hours for action ticked away. Party leaders, too, may rush measures to the floor that are popular with the public or that lawmakers want to consider quickly.

A second reason is partisanship. Majority party leaders may want to avoid review by a committee divided by sharp partisan disagreements. In their estimation, the minority party should not be provided two opportunities—in committee and on the floor—to frustrate the majority and to showcase its agenda. The partisan infighting associated with committee consideration of a politically potent issue and the negative media coverage it will generate is something the majority leadership prefers to avoid. Party leaders may also want to circumvent committee consideration to force a floor vote on a so-called "wedge" issue (something that energizes one party

109TH CONGRESS ⎫
  1st Session ⎬ HOUSE OF REPRESENTATIVES ⎰ REPT. 109–33
                 ⎭   ⎱   Part 1

FAMILY ENTERTAINMENT AND COPYRIGHT ACT OF 2005

APRIL 12, 2005.—Committed to the Committee of the Whole House on the State of
the Union and ordered to be printed

Mr. SENSENBRENNER, from the Committee on the Judiciary,
submitted the following

R E P O R T

together with

MINORITY VIEWS

[To accompany S. 167]

[Including cost estimate of the Congressional Budget Office]

The Committee on the Judiciary, to whom was referred the bill
(S. 167) to provide for the protection of intellectual property rights,
and for other purposes, having considered the same, reports favorably thereon without amendment and recommends that the bill do
pass.

CONTENTS

39–006

FIGURE 3-1 House Committee Report

but divides the other) that can be used in the next election against members of the other party.

A third factor is committee gridlock. Factional disputes within the majority party, combined with strong resistance from the minority party, may prevent committees from reaching agreement on measures deemed important to the majority party. As a result, party leaders will intervene to bypass the stalled committee stage and bring the legislation to the floor. Occasions also may arise when committees are substantively out of sync with the policy preferences of their party or with political imperatives that require the House or Senate to act expeditiously on legislation.

A fourth reason is electoral salience. Certain compelling issues are of such political importance to the majority party in terms of their appeal to the general public or to their party's core supporters that the leadership will circumvent the committee process to keep tight control of them. The Speaker, for example, will use his authority over the House Rules Committee to have his preferred version of a bill sent to the floor under debate and amendment procedures that advantage the majority party. The Senate majority leader might convene closed door drafting sessions or invoke a procedure (Rule XIV) that places a measure directly on the legislative calendar, preventing it from being referred to committee.

A fifth factor is consensus: the relevant committee of jurisdiction, and perhaps a majority of the membership or at least the majority party, supports circumvention. Committees may waive consideration on the grounds that they have conducted hearings and markups on the legislation for several successive Congresses. Some proposals, too, may be debated year after year by the House and Senate so that lawmakers are familiar with the pros and cons of the legislation. "This bill [heading directly to the floor] is pretty straightforward," remarked a House member. "I don't know that it needs much scrubbing by a committee." [73]

When a bill has been reported from committee, it is ready to be scheduled for floor action. Like the winnowing process that occurs in committee, scheduling involves budgeting congressional time. Important political choices must be made in determining the order in which bills will be considered on the floor, how much time will be devoted to each measure, and to what extent the full chamber will be permitted to reexamine a committee decision.

NOTES

1. Janofsky, "Scent of Ballots Is in Air, and Energy Bills are Blooming," *New York Times,* June 20, 2006, A11.
2. Chrissie Long, "Lawmakers Turn To Catchy Names for Bills," *The Hill,* April 21, 2005, 6.
3. National Journal's CongressDailyPM, "The Final Word," March 9, 2005, 9.
4. *CongressDailyAM* (*National Journal*), May 20, 2003, 3.
5. David Francis, "Estate Tax Fight Hinges On Money, Morality," *Christian Science Monitor,* July 13, 2005, 2.

6. Julie Rovner, "Senate Committee Approves Health Warnings on Alcohol," *Congressional Quarterly Weekly Report*, May 24, 1986, 1175.
7. David C. King, *Turf Wars: How Congressional Committees Claim Jurisdiction* (Chicago: University of Chicago Press, 1997), 11.
8. Jill Barshay, "A Rough but Steady Hand at Helm of Ways and Means," *CQ Weekly*, July 5, 2003, 1670.
9. Philippe Shepnick, "Moynihan Is Champion Bill Writer," *The Hill*, March 10, 1999, 6.
10. *Congressional Record*, May 14, 2003, H4021.
11. *Congressional Record*, January 7, 2003, H13.
12. Nicole Duran, "Dingell's Valentine Wish: A Record," *Roll Call*, August 1, 2005, 13.
13. Allison Stevens, "House Revisits Capitol Slave Labor Issue," *CQ Weekly*, July 12, 2003, 1723.
14. On rare occasions, a member introducing a bill may ask unanimous consent that it be passed. Unanimous consent is more likely to be granted in the Senate than in the House and only on a noncontroversial measure or one on which all members agree that immediate action is required.
15. Article I, Section 3, of the Constitution provides that the vice president is president of the Senate, but vice presidents preside over that body infrequently. The Constitution also provides for a president pro tempore. By custom, that position is held by the most senior member of the majority party. Usually, however, junior members designated by the majority leader preside over the daily sessions of the Senate. Each chamber has a parliamentarian, who is an expert on rules of procedure. During a session, the parliamentarians or one of their assistants are present to advise the chair on all points of order and parliamentary inquiries.
16. Committee structure and jurisdiction are not identical in the House and Senate.
17. *CongressDailyPM*, May 4, 1998, 6.
18. *CQ Daily Monitor*, March 1, 2000, 8.
19. David C. King, "The Nature of Congressional Committee Jurisdictions," *American Political Science Review* (March 1994): 49.
20. *CongressDailyAM*, November 7, 1997, 8.
21. Lawrence E. Filson, *The Legislative Drafter's Desk Reference* (Washington, D.C.: CQ Press, 1992).
22. Michael Sandler, "Not a Job for Judiciary Committee? House Ag Handles Eminent Domain Bill," *CQ Today*, August 8, 2005, 7.
23. *CongressDailyPM*, April 24, 1998, 6.
24. "Senate Parliamentarian Can Control Course of Bills," *C-Span Update*, January 14, 1990, 6.
25. *Congressional Record*, January 4, 2005, H26.
26. *Ibid.*, H14.
27. *Congressional Record*, January 30, 1995, H849. When the 110th Congress convened, chairs of the House Committees on Homeland Security and Transportation and Infrastructure signed a memorandum of understanding clarifying their respective jurisdictions over the Federal Emergency Management Agency and the Coast Guard. See *Congressional Record*, January 4, 2007, H15–H16.
28. *CQ Daily Monitor*, May 14, 1998, 15.
29. See Bruce I. Oppenheimer, "Policy Effects of U.S. House Reform: Decentralization and the Capacity to Resolve Energy Issues," *Legislative Studies Quarterly*

(February 1980): 5–30; and David J. Vogler, "Ad Hoc Committees in the House of Representatives and Purposive Models of Legislative Behavior," *Polity* (Fall 1981): 89–109.

30. *Congressional Record,* June 19, 2002, H3694.
31. *Congressional Record,* January 4, 1995, H36.
32. *Congressional Record,* January 19, 2007, H341.
33. *Congressional Record,* January 7, 2003, H11.
34. All Senate committees have the authority to draft an original bill and report it out without referral of the measure back to the committee after its introduction by the committee chair. In the House, only a small number of committees, such as the Appropriations Committee, has the authority to report original legislation.
35. Randall B. Ripley, *Congress: Process and Policy* (New York: Norton, 1975), 75.
36. *Congressional Record,* May 9, 1994, H3181.
37. *Washington Post,* May 21, 1995, A4.
38. Members of Congress rely heavily on committee staff for assistance in organizing hearings, selecting witnesses, and drafting bills, as well as for many other key support functions. The chair's control of committee staff therefore is an important resource in his or her control of the legislative process.
39. Matthew Tully and Emily Pierce, "Senate Republicans Adjust Their Committee Term-Limits Rule," *CQ Daily Monitor,* June 26, 2002, 4.
40. Susan Ferrechio, "House Democrats Stick with Seniority," *CQ Weekly,* December 11, 2006. 3295/
41. Deborah Solomon, "It's Their Party," *New York Times Magazine,* May 8, 2005, 14.
42. Josephine Hearn, "Democrats Stick with Seniority in Round One," *The Hill,* December 6, 2006, 1. However, the issue of term limits may be revisited. See Susan Ferrechio, "Democrats Far From Settled on Term Limits for Committee Chairmen." *CQ Today,* January 8, 2007, 5.
43. *Wall Street Journal,* April 11, 1986, 54.
44. Members unable to attend a committee session frequently assign committee staffers to attend the meeting and brief them later. Staff aides can ask questions of witnesses if authorized by committee rules or by the chair.
45. *Workshop on Congressional Oversight and Investigations,* 96th Cong., 1st sess., 1979, H. Doc. 96–217, 25.
46. *Washington Post,* September 23, 1998, A23.
47. Warren Leary, "When Astronauts Brief Congress, A Little Levity Goes a Long Way," *New York Times,* June 15, 2005, A16.
48. *Washington Post,* May 9, 1986, D8.
49. Bob Pool, "Survivors Take Stock of Gains against Cancer," *Los Angeles Times,* May 30, 1997, B1.
50. *Christian Science Monitor,* November 27, 1985, 28. See also Barbara Vobejda, "Children Show Congress Scars of Gun Violence," *Washington Post,* March 11, 1993, A16.
51. Jackie Calmes, "New Round of Senate Hearings on IRS Risks Overkill," *Wall Street Journal,* March 31, 1998, A24.
52. Elizabeth Bumiller, "Lengthy Practices Prepare Court Nominee for His Senate Hearings," *New York Times,* September 11, 2005, A11.
53. Josephine Hearn, "Democrats To Conduct Web 'e-hearing' On Prison Reform," *The Hill,* May 25, 2005, 4. Also see John Stanton, "Democrats Put Money on New Oversight Plan," *Roll Call,* January 25, 2006, 19.

54. Maura Reynolds, "Reid Says Democrats Will Restore 'Checks and Balances',"
    Los Angeles Times, November 11, 2006 (online version).
55. William Greider, "Pelosi's Moment," *The Nation,* October 20, 2006, 21.
56. Keith Perine, "It's Not Used Much, But House Democrats Invoke Rule 11 To Get
    Extra Exposure on Gitmo," *CQ Today,* June 10, 2005, 12.
57. Mike Allen, "Panel Chairman Leaves Hearing," *Washington Post,* June 11, 2005,
    A4.
58. *State Government News,* April 1982, 4.
59. *Congressional Record,* July 20, 1983, S10430.
60. *Washington Post,* May 6, 1984, F5.
61. Ronald Elving, "Smoking Ban for Short Flights Likely to Ignite Senate Scrap,"
    Congressional Quarterly Weekly Report, October 3, 1987, 2409.
62. *CQ Daily Monitor,* March 21, 2000, 1.
63. *Congressional Record,* January 7, 2003, H18.
64. *Washington Post,* February 6, 1976, A6.
65. Elizabeth Palmer, "Roth's Parliamentary Moves Halt Hatch Act Reform," *Congressional Quarterly Weekly Report,* March 7, 1992, 534.
66. *New York Times,* October 15, 1985, D25.
67. Dana Priest and Spencer Rich, "Key Hill Committees Take Up Health Care Legislation," *Washington Post,* May 19, 1994, A23.
68. *CongressDailyAM,* March 30, 2000, 13.
69. Paul Simon, "Trying on the Senate for Size," *Chicago,* November 1985, 150.
70. *Washington Post,* November 25, 1985, A4.
71. *Washington Post,* February 24, 1988, A22.
72. Robert A. Katzmann, "Justice Breyer: A Rival for Scalia on the Hill's Intent," *Roll
    Call,* May 30, 1994, 5. See Joan Biskupic, "Congress Keeps Eye on Justices as
    Court Watches Hill's Words," *Congressional Quarterly Weekly Report,* October
    5, 1991, 2863–2867; and Joan Biskupic, "Listening In on the 'Conversation' between Court and Congress," *Washington Post,* May 1, 1994, A4. See also
    Michael Koby, "The Supreme Court's Declining Reliance on Legislative History:
    The Impact of Justice Scalia's Critique," *Harvard Journal on Legislation* (summer
    1999): 369–395; and Michael Slade, "Democracy in the Details: A Plea for Substance over Form in Statutory Interpretation," *Harvard Journal on Legislation*
    (Winter 2000): 187–236.
73. *CongressDailyAM,* May 12, 1999, 11.

CHAPTER 4

Scheduling Legislation in the House

"THE POWER of the Speaker of the House is the power of scheduling," observed Thomas P. "Tip" O'Neill Jr., D-Mass., who served as Speaker for more consecutive years (1977–1987) than any of his predecessors.[1] Scheduling floor activities in the House is fundamentally the prerogative of the Speaker and the majority party leadership. For example, Speaker Nancy Pelosi, D-Calif., got fast action at the start of the 110th Congress (2007–2009) on the Democrats' first 100 legislative hours agenda, which included issues such as raising the minimum wage and adopting tougher ethics rules. Why the emphasis on the 100-hour agenda? To impose unity on the Democratic party, build momentum for other legislation, and perhaps most importantly, demonstrate to the electorate that the Democrats have a positive agenda, that they stand for something, and that they can govern effectively. The politics and strategies of scheduling can strongly influence a bill's fate. Determining when (if at all), what, how, and in which order measures are brought to the floor is part of the arsenal of legislative tools that the majority leadership uses to produce winning coalitions, provide political protection to members, mobilize bipartisan support, engineer a record of accomplishment, or advance its own partisan agenda.

The complexities and uncertainties of scheduling are illustrated by this example. During the lame-duck session following the November 2004 elections, President George W. Bush insisted that Speaker Dennis Hastert, R-Ill., move quickly to pass legislation overhauling the intelligence community, including the creation of a new director of national intelligence (DNI) to oversee domestic and foreign intelligence-gathering. Hastert resisted the president's repeated requests for two reasons: divisions within his party and his governing strategy requiring a "majority of the majority party" to support legislation before it is scheduled for floor action. "What good is it to pass something," said the Speaker's spokesperson, "where most of our members don't like it."[2]

One of the key opponents of the bill was Judiciary Chairman James Sensenbrenner, R-Wis. He wanted strict immigration provisions (banning drivers' licenses for illegal immigrants, for instance) included in the overhaul measure. Sensenbrenner viewed those provisions as essential to protecting national security. Hastert persuaded Sensenbrenner to stop his effort to defeat the overhaul measure by promising to bring his immigration reform proposals to the floor early in the 109th Congress. In the end, President Bush signed into law (P.L. 108–458) the biggest revamping of the intelligence community in fifty years, and Hastert fulfilled his commitment to Sensenbrenner.[3]

Scheduling legislation for House floor debate may be simple or complex. Priorities for floor consideration of the bills reported from committee are established by the majority leadership (the Speaker, the majority leader, and the majority whip), sometimes in consultation with the minority leader. Numerous factors influence their decisions: House rules, budgetary timetables, bicameral considerations, election-year activities, the pressure of national and international events, the administration's programs, the leadership's policy and political preferences, whip counts, and the actions of the House Rules Committee. All these elements interact as legislators, pressure groups, and executive agencies maneuver to get favored legislation on the floor.

Scheduling involves advance planning of annual recesses and adjournments, coordinating committee and floor action, providing a steady and predictable weekly agenda of business, anticipating legislative priorities during the end-game rush to adjourn, regulating the flow of bills to the floor during slack or peak periods, and devising a workload that takes into account members' family needs, such as scheduling recesses around school vacations. Plainly, scheduling can be a challenge especially given the traditional "Tuesday-Thursday" work week (lawmakers depart for their constituencies Thursday evening or Friday morning and return on Monday).

When Democrats won control of the 110th House (2007–2009), Speaker Pelosi and Majority Leader Steny Hoyer, Md., announced a five-day work schedule for the House. "Most weeks—not every week—but most weeks," said Hoyer, "yes, we will be working Monday, we will come in Monday at 6:30 p.m. and be working on Friday, as we used to do, until about [2 p.m.] to give people time so they can get home" to their districts.[4] During the November 2006 mid-term elections, Democrats railed against the "do-less than do-nothing" second session of the GOP-controlled 109th Congress, which usually started the work week late on Tuesdays and ended it by Thursday afternoon. The 109th House was in session fewer days (103) than the GOP-controlled 80th Congress in 1948 (110 days). Harry Truman, in his successful 1948 campaign for the White House, made the remark that became famous when he called the 80th Congress the "do-nothing" Congress.

The Democratic leadership's objective is not just to differentiate their management of the House from the Republicans' but to provide more time for committees and members to consider and debate legislation and to oversee the GOP-run executive branch. Minority Republicans quickly dubbed the new schedule, "family-unfriendly." Further, Minority Whip Roy Blunt, Mo., said a five-day schedule provides electoral advantages for the GOP, because freshman Democrats in competitive seats will find it "incredibly difficult to . . . establish themselves in their district. So we're all for it." [5] Democratic leaders reply that good politics is doing the business of the American people.

Scheduling even has some mystery as majority party leaders assess the political climate. As Jim Wright, D-Texas, who served as Speaker from 1987 to June 1989, once noted:

In scheduling the program for the Congress one must be constantly aware of the importance of maintaining a little suspense. I learned this from Agatha Christie. Always hold something back and keep people guessing a little bit. And that is what we are doing with this bill, quite frankly. We are maintaining a little suspense in the schedule [while we determine the best time for taking up this legislation].[6]

Needless to say, the best time for the majority leadership to bring up its preferred measures is when it believes it has the votes. A Speaker who finds that a bill lacks the support to pass may delay in taking it up or yank it off the floor if it is already under consideration. The Speaker, too, may periodically organize the schedule to highlight party priorities such as "health week," "energy week," or "bureaucratic red-tape termination week." The agenda, too, is crafted to appeal to specific voting groups such as Hispanics, or lay claim to cultural values, such as patriotism, that energize core electoral supporters. During the dozen years (1995–2007) when Republicans were in charge, the House voted six times to approve a constitutional amendment banning flag burning. Unsurprisingly, the vote on this "hot button" proposal was scheduled on or about Flag Day in mid-June or July 4. Family values legislation might be taken up around Mother's Day or tax cut bills on or near April 15.

It is common for the minority party to advocate and advertise its agenda of legislative priorities. The minority's agenda is often geared toward message-sending for the next election. For example, to demonstrate to voters that they are the party of new ideas, the minority may advocate an "Innovation Agenda" that includes, for example, more investment in basic research and development. Minority agenda items are often a counterpoint to majority proposals. However, in a closely divided and highly partisan chamber, majority party leaders are unlikely to permit consideration of politically attractive minority initiatives, and only if they have a compelling alternative and the votes to reject the minority's idea. Despite its general powerlessness in agenda-setting, the minority party articulates an agenda to energize its electoral supporters, attract public attention, foment legislative debate, and demonstrate that it has a vision of what to do if it wins control of the House.

The procedures for managing the flow of bills to the floor have evolved throughout the history of Congress and still undergo frequent change. At first glance, they may appear needlessly complex and cumbersome, but they have an internal logic and serve the needs of the House.

THE HOUSE LEGISLATIVE CALENDARS

The House maintains four legislative calendars, which aid in the scheduling of floor action. All measures reported from committee are assigned, in chronological order, by the clerk of the House to the Union Calendar, the House Calendar, or the Private Calendar. In addition, measures may be placed on the Discharge Calendar.

Legislation dealing with raising, authorizing, or spending money is assigned to the Union Calendar (technically, the Calendar of the Committee of the Whole House on the state of the Union). Non-money measures, such as proposals to amend the Constitution, are put on the House Calendar. Bills of a private nature ("for the relief of")—that is, those not of general application and usually dealing with individuals or specific entities—are assigned to the Private Calendar. The Discharge Calendar lists bills removed from committees through special, and infrequently successful, procedures. In 1995, at the behest of Speaker Newt Gingrich, R-Ga., the House created a new Corrections Calendar to repeal unnecessary and overly burdensome rules and regulations, and, as Gingrich said, "the dumbest things the federal government is doing." [7] Little used, the Corrections Calendar was dropped from the House's rulebook at the start of the 109th Congress (2005–2007).

When the House is in session, members receive a daily document, the *Calendars of the United States House of Representatives and History of Legislation,* which lists all House and Senate measures that have been reported from committee (see Figure 4-1). Not every measure listed is called up and considered by the House.

Regardless of the legislative calendars, any lawmaker can ask unanimous consent at almost any time the House is in session to pass legislation. However, since the mid-1980s all Speakers on the opening day of a new Congress have announced that they will confer recognition ("For what purpose does the gentlelady rise?") for "unanimous consent requests only when assured that the majority and minority floor leadership and the committee and subcommittee chairmen and ranking minority members have no objection." The Speaker's recognition power is an unchallengeable prerogative of the chair.

MINOR AND NONCONTROVERSIAL BILLS

As with many legislative assemblies, the House has different procedures for handling minor and noncontroversial measures compared to major bills. Legislation on the Private Calendar is in order only during certain days of the month. The House also processes noncontroversial measures that are on the Union or House Calendars under procedures that grant them privileged access to the floor during certain designated days of the week or month. These include measures brought to the floor under the widely-used suspension of the rules procedure and bills dealing with the District of Columbia. Most of the legislation that comes before the House is passed by use of suspension procedure.

Suspension of the Rules

The principal legislative shortcut and increasingly utilized source of agenda control by the Speaker—sometimes for important as well as minor public bills, resolutions, and conference reports—is suspension of the rules ("I move to suspend the rules and pass H.R. 1234."). Until the 108th Congress

ONE HUNDRED TENTH CONGRESS

FIRST SESSION { CONVENED JANUARY 4, 2007

SECOND SESSION {

CALENDARS

OF THE UNITED STATES
HOUSE OF REPRESENTATIVES
————————————AND————————————
HISTORY OF LEGISLATION

LEGISLATIVE DAY 1   CALENDAR DAY 1

Thursday, January 4, 2007

HOUSE MEETS AT 12 M.

SPECIAL ORDERS

(SEE NEXT PAGE)

PREPARED UNDER THE DIRECTION OF KAREN L. HAAS, CLERK OF THE HOUSE OF REPRESENTATIVES:
By the Office of Legislative Operations

The Clerk shall cause the calendars of the House to be printed and distributed each legislative day. Rule II, clause 2(e)   *Index to the Calendars will be printed the first legislative day of each week the House is in session*

U.S. GOVERNMENT PRINTING OFFICE: 2007   59–038

FIGURE 4-1   *Calendars of the United States House of Representatives and History of Legislation*

(2003–2005), the suspension procedure was in order every Monday and Tuesday and during the last six days of a session of Congress. On an experimental basis, the GOP-controlled 108th House added Wednesday as another suspension day. When the 109th Congress began, Rules Chairman David Dreier, R-Calif., explained that Wednesday now would be a permanent suspension day "after the very successful experiment we had with suspensions on Wednesday in the 108th Congress." [8] Democrats also kept Wednesdays as a suspension day, when they took charge of the 110th House. (The Rules Committee sometimes reports resolutions, subject to House approval, that authorize the Speaker to entertain motions to suspend the rules on days other than Monday, Tuesday, and Wednesday.) Informally, lawmakers often refer to measures on the "suspension calendar" even though there is no formal calendar for this purpose.

Three key rules govern suspension procedure and limit its use on most occasions to noncontroversial measures that enjoy broad bipartisan support, such as naming post offices after deceased lawmakers. First, debate on suspension bills is limited to forty minutes, evenly divided between proponents and opponents. Second, the motion to suspend the rules and pass a bill may include amendments, but only if they are stipulated in the motion offered by the majority floor manager ("I move to suspend the rules and pass H.R. 1234, with an amendment."); otherwise, amendments from the floor are not permitted. Third, the final and only vote on the measure is both to suspend the rules and to pass the bill—by a two-thirds vote, a quorum (218) being present. Bills that fail to gain the necessary two-thirds support may be considered again under regular House procedures (i.e., a special rule granted by the Rules Committee or, far less likely, even another suspension attempt). Sometimes majority party leaders schedule bills they dislike for suspension procedure because the two-thirds requirement makes them easier to defeat.

To accommodate lawmakers' constituency activities—many members travel to their districts on Friday and return the following Monday—the House instituted a cluster voting rule. The Speaker announces that recorded votes on a group of bills considered under the suspension procedure will be postponed until later that day or until the next day. The bills then are brought up in sequence and disposed of without further debate. On the first clustered vote in a series, members have a minimum of fifteen minutes in which to vote; on the remaining votes the Speaker may reduce the time on each one to a minimum of five minutes.

The Speaker is in complete charge of measures considered under the suspension procedure. Committee chairs, usually with the concurrence of their ranking minority colleagues, write the Speaker requesting that certain bills be taken up via the suspension route. Typically, these bills were reported by committee. But any measure—reported or not, previously introduced or not, including conference reports and constitutional amendments—can be brought to the floor under suspension of the rules if the Speaker chooses to recognize the representative offering the suspension motion. Speaker Thomas

"Tip" O'Neill, D-Mass., for example, brought a constitutional amendment, the Equal Rights Amendment (ERA), to the House floor in 1983 under suspension procedure to prevent opponents from offering controversial floor amendments on abortion and the military draft. However, the ERA failed to attract the required two-thirds vote, in part because even its supporters objected to taking up such a significant issue under procedures that limited debate and prevented amendments.

The majority Democrats have guidelines that govern the consideration of measures under the suspension method. Under Democratic Caucus rules, there are provisions that state, for example, that the Speaker will not schedule measures for suspension procedure that are considered major legislation; that are opposed by one-third of any committee reporting such legislation; and that are not available to lawmakers at least three calendar days in advance of consideration (including the day of consideration). The leadership "does not ordinarily schedule bills for suspensions unless confident of a two-thirds vote." [9]

The suspension procedure enables the House to bypass normal floor procedures and quickly approve legislation that can attract an overwhelming voting majority. Committee chairs generally support the suspension of the rules because the procedure protects their bills from floor amendments and points of order. Party leaders, too, use the suspension route to expedite emergency legislation or to move their issue agenda. At times, the minority party gets upset with the majority leadership for not scheduling enough of their bills via suspension procedure. To protest, minority party members may vote against suspension bills until more of their routine measures are taken up on the floor. They may also castigate the majority leadership for using suspension of the rules procedure on bills that in their estimation merit more debate than forty minutes and require the offering of stand-alone amendments.[10]

Table 4-1 highlights the use of suspension procedure from the 100th through the 108th Congresses. As it indicates, the use of suspension procedure is on the increase. For example, during the 107th Congress (2001–2003), nearly "eight out of every 10 bills enacted into law were brought to the House floor under the procedure. Two decades ago, roughly a third of enacted laws were brought to the House floor under the same process." [11] But why, in an increasingly polarized House, is a procedure that requires some support from the minority party being used more often? One explanation is that majority party leaders "keep the peace" in the House and maintain agenda control over major bills by being "more generous in giving members opportunities under suspension to offer minor bills of importance to them," while, at the same time, limiting member opportunities to amend major legislation.[12] In short, greater use of the suspension procedure serves a safety-valve function. It gives lawmakers who are frustrated by their inability to modify major bills a chance to offer additional suspension measures that serve their constituents, make policy, and enhance their influence in the chamber.

TABLE 4-1   Motions to Suspend the Rules in the House, by Party of Sponsor, 100th to 108th Congress

| Congress | Measure Sponsored by | | | | Total |
| | Democrat | | Republican | | |
	Number	Percent	Number	Percent	
100th (1987–1989)	512	83.4	102	16.6	614
101st (1989–1991)	468	80.3	115	19.7	583
102d (1991–1993)	513	83.4	102	16.6	615
103d (1993–1995)	412	88.2	55	11.8	467
104th (1995–1997)	69	17.2	332	82.8	401
105th (1997–1999)	126	20.4	491	79.6	617
106th (1999–2001)	207	23.2	686	76.8	893
107th (2001–2003)	154	22.5	531	77.5	685
108th (2003–2005)	273	29.5	651	70.5	924

SOURCE: Thomas P. Carr, "Suspension of Rules in the House: Measure Sponsorship by Party," CRS Report 97-901, January 16, 2005, 2.

During the hectic last days of a congressional session, suspension of the rules is used more frequently—and even on important measures. Dozens of bills may be scheduled daily for suspension votes. The parliamentary situation also is somewhat different during this period. Members who at an earlier time in the session might have voted against a bill brought up under suspension, because they had no opportunity to offer amendments to it or because it was a major bill, might vote for the same legislation during the end-of-the-session crunch, rationalizing that it is that version or nothing. The minority party's role is also enhanced during this pressure-packed, rush-to-adjourn time, because suspension votes virtually always require some bipartisan support.

District of Columbia Legislation

The federal capital is a unique governmental unit. Residents of the District of Columbia have no voting representation in Congress. (They have a nonvoting delegate in the House and no representation in the Senate.)

In a rules change initiated by D.C. Delegate Eleanor Holmes Norton, the 103d Congress (1993–1995) permitted Norton, the three territorial delegates, and the one resident commissioner—all Democrats—to vote in the Committee of the Whole. However, if their votes determined the outcome of an amendment, an automatic revote would be taken without their participation. Republicans vehemently protested granting the delegates and resident commissioner the right to vote in the Committee of the Whole. In a good example of the majority rule principle in action, they dropped this provision from the House's rulebook when they took control in the 104th Congress.[13] Democrats reinstated this rule for all nonstate delegates when they took control of the 110th House.

Despite home rule for the capital, the House exercises control over the District principally through two committees, Appropriations and Oversight and Government Reform. House rules set aside the second and fourth Mondays of each month for District legislation reported by the Oversight and Government Reform Committee. District bills are typically considered in what is called "the House as in Committee of the Whole"—a hybrid entity that combines procedural features of the House and the Committee of the Whole. For example, general debate is not permitted but debate and amendment may occur under the five-minute rule. Appropriations bills for the District do not come up during those special days. Instead, they are considered under the privilege (access to the floor) given legislation reported by the Appropriations Committee.

The Private Calendar

Private bills are designed to provide legal relief to specified persons or entities adversely affected by laws of general applicability. The constitutional basis for private bills rests on the right of the people, under the First Amendment, "to petition the Government for a redress of grievances." Most private bills deal with immigration and naturalization cases and claims against the federal government. For example, general immigration requirements may be waived or expedited to permit foreign-born athletes to join the U.S. Olympic team or to allow a Philadelphia woman to marry a Greek man. Most private bills are referred to the House and Senate Judiciary Committees for review, and, like other bills, private bills passed by both chambers are sent to the president for signature or veto.

Under House procedures, the Speaker is required to call private bills on the first Tuesday of each month (unless the rule is dispensed with by a two-thirds vote, or unanimous consent is obtained to transfer the call to some other day of the month) and, at the Speaker's discretion, on the third Tuesday as well. Because few lawmakers have the time to review private bills, the Private Calendar Objectors Committee is assigned that task. The panel is composed of three members of each political party appointed by the majority and minority leaders.

Bills must be placed on the Private Calendar seven days before being called up to give the objectors time to screen them for controversial provisions. (Committee reports on private measures must also be available to the objectors for three calendar days.) The objectors attend House sessions on Private Calendar days to answer any questions about the pending measures. If two or more members of the House object to a bill on the first Tuesday, it automatically is sent back to the committee that reported it, although at the request of a member it may at this time be "passed over without prejudice" for later consideration. Generally, private bills are not subject to lengthy consideration and are disposed of by voice vote.

The number of private bills introduced each Congress has declined sharply. From the 1,269 private claims bills introduced during the 80th Congress (1947–1949), the number fell to 132 in the 109th Congress (2005–2007). In the 82d Congress (1951–1953), Congress cleared 1,023 private bills that became private law; the 103d Congress (1993–1995), 8; the 104th, only 4; the 107th and 108th, only 6 each Congress; and 1 in the 109th. Several factors account for the drop-off. First, various scandals were associated with the introduction of private bills for pay. For example, in the so-called Abscam scandal of 1980, FBI agents dressed as Arab sheiks paid several lawmakers to introduce private immigration bills for them. These scandals led to stricter procedures for the consideration of such bills. Second, Congress authorized administrative agencies and the U.S. Court of Claims to handle the bulk of these cases. Third, private bills often require an enormous amount of time to handle and in the end the claims can prove to be incorrect or fraudulent. Finally, congressional staff aides have suggested that legislators feel uncomfortable approving private claims bills that benefit only a few people when so many other programs affecting larger numbers of people are being cut.[14]

PRIVILEGED LEGISLATION

Under House rules, five standing committees have direct access to the floor for selected bills. The Appropriations and Budget panels report measures to finance the operations of the government; the Standards of Official Conduct Committee deals with matters involving the public reputation of the House; the House Administration panel handles necessary housekeeping proposals; and the Rules Committee plays a major role in determining which measures the House considers. The committees and types of legislation eligible to be called up for immediate debate are listed in Table 4-2.

Unlike the other standing committees, which act only on legislation referred to them, these panels have the authority to originate, or initiate, specific measures. The bills may be called up when other matters are not already pending on the House floor. Despite the privilege, most of these bills cannot be considered for at least three days so that members have time to read the committee reports. (Observance of these rules can be set aside via waivers granted by the Rules Committee.) Special rules from the Rules Committee must lay over only one day, whereas reports on budget resolutions must be available to members for ten days. (A few other matters, such as declarations of war, are exempt from the three-day layover rule.) Privileged measures are matters of special import to the House as an institution or to the federal government.

Even privileged measures are subject to points of order (parliamentary objections that any member may raise at an appropriate time) on the grounds that they violate certain rules of the House. If upheld, such points of order return the measure to the committee that considered it. Committees with privileged access, therefore, will usually ask the Rules Committee to waive points of order against their bills. The Appropriations Committee, for example, may violate House rules banning unauthorized appropriations or legislative provisions (policy provisos) in general appropriations bills and will protect the panel's bills from points of order by persuading the Rules Committee to issue

TABLE 4-2 Committees with Direct Access to the Floor for Selected Legislation

Committee	Legislation
Appropriations	General appropriations bills; continuing appropriations resolutions if reported after September 15
Budget	Budget resolutions and reconciliation bills under the Congressional Budget and Impoundment Control Act of 1974
House Administration	Matters relating to enrolled bills, contested elections, and House expenditures, including committee funding resolutions
Rules	Rules and the order of business
Standards of Official Conduct	Resolutions recommending action with respect to the conduct of a member, officer, or employee of the House

waivers. (There are occasions when the Appropriations Committee will bypass the Rules Committee. Instead, a majority committee member will ask and receive the unanimous consent of the House to define the procedural framework for debating and amending an appropriations bill.)[15]

MAJOR LEGISLATION

Most major bills do not go automatically from committee to a calendar and then to the House floor. Simply put, most major bills lack "privilege." Privilege is a parliamentary term that grants certain legislative business precedence "over the regular order of business. It is business that can supersede or interrupt other matters that might otherwise be called up or pending before the House." [16] Recall that only a few matters, such as general appropriations bills, are accorded privilege by the House rulebook. In addition, the House rulebook makes certain measures (suspension and private bills) privileged for floor consideration during specified days of the week or month. Major bills are not accorded privileged access to the floor by the House rulebook. Thus, the route to the floor for major legislation is through the Rules Committee. It can grant privilege to measures that lack this special status.

Brief Overview

The Rules Committee is among the oldest of House panels. The First Congress in April 1789 appointed an eleven-member rules body to draw up its procedures. With a few early exceptions, each succeeding Congress has done the same, although for nearly a century the Rules panel was a select (temporary) committee that prepared procedures for the incoming Congress and then went out of existence.

In 1858 the Speaker became a member and leader of the Rules Committee. In 1880 the Rules Committee became a standing (permanent) committee, and in 1883 it initiated the practice of reporting special orders, or rules, which, when agreed to by majority votes of the House, controlled the amount of time allowed for debate on major bills and the extent to which they could be amended from the floor.

Speakers during and after the 1880s permitted the Rules Committee to acquire authority over the House's agenda and the order of business. Speaker Joseph G. Cannon, a Republican from Illinois who was Speaker from 1903 to 1911, abused these and other powers, with the result that the House revolted in 1910 and removed the Speaker from the Rules Committee. The House majority leadership, however, retained—and still retains, in cooperation with the Rules Committee—fundamental control over the flow of legislation reaching the floor.

A notable exception was maverick Rules Committee chairman Howard W. Smith, D-Va. (1931–1967), who presided over the committee with an iron hand from 1955 to 1967. Smith was no traffic cop simply regulating the flow of bills to the floor. He firmly believed the committee should "consider the substance and merits of the bills," and he often blocked measures he disapproved of and advanced those he favored, sometimes thwarting the will of the majority.[17]

The Rules Committee lacks authority to amend bills, but the Smith-led panel bargained for changes in return for granting rules. (During the Smith era, frustration with the panel stemmed from its refusal to issue rules; today, it is the character of special rules—whether and how many amendments are permitted—that often arouses the ire of legislators.) In an attempt to lessen the power of the conservative coalition of southern Democrats and Republicans that controlled the committee from the mid-1930s to the early 1960s, House liberals succeeded in adopting a series of rules changes beginning in the late 1940s. But the independent power of the chair was not substantially curbed until the membership of the committee was expanded in 1961.[18] This expansion resulted from a titanic battle between Speaker Sam Rayburn, D-Texas, and Rules Committee chairman Smith. In a rare event for any president, newly elected president John F. Kennedy directly intervened in the internal affairs of the House—in the matter of House rules. Kennedy supported Rayburn's successful effort to enlarge the Rules Committee, thereby changing its ideological complexion so that conservative members could not kill the president's New Frontier program.

By the 95th Congress (1977–1979), the Rules Committee had become closely linked to the Speaker. In 1975 the Democratic Speaker was authorized by his party caucus to appoint, subject to party ratification, all majority party members of the Rules Committee. In 1989 House Republicans authorized their leader to name all the GOP members of the Rules Committee. The committee's composition in the 110th Congress (2007–2009) was nine Democrats and four Republicans. Thus in the 110th Congress, Speaker Pelosi named the chair—Louise Slaughter, N.Y., the first female to head the panel—and the other eight Democratic members, and Minority Leader John Boehner, R-Ohio, appointed the four GOP members. (Traditionally, the panel has had a disproportionate partisan ratio to ensure majority control.) Today, the committee is one of the few centralizing panels in a decentralized House. It is the "Speaker's Committee" and functions to implement the program of the majority party. Its rule-writing responsibilities mean that it has the job of ensuring that legislation brought before the House is considered in a coherent and systematic manner and under procedural ground rules that advantage the majority party. As former Speaker Jim Wright, D-Tex., stated:

> The Rules Committee is an agent of the leadership. It is what distinguishes us from the Senate, where the rules deliberately favor those who would delay. The rules of the House, if one understands how to employ them, permit a majority to work its will on legislation rather than allow it to be bottled up and stymied.

The leader of the GOP Conference expressed the same idea: "It's the committee that makes the difference between the House and Senate. It's the committee that makes the House more efficient." [19] Or as a GOP Rules vice chairman said about the panel's relations with the Speaker: "How much is the Rules Committee the handmaiden of the Speaker? The answer is, totally." [20]

Still, the Rules Committee's power should not be underestimated. The Speaker cannot track every major and minor bill or issue instructions constantly to the panel. The history of the Rules Committee is "one of the committee's accommodating the leadership on the one hand and seeking independent status on the other." [21] Today, the emphasis is on accommodating the Speaker.

Role of the Rules Committee

The power of the Rules Committee lies in its scheduling responsibilities: its traffic cop role. Besides deciding whether to grant a rule, the committee must craft rules to accomplish diverse purposes, such as providing for orderly review of major policy alternatives on the floor, protecting partisan objectives, focusing House debate on the main proposals in contention, and expediting consideration of priority measures.

As public bills are reported out of committee, they are entered in chronological order on one of the two main calendars, the Union Calendar or the House Calendar. All revenue bills, general appropriations bills, and measures that directly or indirectly appropriate money or property (including all authorization measures) are placed on the Union Calendar; all remaining public bills, such as constitutional amendments or resolutions recognizing the anniversary of a country, go on the House Calendar. If all measures have to be taken up in the order in which they are listed on the calendars, as was the practice in the early nineteenth century, many major bills would not reach the

House floor before Congress adjourns. Instead, major legislation reaches the floor in most instances because it has been granted precedence through a special order (rule) obtained from the Rules Committee. A rule is a simple resolution (H. Res.). A written request for a rule is usually submitted to the Rules Committee chair by the chair of the committee reporting the bill.

The Rules Committee then holds a hearing on the request—witnesses are limited to lawmakers—and debates the proposal in the same manner that other committees consider legislative matters. One congressional scholar has called hearings the "dress rehearsal" function of the Rules Committee:

> Rules members comprise the first audience for a piece of legislation outside the narrow confines of the committee and subcommittee that reported it. As such, the hearing on a rule request serves as a "dress rehearsal" for bill managers before they take the legislation to the House floor. The hearing on a rule is an opportunity for them to present their case and test the reaction from Rules members.[22]

After the hearings, Rules members (particularly of the majority party) craft their rule and vote it out of committee. (In a rare occurrence involving the bill to establish the Department of Homeland Security, the special rule "governing consideration of this legislation [was] jointly recommended by the Speaker and the Democratic leader and then brought to the Committee on Rules.")[23] Once reported by the panel, the rule is considered on the House floor as privileged matter, which essentially means it is subject to one hour of debate and no amendments, and it is voted on in the same fashion as regular bills. In effect, a rule provides a tailor-made process for floor consideration of a bill—that is, it is a departure from the procedures provided in the standing rules of the House. A rule, then, serves several important purposes:

- It bumps a bill up the ladder of precedence, eliminating the waiting time that would be needed if chronological order were observed. The Rules Committee, in effect, shuffles the Union and House Calendars by holding back rules for some bills and reporting them for others.
- It governs the length of general debate on the bill as opposed to allowing any member to speak for up to one hour on it.
- It usually dispenses with the first reading of the bill and the reading of amendments that are preprinted in the *Congressional Record* or in the report of the Rules Committee accompanying the rule.
- It usually limits the number of amendments that may be offered and the time for debate on any amendment, as opposed to allowing any member to offer and debate as many germane amendments as he or she wants.
- It orders the previous question—that is, debate ceases, no amendments are permitted, and the House votes immediately on the issue at hand—as opposed to allowing the House to further amend and debate the bill after it has been reported from the Committee of the Whole.

In blocking or delaying legislation from reaching the floor, the Rules Committee is not necessarily playing an obstructionist role. It may be providing political cover by drawing fire away from the leadership, certain committees, and individual members. Representatives sometimes request that the Rules Committee prevent unwanted bills or amendments from reaching the floor. As Speaker O'Neill once said, "It takes the heat for the rest of the Congress, there is no question about that."[24]

The committee also acts as an informal mediator of disputes among other House committees and members. Because of overlapping jurisdictions, one committee may report a measure that trespasses on the authority of another. In such a case, the Rules Committee may resolve the dispute by authorizing the second committee to offer amendments or by refusing to waive points of order on the floor, thus giving members of the second committee an opportunity to attempt to delete the offending matter. The Rules Committee also may mediate intraparty conflicts, so that majority party members are not hanging their dirty linen in public when contentious issues reach the floor. Interparty differences are reconciled to the extent that bills enjoy cross-party support.

The Rules Committee also plays a jurisdictional arbitration role on multiply referred legislation. As a precondition for a rule, the committee may urge or require competing committees to agree on the vehicle—one of the committee's reported bills, some consensus product, or something else—for floor debate and amendment. This practice limits floor fights among rival committees, simplifies floor decision making, expedites the processing of legislation, and avoids putting the Rules Committee in the position of deciding which panel's bill to use for floor discussion.

The Rules Committee also has substantive (or original jurisdiction) responsibilities. It has reported out major measures such as the Legislative Reorganization Act of 1970, the Congressional Budget and Impoundment Control Act of 1974, the Legislative Transparency and Accountability Act of 2006, and resolutions providing for the creation of a permanent Select Intelligence Committee and the televising of House floor sessions. As part of its jurisdiction over the House rulebook, the panel regularly recommends a variety of procedural changes. For example, the panel supported the use of points of order, which it cannot waive, against the imposition of unfunded mandates on states and localities and the private sector. If, for example, a lawmaker both raises a point of order against a rule that permits consideration of measures that contain unfunded mandates on states and localities in excess of $50 million and specifies the precise violation, the Speaker does not rule but puts the question ("Will the House now consider the resolution?") to the membership. Twenty minutes of debate are permitted (ten per side), and then the House votes on whether it will take up the rule.[25] Finally, since the September 11, 2001, terrorist attacks, the Rules Committee has taken action to address the continuity of Congress should a catastrophic event kill or incapacitate scores of House members. A key continuity issue is how to re-populate the House quickly so it can conduct the people's business.

Traditional Types of Special Rules

The Rules Committee traditionally grants three basic kinds of rules: open, closed, and modified. The distinction among them goes solely to the question of the amendment process. All three types almost always provide a fixed number of hours for general debate. In addition, any of these types may contain waivers of points of order. An example of a rule from the Rules Committee, with an explanation of its basic features, is shown in Box 4-1.

Open Rules. Open rules were common for most bills until about the 95th Congress (1977–1979)—in the previous Congress, for example, 81 percent of the rules were open—when restrictive rules began to increase in number, as Table 4-3 shows.[26] At the end of his thirty-eight-year career in the House, the last fourteen (1981–1995) as GOP leader, Robert H. Michel, Ill., wrote that during this period when Democrats controlled the House, they "clamped down on the granting of open rules, making it more and more difficult for Members to offer amendments to legislation." [27] Given their frustrating and even embittering experience with rules that often restricted their right to offer amendments, Republicans, when they took control of the House in the 104th Congress, wanted the Rules Committee to provide more amendment opportunities for all lawmakers. This goal proved to be short-lived, however.

Under an open rule, germane amendments to a bill may be offered from the floor so long as they comply with House rules and precedents, such as the requirement that amendments must be in writing at the time they are offered. Amendments may be simple or complex. For example, an amendment may extend the funding of a program from two to four years or it may rewrite whole sections of a bill. Some committees, such as Science, customarily request the Rules Committee to grant an open rule for their legislation.

Although open rules permit any and all germane amendments, they do have a downside in the length of time it may take to complete action on legislation and in the unpredictable character of the many amendments that might be offered. After two weeks of debate and with nearly 170 amendments still pending to one of their Contract with America measures, Republicans began to have some doubts about open rules. (The Contract with American was the GOP's governing document when they took control of the House following the November 1994 elections.) They believed Democrats were offering scores of amendments to an unfunded mandates bill to prevent Republicans from considering all their contract bills within the first one hundred days of the 104th Congress (1995–1997), as promised. Thus, the GOP voted to limit debate to ten minutes for each of the pending amendments. The Rules Committee chairman added, "It looks like we're going to have to increasingly restrict rules if the Democrats won't cooperate." [28]

Lack of minority party cooperation is only one of a variety of factors that produced a decline in the number of open rules during GOP control

TABLE 4-3 Open versus Restrictive Rules, 95th to 108th Congresses

		Open Rules		Restrictive Rules	
Congress		Number	Percent	Number	Percent
95th	(1977–1979)	179	85	32	15
96th	(1979–1981)	161	75	53	25
97th	(1981–1983)	90	75	30	25
98th	(1983–1985)	105	68	50	32
99th	(1985–1987)	65	57	50	43
100th	(1987–1989)	66	54	57	46
101st	(1989–1991)	47	45	57	55
102d	(1991–1993)	37	34	72	66
103d	(1993–1995)	31	30	71	70
104th	(1995–1997)	86	54	65	43
105th	(1997–1999)	58	42	81	58
106th	(1999–2001)	91	51	88	49
107th	(2001–2003)	40	37	67	63
108th	(2003–2005)	34	26	99	74

SOURCE: Donald Wolfensberger, *The Congress Project,* Woodrow Wilson Center, Washington, D.C., 2003.

(1995–2007) of the House. The narrow divide in numbers between the parties combined with sharp partisan polarization and the wide ideological divergence between Democrats and Republicans are just some of the factors that make open rules scarce in the contemporary House. Rules Committee member James P. McGovern, D-Mass., even urged his colleagues to examine a specific open rule "very closely, to study it, because it is a very, very rare specimen." He added, "Whenever an issue is the least bit contentious, whenever there is even a hint of disagreement about a bill, the majority clamps down on its Members, chokes debates, and forces a closed rule through this House." [29] He further added that in the 109th Congress, "only one non-appropriations bill was considered under an open rule." [30] Recall that appropriations measures are traditionally considered under an open amendment procedure. Republicans responded to the Democratic complaints by citing, among other things, that they are fairer to the minority than when Democrats ran the House, that the electorate made the GOP the governing majority and it expects them to advance the public's agenda, and that the minority is more interested in making political points than engaging in bipartisan policymaking.

Speaker Pelosi and the other Democratic leaders vowed that the 110th House would be run in a different manner. Speaker Pelosi, for instance, articulated several principles for running the House in a bipartisan and civil manner, such as ensuring the rights of the minority and consulting regularly with the minority leadership.[31] Majority Leader Hoyer also emphasized that

BOX 4-1   Reading a Special Rule

H. Res. 289
[Report No. 106-317]

Original Text of the Resolution

Resolved, That at any time after the adoption of this resolution the Speaker may, pursuant to clause 2(b) of the rule XVIII, declare the House resolved into the Committee of the Whole House on the state of the Union for consideration of the bill (H.R. 1655) to authorize appropriations for fiscal years 2000 and 2001 for the civilian energy and scientific research, development, and demonstration and related commercial application of energy technology programs, projects, and activities of the Department of Energy, and for other purposes.

EXPLANATION: *Authorizes the Speaker to transform ("resolve") the House into the Committee of the Whole House to consider the measure after adoption of the special rule.*

The first reading of the bill shall be dispensed with. General debate shall be confined to the bill and shall not exceed one hour equally divided and controlled by the chairman and ranking minority member of the Committee on Science.

EXPLANATION: *Dispenses with the first reading of the bill. (Bills must be read three times before being passed.) Sets the amount of general debate time—one hour—and specifies which members control that time—in this instance, the chair and ranking minority member of the Committee on Science. Specifies that debate should be relevant to the bill.*

After general debate the bill shall be considered for amendment under the five-minute rule.

EXPLANATION: *Sets reading for amendment one section at a time (or one paragraph at a time for appropriations bills), and provides that each member can speak for five minutes on each amendment. Because this special rule sets no limitations on amendments that can be offered, it is an open rule. Nonetheless, amendments still must comply with the House's standing rules, such as germaneness.*

It shall be in order to consider as an original bill for purposes of amendment under the five-minute rule the amendment in the nature of a substitute recommended by the Committee on Science now printed in the bill. Each section of the committee amendment in the nature of a substitute shall be considered as read.

EXPLANATION: *Identifies text to be open to amendment in the Committee of the Whole. A special rule can provide that a committee-reported substitute be considered as an original bill for the purpose of amendment. Allowing a full-text substitute to be considered as an original bill is usually done to permit second-degree amendments to be offered.*

During consideration of the bill for amendment, the Chairman of the Committee of the Whole may accord priority in recognition on the basis of whether the Member offering an amendment has caused it to be printed in the portion of the Congressional Record designated for that purpose in clause 8 of rule XVIII. Amendments so printed shall be considered as read.

EXPLANATION: *Determines recognition order for offering amendments. Open rules customarily grant the chair of the Committee of the Whole discretion to give priority recognition to members who submitted their amendments for preprinting in the* Congressional Record. *Absent this provision, the chair would follow the custom of giving preferential recognition to members, based on seniority, who serve on the reporting committee, alternating between the parties.*

The Chairman of the Committee of the Whole may: (1) postpone until a time during further consideration in the Committee of the Whole a request for a recorded vote on any amendment; and (2) reduce to five minutes time for electronic voting on any postponed question that follows another electronic vote without intervening business, provided that the minimum time for electronic voting on the first in any series of questions shall be 15 minutes.

EXPLANATION: *A special rule that allows amendments to be offered might allow the chair of the Committee of the Whole to postpone votes on amendments, as shown here. The chair may reduce to five minutes the time for electronic voting on a postponed question, provided that the voting time on the first in any series of questions is not less than fifteen minutes.*

At the conclusion of consideration of the bill for amendment the Committee shall rise and report the bill to the House with such amendments as may have been adopted.

EXPLANATION: *Provides for transformation ("to rise") back to the House from the Committee of the Whole. This provision eliminates the need for a separate vote on a motion to rise and report.*

Any Members may demand a separate vote in the House on any amendment adopted in the Committee of the Whole to the bill or to the committee amendment in the nature of a substitute.

EXPLANATION: *Enables separate votes to occur in the House on each first-degree amendment approved by the Committee of the Whole. House rules require the House to vote on each first-degree amendment approved by the Committee of the Whole.*

The previous question shall be considered as ordered on the bill and amendments thereto to final passage without intervening motion except one motion to recommit with or without instructions.

EXPLANATION: *Expedites final passage. By automatically imposing the "previous question," intervening debate and the offering of motions is precluded. The only motion allowed is a motion to recommit.*

SOURCE: Michael L. Koempel and Judy Schneider, *Congressional Deskbook 2005–2007* (Alexandria, Va.: TheCapitol.Net, 2005), 258–259. www.CongressionalDeskbook.com. Reprinted with permission.

the Democratically managed House would permit minority alternatives to be offered to pending legislation. "We intend to have a Rules Committee and Mrs. Slaughter leading the Rules Committee that gives opposition voices and alternative proposals the ability to be heard and considered on the floor of the House," said Hoyer.[32] To be sure, allowing the minority party to offer amendments does not mean that measures will always be brought to the floor under an open rule.

Significantly, open rules raise the important question of where the fundamental deliberations on legislation should take place: in the committee setting among a relatively small number of lawmakers who specialize in the subject area or on the House floor with the entire membership having a say in policy formulation. Further, can a House of 435 members function without some limits on debate and amendments during floor action on major and controversial bills?

Closed Rules. Closed rules prohibit floor amendments, except at times, those offered by the reporting committee or committees. Recent years have seen an increase in the number of closed rules that require a bill to be considered in the House and not in the Committee of the Whole under procedures that limit debate to one hour and restrict or prohibit amendments. The rule also automatically orders the previous question on the bill. For example, a major domestic initiative (H.R. 1, the Medicare Prescription Drug and Modernization Act of 2003) was considered in the House and not the Committee of the Whole to expedite its consideration. Language in the special rule stated that the "previous question shall be considered as ordered on the bill and any amendment thereto to final passage without intervening motion," except for three hours of debate on the bill and one amendment if offered by Rep. Charles Rangel, D-N.Y., or his designee. As noted earlier, "ordering the previous question" means that, unless a special rule provides exceptions such as for H.R. 1, debate ceases, no amendments are permitted, and the House votes immediately on the issue at hand.

Critics say closed rules (also called "gag" rules) hamper the legislative process and violate democratic norms. A House Democrat put it this way:

> In most cases, closed rules say that we as individual Members are willing to allow a small portion of the whole to decide what information we need to consider, what complexities our minds are able to master, and from what alternatives we should choose. Furthermore, many times closed rules indicate either an arrogance on the part of the proponents of a bill or an insecurity about the bill's merits or abilities to stand up against competing ideas.[33]

Supporters of closed rules say they are needed for complex measures that are subject to intense lobbying. In addition, legislation related to a national emergency sometimes must be expedited by the closed rule procedure.

Tax bills provide a good illustration of the pressures surrounding closed rules. For decades and even today, the House considers tax measures under closed rules, agreeing with the argument of Wilbur D. Mills, D-Ark.

(1939–1977), chairman of the Ways and Means Committee from 1958 to 1974, that tax legislation was too complex and technical to be tampered with on the floor. If unlimited floor amendments were allowed, Mills argued, the Internal Revenue Code would soon be in shambles and at the mercy of pressure groups. However, the Rules Committee may permit complete substitutes—the functional equivalent of an alternative bill—to be offered to Ways and Means-reported tax bills. As former Majority Leader Tom DeLay, R-Tex., noted: "We have always as a tradition discouraged [discrete] amendments, but we have encouraged substitutes." [34]

An indirect way to amend tax (or other) legislation is via a self-executing feature (see the discussion below on self-executing rules), a provision that can be contained in a closed rule. For example, after the Ways and Means Committee reports a tax bill, the chair may learn that there are not enough votes to pass the legislation because of concerns raised by various lawmakers. An option for the chair is to recommend changes in the tax-reported bill to the Rules Committee. The changes are designed to attract the support of wavering lawmakers by addressing their policy concerns. These substantive changes (or amendments) are automatically incorporated, or self-executed, into the text of the bill.

Modified Rules. This third category of special rules comes in two versions—modified open rules and modified closed rules—but these designations are somewhat subjective. A modified open rule might indicate that all parts of a bill are open to amendment except a specific title or section. A modified closed rule could state that an entire bill is closed to amendment except a certain title or section. Or the distinction between the two is based on the number of amendments allowed by the Rules Committee. Fundamentally, modified open rules provide more amendment opportunities than modified closed rules. During the early 2000s, the special rule of choice for the then GOP majority leadership, operating with a small majority, has often been the modified closed rule, which may permit the minority only one amendment that is a complete substitute for the underlying bill.

Sharp Democratic criticism of the GOP's management of the House, particularly the curtailment of amendment opportunities for the minority, led to an informal development in the 109th Congress (2005–2007). Republicans, but not Democrats, no longer mentioned "modified closed" rules. Instead, Rules Republicans characterized modified closed as "structured" rules. (See the discussion below on structured rules.) This change in terminology is a mini-example of the contemporary emphasis on language in framing political communication. "Closed" implies exclusion whereas "structured" suggests a fair and systematic procedure for taking up amendments.

Waiver Rules. Under these rules, which appear in open, closed, and modified rules, specific House procedures or points of order are temporarily set aside. Without such waivers, measures in technical violation of House procedures could be blocked from floor consideration or important parts of bills could be deleted for technical reasons during floor debate. "If we went strictly by the House rules," remarked one House member, "I am sure this body would have a very difficult time operating." [35]

The sole purpose of some rules is to waive points of order against the consideration of legislation that is privileged, such as conference reports, but that also has violated various House rules. The Rules Committee may issue a "same day"(also called "martial law") rule. The purpose of this special rule—typically employed when the House is trying to wrap up its end-of-session business quickly—is to allow the Rules Committee to bring priority legislation to the floor on the same day the panel approves a special rule. The House rulebook specifies that special rules brought to the floor on the same day they are approved by the panel require a two-thirds vote for adoption instead of the usual majority vote. Martial law, or same day, rules set aside, or waive, the two-thirds requirement.

Generally, waivers are of two types: (1) exemptions from specific House rules and procedures, or (2) blanket waivers of all points of order against pending legislation. For example, the Rules Committee may waive the House rule requiring committee reports on legislation to be available to lawmakers for at least three calendar days (excluding Saturdays, Sundays, and legal holidays) before the House can take up a measure. In the minority, Republicans objected strenuously to the large number of waivers. But when they assumed majority control of the House in the mid-1990s, Republicans amended the rules of the House to require the Rules Committee, to the maximum extent possible, "to specify in any special rule providing for the consideration of a measure any provisions of House rules being waived." [36] Today, waivers are granted routinely to advance party and substantive objectives. During the 108th Congress, for instance, the three-day layover provision in House rules for committee-reported legislation—granting time to non-committee members to become familiar with the bill before it is considered on the floor—was waived thirty-one times to expedite consideration of the majority's agenda.[37] Sometimes, members refer to open plus rules, which means an open amendment process with the plus of having waivers that provide protection for certain amendments against valid points of order.

The Rules Committee may establish informal practices of its own with respect to waivers. Although general appropriations bills are privileged under House rules, these measures are commonly regulated by special rules that waive appropriate points of order. When Republicans took control of the House in 1995, the GOP leadership established a protocol relating to waivers of unauthorized programs and legislative language (policy) in general appropriations bills. As the Rules Committee chairman explained:

> Under this protocol, the Committee on Rules would provide the necessary waivers to enable the bill to come to the floor if the authorizing committee chairmen did not object to them. If the authorizing chairmen objected to the waivers, then under the leadership's protocol, the Committee on Rules would leave the specific language in question exposed to a point of order on the floor.[38]

For example, during consideration of a special rule governing consideration of the agriculture appropriations bill for fiscal year 2007, Rules Republican Doc Hastings, Wash., responded to Democratic criticism that the procedural resolution prevented the offering of a dairy program amendment. Hastings replied: "[W]e have a long-standing tradition in the Rules Committee that when the authorizing committee has a problem with amendments or policies. . . that they feel is under their jurisdiction," those amendments are not granted waivers that protect them against points of order.[39] This informal policy is also observed by the Democratic majority of the 110th House.

Creative Rules for the House

Fundamental changes in the workings of the House that began during the 1970s and continue into the 2000s triggered the rise of "creative rules." The House witnessed a dramatic redistribution of internal influence from powerful, seniority-chosen committee chairs to scores of individual lawmakers, including subcommittee chairs, faction leaders, and rank-and-file members. Party leaders and caucuses gained influence too: the Speaker received multiple referral authority and the party caucuses were allowed to approve (or disapprove) committee chairs (or ranking minority members). Partisan polarization also enveloped the House, as did the intensity of outside pressures such as press and media coverage of congressional affairs and special interest involvement in lawmaking and campaigning.

Substantive and procedural complexity triggered the need for creative rules as well. Not only did measures become bigger and more complex, but also new procedures—multiple referrals, the requirements of the 1974 budget act, and various statutory provisions providing special procedures for certain bills—required the Rules Committee to sort through the complications and devise an orderly procedure for debating and amending legislation. The House also amended its rules in ways that encouraged lawmakers to ask for more recorded votes. The House permitted recorded votes in the Committee of the Whole in 1971 (votes had been unrecorded in this main amending forum), and electronic voting was authorized two years later.

All these changes produced a basic shift in the political culture of the House. It moved from the "to-get-along, go-along" spirit of Speaker Rayburn's era to an entrepreneurial and participatory style within which even freshmen lawmakers have many opportunities to voice their views and exert their influence in all phases of lawmaking. The Rules Committee responded to the new climate during most of the 1970s by providing members with wide-open amending opportunities on the floor. As one scholar pointed out:

Fewer than 900 amendments were offered in the 91st Congress (1969–1970) and fewer than 800 were offered in the 92d Congress (1971–1972), but over 1,400 were offered in the 93d Congress (1973–1974) and nearly 1,400 were offered in the 94th (1975–1976). In the 95th, floor amendments peaked at nearly 1,700. Clearly, the incentive to put oneself or one's opponents on the record helped to stimulate more amending activity. . . . [Further, a] group of Republicans—John Ashbrook of Ohio, Robert Bauman of Maryland, and John Rousselot of California—deliberately badgered Democrats with many amendments and requests for recorded votes.[40]

By the end of the 1970s, Democratic leaders and lawmakers wanted the Rules Committee to exert greater control over floor procedures. Members wanted greater certainty in an environment grown more conflict-ridden and unpredictable. The open amendment process produced longer sessions, disruptions in members' schedules, more dilatory tactics, and numerous challenges to committee-reported measures that often undercut the carefully crafted compromises negotiated in advance of floor consideration. For example, when President Jimmy Carter's proposal to create a Department of Education went to the floor in June 1979, "Republican opponents prepared nearly 200 amendments, for the express purpose of delaying a final vote and blocking passage." [41]

Other factors also contributed to the need for creative rules and the procedural crackdown that limited members' amendment opportunities. They included the use of multiple referrals, which required the Rules Committee to play a larger coordinative role in arranging floor action on legislation reported by several committees; the rise of megabills hundreds of pages in length that contained priorities the Speaker did not want picked apart on the floor; and the escalation of sharp partisanship, especially in the aftermath of Republican Ronald Reagan's election as president in November 1980 while the House remained in Democratic hands. GOP lawmakers, for example, sponsored floor amendments designed to embarrass Democrats and to supply Republican House challengers with campaign ammunition.

In response to these diverse circumstances, the Democratic-controlled Rules Committee tightened opportunities for floor amendments and devised a variety of innovative and procedurally creative rules, which remain available today. Their primary objectives are to expedite floor decision making, protect party programs by limiting or blocking minority amendments, focus member attention on the major policy alternatives, enhance partisan goals, and strengthen committee prerogatives. Among these creative procedures are structured rules, self-executing rules, king-of-the-hill rules, and multiple-stage rules.

Structured Rules. Structured rules limit the number of floor amendments; establish a specific order in which those amendments are to be offered, frequently identifying the member who can offer each amendment; and typically prohibit any change in the amendments made in order. These rules also may prescribe debate limits for the entire amendment process or for each amendment made in order. Structured rules may require as well that all amendments be published in the *Congressional Record* prior to floor action on the legislation. This requirement aids the floor managers. "Newer chairmen are kind of unsure of themselves," said Rep. J. Joseph Moakley, D-Mass., who served as Rules Committee chairman from 1989 to 1995. "They ask for amendments to be printed [in advance, in the *Record*] so they can be ready for anything." [42]

On the one hand, these rules restrict members' general right to offer floor amendments—something that frequently arouses the ire of minority party members. On the other hand, structured rules can expand the range of policy options put before the membership. Issues that are not eligible under normal parliamentary procedures can be made eligible for floor consideration. The Rules Committee can allow consideration of nongermane amendments, legislation stuck in committee, or even measures that have never been introduced.

Whether restrictive, expansive, or both, a fundamental purpose of structured rules is to define the sequence in which specific amendments are to be voted on—often to benefit the committee that reported the legislation, sometimes to grant other members an opportunity to revamp the reporting committee's priorities. The Rules Committee's ability to determine the sequence of action can influence the ultimate outcome. For example, the majority leadership may support a less costly initiative over an expensive one advocated by the minority leadership. The Rules Committee could fashion a rule that permits votes on only three policy alternatives: the costly version; the less costly version; and a compromise midway between the two, advanced by the majority leadership and designed to attract broad support. Members can then explain to constituents who opposed both the budget-buster and inadequate alternative that they voted for the reasonable option.

Self-Executing Rules. This kind of rule embodies a two-for-one procedure—that is, when the House adopts a rule it also automatically agrees to dispose of a separate matter, which is specified in the rule itself. Self-executing language in the special rule often states something like the following: "The amendment printed in [section 2 of this resolution or in part 1 of the report of the Committee on Rules accompanying this resolution] shall be considered as adopted in the House and in the Committee of the Whole." Thus, a self-executing rule may stipulate that a discrete policy proposal is deemed to have passed the House and been incorporated in the bill to be taken up. The effect is that neither in the House nor in the Committee of the Whole will lawmakers have an opportunity to amend or to vote separately on the self-executed provision. For example, to minimize a floor battle with tobacco-state lawmakers, the House adopted a rule that automatically incorporated into the text of the bill made in order for consideration a provision that prohibited smoking on domestic airline flights of two hours or less duration.

A self-executing rule saves the House time by avoiding multiple subsequent votes, and it allows members to escape a direct recorded vote on a controversial issue. Such rules can also assist party leaders in constructing winning coalitions. Post-committee revisions to reported legislation, as mentioned earlier, strengthen proponents' vote-mobilization efforts.

While in the minority, House Republicans complained mightily about self-executing rules because they avoided a separate debate and vote on the amendment(s) being folded into a bill by virtue of the special rule's adoption. Yet once in the majority, the Republican leadership found such devices an increasingly attractive means of altering legislation at the last minute to nail down wavering votes to ensure passage. Whereas the 103rd Democratic Congress issued thirty self-executing rules, making up 22 percent of all special rules, the GOP-led Houses under Speaker Newt Gingrich, R-Ga., witnessed 38 self-executing rules (25 percent of all rules) in the 104th Congress (1995–1997) and 52 (35 percent of all rules) in the 105th Congress (1997–1999). Under Speaker Dennis Hastert, "there were 40, 42, and 44 self-executing rules in the 106th, 107th, and 108th Congresses (22 percent, 37 percent, and 22 percent, respectively)." [43]

King-of-the-Hill Rules. The early 1980s witnessed another procedural innovation: the king-of-the-hill (or king-of-the-mountain) rule. During a May 1982 debate on a rule governing consideration of the concurrent budget resolution, Rules Committee chairman Richard W. Bolling, D-Mo., pronounced the procedure "unique." [44] The rule is unusual in a parliamentary sense for two major reasons. First, it permits the House to vote on an array of major policy alternatives—so-called substitutes that are equivalent to new bills, such as three different budget proposals—one after the other. Significantly, no matter the outcome—yea or nay—on any of the substitutes, the king-of-the-hill rule typically stipulates that the vote on the last substitute is the only one that counts for purposes of accepting or rejecting a national policy.

Gingrich, then House minority leader, highlighted the partisan importance of structuring the sequence of amendments for lawmakers. "[If] you are the Democratic leadership, what you do is you set up the bills and you say to your Members, vote for anything you want to, but when you get to the last one, vote for ours." [45] The king-of-the-hill rule has several key advantages. First, it provides legislators with political cover; they can cast votes on several policy alternatives and explain their actions to constituents in any manner they choose. Second, the rule limits criticism of the Rules Committee. The panel can allow votes on major policy alternatives advocated by different House factions without taking sides among them.

And, finally, the king-of-the-hill rule waives scores of procedures and precedents. For example, parliamentary principles state that once part of a bill is amended, re-amending it is generally not in order unless another amendment, broader in scope, changes the part by taking a bigger bite of the legislation. The massive substitutes made in order by the king-of-the-hill rule amend everything in the pending legislation. Technically, nothing is left to be changed and the amending process automatically terminates under traditional House procedures. Traditional procedures, however, are not followed when this type of rule is used, because political and policy objectives are of overriding concern. Republicans objected to the undemocratic character of king-of-the-hill rules when they were in the minority and did not use them during their twelve-year (1995–2007) control of the House.

Multiple-Stage Rules. At times, the Rules Committee will issue several rules for the same bill to facilitate coherent consideration of the issues it raises or to expedite action on the legislation. Legislation will be considered with a series of rules that separates general debate from the amendment process. For example, the initial rule on a defense bill may govern the terms for the general debate. The rule is intended to focus House deliberation on the major issues and to apportion debate fairly among the interested parties. A second rule will govern the amendment process on the principal military issues. All related amendments might be grouped together and debated under specific time limits. A third or even fourth rule might then regulate how all the remaining amendments will be considered by the membership. The time lapse among multiple-stage rules can be hours, days, or even weeks.

A variation of the multiple-stage rule is the "shutdown" rule, which is issued when a bill has become bogged down in a filibuster by amendments under an open rule. Failing unanimous consent or a series of motions to limit debate on amendments, the committee in charge of the bill, with the support of the majority leadership, will ask the Rules Committee to issue a new rule to limit the number of remaining amendments or the time for consideration of further amendments.

GOP Innovations

When Republicans assumed majority control of the House in 1995, they promised to provide a fair and open amendment process. This promise, as noted earlier, was also articulated by the Democratic leaders after they won majority control of the House following the November 2006 elections. The House Democrats decided not to allow amendments during the legislative push to pass their opening agenda in the first 100 legislative hours.[46] The dilemma of the Democratic leadership demonstrates how the goal of an open amendment process clashes with a fundamental objective of any majority party: passage of priority measures even if that means restricting lawmakers' amendment opportunities.

At least three creative rules employed by the GOP-controlled Rules Committee are of note: queen-of-the-hill rules, time-structured rules, and bifurcated rules.

Queen-of-the-Hill Rules. When they were in the minority, as noted earlier, Republicans objected to the king-of-the-hill rule because it "allowed lawmakers to be on both sides of an issue and violated the democratic principle that the position with the strongest support should prevail." [47] As a result, Republicans rejected the king-of-the-hill rule in favor of the queen-of-the-hill rule, which stipulates that whichever substitute amendment wins the most votes in the Committee of the Whole is forwarded to the full House for a vote on final passage. In the event that two or more amendments receive the same number of affirmative votes, then the last one voted on is considered to be finally approved.

In 1998 the GOP leadership devised a queen-of-the-hill rule to frustrate House approval of campaign reform legislation that would prohibit the parties from receiving or spending soft money—unregulated campaign contributions used for party building and get-out-the-vote drives but not for advocating the election or defeat of specific candidates. To kill this proposal, sponsored by Reps. Christopher Shays, R-Conn., and Martin T. Meehan, D-Mass., the Rules Committee made in order eleven substitute amendments, thereby forcing the soft money ban to compete against all the other recommendations. For example, one of the substitutes proposed the creation of a bipartisan commission on campaign finance reform. GOP leaders generally expected this noncontroversial proposal to receive an overwhelming number of "yes" votes and easily trump the soft money alternative. However, Representatives Shays and Meehan persuaded many who supported the commission idea to vote either "no" or "present," fully mindful that under the queen-of-the-hill procedure the amendment receiving the most votes becomes the House bill. In the end, the strategy worked, and their proposal was agreed to by the House. It later died, however, in the Senate. (In 2002 President Bush signed the Bipartisan Campaign Reform Act into law.) Queen-of-the-hill rules were seldom issued by the Rules Committee, in part because the process is like a "beauty contest": all the amendments appear attractive to numerous lawmakers with the result that the "most votes" winner might not represent the preferred policy of the majority leadership.

Time-Structured Rules. To accommodate the GOP leadership's pledge to adopt open rules but still meet its need to act on priority bills, the Rules Committee began to issue rules that establish debate limits on the entire amendment process. A ten-hour cap for debating and voting on amendments is an example of such a rule. Democrats criticized these rules as not being genuinely open. Because the time for voting on amendments is counted against the cap, a ten-hour restriction may leave, for example, only seven hours for debating amendments. Time limits, they say, encourage dilatory tactics. Recorded votes may be called on amendments that could pass by voice vote "in order to consume time allotted for considering amendments." [48] Republicans responded that Democrats should consult in advance with their leaders to identify priority amendments that need to be offered inside the cap.

Bifurcated Rules. Bifurcated rules make at least two separate bills in order for back-to-back consideration in the chamber. Under bifurcated rules, the House first debates, amends, and passes one bill, and then proceeds to consider another related but different bill. These actions can occur on separate days. Once the House agrees to the second measure, the rule provides that the two bills will be combined into one measure and sent to the Senate. A separate vote is not taken on the combined legislation.

The basic purpose of this kind of rule was twofold: provide Republicans with political cover on issues on which Democrats had the momentum and mobilize winning majorities for party priorities. For example, in the 106th Congress (1999–2001), the GOP leadership opposed the idea of raising the minimum wage—a key priority of nearly every House Democrat. However, the Republican leadership recognized that some moderate Republicans strongly supported raising the minimum wage and that the combination of the two blocs—Democrats and moderate Republicans—made it a winning coalition. The GOP leaders thus faced a potential revolt within their ranks if they did not bring minimum wage to a vote on the floor. They also realized that without a vote on minimum wage some of their vulnerable moderates could be hurt in the November elections.

The Rules Committee therefore crafted a bifurcated rule designed to neutralize the issue's campaign potency in Republican-held districts where organized labor's influence remains strong. The rule first permitted consideration of a bill providing $122 billion in tax cuts over ten years, which appealed to both GOP moderates and conservatives and which took the sting out of the wage hike for the Republican-leaning business community. No amendments were permitted to the tax bill—a closed rule process. The second bill, raising the minimum wage, was then taken up and debated under a modified closed rule procedure (two amendments were made in order). The House passed both bills by a separate vote. Then, under the bifurcated rule, they were combined into one measure (in this instance, the wage hike was added to the tax cut bill) and sent to the Senate without ever having been voted on as a single piece of legislation. Combining two bills into a single package presents a potential problem, however, if the combined bill is sent to the president. If the chief executive favors one proposal but not the other, a veto ends up killing both.

During the 108th Congress (2003–2005), Republicans employed a bifurcated rule to win the votes of conservative lawmakers on the Medicare prescription drug plan. The bifurcated rule first made H.R. 1 in order under a modified closed rule, after which the Health Savings and Affordability Act (H.R. 2596)—which would permit citizens to establish medical savings accounts—was brought up under a closed rule. A GOP Rules member explained that "upon passage of both pieces of legislation, the text of H.R. 2596 shall be added as a new matter at the end of H.R. 1. In simple terms, these two bills shall become one." [49] The bifurcated rule was part of an intense effort by GOP leaders "to win the support of holdout conservatives, who have long backed establishing medical savings accounts for all citizens." [50] The GOP strategy was a success.

Creative rules affect House operations in important ways. They enable the majority party to advance its policy and political agenda and to cope effectively with today's substantive and procedural complexities. They exacerbate partisan tensions when minority lawmakers are shut out from proposing their favorite amendments. Regularly, said a minority lawmaker, the majority Republicans "vote for procedures that prevent amendments from coming to the floor. Then they vote for the bills unamended and say. 'Well, I had no choice. I would have been in favor of an amendment, but it wasn't offered.' " [51]

Innovative rules also promote greater certainty and predictability in floor decision making and in the overall scheduling of House activities. And, in this era of video or message politics and partisan polarization, creative rules may protect many lawmakers from casting politically troublesome votes.

Adoption of the Rule

All rules must be approved by a majority vote of the House. Rules are reported to the House by the Rules Committee and are debated for a maximum of one hour, with the time equally divided by custom between the Rules chair, or a designee, and the ranking minority member of the committee, or a designee. The hour rule is the basic rule of floor debate in the House. Theoretically, it permits each member one hour of debate on any question. The hour rule is never followed in practice, however. A member who controls the debate time under the hour rule, in this case the Rules chair or the chair's designee, always moves the previous question at the end of this hour (or before the full hour is used if no member seeks time for debate). Adoption of this motion by majority vote, as noted earlier, stops all debate, prevents the offering of amendments, and brings the House to an immediate vote on the main question, the rule itself in this context.

The main strategy, then, for a member wishing to amend a rule is to defeat the previous question, a rare occurrence. "I am urging my colleagues to vote against the previous question on this rule so that we can offer a substitute rule" is a common refrain from members who oppose the rule. Under House precedents, the member who led the fight against approval of the previous question is recognized by the Speaker to propose a substitute rule. The significant vote here often is not on adoption of the rule but on approval of the previous question.

If there is no controversy, rules are adopted routinely by voice vote after a brief discussion. Under a 1977 procedural change, the Speaker may postpone votes on rules and permit them to be voted on at five-minute intervals later in the day or any time within the next two days. The procedure is similar to cluster voting under suspension of the rules.

The House seldom rejects a rule proposed by the Rules Committee. Thomas "Tip" O'Neill once remarked, "Defeat of the rule on the House floor is considered an affront both to the Committee and to the Speaker." [52] The Rules Committee generally understands the conditions the House will accept for debating and amending important bills. Furthermore, the majority party expects support for rules to be a given, and deviations from this behavioral norm could be held against a lawmaker when, for example, plum committee assignments are handed out. The record number of rules defeated during the 103d Congress—seven—highlighted the fissures within Democratic ranks that doubtlessly contributed to their loss of the House in November 1994 after forty years of continuous control. (Six rules were rejected in the 100th Congress, three in the 101st, none in the 102d, one in the GOP-run 104th, five in the 105th, none in the 106th, two in the 107th, and none in the 108th and 109th.) There are occasions, too, when the majority leadership will either not take up a rule or yank it off the floor if the House appears likely to turn it down.

LEGISLATION BLOCKED IN COMMITTEE

What happens when a standing committee refuses to report a bill that many members support, or when the Rules Committee fails to grant a rule to legislation having substantial support? Several procedures are available to bring such legislation to the floor, and the procedure used depends on the nature of the legislation. Suspension of the rules is appropriate if the measure is relatively noncontroversial or minor. If a major bill is being blocked, extraordinary procedures can be employed to spring the bill from committee. These procedures are difficult to implement, but if the House is determined, committees can be compelled to yield legislation.

The Discharge Petition

The discharge procedure, adopted in 1910, provides that if a bill has been before a standing committee for thirty legislative days (that is, days on which the House met), any member can introduce a motion to relieve the panel of the measure. A clerk of the House then prepares a discharge petition, which is made available for members to sign when the House is in session. If the requisite number of members (218) signs the petition, this procedure permits a majority of the House to bring a bill to the floor even if it is opposed by the committee that has jurisdiction over the measure, the majority leadership, and the Rules Committee. This procedure is difficult to use in part because majority party leaders often urge their partisan colleagues not to sign petitions.

Until 1993 House precedents prohibited public disclosure of the names of lawmakers who signed discharge petitions until the required 218 signatures had been obtained. Then the names were published in the *Congressional Record*. Critics of this procedure successfully changed House rules to require the signers' names to be made public as soon as a discharge petition is introduced instead of when a majority is achieved. The sponsor, James M. Inhofe, R-Okla. (House, 1987–1994; Senate, 1994–), and backers such as 1992 Reform Party presidential candidate H. Ross Perot, conservative talk show hosts, the *Wall Street Journal,* and freshmen lawmakers, including Democrats, argued that the change would help eliminate secrecy and hypocrisy by ending the practice whereby House members introduce, cosponsor, or publicly proclaim support for bills but then refuse to sign discharge petitions that might facilitate getting those same measures to the floor. Without public disclosure, they said, party and committee leaders could pressure members either not to sign or to remove their name if they had signed a discharge petition. The House amended its rules in 1995 to require weekly publication in the *Congressional Record* of members who have signed a discharge petition and daily availability in the clerk's office of the cumulative list of signers.

When 218 members have signed the petition, the motion to discharge is put on the Discharge Calendar. After seven legislative days on the calendar, it becomes privileged business on the second and fourth Mondays of the month (but not during the last six days of a session). Any member who signed the petition may be recognized to offer the discharge motion. When the motion is called up, debate is limited to twenty minutes, divided between proponents and opponents. If the discharge motion is rejected, the bill is not eligible again for discharge during that session. If the discharge motion prevails, any member who signed the petition can make a motion to call up the bill for immediate consideration. It then becomes the business of the House until it is disposed of. A vote against immediate consideration assigns the bill to the appropriate calendar, with the same rights as any bill reported from committee.

Few measures are discharged from committee. From 1931 through 2006 (which roughly coincides with the period during which the modern version of the rule has been in effect), 546 discharge petitions were filed, but only forty-seven attracted the required signatures and only nineteen bills were discharged and passed by the House.[53] Of those, only three became law: the Fair Labor Standards Act of 1938, the Federal Pay Raise Act of 1960, and the Bipartisan Campaign Reform Act of 2002.

Several factors account for the general failure of the discharge procedure. Members are reluctant to second-guess a committee's right to consider a bill. The discharge rule violates normal legislative routine, and even members who support a bill blocked in committee may refuse to sign a discharge petition for this reason. Committees, too, may nullify the discharge attempt by reporting the bill. Because it no longer has the measure, the committee cannot be discharged.

Legislators also are reluctant to write legislation on the House floor without the guidance and information provided in committee hearings and reports. Particularly for complicated legislation, many members want committee interpretation. Then too, obtaining 218 signatures is not easy. Finally, members are hesitant to employ a procedure that one day may be used against committees on which they serve.

But for all its limitations, the discharge rule serves important purposes. It focuses attention on particular legislative issues, and the threat of using it may stimulate a committee to hold hearings or report a bill or the majority leadership to schedule floor debate on an issue. Discharge petitions also provide a way for the minority party to gain some visibility for its key agenda items. Minority members often launch petition drives on their message priorities. This discharge effort is "part of our message strategy, not our legislative strategy," remarked a minority party aide.[54] However, if the minority party fails to attract sufficient discharge signatures for its priority items, it can undermine any message of party unity. "How do you say the [minority] caucus is united—that we want this [bill] on the floor—with only 140 signatures?" said an exasperated minority aide.[55]

Rules Committee's Extraction Power

The Rules Committee has an extraordinary authority that it seldom exercises: it can introduce rules for bills that the committee of jurisdiction does not want to report. The power of extraction is based on an 1895 precedent, which the committee has rarely invoked. Extraction, a highly controversial procedure, evokes charges of usurpation of other committees' rights.

On one of the rare occasions when extraction was used, the Education and Labor Committee refused on February 9, 1972, to approve a dock strike measure, but the Rules Committee reported a rule for floor action on the bill. Despite the vigorous opposition of Speaker Carl Albert, D-Okla. (1947–1977), the House adopted the rule by a 203–170 vote, thus springing the bill from the committee. The House then passed the bill.

The threat of extraction by the Rules panel in itself can break legislative logjams. In 1967 the Judiciary Committee balked at reporting an antiriot bill. Rules Committee chairman William M. Colmer, D-Miss., announced that his committee would soon hold hearings on a rule for the bill. This was enough to prompt the Judiciary Committee to report the legislation.[56]

A Rules Committee chair can try to make any measure in order for floor action, even if it has not received committee consideration. In 1988 Chairman Claude Pepper, D-Fla., "used his position to circumvent Ways and Means and clear his home-care health bill for floor action without hearings, debate, or markup in the committee of jurisdiction—a rare use of the Rules Committee's chairman's power." [57]

In 1995, when the GOP-controlled Government Reform Committee rejected legislation changing the federal retirement system, the Rules Committee included the change as part of a major tax bill. "In what is clearly an extraordinary departure from usual procedures," declaimed the ranking minority member on the Government Reform panel, "the Rules Committee has chosen to take a course of action which negates the very existence of the authorizing committees." [58] Despite that protest and that of others, the House agreed with the action of the Rules Committee.

Discharging the Rules Committee

The discharge rule also applies to the Rules Committee. The main reason a discharge petition is sometimes filed on a special rule is to control the terms of debate and amendment on the bill the special rule would make in order. The bill itself must still have been pending for at least thirty legislative days before a standing committee. A motion to discharge the Rules Committee is in order seven legislative days—instead of thirty—after a special rule has been referred to the panel.

Because the Rules Committee reports rules as a matter of original jurisdiction, members who wish to discharge a rule (making the stalled bill in order) have to draft and introduce one of their own so there will be something to discharge. (This introduced rule, according to the House rulebook, can neither allow for nongermane amendments nor make more than one bill in order.) Then, once the rule has been pending before the Rules Committee for seven legislative days, House precedents state it is in order to bring before the House "a measure pending before a standing committee for 30 legislative days." If the Rules Committee determines that a discharge attempt might be successful, it can report its own special rule for considering the bill on which discharge is sought. As congressional scholar Richard Beth has noted:

> Increasingly often in recent years, the Committee on Rules has responded to discharge efforts by reporting its own special rules for considering the measures involved. It often does so even when the petition is not completed, especially for petitions filed on special rules, rather than on the measures themselves. Since 1967, measures on which this form of petition was filed have had over twice as much chance of reaching the floor . . . as when the petition was filed on the measure itself. Perhaps as a result, this form of discharge has become more popular, amounting to almost 70 percent of petitions filed during the past decade (1993–2002).[59]

Calendar Wednesday

Under House procedures, every Wednesday is reserved for standing committees to call up measures (except privileged bills) that have been reported but not granted rules by the Rules Committee. The Speaker calls the roll of standing committees in alphabetical order. Each chair (or designated committee member) then decides whether to bring up for House debate a measure pending on the House or Union Calendars. The rule may be dispensed with by unanimous consent—that is, without objection—or by a two-thirds vote of the House. The Rules Committee may not report a rule setting aside Calendar Wednesday.

The Calendar Wednesday rule was adopted to circumvent Speaker Joe Cannon's (1903–1911) control of the legislative agenda. Today, it is seldom employed and usually dispensed with by unanimous consent. During the 98th Congress (1983–1985), however, a group of Republicans led by Representative Gingrich objected regularly to dispensing with Calendar Wednesday proceedings. Their purpose was to generate political heat on the majority leadership to schedule nonprivileged measures (a constitutional balanced budget amendment, school prayer measures, criminal code reform, and so on). Republicans called their list of priority measures the Agenda of the American People (precursor of the Contract with America). In 1984 the House even adopted an agriculture bill under its Calendar Wednesday procedure.[60] Objections to dispensing with Calendar Wednesday soon ended because of the inherent limitations of the procedure.

Since 1943 fewer than fifteen measures have become law under Calendar Wednesday proceedings.[61] House consideration of the 1984 agricultural measure was the first time the procedure had been used in a quarter-century. Five factors account for the limited use of this procedure: (1) only two hours of debate are permitted, one for proponents and one for opponents, which may not be enough for complex bills; (2) a committee far down in the alphabet may have to wait weeks before its turn is reached; (3) a bill not completed on one Wednesday is not in order the next Wednesday unless two-thirds of the members agree; (4) the procedure is subject to dilatory tactics because the House must complete action on the same day; and (5) only the chair or a member authorized by the committee may bring up a bill under Calendar Wednesday.

FINAL SCHEDULING STEPS

After a bill has been granted a rule, the majority party leaders decide when the measure will be debated. The leadership prepares daily and weekly schedules of floor business and adjusts them according to shifting legislative situations and demands. A bill the majority has scheduled for consideration may be withdrawn if it appears to lack sufficient support. Nothing in the House rules requires the majority leadership to provide advance notice of the daily or weekly legislative program. However, as a matter of long-standing custom, majority party leaders make announcements about floor action, often in response to a query from a minority leader, as Box 4-2 shows. The legislative program for the next day for both chambers also is published in each issue of the *Congressional Record,* in a section called the "Daily Digest." The Friday *Record* contains a section called the "Congressional Program Ahead," which lists the next week's legislative agenda and the dates on which floor action has been scheduled.

The majority and minority whip offices also send "whip notices" to their members' offices. Each party whip also maintains a Web site that lists daily and for each week the expected schedule of legislation to be considered on Monday, Tuesday, and so on, along with convening times of the House and other relevant information. For example, the whip notice may state that "On Wednesday and Thursday, the House will meet at 10 a.m. for legislative business," and then list the measures expected to be taken up either under suspension procedure or via a special rule. This information is updated to keep lawmakers informed of changes in the schedule. Telephone recordings also announce the daily and weekly program, legislative actions taken on the floor, and changes in the schedule.

Another agenda-setting action requiring mention is so-called "fast-track" procedures. Fast-track procedures are specified in various statutes to expedite the processing of certain legislation. Known as rule-making provisions, these statutory procedures are enacted under Congress's constitutional authority to "determine the rules of its proceedings." They are equivalent to the formal rules of each chamber, which also means they can be set aside if either body chooses to follow another procedure. Examples of fast-track procedures are timetables established in law for committees to report measures; legislation granted privileged access to the floor; prohibition of floor amendments of any type; imposition of strict debate limits; and counterpart legislation from the other chamber acted on promptly with little or no debate.

Traditionally, trade laws contain fast-track provisions. They are designed to expedite House and Senate committee and floor consideration of trade agreements negotiated by the president and follow-on implementing legislation. Under these laws, Congress delegates trade negotiating authority to the

---

BOX 4-2   A Scheduling Ritual

This typical exchange between House minority whip Roy Blunt, R-Mo., and majority leader Steny Hoyer, D-Md., on scheduling legislation for the following week appeared in the *Congressional Record*.

Legislative Program

(MR. BLUNT asked and was given permission to address the House for 1 minute.)

MR. BLUNT. Mr. Speaker, I yield to the majority leader Mr. HOYER for a discussion of next week's schedule.

MR. HOYER. Mr. Speaker, I thank the gentleman for yielding.

On Monday, Mr. Speaker, the House will not be in session so that Members can join with their communities in observance of the birthday of Martin Luther King, Jr.

On Tuesday, the House will meet at 12:30 p.m. for morning hour debate and at 2 p.m. for legislative business. We will consider several bills under suspension of the rules. You will be getting notice of those, hopefully, by the end of the day. We will consider several bills under suspension. There will be no votes before 6:30 p.m., as has been our practice.

---

president with the explicit understanding that the president must consult with Congress during the negotiations. When the trade agreement and implementing legislation are submitted to Congress, fast-track procedures prohibit any amendments by the House or Senate and impose a timetable for committee and floor action. "The goal of fast track," wrote an analyst, "is to prevent U.S. trade agreements from being amended in Congress in ways that might be unacceptable to the other nation or nations that are parties to the agreements." [62]

Party leaders, in sum, consider many factors and circumstances to advance their agenda-setting objectives. Bills may be scheduled to correspond with well-known dates (back-to-school legislation) or the House floor may be used as a campaign platform to highlight partisan agenda items (message politics), especially as the November elections get nearer. Party leaders may advocate agendas of interest to selected groups or interests, such as the business or labor communities. Legislation may be scheduled for action late at night to minimize public attention. And party leaders practice deadline lawmaking—that is, they may take advantage of various work or electoral cycles to facilitate action on legislation.

On Wednesday and the balance of the week, the House will meet at 10 a.m., although let me say to my friend that I may well be requesting again, as I did for today, unanimous consent that we meet at 9 on Friday. It has historically been the practice to wait until about May, the middle of May, when we get into heavy legislative business, to meet at 10 on Fridays if we were in on Fridays. My view is, however, and I want to say to all the Members, that it will be my intent to make every effort possible to have us adjourn on Fridays prior to or no later than 2 p.m. in consideration of Members' need to get back to their districts where they have events that are going on where they need to be. I want to tell my friend that we will, therefore, quite possibly ask for unanimous consent to come in at 9 rather than 10 next Friday.

In addition to other Suspension Calendar business, and all suspension bills, as I said, will be announced later today, the House will coonsider H.R. 5, a bill to cut in half the interest rates on student loans; and H.R. 6, a renewable energy bill.

In addition to that, I want to give notice to the House, and I have discussed this with Mr. BLUNT and have discussed it with the leader, Mr. BOEHNER, that NANCY BOYDA of Kansas is introducing a bill which will provide that Members who commit felonies while Members of Congress and in the course of their duties will be precluded forom receiving pensions.

SOURCE: *Congressional Record*, January 12, 2007, H-489.

NOTES

1. *Congressional Record*, November 15, 1983, H9856.
2. Sheryl Gay Stolberg, "Republican Defiance on Intelligence Bill Is Surprising, Or Is It?" *New York Times*, November 22, 2004, A8.
3. See, for example, Martin Kady and John Donnelly, "Bush, GOP Leaders Quell Rebellion on Intelligence," *CQ Today*, December 7, 2004, 1; and Seth Stern, "Sensenbrenner's Win on Immigration," *CQ Weekly*, May 9, 2005, 1241.
4. Jennifer Yachnin, "Hoyer: House to Work Monday–Friday in 110th," *Roll Call*, December 6, 2006, 1.
5. Lyndsey Layton, "Culture Shock on Capitol Hill: House to Work 5 Days a Week," *Washington Post*, December 6, 2006, A7.
6. *Congressional Record*, July 2, 1980, H6106.
7. *Washington Post*, January 31, 1995, A13.
8. *Congressional Record*, January 4, 2005, H13.
9. Martin Gold, Michael Hugo, Hyde Murray, Peter Robinson, and A. L. "Pete" Singleton, *The Book on Congress* (Washington, D.C.: Big Eagle Publishing Co., 1992), 124.
10. *Congressional Record*, December 17, 2005, H12057.

11. Damon Chappie, "House Caught in a State of Suspension," *Roll Call,* January 27, 2003, 22. This article was based on a study of the suspension procedure by Donald R. Wolfensberger, director of the Congress Project, Woodrow Wilson Center, Washington, D.C.

12. Donald R. Wolfensberger, "Suspended Partisanship in the House: How Most Laws Are Really Made" (paper prepared for delivery at the 2002 annual meeting of the American Political Science Association, Boston, August 29–September 1, 2002), 29.

13. See Justin Gelfand, "Members without a Vote Are Raising Their Voices on Hill," *The Hill,* July 23, 2003, 6.

14. Jeffrey S. Hill and Kenneth C. Williams, "The Decline of Private Bills: Resource Allocation, Credit Claiming, and the Decision to Delegate," *American Journal of Political Science* (November 1993): 1017.

15. *Congressional Record,* July 14, 2003, H6655.

16. William Holmes Brown and Charles W. Johnson, *House Practice: A Guide to the Rules, Precedents, and Procedures of the House* (Washington, D.C.: Government Printing Office, 2003), 657.

17. *Nation's Business,* February 1956, 103.

18. See, for example, James A. Robinson, *The House Rules Committee* (Indianapolis: Bobbs-Merrill, 1963); Charles O. Jones, "Joseph G. Cannon and Howard W. Smith: An Essay on the Limits of Leadership in the House of Representatives," *Journal of Politics* (September 1968): 617–646; and Robert L. Peabody, "The Enlarged Rules Committee," in *New Perspectives on the House of Representatives,* 2d ed., ed. Robert L. Peabody and Nelson W. Polsby (Chicago: Rand McNally, 1969).

19. Jonathan Allen, "What's the Deal with the House Rules Panel Usually Meeting Late at Night?" *CQ Today,* May 22, 2003, 6.

20. *New York Times,* April 2, 1995, 20.

21. *New York Times,* December 18, 1987, A34.

22. *A History of the Committee on Rules,* 97th Cong., 2d sess. (Washington, D.C.: Government Printing Office, 1983). See also Bruce I. Oppenheimer, "The Changing Relationship between House Leadership and the Committee on Rules," in *Understanding Congressional Leadership,* ed. Frank H. Mackaman (Washington, D.C.: CQ Press, 1981).

23. *Congressional Record,* June 19, 2002, H3696.

24. Spark M. Matsunaga and Ping Chen, *Rulemakers of the House* (Urbana: University of Illinois Press, 1976), 21. See also Alan Ehrenhalt, "The Unfashionable House Rules Committee," *Congressional Quarterly Weekly Report,* January 15, 1983, 151.

25. For an example of the use of this procedure, see *Congressional Record,* June 10, 1998, H4338–H4343.

26. Stanley Bach and Steven Smith, *Managing Uncertainty in the House of Representatives* (Washington, D.C.: Brookings, 1988), 50.

27. Bob Michel, "Beyond the Political Wilderness: Reforming 40 Years of One-Party Rule," *CommonSense* (fall 1994): 56.

28. Jonathan Salant, "Under Open Rules, Discord Rules," *Congressional Quarterly Weekly Report,* January 28, 1995, 277.

29. *Congressional Record,* June 5, 2003, H4986.

30. *Congressional Record,* December 7, 2006, H8896.

31. John Bresnahan, "Democrats Vow Fairness on Rules," *Roll Call,* November 2, 2006, 3.

32. Lynn Sweet, "New Congress, New Rules," *The Hill,* December 7, 2006, 27.

33. *Congressional Record,* December 15, 1987, H11436.

34. *Congressional Record,* March 4, 2004, H843.

35. *Congressional Record,* July 14, 1987, H6282.

36. *Congressional Record,* January 4, 1995, H32.

37. *Congressional Record,* January 4, 2005, H29.

38. *Congressional Record,* July 10, 1997, H5049.

39. *Congressional Record,* May 23, 2006, H3027.

40. *Floor Deliberations and Scheduling, Hearings before the Joint Committee on the Organization of Congress* (Washington, D.C.: Government Printing Office, 1993), 216–217.

41. Alan Ehrenhalt, "O'Neill Studying Moves to Counter GOP 'Obstructionism,'" *Washington Star,* August 5, 1979, A3.

42. Janet Hook, "GOP Chafes under Restrictive House Rules," *Congressional Quarterly Weekly Report,* October 10, 1987, 2452.

43. Don Wolfensberger, "House Executes Deliberation With Special Rules," *Roll Call,* June 19, 2006, 8. Mr. Wolfensberger is a former staff director of the House Rules Committee.

44. *Congressional Record,* May 21, 1982, H2519.

45. *Congressional Record,* August 8, 1994, H7181.

46. Lyndsey Layton and Juliet Eilperin, "Democrats to Start Without GOP Input: Quick Passage of First Bills Sought," *Washington Post,* January 2, 2007, A01.

47. *National Journal,* January 21, 1995, 183.

48. *Congressional Record,* February 27, 1995, H2235.

49. *Congressional Record,* June 26, 2003, H5952.

50. Mary Agnes Cary, Kelly Field, and David Nather, "Medicare Drug Benefit Approaches Final Lap," *CQ Today,* June 27, 2003, 1, 4.

51. Mary Lynn F. Jones, "The Republican Railroad," *The American Prospect,* April 2003, 16.

52. "Switched Votes for Gas Bill," *Congressional Quarterly Weekly Report,* February 14, 1976, 313.

53. Richard S. Beth, "The Discharge Rule in the House: Recent Use in Historical Context," CRS Report 97–856, April 17, 2003, 1.

54. Richard E. Cohen, "A Strong Sense of Entitlement," *National Journal,* April 27, 2002, 1226.

55. Ethan Wallison, "House Democrats Split on Strategy," *Roll Call,* February 17, 2000, 28.

56. Matsunaga and Chen, *Rulemakers of the House,* 25.

57. Julie Kosterlitz, "Still Going Strong," *National Journal,* January 2, 1988, 15.

58. *Congressional Record,* April 5, 1995, H4204.

59. Beth, "Discharge Rule in the House," Summary.

60. *Congressional Record,* January 25, 1984, H126–H139.

61. Information compiled by Richard Beth, congressional specialist, Government Division, Congressional Research Service, Library of Congress.

62. Bob Benenson, "Removal of 'Fast Track' May Put GATT in the Fast Lane," *Congressional Quarterly Weekly Report*, September 17, 1994, 2561. Also see I. M. Destler, *American Trade Politics*, 2d ed. (Washington, D.C.: Institute for International Economics, 1992), 71–76.

CHAPTER 5

House Floor Procedure

VISITORS TO the House gallery may be surprised by what they observe on the House floor. For one thing, the floor activity appears quite disorganized. People come and go in an endless stream. Motions are offered, amendments are proposed, and points of order are raised. Amid all this activity, representatives on the floor display little interest in what is going on. Legislators talk in small groups or read newspapers while their colleagues make speeches. Furthermore, attendance is often sparse during floor debates. Members may be in committee sessions, meeting with constituents, or attending to numerous other tasks. Members can reach the floor quickly, however, to respond to quorum calls, participate in debate, or vote.

The House chamber itself is divided into two levels. Above the floor are the galleries for visitors, diplomats, reporters, and other observers. Visitors sit on either side of the chamber or facing the Speaker's rostrum; the press sits above and behind the rostrum. Unlike senators, representatives have no desks in the chamber. Seats, which are unassigned, are arranged in semicircular rows in front of the Speaker. Aisles divide groups of seats, and a broad center aisle divides the majority and minority parties (see Figure 5-1).

While in session, the House normally convenes daily, except Saturdays and Sundays, often at noon or earlier.[1] Buzzers ring in committee rooms, members' offices, and in the Capitol, summoning representatives to the floor. Rules and informal practices set the daily order of business: an opening prayer, approval of the *Journal* (a record of the previous day's proceedings as required by the Constitution), the Pledge of Allegiance, receipt of messages from the Senate or the president, one-minute speeches, and other routine business. On some days, a morning hour debate is held prior to the start of formal legislative business. The House convenes from an hour to an hour and a half earlier to accommodate lawmakers who want to discuss various issues of the day. The time is equally divided between the two parties.[2] With the escalation of partisanship, each party has begun to use its own theme team or message group to orchestrate the daily speeches during the one-minute or other debate periods.

Under the Constitution, a majority of the House (218 of the 435 members) constitutes a quorum to conduct business. House rules and precedents define what constitutes "business" for quorum purposes. For example, a House rule "specifically prohibits the entertainment of a point of order of no quorum unless a question has been put to a vote. The House has determined by adopting such a rule that the mere conduct of debate, where the Chair has not put the pending proposition to a vote, is not 'conducting business.' "[3] Whether

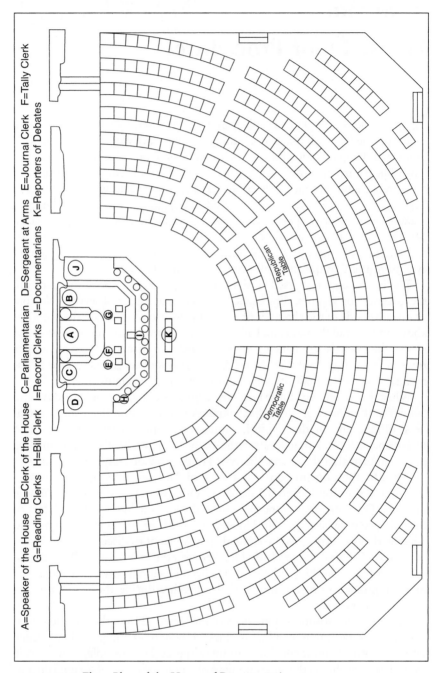

A=Speaker of the House B=Clerk of the House C=Parliamentarian D=Sergeant at Arms E=Journal Clerk F=Tally Clerk G=Reading Clerks H=Bill Clerk I=Record Clerks J=Documentarians K=Reporters of Debates

Republican Table

Democratic Table

FIGURE 5-1 Floor Plan of the House of Representatives

or not a quorum has been established, it is assumed to be present unless officially discovered otherwise. Thus, any member may make a point of no quorum whenever a vote is pending. Informally, the House frequently operates with far fewer members.

While in session, the House usually convenes Monday through Friday. Mondays are reserved mainly for routine legislation. The workload on Fridays is generally light because many members want to return to their home districts on weekends. Most major business is usually conducted from Tuesday through Thursday. Other scheduling arrangements are sometimes employed at different times, such as around-the-clock daily sessions during the hectic last days of a legislative session. The House has also tried for years to make its schedule more predictable and therefore family-friendly, but that is hard to accomplish because the legislative job is not a 9:00 a.m. to 5:00 p.m. routine. Typically, the House meets less frequently during the second session (an election year) than the first session.

Although no one day on the House floor is the same—some days the House meets only briefly, while at other times it meets all night, for example—a recurring pattern of daily activity has emerged. In considering major bills, the House usually follows the steps listed below. Each merits some discussion.

1. Adopt the rule granted by the Rules Committee.
2. Resolve the House into the Committee of the Whole.
3. Proceed with the general debate.
4. Undertake the amending process, if permitted.
5. Consider any motions to recommit.
6. Take final action (full House).

ADOPTION OF THE RULE

The first step in bringing a major bill to the floor is House adoption of a special rule issued by the Rules Committee. A rule sets the conditions under which a measure will be considered, decreeing whether floor amendments will be permitted and how much debate will be allowed.

The House rarely rejects a rule, as noted in Chapter 4, largely because it normally receives overwhelming support from majority party members. Majority party leaders make it clear to partisan colleagues that procedural votes are party-line votes. Their advice is regularly followed, but not always. For example, upset with what they viewed as runaway spending by the federal government, 29 conservative Republicans voted against a rule (which was adopted with Democratic support) permitting floor consideration of an emergency spending bill. The vote against the rule was "a strong signal from House conservatives that a number of us are willing to do whatever it takes to slow spending," stated Representative Jeff Flake, R-Ariz.[4] House members realize that at some point in the future they may need a rule from the Rules

Committee for one of their own bills, and so challenging the committee is unwise. In general, when a rule is rejected, it usually reflects sharp divisions in the House; disagreements within the majority party; heavy lobbying by pressure groups, the president, or federal agency officials; or broad agreement that the reporting committee did a poor job of drafting the bill.

Voting down a rule is often a procedural kill. As one House leader stated, it enables members "to get rid of the bill without putting their fingerprints on the trigger." [5] Such actions demonstrate how procedural matters can have a critical impact on policymaking. Without favorable action on a rule, the House may lose the chance to consider a measure and face subsequent delays in taking it up. For example, as the 107th Congress headed for final adjournment, GOP leaders suffered a rare defeat on a rule when they decided to take up a bankruptcy conference report. The House voted down 172-243 the rule making the conference report in order for floor consideration.[6] The rule's rejection, even with Speaker Dennis Hastert, R-Ill., casting a vote in favor, sounded the death knell for bankruptcy reform. Action was blocked on the conference report by an unusual coalition of Democrats and religiously oriented conservative Republicans. Democrats opposed the conference agreement because they viewed it as anti-consumer and pro–credit card companies; conservative Republicans rebelled against a provision in the conference report that prohibited antiabortion protesters from filing for bankruptcy to avoid paying court-ordered fines for blocking abortion clinics. Republican defections were encouraged by antiabortion Christian groups that "flooded Republican offices with phone calls and e-mails . . . railing against the bill and splitting the [GOP] Conference between business-friendly Republicans and social conservatives." [7] (The antiabortion provision also doomed bankruptcy reform in the 108th Congress, but finally the bill was signed into law early in the 109th Congress. The antiabortion amendment was defeated in the Senate, which acted first on the legislation, and the House then approved the Senate bill without change in April 2005.)

COMMITTEE OF THE WHOLE

After the House votes to adopt a rule, the Speaker declares the House resolved into the Committee of the Whole. The Committee of the Whole is the House in another form. Every legislator is a member. House rules require all revenue-raising or appropriations bills to be considered first in the Committee of the Whole. The staff director of the House Rules Committee once wrote that, with its special authority for revenue and spending bills, the Committee of the Whole "is the very essence of the House exercising its special [fiscal] powers and prerogatives under the Constitution." [8]

Technically, there are two such bodies. One is the "House as in Committee of the Whole," which is a forum that can be used for considering private bills and District of Columbia legislation.[9] The other and more important body is the Committee of the Whole House on the state of the Union, com-

TABLE 5-1 Major Characteristics, House and Committee of the Whole

House	Committee of the Whole
Mace raised	Mace lowered
Speaker presides	Chair presides
More than half the House (218) is a quorum	One hundred is a quorum
One-hour rule for amendments	Five-minute rule for amendments
Previous question in order	Motion to limit debate on amendments, but not the previous question motion, in order
Forty-four members or one-fifth of the House quorum of 218 trigger a recorded vote	Twenty-five members trigger a recorded vote
Motion to recommit in order	Motion to recommit not in order

SOURCE: Adapted from *Manual on Legislative Procedure in the U.S. House of Representatives,* 6th ed., 99th Cong., prepared under the auspices of the House Republican leader, May 1986.

monly shortened to Committee of the Whole, which considers public measures. The Committee of the Whole has its origins, like many congressional practices, in the British Parliament. During the seventeenth century, the Parliament and the Crown regularly clashed over finances and taxes. To ensure that all members of the House of Commons participated in debates involving the expenditure of money, Parliament established the Committee of the Whole to review and check the financial proposals made by parliamentary committees, which were sometimes stacked with the king's or queen's supporters. A further elaboration of the Committee of the Whole's origins is provided by a scholar and former member of the House of Representatives, De Alva Stanwood Alexander, R-N.Y. (1897–1911):

> It originated in the time of the Stuarts, when taxation arrayed the Crown against the Commons, and suspicion made the Speaker [of the House of Commons] a talebearer to the King. To avoid the Chair's espionage the Commons met in secret [in a Committee of the Whole], elected a chairman in whom it had confidence, and without fear of the King freely exchanged its views respecting [financial] supplies.[10]

The Committee of the Whole uses rules different from those of the House; they are designed to speed up floor action. Table 5-1 sets out several rules or customs that distinguish the conduct of business in the full House from proceedings in the Committee of the Whole.

First, a quorum is only one hundred members in the Committee of the Whole; 218 members constitute a quorum in the House. Second, by custom, the Speaker does not preside over the Committee of the Whole. Instead, the Speaker appoints a colleague, who is also a member of the majority party, to fill that role—a practice that can be traced to English precedent. The Speaker is permitted to remain in the chamber and take part in debate, but rarely participates except to make closing remarks on tightly contested major bills. By tradition, the Speaker seldom votes in the Committee of the Whole (or the House), except to break a tie. Third, it is in order in the Committee of the Whole to close or limit debate on sections of a bill by unanimous consent or majority vote of the members present; the prime debate-ending motion in the House is the previous question. Fourth, various motions that are in order in the House are not permitted in the Committee of the Whole, such as the previous question motion or motions to recommit, adjourn, or reconsider the vote by which an amendment was agreed to or rejected. Fifth, amendments to bills are introduced and debated under the five-minute rule in the Committee of the Whole, not under the hour rule as in the House.[11] Sixth, in the Committee of the Whole twenty-five members can trigger a recorded vote; in the House forty-four members can do so (one-fifth of a quorum).

Finally, the position of the mace, a forty-six-inch column of ebony rods bound together by silver and topped by a silver eagle, indicates whether the House is in the Committee of the Whole. The mace, symbol of the authority of the sergeant at arms, is carried by him, if called upon, to enforce order on the floor. It rests on a pedestal on a table at the right of the Speaker's podium. It is taken down from the table when the Speaker hands the gavel to the chair of the Committee of the Whole. When the committee rises (dissolves) and the Speaker resumes the chair, the mace is returned to its place.[12]

GENERAL DEBATE

The first order of business in the Committee of the Whole is general debate on the entire bill under consideration.[13] One hour of debate is usually allowed, equally divided between the minority and majority parties. For most bills, one hour is authorized; for complex and highly significant legislation, as many as ten or more hours may be scheduled. The chair of the Committee of the Whole presides over the proceedings and wields the gavel to maintain order and fairness. "It's an art form," said a lawmaker. "It takes an ability to sense the mood of the House, track the chemistry of what is going on on the floor, apply the gavel lightly or hard, depending on what is warranted." [14]

Each party has a floor manager from the committee of original jurisdiction who controls time, allotting segments to supporters or opponents, as the case may be. (On multireferred measures, there may be two or more pairs of floor managers.) Almost without exception, the floor manager for the majority party is the spokesperson for the bill. When both sides favor passage of a bill, both floor managers rise in support. During debate on controversial legislation, both floor managers may declare their support for the bill's aims but have differences of opinion on specific sections or amendments.

The term *general debate* can be misleading, as most members deliver prepared speeches and engage in a minimum of give-and-take. Because committees and subcommittees shape the fundamental character of most legislation, only a limited number of representatives participate in the debate, and those who do are usually members of the committee that drafted the legislation. Yet general debate has an intrinsic value that is recognized by most House members and experts on the legislative process.

Because of its large size and workload, the House imposes strict debate limits on lawmakers. Nearly every second of debate time (the hour rule, the five-minute rule, forty minutes for suspensions, and so on) is regulated by some rule or practice. The House did experiment with three Oxford-style floor debates in 1994 on agreed-on national issues—health, welfare, and trade—where teams of lawmakers engaged each other in sustained discussions of these topics. This British debating format has not been used since by the House, in part because lawmakers prefer debate to be tied directly to specific legislation.

However, there are two debate formats used almost every legislative day. They allow members to engage in "non-legislative" debate on topics of their choosing: one-minute speeches and special order speeches. A limited number of one-minute speeches (governed by the Speaker through his recognition power) commonly occurs following the opening proceedings. Special order speeches take place at the end of each legislative day when the formal program of the House is concluded. Members may reserve up to an hour and speak on any issue. In addition, since the 103d Congress, there are "morning hour" speeches that occur on Mondays and Tuesdays ninety minutes before the House convenes for formal business. During this period, lawmakers typically address any issue for up to five minutes.

Purposes of General Debate

General debate is both symbolic and practical. It assures both legislators and the public that the House makes its decisions in a democratic fashion, with due respect for majority and minority opinion. "Congress is the only branch of government that can argue publicly," noted a House Republican some years ago. "Debate appropriately tests the conclusions of the majority." [15] General debate forces members to come to grips with the issues at hand; offers a forum for explaining difficult and controversial sections of a bill; alerts constituents and interest groups to a measure's purpose through press coverage of the debate; gives floor leaders an opportunity to assess member sentiment; builds a public record, or legislative history, for administrative agencies and the courts, indicating the intentions of proponents and opponents alike; allows legislators to take positions for reelection purposes; and, occasionally, influences fence-sitters. General debate also permits Republicans and Democrats, especially in election years, to raise issues that are of concern to their respective constituencies.

Some legislators doubt that debate can change views or affect the outcome of a vote. But debate, especially by party leaders just before a key vote, can change opinion. For example, a House member noted that an address by the Speaker marked "one of the few times on the House floor when a speech changed a lot of votes." [16] Robert H. Michel, R-Ill., House minority leader from 1981 to 1995, also highlighted the importance of having informed and persuasive speakers take part in floor debates.

> A classic example . . . occurred during our debate on the nuclear freeze in 1983. A Democratic colleague challenged my Illinois colleague, [Republican] Henry Hyde, who had just criticized a prominent woman advocate of the freeze. The Democrat said: "Yes, she is, as you say the mother of the freeze. But President Reagan, through his lack of arms control progress, is the father of the freeze." And, without missing a beat, Henry Hyde shot back: "And that makes you a son of a freeze." The debate went our way after that.[17]

Reasoned deliberation is important in decision making. Lawmaking consists of more than logrolling, compromises, or power plays. General debate enables members to gain a better understanding of complex issues, and it may influence the collective decisions of the House. The dilemma members often face, said one House member, "is to know what is right, and to make the right decisions" even though information may be skimpy, incomplete, or simply unavailable.[18] This was certainly the case in 1991 when the House debated authorization for President George Bush to use military force against Iraq's invasion of Kuwait. The legislation amounted to a declaration of war, said Speaker Thomas S. Foley, D-Wash., and general debate on it was "the longest in the modern history of the House of Representatives, extending over 20 hours." [19] Similarly, in 2002 House members debated twenty hours over the joint resolution authorizing President George W. Bush to launch a preemptive military strike against Iraq. "Just as in 1991," said Rules Committee chair David Dreier, R-Calif., "every single Member will have a chance to be heard" on the threat that the Saddam Hussein–led regime poses to the United States.[20]

Four years later, during June 15–16, 2006, with public disenchantment over Iraq rising in an election year, House GOP leaders scheduled a ten-hour debate on a nonbinding Republican-crafted resolution endorsing the administration's "stay the course" policy in Iraq and its assertion that Iraq is central to the global war on terrorism. The resolution also rejected any arbitrary deadline for the withdrawal of American troops from Iraq. Every lawmaker had the opportunity to be heard, but the two-day debate was often harsh, intense, and partisan. Democrats, for example, lamented that the Pentagon distributed a partisan briefing document (the "Iraq Floor Debate Prep Book") to GOP lawmakers containing talking points bolstering the president's war policy.[21] Democrat Jim McGovern, Mass., exclaimed that the event should not even be called a debate "when no Member will have the opportunity to vote on competing policy proposals." [22] (The resolution was considered under a closed rule.) GOP leaders, for their part, spotlighted the Democrats' lack of a unified party position on Iraq and framed the discussion as a choice between the Republicans' strong national security commitment versus the weak Democratic approach to national security. If anything, the debate underscored that a majority of the members appeared willing at that particular time to stick with the administration's alleged policy course in Iraq. The resolution was adopted on a 256 to 153 vote.

Floor Managers' Role

Long-standing customs may govern much of the action on the House floor, but the floor managers direct the course of debate on each bill. The manager for the majority side is often the chair of the committee that reported the bill or an appointed committee colleague. The ranking minority committee member, or an appointed surrogate, is usually the floor manager for the minority party. Floor managers generally can count on support from their party leadership.

During the debate, the floor managers sit at long tables near the center of the chamber, with the main aisle separating the Democratic side from the Republican side. They also are permitted to have up to five of their committee's staff members on the floor during debate, ready to research rules and precedents, draft amendments, answer technical questions about the bill, or prepare statements.

In guiding their bill through final disposition by the House, the floor managers principally inform colleagues (and by inference the general public and media) about the contents of the bill; explain the issues in controversy and why the committee made the decisions it did; and provide lawmakers with reasons to vote for the legislation and to reject alternatives. In addition, they must:

- plan strategy and parliamentary maneuvers to meet changing floor situations;
- respond to points of order;
- attempt to protect the bill from amendments the majority considers undesirable;
- alert supporters to be on the floor to vote for or against closely contested amendments;
- advise colleagues on the meaning and importance of the amendments;
- judge when amendments of committee members should be offered or deferred;
- inform party leaders of member sentiment and the mood of the House toward their bill;
- control the time for general debate and, if necessary, act to limit debate on amendments, sections, or titles of the bill, or on the entire measure;
- arrange the sequence of speakers on major amendments to ensure that the best supporting orators are matched against those of the opposition; and
- mobilize outside support to build winning coalitions on the floor.

The fate of much legislation depends on the skill of the floor managers. Effective floor management increases the chances for smooth passage. For example, enactment of the landmark Congressional Budget and Impoundment Control Act of 1974 was credited in large part to its skillful floor manager, Rep. Richard W. Bolling, D-Mo. (1949–1983).

Floor managers are given several advantages over their colleagues. They customarily lead off debate in the Committee of the Whole and therefore have the first opportunity to appeal for support. During the debate, they receive priority recognition from the chair. Floor managers may take the floor at critical moments ahead of other legislators to defend or rebut attacks on the bill, or they may offer amendments to coalesce support for the measure. And floor managers, who are entitled, by custom, to close the debate on an amendment, have the last chance to influence sentiment. As a result of committee hearings, discussion, and markup, the managers have a reservoir of knowledge about the technical details of a measure and are in a good position to judge which amendments to accept and reject, and the best arguments to employ for or against them.

Delaying Tactics

Despite the generally tighter rules on debate in the House than in the Senate, representatives have various ways to prolong or delay proceedings. They may raise numerous points of order, make scores of parliamentary inquiries, or offer trivial amendments. For example, during consideration of a bill creating the Department of Education, an opponent offered two unsuccessful but dilatory amendments. One would have changed the department's name to the Department of Public Education (DOPE), the other to the Department of Public Education and Youth (DOPEY).[23] Members may also demand recorded votes on every amendment and motion, ask unanimous consent to speak for additional minutes on each amendment, make certain that all time for general debate is used, appeal rulings of the chair, or move that the Committee of the Whole rise.

Until a 1971 rules change, a reading of the *Journal* was used as a delaying tactic. Before then, the reading could be dispensed with only by unanimous consent or by a motion to suspend the rules, requiring a two-thirds vote. Since then, the Speaker has been authorized to examine the *Journal* and announce his approval, although a vote can be demanded on its approval. However, the chair can postpone the vote on the *Journal*'s approval until later in that legislative day.

Often the purpose of delaying tactics is to stall action on a measure to allow more time to gather support (if those using such tactics favor the bill) or to kill it (if they are opposed). At times, delay is intended to force action and other times to prevent it. Delay is often employed by the minority party for a number of reasons: to protest the heavy-handed actions of the majority, to attract publicity for their agenda, to energize or rally their electoral supporters, to extract policy concessions, or to promote party unity.

When they were in the minority from 1995 to 2007, Democrats employed many of the parliamentary guerrilla warfare tactics used by Republicans when they were in the minority, such as raising parliamentary objections; clashing verbally with lawmakers on the other side of the aisle; demanding roll call votes; forcing votes on the motion to adjourn the House, to reconsider a vote by which a measure was just agreed to, or to reconsider the vote by which engrossment (preparation of the official copy of the bill as passed by the House) and third reading (the obligatory reading of the bill, by title, just before the vote on final passage) is ordered; and offering floor amendments (if the special rule allows) designed to foment reelection difficulties for members of the opposing party who must vote against them. "The job of the minority is to make trouble for the majority," remarked a GOP leader, "and they are doing a very good job of this." [24]

Democrats also added to the repertoire of stalling tactics, as illustrated by these two examples. First, House Democrats, including the minority leader, employed questions of privilege in a systematic manner.[25] Questions of privilege involve the rights of the House collectively, its safety, dignity, and the integrity of its proceedings. This kind of question is brought before the House in the form of a resolution, and it has precedence over every other motion except a motion to adjourn. Any lawmaker may offer this privileged resolution after providing one day's notice on the House floor of the resolution's language. The Speaker then has up to two days to schedule it for floor consideration and also to rule on its legitimacy. The majority leader and the minority leader are exempt from these requirements and may offer these privileged resolutions at any time. If the resolution is not immediately tabled (or killed), and after the Speaker states that it does present a question of the privileges of the House, the resolution is debated under the one-hour rule equally divided between the proponent and an opponent.

During a two-week period from late October 1997 to early November, Democrats offered fourteen privileged resolutions to end a controversial 1996 contested-election investigation. The case involved GOP incumbent Bob Dornan, Calif., and Democrat Loretta Sanchez, who won the election but was challenged on the ground that there was illegal voting by noncitizens. (The Speaker acknowledged that the resolutions constituted a legitimate question involving the privileges of the House.) To compel as many votes as possible, each resolution had to be phrased differently. Not only did repeated use of the resolution irk Republicans, but the phraseology of some resolutions angered them as being frivolous and disrespectful of the House. For example, a Democratic lawmaker included the following "whereas" clauses in her resolution to differentiate it from the others: "Whereas Loretta Sanchez of the Golden State smiles brighter than Bob Dornan even on a cloudy day; and Whereas, many feel that the real bottom line in all of this is that Bob Dornan needs to get a life—and a job." [26]

When GOP frustrations with the stalling tactics of Democrats finally reached a boiling point—Republicans during one week tabled eight questions of privilege as soon as they were offered—the Rules Committee reported a rule, which the House adopted after sharp debate, that prohibited any lawmaker, except the majority and minority leaders, from offering a privileged resolution for the remainder of the session. The rule said that "the Speaker may not recognize a Member other than the majority leader or the minority leader to offer from the floor, or to announce an intention to offer, a resolution as a question of privileges of the House." [27] Much of the controversy over the Sanchez-Dornan case could be traced to a 1984 election, which Republicans contended that Democrats stole from them. With Democrats then in charge, Frank McCloskey, D-Ind., was declared the victor by the House by four votes over Republican Richard D. McIntyre. When the decision was announced, Republicans walked en masse from the House chamber.

Democratic leader Nancy Pelosi, Calif., used questions of privilege at least ten times to castigate Republicans on their management of the House and to spotlight what she called the GOP's "culture of corruption"—a campaign theme that proved to be important for Democrats in many of the 2006 House elections. Although most were immediately tabled on a party-line vote, Pelosi got Republicans on record as voting against disapproving the validity of a Ways and Means Committee markup (see the discussion below); a bipartisan ethics process; an investigation into the ethical conduct of then Majority Leader Tom DeLay, Tex.; the creation of a bipartisan ethics task force; investigations relating to the Iraq War and the lack of committee oversight of the executive branch; ending abuses of the voting process, such as the three-hour roll call on the Medicare prescription drug bill; investigating whether a budget reconciliation bill signed into law actually passed the House; and investigating the lawmakers and staff implicated in the criminal activity of lobbyist Jack Abramoff.[28] Questions of privilege, according to a congressional expert, are "helping the minority to document their case and rally their troops against Republican rule." [29]

In the second example, Democrats walked en masse to the chamber when they learned that the Ways and Means chair had earlier in the day called the Capitol police to evict Democratic members of the panel from the committee's library. Angry at the chair's behavior, Democratic leader Pelosi marched to the floor with her party colleagues to introduce a privileged resolution reprimanding the Ways and Means chair for his extraordinary action. The result was a bitter debate between the two parties.

Republicans argued that the chair had called the police to restrain the only Democrat on the committee who remained in the room with the other GOP members during a markup. The Republicans alleged that the Democrat was about to start a fight with a Republican member of the panel. Democrats disputed the allegation and contended that the chair had called the police to oust them from the library where they had gone to plan strategy on a pension reform bill that was slated to be marked up that day. "I want to focus on how the chairman can call upon the Capitol Police to evict Members at his whim from the committee space," exclaimed Pelosi. "We cannot let this stand. We cannot let this go unchallenged." [30] In the end, the House voted down Pelosi's resolution, but five days later the chair apologized to the House and admitted his mistake in calling the police on the Ways and Means Democrats.

Democrats, however, were not mollified by the apology. They remained angry at the GOP majority for not permitting them much say in policymaking, especially over a child care tax credit proposal. Pelosi threatened disruptions during the week preceding the chamber's traditional August recess. "I say this as a promise not a prediction: This will be a week from hell for Republicans," declared Pelosi. "We will be disruptive on the floor until we get a child tax credit." [31] Democrats then proceeded to employ various parliamentary tactics to stall House action, such as offering motions to adjourn and forcing votes on usually noncontroversial procedural matters. During debate on the special rule making in order for a GOP-sponsored bill (H.R. 2210) revamping the preschool Head Start program, Rules Democrat Alcee Hastings, Fla., yielded to twenty-three Democrats to make unanimous consent requests to revise and extend their remarks; all the requests were granted by the House. In their remarks, every Democrat said virtually the same thing, such as "Mr. Speaker, H.R. 2210 would cynically dismantle Head Start, so I rise in opposition," or "Mr. Speaker, H.R. 2210 will dismantle the successful Head Start program," or "Mr. Speaker, H.R. 2210 will dismantle Head Start and rob single moms of the best early childhood education for their children." [32] The bill passed the House by one vote. To be sure, minority Republicans in the 110th House can work to frustrate the Democratic majority by employing these and other dilatory and party-bashing tactics.

THE AMENDING PROCESS

The complex amending process is the heart of decision making on the floor. Amendments can be categorized by (1) form—whether they add or insert language, take out or strike matter, or do both, strike and insert; (2) differentiated by their degrees (described later in this chapter); and (3) distinguished by how much they may change a bill or a pending amendment. A "perfecting amendment" (here *perfecting* does not mean *improving* in the dictionary sense) modifies less of the language open to amendment than a "substitute amendment," which replaces the entire text (every word) of a pending first-degree amendment. An alternative for an entire bill is called "an amendment in the nature of a substitute" (see the discussion below on "substitute amendments"). Under an open rule, amendments—which are policy alternatives—determine the final shape of bills passed by the House. At times, amendments become more important or controversial than the bills themselves.

Since at least the past two decades, opportunities to amend legislation under an open rule, as discussed in the previous chapter, have been on the decline. As a result, an open amendment process occurs more frequently during committee markups than on the House floor. Measures of high priority to the majority leadership are typically considered with a "scripted" amendment process devised by the Rules Committee. An example of the scripted procedure is discussed later in this chapter.

The Five-Minute Rule

House rules require that all bills and joint resolutions be read three times to give members every opportunity to become familiar with the measures they are considering. In practice, though, bills are not read word for word. Verbatim readings generally are dispensed with by unanimous consent or by a rule that stipulates that each section of the bill is considered to have been read.

The first "reading" is held when a measure is introduced and referred to committee. The bill is not read aloud; the bill's number and title are published in the *Congressional Record*. The second reading occurs in the Committee of the Whole. And the third, by title (the name of the bill only), is held just before the vote on final passage.

Bills are considered, or read, as specified in the rule from the Rules Committee, usually section by section. The Rules Committee might specify a reading by title instead of by section to permit larger, interrelated parts of the measure to be open to amendment. Customarily, general and supplemental appropriations measures are read for amendment paragraph by paragraph.

At the end of general debate, a bill is read for amendment under the five-minute rule. Under this House rule, any Member "shall be allowed five minutes to explain the amendment, after which the Member who shall first obtain the floor shall be allowed to speak in opposition to it. There shall be no further debate thereon." [33]

Actual practice differs from the rule. Amendments are regularly debated for more than the ten minutes allowed. Members gain the floor by offering pro forma amendments, moving to strike the last word or to strike the requisite number of words. Although technically these are amendments, no alteration of the bill is contemplated by the sponsors; their purpose is to extend the debate. (Pro forma amendments are not in order under a closed rule.) In addition, members may ask for unanimous consent to speak longer than five minutes, and they may yield part of their time to other legislators.

Debate on amendments cannot extend forever, however, and a floor manager can move that discussion be terminated at a specified time. Time limits on amendments can be critical to the fate of legislation. For example, a time limit on debate on a Labor–Health and Human Services (HHS) appropriations bill, engineered by the chairman of the HHS Appropriations Subcommittee, effectively prevented amendments from being offered on sensitive social topics such as abortion, which in years past had mired the funding bill in controversy. [34]

Amendments are in order as soon as the section to which they apply has been read, but they must be proposed before the clerk starts to read the next section. If the clerk has passed on to a succeeding section, a member must be granted unanimous consent to offer an amendment to the previous section. In addition to being timely, amendments must be germane to the bill, the section under consideration, or to a pending amendment. Reading by section or title helps structure rational consideration of complex bills, but on noncontroversial measures the floor manager usually asks unanimous consent that the entire bill be considered as read. In that case, the entire measure is open to amendment at any point. Thus, under the regular (customary) order, as explained by the Rules Committee:

> [A]s each section is read, any amendments recommended by the reporting committee are automatically considered first without having to be offered from the floor. Quite often a special rule will provide that if the committee amendment is adopted, it becomes part of the base text for the purpose of further amendment so as not to block other members from amending that portion of the bill. Traditionally, the Chair next recognizes other members with amendments to that section. If two or more Members seek recognition, the Chair gives priority to Members of the committee(s) of jurisdiction over the bill, taking account of their seniority. Members of the primary committee of jurisdiction are recognized before secondary committee Members. The Chair will alternate between the parties in recognizing Members to offer amendments. Special rules commonly authorize the chairman of the Committee of the Whole to give priority in recognition to Members who have pre-printed their amendments in the [*Congressional*] *Record*.[35]

House rules permit a nondebatable motion to be made in the Committee of the Whole to dispense with the reading of an amendment if it was either published in the *Congressional Record* or printed in the bill reported by a committee. The reading of amendments may also be dispensed with by unanimous consent or, commonly, by special rule. Indeed, the Rules Committee often requests (or may require) that lawmakers have their proposed amendments to bills printed in advance in the amendment section of the *Congressional Record*. The special rule will then state that the "amendments so printed are to be considered as read." The prenotification of amendments strengthens the reporting committee's role on the floor by enabling it to prepare advance arguments, alternatives, or modifications to each prenoticed change. Advance notice of amendments also provides some degree of predictability in floor decision making, an objective favored by the floor managers and the majority leadership.[36]

Scripted Amendment Process

On major bills, it is common for the Rules Committee to sift through one hundred or more proposed amendments before the majority members decide, after consultation with the Speaker and other key actors, which, when, and how many amendments will be made in order for floor consideration. It is this political-procedural process that determines the restrictiveness of the amendment process on priority legislation. A bill governed by a scripted amendment procedure is brought to the floor via a structured rule.

Take the REAL ID Act (H.R. 418), an immigration measure that addressed, among other things, the closing of asylum loopholes and strengthening deportation laws. The general amendment procedure was specified in the rule

(H. Res. 75) but the specifics were contained in the Rules Committee report (H. Rept. 109–4) accompanying the rule. The special rule for the ID Act noted that the amendment printed in Part A of the panel's report was considered adopted (a self-executing provision) and that the bill, as amended, would be considered as an original bill for purposes of further amendment. The special rule then stated that only the five amendments printed in Part B of the Rules Committee report could be offered, only in the order printed in the report, and only by a member named in the report. In addition, the special rule stipulated that the Part B amendments could not be amended, that each amendment would be debated for twenty minutes only, and all points of order were waived against the five amendments.[37] Sometimes only GOP-sponsored amendments are made in order; in this case, the distribution was three amendments for Republicans (all adopted) and two by Democrats (both rejected).

Typically, a scripted amendment process governs floor consideration of numerous important measures. From the majority party's perspective, the substantive and political risks are too high and the benefits too low to permit an unfettered amendment process. Needless to say, a narrowly divided House—combined with the reality that few minority members are likely to vote with the majority to enact their priority issues—contributes to the clampdown on amendment opportunities for lawmakers. From the minority's perspective, the limitation on amendments prevents them from defining their policy differences with the majority party and offering solutions to problems that may attract bipartisan support.

Rationale for Amendments

Amendments serve diverse objectives. Some are offered in deference to pressure groups, executive branch officials, or constituents; others are designed to attract public notice, to stall the legislative process, to demonstrate concern for an issue, to test sentiment for or against a bill, and, of course, to alter the pending bill; and still others are politically motivated in that they are designed to force controversial votes and thus provide electoral ammunition to congressional challengers, and to energize a party's core electoral supporters. "I want the Republicans on record having endorsed all these shortfalls in key programs the public wants, for education, veterans, housing, the environment," declared Representative Obey, the Democratic leader of the House Appropriations Committee.[38] Some amendments are more technical than substantive; they may renumber sections or titles of a bill or correct typographical errors.

Committees do not have final authority to amend bills or measures during their markups. Only the full House has the authority to approve or disapprove of proposed changes to legislation. Committee amendments, then, are recommendations to the full House, where they are granted priority consideration ahead of amendments proposed by individual lawmakers. Committee amendments are usually subject to amendment. Committee amendments, floor amendments, and substitutes are different types of amendments that merit some mention, along with the House's requirement that amendments must be germane.

Committee and Floor Amendments. As just noted, House precedents grant priority to amendments recommended by the reporting committee(s). These precedents state: "Committee amendments to a pending section are normally considered prior to amendments offered from the floor." [39] This condition is another example of the parliamentary advantage accorded committees by House rules and precedents. Committees receive most of the bills introduced in the House, influence the kind of rule their bills receive from the Rules Committee, and control general debate on the floor.

Until the 1970s or so, the House was inclined to defer to the committees' recommendations, but that changed. The committee monopoly over policy-making diminished as the Capitol Hill environment became more permeable to outside influences. Now committees may be bypassed in whole or in part by various means, such as informal or leadership task forces established to draft legislation. The multiple referral of measures to several committees also undercuts jurisdictional monopolies. The trend away from committee autonomy has been reinforced by partisan actions that further consolidate power in the office of the Speaker and the majority party caucus.

With most committees open to greater challenges on the floor (subject to the character of the rule), chairs not surprisingly may look to the suspension procedure as a way to protect their measures from floor amendments. Or the Rules Committee may make it clear that if legislation gets bogged down during an open amendment process, the panel will reconvene and report a shut-down rule that limits amendments and expedites action on the bill.

Germaneness. Amendments that are extraneous to the subject matter of a bill are far more common in the Senate because House rules require amendments to be germane or relevant to the pending matter. Any member can question the relevance of a proposed amendment by raising a point of order, on which the chair must rule. (A lawmaker whose amendment is challenged on germaneness grounds is automatically considered "guilty" and must marshal arguments to prove that the amendment is relevant to the bill or pending amendment.) Such points of order are not always raised, however, either because the rule from the Rules Committee may waive them, or because members are in general agreement with the provision. "I don't make points of order on all [nongermane amendments]," a member once observed, "because some may be necessary due to changing conditions." [40] The House's strict rule requiring that committee and floor amendments be germane is not self-enforcing.

A fundamental objective of the germaneness rule ("no motion or proposition on a subject different from that under consideration shall be admitted under color of amendment") is to focus the House's attention on one subject at a time. In addition, the rule facilitates majority party control of the agenda—by preventing, for example, the minority party from offering unrelated amendments—and bolsters the role of committees. Although brief, the germaneness rule, which applies to all amendments (committee and individual), is difficult and complex to apply. For example, if an amendment is proposed to a pending amendment, is the proposed change supposed to be germane to the pending amendment, to the bill, or to both? (The answer is, to the pending amendment.)

House members use scores of precedents and tests to defend their amendments from germaneness points of order, some of which are listed in Box 5-1. A dilemma for lawmakers is that these tests and "precedents do not set down perfectly distinct guidelines for analysis." [41] Two brief examples illustrate the point. Take a bill to cut taxes reported from the Ways and Means Committee. An amendment to increase taxes meets the subject matter and committee jurisdictional tests noted in Box 5-1. However, it fails the fundamental purpose test because the amendment proposes to raise rather than further cut taxes. An amendment challenged on germaneness grounds must meet all the tests if it is to be ruled in order.

As another example, Representative John Conyers Jr., D-Mich., offered an amendment to add crimes of fraud and deception to a bill addressing crimes of violence against children, the elderly, and other vulnerable persons. A germaneness point of order was successfully lodged against Conyers's amendment on the grounds that it did not deal with crimes of violence. Immediately, Conyers offered another amendment—to add environmental crimes (the pollution of the environment) to the underlying bill. Again, a successful germaneness point of order was raised and sustained by the chair, who ruled that Conyers's amendment was "not confined to the subject of crimes of violence" as defined in the U.S. criminal code. Quickly, Conyers proposed a third amendment—to include environmental crimes as a subset of crimes of violence under the appropriate section of the U.S. criminal code. A germaneness point of order was raised, but the chair overruled it on the grounds that Conyers's amendment was confined to the subject of violent crimes against vulnerable persons.[42]

Substitute Amendments. There are two kinds of substitutes, as briefly noted earlier: a substitute amendment and an amendment in the nature of a substitute. The first type is an amendment that deals with part of a bill. For example, when an amendment is made to change part of a bill, a substitute amendment offers alternative language for the entirety of that pending amendment. By contrast, a perfecting amendment seeks to change, but not replace completely, the language in the first offered amendment.

This distinction goes to form rather than substance. This means, as an example, that a first-degree perfecting amendment might simply change a date (from August 27 to August 28) in a section of the bill. A substitute replaces all the language ("in lieu of the matter") in the pending first-degree amendment, but its sole objective is to accomplish the same purpose as the first-degree amendment (perhaps by using similar but not identical language). Strategically, if an unfriendly second-degree perfecting amendment has been offered to the first-degree amendment, the limb available for a friendly amendment is the substitute branch (see Figure 5-2).

Box 5-1   Some Tests of Germaneness

When a Representative raises a germaneness point of order, the burden of proof rests with the sponsor of the amendment to establish its germaneness.

1. *Fundamental Purpose.* A basic test of germaneness is that the fundamental purpose of an amendment must be germane to the fundamental purpose of the bill. In determining this purpose, substantial reliance should not be placed upon the title of the bill as the title need not state the fundamental purpose of the bill, either as introduced or later amended. One must look rather to the text of the bill as the principal tool in determining purpose.

2. *Subject Matter.* The amendment must relate to the subject matter under consideration. One must determine "what is the subject matter under consideration?" Once it is clear just what the subject matter is, the next element is whether or not the amendment relates to that subject matter.

3. *Committee Jurisdiction.* The jurisdiction of a committee is not necessarily controlling as to the germaneness of an amendment. When an argument has been advanced that the subject matter of an amendment lies within the jurisdiction of a committee other than the committee reporting the bill, the Chair has ruled that the germaneness of an amendment is based upon its relation to the bill in its amended form. In short, the subject matter of the bill is the controlling factor, not the description in the Rules of the House of the various committees' jurisdiction.

SOURCE: Excerpted from *Manual on Legislative Procedure in the U.S. House of Representatives*, 6th ed., 99th Cong., prepared under the auspices of the Republican leader, May 1986.

The second kind of substitute recommends new language for the entire bill. Amendments in the nature of substitutes are commonly reported by the standing committees. They have increased in importance in recent years, in part because of the complexity and interrelatedness of contemporary issues and in part because of multiple referrals. For example, committees that consider the same bill may report dissimilar versions of it. Sometimes, such differences are resolved through intercommittee cooperation. Members and staff from each panel might blend their products into a consensus bill that will be offered on the House floor as an amendment in the nature of a substitute for the bill as originally introduced. Usually, the Rules Committee will accommodate the committees by giving such a substitute special status by making it, instead of the original bill, the vehicle for House debate and amendment. The rule typically states that the consensus or substitute text will be considered an "original bill for the purpose of amendment."

Degrees of Amendments

A basic parliamentary principle permits only two degrees of amendments: an amendment and an amendment to it. Any further motion to amend is a third-degree proposal (an amendment to an amendment to an amendment) and is out of order. "The line must be drawn somewhere," Thomas Jefferson wrote, "and usage has drawn it after the amendment to the amendment." [43]

When a bill is open to revision in the House, only four amendments may be pending simultaneously: (1) an amendment to the bill itself, (2) an amendment to the first amendment, (3) a substitute amendment, and (4) an amendment to the substitute amendment. Once an amendment to a bill has been offered (the first degree), the other three may be offered and be pending simultaneously. Once either of the second degrees is adopted or rejected, another may be offered until there is no unamended text left to change in the pending alternatives (the first-degree perfecting and the substitute for it). If a substitute is adopted, its effect is to replace the language of the original first-degree proposal and any second-degree changes to it that might have been adopted.

The four amendments, with the degrees that are permissible and the order of voting on each, are depicted in Figure 5-2. This representation of the common amendment tree has two first-degree amendments—the amendment to the text and the substitute amendment—and two amendments in the second degree. House Rule XVI states: "When a motion or proposition is under consideration a motion to amend and a motion to amend that amendment shall be in order, and it shall also be in order to offer a further amendment by way of a substitute, to which one amendment may be offered."

Second-degree amendments are voted on first, and the second-degree amendment to the original amendment to the bill is voted on before the second-degree amendment to the substitute. A short-hand way to remember the voting order is this: perfect the amendment, perfect the substitute, vote on the substitute, and then vote on the original amendment, as or if modified. The first degree is the last voted upon to give lawmakers ample opportunity to perfect it before they decide whether to adopt it. Thus, a lawmaker faces a series of binary voting choices: on the first vote, do I like the original amendment or do I prefer the amended version? On the second vote, do I prefer the substitute or the alterations to it? On the third vote, do I favor the amendment first offered (no doubt as amended) or the substitute, possibly as amended? On this vote, if the substitute prevails, it replaces all the language in the original amendment. In this case, it is plain that this is the preferred option of most lawmakers. Finally, the last vote, which is likely to be pro forma, amounts to this choice: accept the first amendment offered (as or if modified) or stay with the language in the original bill.

There is no necessarily "right" place on the amendment tree. Members understand that the initial first-degree amendment is likely to be the target for change by either a first-degree substitute or one or more second-degree perfecting amendments. If proponents of the first-offered amendment have the votes, they can defeat any of the proposed changes and prevail in the end. If they lack the votes, the proponents could end up voting against their own proposal because it was amended with unwanted changes. Lawmakers often

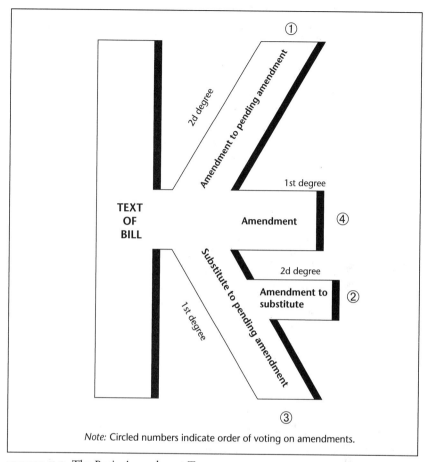

Note: Circled numbers indicate order of voting on amendments.

FIGURE 5-2 The Basic Amendment Tree

want the first vote—the second-degree perfecting amendment—because it cannot be further amended (that would be a third-degree proposal). So a lawmaker whose amendment occupies this slot gets a "clean" vote on the proposition.

Strategically, the amendment procedure can be critical to policy formulation. Either side of an issue may be aided by the voting sequence—whether the amendment is voted on first or last. During House consideration of a nuclear freeze proposal, the proponents wanted the House to vote first on their policy recommendation. As a result, they waited for opponents to offer a first-degree amendment before they countered with a second-degree amendment to their liking. This approach gave backers of the freeze the opportunity "to formulate the final version of any amendment." [44] The first vote, therefore, was on the freeze backers' alternative amendment to the opponents' amendment revising the text of the freeze resolution. The strategy of "fighting fire with fire" means that "threatening amendments by opponents are . . . met with counteramendments" by proponents.[45] The reverse approach is to arrange for a colleague to offer a "friendly" second-degree amendment to the first-offered proposal so as to block opponents from trying to undermine the original amendment with poison-pill changes. (Worth remembering is that the Rules Committee, subject to House approval, can establish a unique amendment tree for legislation, setting aside the traditional amendment process.)

Maneuvering for Advantage: Common Tactics

Proponents and opponents of bills constantly seek to advance their policy objectives through the amending process. Skillful use of various motions, dilatory tactics, or shrewd drafting of the wording of amendments can influence which side carries the day. Customarily, the minority party has self-appointed floor watchdogs who seek to protect party interests and stymie majority steamrollers by raising points of order or making parliamentary inquiries. Timing, too, is all-important to the success of many floor maneuvers, especially preferential motions and amendments to sweeten bills.

Strike the Enacting Clause. Certain motions from the floor take preference over other House business. One is the motion to strike the enacting clause—"Be it enacted by the Senate and House of Representatives of the United States of America in Congress assembled, . . ." This clause, which opens every House and Senate bill, makes a bill an operative law once the bill is approved by Congress and signed by the president. Under House rules, approval of a motion to strike the enacting clause is equivalent to rejecting the measure. A motion to strike the clause is in order at any time during the amending process. The preferential motion is phrased as follows: "I move that the Committee [of the Whole] do now rise and report the bill to the House with the recommendation that the enacting clause be stricken out." This privileged motion must be disposed of before the House takes up any further business on the bill. Debate on the motion is limited to ten minutes, five for and five against. The motion is in order only once, unless the bill is materially changed by adoption of major amendments, a determination the chair makes if a point of order is raised against a second motion to strike.

It is not unusual for the motion to be made either to get debate time or to make a political point. For example, immediately after the Speaker declared the House to be in the Committee of the Whole for the further consideration of an appropriations bill that reduced spending for many programs, a lawmaker who opposed the cuts made the preferential motion to rise. He said: "What I would simply say to you is this: We believe that this bill is warped and we believe there is no underlying sense of decency in the way the cuts are focused in this bill." The Appropriations chair responded that the bill represents "the first step toward fiscal sanity and a balanced budget and it must be taken." [46] The motion to rise was rejected, 187-228.

Sweeteners. Members can make measures considered unpalatable more acceptable by proposing changes—that is, sweetening the measures—to attract broader support. Changes might include amendments granting members more staff or additional office allowances, or pork barrel provisions for the construction of dams, highways, port facilities, airports, and the like in various congressional districts. Because lawmakers and others have criticized pork barrel spending, amendment sweeteners that reduce spending, streamline federal regulations, or cut bureaucratic red tape may also appeal to voters.

Poison Pills. Killer or poison-pill amendments aim to turn a majority against the legislation.[47] For example, adoption of an amendment to include primaries in a congressional public financing bill is almost certain to kill the legislation because many House incumbents, particularly those from safe and one-party districts, oppose any measure that aids party challengers. Or, as a recent Speaker said to proponents of an amendment he strongly opposed, "If that is your goal, if you just want to find a cynical way to burden down the committee bill and make it unpassable, then you might want to vote for the [amendment]." [48]

Importance of the Amending Process

Subject to the character of the special rule from the Rules Committee, lawmakers try to amend controversial bills when they are considered in the Committee of the Whole. The amending process is a critical—and complex—stage for any bill. To summarize, some of the main features of the process are:

- Amendments in the Committee of the Whole are usually offered section by section under the five-minute rule.
- All amendments must be offered from the floor in written form.
- Amendments may not be repetitious. When an amendment is rejected, a member may not offer exactly the same proposal later.
- Any amendment may be challenged on a point of order before debate on the amendment has begun.
- Committee amendments are considered before those introduced by other legislators.
- Pro forma amendments ("Mr. Chairman, I move to strike the last word.") enable members to discuss the bill under consideration for five minutes, even though no change is intended.
- Amendments must be germane to the subject under consideration. Occasionally, nongermane amendments may slip by, either because members generally agree on their intent or because the Rules Committee has barred points of order against them.

The amending process is a key feature of lawmaking. Yet it is important to note that in today's House there are fewer opportunities for members to propose changes to legislation. The combination of wider use of the suspension procedure—which prohibits free-standing amendments—and greater use of structured or modified closed rules means that lawmakers often confront a restrictive amendment environment. Proposing amendments in the contemporary House is sometimes a privilege granted to certain members rather than a legislative right accorded to everyone.

VOTING

The House uses a variety of methods for voting, and many of its votes take place in the Committee of the Whole. (The methods are listed in Box 5-2.) A significant change in voting occurred on January 23, 1973: electronic voting was introduced. In electronic voting, which was authorized by the Legislative Reorganization Act of 1970, members insert a personalized card about the size of a credit card into one of the more than forty voting stations located on the House floor and press one of three buttons: "yea," "nay," or "present." Each member's vote is displayed behind the Speaker's desk and on the wall panels over the press gallery. The system is also used to establish quorums. If electronic voting malfunctions, traditional methods are used. GOP House leader Robert Michel was not a fan of electronic voting because it quickened the pace of the House: "It eliminates the time for informal chats with other members. C-SPAN is even more of a problem. Members now follow the affairs of the House from their offices, rushing to the floor to vote only at the last minute. Again, valuable face-to-face contact is gone." [49]

These technological changes have placed additional pressures on the floor managers. Electronic voting cut balloting time in half, from about thirty minutes under the traditional roll call method to no less than fifteen minutes. The chair has discretionary authority either to close the vote after the expiration of fifteen minutes or to keep the vote open, allowing additional time for lawmakers to vote or more opportunities for party leaders to persuade reluctant members to vote their way. The voting period ends when the chair announces the final result. Recent changes in the rules have permitted the Speaker to postpone votes and schedule votes in clusters on matters such as passing bills or agreeing to suspension of the rules motions. The Speaker may reduce the time allowed for each vote in this procedure to five minutes.

However, on the opening day of the 110th House (2007–2009), the membership adopted a new rule designed to prevent the Speaker from keeping a vote open indefinitely, as occurred during a three-hour vote on a Medicare drug prescription bill (see the discussion below). The new House rule states: "A record vote by electronic device shall not be held open for the sole purpose of reversing the outcome of such a vote."

From the floor managers' standpoint, the modern system has advantages and disadvantages. Managers have computer display terminals that allow them to easily track the progress of a vote. In doing so, they can spot quickly problems such as the absence of one member or the unexpected vote switch.

BOX 5-2   Methods of Voting

In the House. There are four ways of voting in the House: voice, division, yea and nay votes, and recorded votes. A voice vote means that lawmakers call out "yea" or "nay" on one side or the other when a question is put by the presiding officer, and the chair decides the result. A division or standing vote means that those in favor of a proposal and then those opposed stand up while the chair takes a head count. Only vote totals are announced; there is no record of how individual members voted. Yea and nay votes are provided for by the Constitution and are obtained "at the Desire of one fifth of those present" regardless of how few lawmakers are in the chamber. House rules also provide for an "automatic," publicly recorded vote. To obtain an automatic vote, a member says, "I object to the vote on the ground that a quorum is not present, and I make a point of order that a quorum is not present." The actual vote will then determine both issues simultaneously: the presence of a quorum and the vote on the pending question. A recorded vote under House rules is obtained when a lawmaker states, "Mr. Speaker, I demand a recorded vote." If at least one-fifth of a quorum (44 of 218) stand and support the request, then the recorded vote will be taken by electronic device. (There are back-up procedures if the electronic voting system malfunctions.) Recall that the distinction between recorded votes and the yeas and nays goes to the number of lawmakers required to support each request: *one-fifth of a quorum* (44 of 218) for a recorded vote and *one-fifth of those present* for the yeas and nays. Members employ the automatic method when they might not be able to get the support of either a fifth of those present or a fifth of a quorum.

In the Committee of the Whole. Three methods of voting are available in this forum: voice, division, and recorded. The constitutional yea and nay votes are not permitted in this forum. A request for a recorded vote in the Committee—where a quorum is 100 members—is obtained when it is supported by at least twenty-five lawmakers (the member who asked for the recorded vote counts as part of the tally.) If there are few members in the chamber, a member may say, "Mr. (or Madam) Chairman, I request a recorded vote and, pending that, I make a point of order that a quorum is not present." Once the chair determines that a quorum is not present, there is an immediate quorum call and the member who requested the recorded vote can ask twenty-four other colleagues to support his request as they come onto the floor.

Absent members can be summoned to the floor, and vote switchers can be approached by persuasive members of the party. Managers have less time, however, to evaluate opposition to proposals and line up votes. Today, floor managers must work harder to build support before bills reach the floor.

House rules also permit what are called "live" pairs. The practice of live pairs is an informal agreement "between one Member who is present and voting and another on the opposite side of the question, who is absent. . . . By agreement, the voting Member withdraws his vote and records himself as 'present' by submitting an amber 'present' card." [50] A live pair subtracts one vote, yea or nay, from the final tally and could influence the outcome of closely contested issues. Although rarely used, a live pair was in play when the House passed a Medicare reform bill (H.R. 1) by a 216-215 vote in June 2003.[51] House Appropriations Committee chairman Bill Young, R-Fla., attended the funeral of an army sergeant who died from wounds suffered in Iraq. "But Young made sure his absence . . . would not affect the vote. He made arrangements to 'pair' the vote he would have cast for the bill with that of Rep. Ernest Istook, R-Okla., who opposed the bill but voted 'present.' " [52] Pairs are not counted in tabulating the final results of recorded votes, but they are printed in the *Congressional Record* and announced before the vote is finally declared. As Representative Istook stated: "Mr. Speaker, on my vote just recorded I voted 'no.' I have a pair with the gentleman from Florida, Mr. Young, who is at a funeral, and desire to change my vote and be recorded as 'present.' "

Pairs used to take three forms: (1) a general pair meant that two members were listed without any indication as to how either might have voted; (2) a specific pair indicated how the two absent legislators would have voted, one for and the other against; (3) a live pair, as noted, matched two members, one present and one absent. At the start of the 106th Congress (1999–2001), all pair voting except live pairs was eliminated. However, members may indicate in writing whether they would have voted for or against, and these statements appear in the *Congressional Record* immediately after the vote.

Factors in Voting

On any given day, legislators may be required to vote on measures ranging from foreign aid to abortion, from maritime subsidies to tax reform. It is nearly impossible for a member to be fully informed on every issue before the House. As one lawmaker said, "The sheer volume of votes is so great that there's no way you can weigh each and every issue." [53] Many lawmakers, as a result, follow the "rational ignorance" principle. They rely on cue givers for guidance on matters beyond their special competence. These may be committee or party leaders, members of the state congressional delegation, trusted colleagues, staff aides, or floor managers.[54] "You want to know how Members are voting on an issue," a representative said, "you want to know how Members from your delegation vote, and you want to know how Members who always vote the opposite of you are voting." [55]

Party loyalty, constituency interests, and individual conscience are primary factors in determining a member's vote on any issue, but they are not the only factors. Members sometimes vote for proposals they oppose to prevent enactment of something worse or in the expectation that somewhere along the line the proposal will go down to defeat. Members might vote one way on an authorization bill and another on the corresponding appropriations measure. And lawmakers use their votes as trading material. In exchange for voting yea or nay on an issue, they may receive some project or favor that benefits their district.

On controversial and divisive issues, it is not easy to mobilize winning coalitions. A classic example is the Medicare prescription drug bill (H.R. 1) of 2003. Sponsored by Speaker Hastert, the top domestic priority of President Bush, and the largest expansion of an entitlement program for seniors in recent memory, the legislation was viewed as "must win" by Republicans, but enactment was enormously difficult for two main reasons. First, around two dozen small government, deficit-minded Republicans opposed the measure as overly expanding a government entitlement program. Second, then Minority Leader Pelosi worked diligently to promote party unity, arguing that the GOP plan would weaken Medicare and undermine the party's "ownership" of the issue and encourage more seniors to vote Republican. The GOP faced an uphill challenge to find the votes to pass the prescription drug bill.

Earlier in this chapter, there was discussion of the bifurcated rule used successfully to win passage of H.R. 1 in the House by a 216 to 215 vote occurring around 2:30 a.m. (Many major bills may pass the House after the midnight hour.[56]) That vote was held open for fifty minutes beyond the standard minimum of fifteen minutes for recorded votes so GOP and administration leaders could secure passage. The closeness of the vote on House passage repeated itself with even greater drama during adoption of the conference report on H.R. 1.

To expedite action on the conference report, the House on November 21 adopted a special rule waiving the requirement that a two-thirds vote is necessary to take up a rule on the same day that it is reported from the Rules Committee. Rules Democrat Louise Slaughter objected to the same-day rule for various reasons, including the exclusion of Democratic conferees from the bicameral negotiating sessions (see Chapter 8) and the lack of time for lawmakers to read the close to 700-page conference report. (The report was filed at 1:17 a.m. on November 21; House rules state that conference reports are to be available for three legislative days prior to floor action.) Deborah Pryce, Ohio, the chair of the GOP Conference, responded that the conference report was available on the respective Web sites of the Committees on Rules and Ways and Means, and "anyone is free to look it up and read it at their leisure." [57] The House first adopted the same-day rule and then another rule waiving all points of order against the conference report and its consideration.[58]

The conference report was taken up on November 21, but GOP leaders were uncertain whether they had enough votes to adopt it. When the tally began at 3:00 a.m. on November 22, it was evident to GOP leaders that they lacked the votes for passage. Thus, the vote was held open for nearly three hours (around an hour into the vote the tally was 216 for and 218 against) as GOP leaders and executive branch officials used a combination of promises and threats to persuade several lawmakers to switch their vote from "nay" to "yea." They were successful. The conference report was agreed to by a 220 to 215 vote. "A vote is a pressure cooker sometimes," stated Speaker Hastert. "It just took that amount of time to get people to change their minds." [59] Democratic leaders were outraged at the extraordinary length of the vote. However, Rules Chairman Dreier pointed out: "This was in complete compliance with the rules of the House. Members have a minimum of 15 minutes to vote." [60]

Still angry about the three-hour vote, Minority Leader Pelosi on December 8, 2003, offered a privileged resolution denouncing its length as an abuse of power. The resolution was tabled on a party-line vote (207-182).

The Medicare vote illustrates a theme prevalent in the contemporary House: majority party leaders go all out to win their paramount policy priorities. As a spokesperson for Speaker Hastert put it: "We are not going to play unless we play to win. We want to have a public discourse and debate, but we want our position to prevail." [61] Of course, majority party leaders prefer to know in advance through their whip system that a winning coalition has been forged to pass priority measures, but even if not, the majority leadership may not be reluctant to bring major legislation to the floor under dicey circumstances. The combination of tailor-made special rules—artfully constructed to restrict minority amendments—and the persuasive "carrot-and-stick" abilities of party leaders is often enough to bring about chamber passage of party-preferred agenda items.

The voting records of members can become a campaign issue. Representatives who miss numerous votes may have to explain their spotty congressional attendance record. Many interest groups contribute campaign funds to legislators whose votes are in accord with the groups' views. "If I cast a vote, I might have to answer for it," said a House member. "It may be an issue in the next campaign. Over and over I have to have a response to the question: Why did you do that?" [62] Another lawmaker put it this way: "If you don't like fighting fires, don't be a fireman . . . and if you don't like voting, don't be a congressman." [63]

When voting on all amendments has been concluded, the Committee of the Whole rises (dissolves) and reports the bill back to the full House. (Rules from the Rules Committee typically provide that the Committee of the Whole rises automatically at the end of the amending process.) Then the chair hands the gavel back to the Speaker, who resumes his place at the podium. The mace is returned to its pedestal on the table next to the podium, and a quorum becomes 218 members (a majority of the House). As prescribed in the rule, a standard sequence of events takes place prior to the vote on final passage of a bill.

FINAL PROCEDURAL STEPS

After taking the chair, the Speaker announces that "under the rule [from the Rules Committee], the previous question is ordered." This means that no further debate is permitted on the measure or on amendments; no amendments other than those reported by the Committee of the Whole may be considered; and previously adopted amendments are not subject to further amendment. Then members, sitting as the House, consider the decisions taken in the Committee of the Whole.

The Speaker asks all the members to identify amendments on which they want separate recorded votes. The remaining amendments are decided en bloc by voice vote, after which the contested amendments are voted on individually. Except for motions to send a measure back to the reporting committee with instructions, only first-degree amendments adopted in the Committee of the Whole can now be considered. Separate recorded votes are not usually requested on amendments adopted in the Committee of the Whole unless the earlier votes were very close and the amendments highly controversial. On occasion, the House rejects amendments adopted in the Committee of the Whole.[64]

After all floor amendments are disposed of, two more steps remain before the final vote on passage. The first is engrossment and third reading. "The question is on engrossment and third reading of the bill," the Speaker declares. This is a pro forma question, which is commonly approved quickly by voice vote. House rules provide that the bill be read by its title. (Before 1965 any legislator could demand that the bill be read in full, but the rules were changed to prevent this dilatory tactic.) Recall that engrossment is the preparation of a final and accurate version of the bill by an enrolling clerk for transmission to the Senate. This can be a complicated process, particularly if numerous amendments were adopted.

The second step is the recommittal motion, which calls for returning a bill to the committee that reported it. The motion is provided for in the rule from the Rules Committee. This privileged motion, protected and guaranteed by the rules of the House, is the prerogative of the minority party and it is always made by a member opposed to the bill.[65] It gives opponents one last chance to obtain a recorded vote on their own policy alternative. Recommittal is in order only in the House, not in the Committee of the Whole. An example of a recommittal motion can be found in Box 5-3.

The motion can take one of two forms: a simple, or straight, motion to recommit or a motion that contains instructions to the reporting committee. A simple motion (rarely used) to recommit the bill to committee ("I move to recommit the bill to Committee A"), if adopted, kills the bill, although technically it may be returned to the House floor later in the session. No debate is permitted on a simple motion to recommit. Instructions in recommittal motions may embody amendments that were defeated in the Committee of the Whole. This is the only way amendments rejected earlier in the debate can be brought before the full House.

The recommittal motion to instruct (the instructions must be germane to the bill) may be the only opportunity for the minority party to get a vote on its policy alternative given the scarcity of open rules in today's House. When Republicans controlled the House (1995–2007), they often used the guarantee to the minority of the recommittal motion to refute Democratic charges that they ran the House in an unfair manner. As Speaker Hastert said: "We guarantee the minority the right to recommit the bill with instructions, giving them one last chance to make their best arguments to amend the pending legislation." [66] Of course, there are majority members who contend that is all that is necessary to give the minority party. They object to granting the minority "two bites of the apple"—a complete substitute during the regular

---

BOX 5-3   Motion to Recommit

MOTION TO RECOMMIT OFFERED BY MR. MARKEY

MR. MARKEY. Mr. Speaker, I have a motion to recommit at the desk.
THE SPEAKER PRO TEMPORE. Is the gentleman opposed to the bill?
MR. MARKEY. In its current form, I am opposed to the bill.
THE SPEAKER PRO TEMPORE. The Clerk will report the motion to recommit.

The Clerk reads as follows:

> Mr. Markey moves to recommit the bill H.R. 5682 to the Committee on International Relations with instructions to report the same back to the House forthwith with the following amendment:

> In section 4 (b), add at the end the following new paragraph:

> (8) India is fully and actively participating in the United States efforts to dissuade, isolate, and, if necessary, sanction and contain Iran for its efforts to acquire weapons of mass destruction, including a nuclear weapons capability (including the capability to enrich or process nuclear materials), and the means to deliver weapons of mass destruction.

MR. MARKEY. (during the reading): Mr. Speaker, I ask unanimous consent that the motion to recommit be considered as read and printed in the RECORD.

SOURCE: *Congressional Record*, July 26, 2006, H5928.

---

amending phase for the underlying bill (the first bite) and the motion to recommit with instructions (the second bite).

Until 1970 no debate was permitted on a recommittal motion. The Legislative Reorganization Act of that year authorized ten minutes of debate (five per side) on recommittal motions with instructions. On occasion, a rule from the Rules Committee will authorize longer debate on recommittal motions with instructions.

Although House rules today prohibit the Rules Committee from excluding a motion to recommit from a special rule, partisan conflict over the motion to recommit with instructions escalated during the 1980s and early 1990s when Democrats controlled the House. The Democratic-controlled committee issued rules with greater frequency that either eliminated or restricted the recommittal motion with instructions. The GOP staff director of the Rules Committee, Donald R. Wolfensberger, even wrote a report in 1990 entitled "The Motion to Recommit in the House: The Rape of a Minority Right."

The GOP raged against special rules that prohibited Republicans from offering any floor amendments to legislation. The combination of restrictive rules and no recommittal motion with instructions meant that Republican policy alternatives were never considered and voted on. For their part, Democratic Speakers cited a 1934 precedent to overrule any GOP points of order against special rules that did not contain the recommittal motion with instructions. The precedent stated that under House rules the minority was guaranteed the right to offer a simple, or straight, motion to recommit, but it was not guaranteed the recommittal motion with instructions. When the 104th Congress convened, the new GOP majority amended House rules to guarantee the minority's right to offer a motion to recommit with instructions if offered by the minority leader or a designee.[67] (This rule change, which is still in place, was originally proposed in 1993 by the bipartisan Joint Committee on the Organization of Congress.)

Recommittal motions with instructions commonly provide that the committee report "forthwith," which means that the measure never really leaves the floor. If the recommittal motion is adopted, the committee chair immediately reports back to the House in conformity with the instructions, and the bill, as modified by the instructions, is automatically before the House again. The committee chair states: "Mr. Speaker, pursuant to the instructions of the House on the motion to recommit, I report the bill, H.R. 1234, back to the House with an amendment." The House votes separately on this amendment and, if adopted, then again on the pro forma engrossment and third reading questions, and finally on passage of the bill.

Occasionally, the minority will offer a motion to recommit with instructions that the committee (or committees) reports back to the House "promptly." This word is sometimes used instead of "forthwith" for at least three reasons. First, motions to recommit that contain the word "promptly" may outline a general statement of minority party policy—not detailed legislative language—which makes it easier for minority members to vote for it. Second, if the House adopted this kind of motion to recommit, it would kill the bill, which may be the objective of the sponsor. As a Ways and Means Committee chairman explained when a minority member offered a motion to recommit a measure to Ways and Means with instructions that it report back promptly:

> What in the world is the difference between 'promptly' or, let us choose another word, 'forthwith'? The difference is the difference between 'I love you' and 'I hate you.' Why? Because if you include 'forthwith' in the [motion], it means [the bill] would be immediately changed as the gentleman says he wants, it is reported right back on the floor, and we go forward. If you included the word 'promptly,' it kills the bill.[68]

Third, the word "promptly" is employed to avoid any budget points of order. A recommittal motion with "forthwith" instructions immediately brings before the House the minority party's substantive alternative, which could open it to parliamentary challenge on budgetary grounds.

Recommittal motions are seldom successful, but much depends on the size of the minority party in the House and political circumstances. Probably the most dramatic recommittal motion in recent Congresses occurred on September 25, 1984 (only a few weeks before national elections), when the Comprehensive Crime Control Act was enacted via the recommittal route. A GOP lawmaker offered the recommittal motion with instructions containing the recodification of the criminal code, debated it for five minutes, and urged members to pass a crime package that "has been languishing here in the House since March of this year." [69] A Democratic opponent of the recommittal motion then took the floor and urged rejection of the motion in his five minutes.

To the surprise of nearly everyone, the recommittal motion was passed by a 243–166 vote. Then the continuing resolution to which the crime bill was attached was approved by the House. Democratic leaders were chagrined that the crime package had passed in this manner. Speaker O'Neill declared that it was the "wrong way" to pass major crime legislation—after only ten minutes of debate.[70] When the next Congress convened, the House changed its rules, which continue in force today, to permit the majority floor manager—but not the minority floor manager—to request up to an hour of debate, equally divided, on a motion to recommit with instructions. This is a good example of the majority rule principle that undergirds House operations. Another is the comprehensive recodification of House rules that occurred at the start of the 106th Congress, something that had not occurred since the 1880s.

If the recommittal motion is rejected, the Speaker moves to the third step, the final vote on the whole bill. "The question is on the passage of the bill," says the Speaker. Normally, final passage is by a recorded vote. If the outcome is obvious and the members are eager to be done with it, the measure may be passed by voice vote. When the results of the final vote have been announced, a pro forma motion to reconsider is made and laid on the table (postponed indefinitely) to prevent the bill from being reconsidered later. House rules state that a final vote is conclusive only if an opportunity was provided to reconsider it on the same legislative day (a day on which the House is in session) or the succeeding legislative day.

NOTES

1. During the 95th Congress (1977–1979), the House developed a regular system of scheduling floor sessions in response to the desires of members, committees, and party leaders. Members complained about problems in arranging their personal schedules and their inability to make firm commitments for meetings in their districts; committees wanted more time early in the session to work on legislation without being interrupted by floor meetings; and party leaders wished to better synchronize committee and floor action and use the time in session more effectively. As a result, the House, by standing order, varies its starting time: noon on Mondays and Tuesdays, 3:00 p.m. on Wednesdays, 11:00 a.m. on Thursdays and the balance of the week until May 15, when the convening time for Wednesdays through the balance of the week, including Saturdays if the House is in session, is advanced to 10:00 a.m. for the remainder of the session.

2. For guidelines on the morning hour debate, see *Congressional Record,* May 12, 1995, H4901.

3. William Holmes Brown and Charles W. Johnson, *House Practice: A Guide to the Rules, Precedents, and Procedures of the House* (Washington, D.C.: Government Printing Office, 2003), 732.

4. Jonathan Allen, "House Conservatives Rebel," *The Hill,* March 16, 2006, 3.

5. Jeffrey H. Birnbaum and Alan S. Murray, *Showdown at Gucci Gulch* (New York: Random House, 1987), 163.

6. *Congressional Record,* November 14, 2002, H8742–H8757.

7. Susan Crabtree, "Hastert Asserts His Authority," *Roll Call,* November 18, 2002, 18. Also see Jennifer Dlouhy, "Yet Another Blow to Bankruptcy Rewrite," *CQ Weekly,* November 16, 2002, 3021–3022.

8. Donald R. Wolfensberger, "Committees of the Whole: Their Evolution and Functions," *Congressional Record,* January 5, 1993, H31.

9. The "House as in Committee of the Whole" is a hybrid body that combines several procedures employed in the House and in the Committee of the Whole. The principal features of this hybrid entity are that there is no general debate, bills are open to amendment at any point under the five-minute rule, the previous question is in order, a quorum is half the House plus one, and the Speaker may preside over the proceedings.

10. De Alva Stanwood Alexander, *History and Procedure of the House of Representatives* (New York: Burt Franklin, 1916), 257.

11. In the House sitting as the House, an hour is permitted for debate on amendments. "No member," the rule states, "shall occupy more than one hour in debate on any question in the House." Technically, then, all matters could be debated for 440 hours—one hour each for the 435 representatives, 4 delegates (from the District of Columbia, the Virgin Islands, American Samoa, and Guam), and 1 resident commissioner (from Puerto Rico). In practice, measures are debated for only one hour in total and then are voted on.

12. For a description of the seventeenth-century English origins of the Committee of the Whole, see Alexander, *History and Procedure of the House of Representatives,* 257–258.

13. Technically, the first order of business in the Committee of the Whole is the reading of the bill. But this step is usually dispensed with either by unanimous consent or by the terms of the rule, which is the ordinary practice today.

14. Lizete Alvarez, "Taking a Job That Others Would Not," *New York Times,* December 19, 1998, B2.

15. *U.S. News and World Report,* August 20, 1984, 30.

16. *Washington Post,* October 22, 1983, A19.

17. *Congressional Record,* September 12, 1989, E3001.

18. *Congressional Record,* May 24, 1983, H3257.

19. *Congressional Record,* January 12, 1991, H441. See Joseph M. Bessette, *The Mild Voice of Reason: Deliberative Democracy and American National Government* (Chicago: University of Chicago Press, 1994).

20. *Congressional Record,* October 8, 2002, H7178.

21. Robin Toner, "House Rejects Timetable for Withdrawal From Iraq," *New York Times,* June 17, 2006, A7.

22. *Congressional Record,* June 17, 2006, H4022.

23. *Congressional Record,* June 11, 1979, H14213–H14215.

24. Nancy Roman, "Disaster Measure Doubles in Its Cost," *Washington Times*, June 5, 1997, A3.
25. See Donald R. Wolfensberger, "Questions of Privilege in the House: Minority Party Tools for Unity, Accountability, and Reform," paper prepared for the annual meeting of the American Political Science Association, September 1–4, 2005. Mr. Wolfensberger is the director of The Congress Project at the Woodrow Wilson Center for International Scholars and a former staff director of the House Rules Committee.
26. *Congressional Record*, October 31, 1997, H9834.
27. *Congressional Record*, November 6, 1997, H10112.
28. See *Congressional Record*, July 18, 2003, H7148; July 23, 2003, H7336; October 8, 2004, H8993; March 15, 2005, H1435; April 14, 2005, H1992; June 9, 2005, H4318; November 3, 2005, H9566; December 8, 2005, H11264; February 16, 2006, H351; and April 5, 2006, H1513.
29. Wolfensberger, "Questions of Privilege in the House," 26.
30. *Congressional Record*, July 18, 2003, H7149.
31. Mark Wegner, "Pelosi Threatens 'Week from Hell' Absent Vote on Child Tax," *CongressDailyAM*, July 22, 2003, 16.
32. *CongressDailyAM*, July 24, 2003, H7519–H7521.
33. *Constitution, Jefferson's Manual, and Rules of the House of Representatives*, 109th Congress, 2005, H. Doc. 108–241, 757.
34. Julie Rovner, "House Passes Labor-HHS Appropriations Bill," *Congressional Quarterly Weekly Report*, August 8, 1987, 1790.
35. "Amendment Procedure in the Committee of the Whole: A Brief Synopsis," Parliamentary Outreach Program, Committee on Rules, June 3, 1997.
36. The Legislative Reorganization Act of 1970 provided that amendments published in the *Congressional Record* at least one day prior to their consideration in the Committee of the Whole are guaranteed ten minutes of debate time, regardless of any committee agreements to end debate on the bill. The objective is to prevent arbitrary closing of debate when important amendments are pending. The Rules Committee can waive this requirement.
37. *Congressional Record*, February 10, 2005, H527.
38. Peter Cohn, "Obey's FY04 Strategy: Get Republicans 'On the Record,'" *CongressDaily (National Journal)*, August 7, 2003, 2.
39. *Procedure in the U.S. House of Representatives*, 97th Cong., 4th ed. (Washington, D.C.: Government Printing Office, 1982), 526.
40. Richard F. Fenno Jr., *The Power of the Purse* (Boston: Little, Brown, 1966), 74.
41. Martin Gold, Michael Hugo, Hyde Murray, Peter Robinson, and A. L. "Pete" Singleton, *The Book on Congress* (Washington, D.C.: Big Eagle Publishing Co., 1992), 226.
42. See *Congressional Record*, May 7, 1996, H4482–H4484.
43. *Constitution, Jefferson's Manual, and Rules of the House of Representatives*, 226–227.
44. Pat Towell, "After 42 Hours of Debate: Nuclear Freeze Resolution Finally Wins House Approval," *Congressional Quarterly Weekly Report*, May 7, 1983, 869.
45. Barry R. Weingast, "Fighting Fire with Fire: Amending Activity and Institutional Change in the Postreform Congress," in *The Postreform Congress*, ed. Roger H. Davidson (New York: St. Martin's Press, 1992), 165.
46. *Congressional Record*, March 16, 1995, H3282.

47. See James M. Enelow and David H. Koehler, "The Amendment in Legislative Strategy: Sophisticated Voting in the U.S. Congress," *Journal of Politics* (May 1980): 396–413; and James M. Enelow, "Saving Amendments, Killer Amendments, and an Expected Utility Theory of Sophisticated Voting," *Journal of Politics* (November 1981): 1062–1089.

48. *Congressional Record*, May 25, 1982, H2824. The amendment was not adopted.

49. Donnie Radcliffe, "Many Hits, One Era," *Washington Post*, March 9, 1994, C4.

50. Brown and Johnson, *House Practice*, 926.

51. *Congressional Record*, June 27, 2003, H5256.

52. *CongressDaily*, July 1, 2003, 5.

53. *New York Times*, June 29, 1983, A14.

54. On factors influencing votes, see, for example, John W. Kingdon, *Congressmen's Voting Decisions* (New York: Harper and Row, 1973); and Donald P. Matthews and James A. Stimson, *Yeas and Nays* (New York: Wiley, 1975).

55. *Congressional Record*, July 16, 1986, H4558.

56. Jonathan Weisman, "House Voting More Often in the Wee Hours," *Washington Post*, December 20, 2005, A19.

57. *Congressional Record*, November 21, 2003, H12176.

58. *Ibid.*, H12230–H12246.

59. Jackie Koszczuk and Jonathan Allen, "Late-Night Medicare Vote Drama Triggers Some Unexpected Alliances," *CQ Weekly*, November 29, 2003, 2958.

60. Robert Pear and Robin Toner, "Sharply Split, House Passes Broad Medicare Overhaul; Forceful Lobbying by Bush," *New York Times*, November 29, 2003, 21.

61. Isaiah J. Poole, "Two Steps Up, One Step Down," *CQ Weekly*, January 9, 2006, 82.

62. *New York Times*, May 13, 1986, A24.

63. Jack Anderson and Michael Binstein, "Synar Stands His Ground," *Washington Post*, August 22, 1993, C7.

64. See, for example, Martha Bridegam and Pat Towell, "'Goodwill Games' Spark Sharp Exchange," *Congressional Quarterly Weekly Report*, June 27, 1987, 1386.

65. Representative Ray LaHood, R-Ill., has made a point of noting that some minority members who say they are opposed to the bill in "its current form" and are recognized to offer the motion to recommit end up voting for final passage of the bill. He wants to change this rule at the start of the 110th Congress. See Jennifer Yachnin,"LaHood's Rule: Don't Be Against, Then for, a Bill," *Roll Call*, May 9, 2006, 3.

66. *The Cannon Centenary Conference: The Changing Nature of the Speakership*, House Document No. 108–204 (Washington, D.C.: Government Printing Office, 2004), 62. Also see Donald Wolfensberger, "The Motion to Recommit in the House: The Creation, Evisceration, and Restoration of a Minority Right," paper prepared for presentation at a conference on the History of Congress, University of California, San Diego, December 5–6, 2003.

67. But some controversy surrounded Minority Leader Richard A. Gephardt's motion to recommit with instructions to a tax bill. See *Congressional Record*, April 5, 1995, H4331–H4332; April 6, 1995, H4340–H4341.

68. *Congressional Record*, February 5, 2003, H311.

69. *Congressional Record*, September 25, 1984, H10129.

70. See Charles R. Wise, *The Dynamics of Legislation* (San Francisco: Jossey-Bass, 1991).

CHAPTER 6

Scheduling Legislation in the Senate

REPRESENTATIVES AND Senators work long days, not only on the floor and in committee but also in meetings with executive branch officials, constituents, interest groups, and the media. Moreover, they must maintain contact with the diplomatic community, party leaders, and state and local officials. And then there are the periodic trips home to attend important political functions, meet with constituents, or appear at campaign fund-raising events. As Sen. Arlen Specter, R-Pa., said, "A big part of the job is taking the pulse of our constituents." [1]

Of legislators in the two houses of Congress, senators lead the more harried existence. The legislative and committee workload is as heavy in the Senate as in the House, but it must be carried out by fewer lawmakers (100 senators compared with 435 House members), and in most cases senators represent a larger number of constituents. Senators are more often in the public eye and are called on more frequently to comment on national and international policy. Senators not uncommonly are expected to be in two or more places at the same time. See Box 6-1. In such a situation, a senator must select the top-priority event to attend in person and delegate staff members to cover the rest or rely on a fellow senator to recount what took place.

Because of the role senators must play, the time restraints on them, and the smaller size of the Senate, the chamber's legislative scheduling system is much more flexible than that of the House, as Table 6-1 shows, and its deliberative process is more informal. The Senate has formal rules dictating floor procedure, but they are routinely set aside. Instead, the chamber relies on unanimous consent agreements (UCAs). Senators also have significant parliamentary prerogatives, especially with respect to their ability to stymie floor action, and senators are not reluctant to wield these prerogatives to achieve individual or partisan objectives. As a result, floor decision making can be an uncertain or unruly affair. And, unlike the House, where the majority party led by the Speaker is in charge of scheduling, the majority and minority leaders in the Senate together largely shape the institution's program and agenda.

FLEXIBLE SCHEDULING SYSTEM

In response to the manifold pressures on members, the Senate has evolved a highly adaptable legislative scheduling system that responds to the needs of the individual members, as well as to the needs of the institution. The system bears little resemblance to what the formal rules specify and rests largely on usage and informal practice. Senators' frustration with delays and uncer-

---

BOX 6-1   A Sample Tuesday for Sen. Jeff Bingaman, D-N.M., 2006

8:15–9:00 AM	Legislative Discussion with Jack Nugent et al.: National Enrichment Facility
9:00–10:00 AM	Democratic Leadership Meeting Location: S219, The Capitol
10:00–11:00 AM	Energy Committee Meeting: Prudhoe Bay Location: 366 Dirksen
11:00–11:30 AM	NM Constituent Meeting: Randy Marshall et al. New Mexico Medical Society Location: Personal Office
12:00–12:30 PM	Legislative Briefing Meetings with staff and assorted experts Location: Personal Office
12:30–12:45 PM	Press Time, CNBC Location:TV Gallery, The Capitol
12:45–2:00 PM	Democratic Caucus Luncheon Location: S211, The Capitol
2:15–2:30 PM	Scheduled Floor Vote Location: Senate Floor, The Capitol
2:30–3:00 PM	Legislative Discussion: Global Warming Location: Personal Office
3:00–3:30 PM	New Mexico Constituent Meeting: Carol Waite et al. New Mexico Restaurant Association Location: Personal Office
3:30–4:00 PM	New Mexico Constituent Meeting: Terri Cole et al. Albuquerque Chamber of Commerce Location: Personal Office
4:00–5:10 PM	Legislative Time: Discussions with staff Location: Personal Office
5:10–5:15 PM	Press Time, Bloomberg News Location: Russell Rotunda
5:15–5:30 PM	Scheduled Floor Vote Location: Senate Floor, The Capitol
5:30–6:30 PM	Legislative Briefing and Policy Reviews with staff Location: Personal Office
6:30–9:00 PM	Reception and Dinner: Alliance to Save Energy Location: National Building Museum

See also, Lindsey Layton, "Capitol's Newcomers Try a Little Openness: In the Name of Transparency, Two Hill Freshmen Make Their Daily Schedules Public," *Washington Post,* February 4, 2007, A6.

TABLE 6-1 House and Senate Scheduling Compared

House	Senate
Important role for the Rules Committee	No equivalent body; instead, unanimous consent agreements govern floor action on measures
Majority party leaders, especially the Speaker, are the predominant force in scheduling	Majority party leaders control the flow of legislation to the floor in close consultation with minority party leaders
More formal process	Less formal process
Only key members are consulted in scheduling measures	Every reasonable effort is made to accommodate the scheduling requests of all senators
Elaborate system of formal calendars and special days for calling up measures	Heavy reliance on informal practice and personal accommodation in scheduling (Senate has only two calendars)
Party leaders can plan a rather firm schedule of daily and weekly business	Party leaders regularly juggle several measures to suit events and senators

tainty in scheduling sometimes prompts changes that may be observed at different times, depending on legislative workload and political circumstances, such as when the Senate is scurrying to move a backlog of business.

Different Options

To pass the twelve general appropriations bills and a few other key legislative priorities during an election year when a third of the membership is busy campaigning, majority leaders may plan several five-day workweeks with votes on Mondays and Fridays.[2] The Senate tried a scheduling system that called for three weeks in session each month followed by one week off to give "Senators some predictability, to schedule their trips back home to their constituencies, or to catch up on committee work here or other work here," said Robert C. Byrd, W.Va., the Senate Democratic leader who instituted the change.[3] Senators did not, however, adhere regularly to the three-week, one-week system, and so it soon lapsed as they reverted to the usual Tuesday to Thursday work pattern.

Figure 6-1 depicts the concentration of Senate work in the Tuesday to Thursday period during the 102d Congress (1991–1993) and contrasts the Senate pattern with the House's. This several-decades-old pattern remains typical of senatorial activity today, although the Democratic majority leader Harry Reid, Nev., of the 110th Senate has promised to "add nearly a month of workdays to the 2007 legislative calendar."[4]

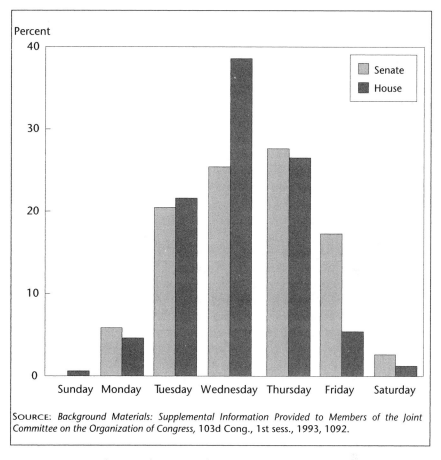

FIGURE 6-1 Distribution of Senate and House Votes, 102d Congress, by Day of Week

Diverse Goals

Although the subject of scheduling improvements comes up perennially, majority leaders (who ultimately are responsible for setting the Senate's schedule) usually strive to ensure certainty, predictability, and family friendliness in the chamber's day-to-day work. "I tried my very best to make sure the Senate in fact is a family friendly workplace," remarked Trent Lott, Miss., when he was Republican leader (1996–2003). "[W]e have tried not to work into the wee hours of the night." [5] Lott provided advice to his successor, Bill Frist, R-Tenn., on how to manage the Senate, but he was critical of Frist's decision to keep the Senate in longer hours. (Lott, who relinquished his GOP leadership position in December 2002 after making remarks interpreted as controversial during Senator Strom Thurmond's, R-S.C., 100th birthday party, made a comeback by winning the position of minority whip of the 110th Senate.)

When Lott was leader, he usually adjourned the Senate by 6:00 p.m. during the week and by noon on Fridays so senators could fly home to their states. Under Frist, the Senate rarely adjourns before 7:00 p.m. and has been in session several nights after midnight and [sometimes] for a full day on Fridays. Frist also opens the Senate at 9:30 a.m., a half hour before Lott did. "I think marathon hours are bad because they almost invariably lead to mistakes and anger," Lott said. "Almost always, when you go beyond 9:00 p.m. something squirrelly will happen." [6]

Senate leaders do try to accommodate each senator's scheduling needs. "I had an inquiry this afternoon on when the votes will occur on Monday," said a GOP leader. "One of our colleagues on this side is attending a Little League baseball tournament where his son is involved and he cannot be back until 3:00 p.m., so he will be accommodated." [7] However, to balance institutional obligations with individual requests is no easy assignment for majority leaders, particularly when senators have children. For example, a 5:00 p.m. Thursday roll call vote "means GOP Sen. Kay Bailey Hutchison can make an evening flight [to Texas] to be with her two newly adopted children. A 6:30 p.m. vote means she can't depart until Friday." [8]

The best-laid scheduling plans can always go awry in the Senate because individual senators have the capacity through various parliamentary devices to frustrate plans for moving the legislative agenda in a predictable fashion. Given the individualistic and increasingly partisan character of today's Senate, Republicans and Democrats commonly battle over agenda control. Understandably, a Democratic or Republican majority leader wants the Senate to focus on their party's agenda; the minority leader wants, by contrast, the opportunity to advance his party's priorities by offering nonrelevant amendments to whatever vehicle or bill lends itself to that objective. In the majority, one GOP senator said, "It's got to be a Republican agenda, not a Ted Kennedy [Sen. Edward M. Kennedy, D-Mass.,] agenda." Added another Republican, "the majority leader must show he's running the calendar, not a member of the minority." [9]

Strategic Considerations

Senate leaders require flexibility in determining the chamber's business; they understand that scheduling is a significant strategic and political resource. If the Senate is in gridlock over a measure because of various stalling tactics, the majority leader might threaten to make members work long days, through the weekend, and even through a planned recess until the impasse is resolved. Alternatively, if senators agree on a date for a final vote on controversial legislation, the majority leader might extend a scheduled Senate recess for another week. Or the majority leader might set a difficult vote for members just before a recess. For example, a majority leader "scheduled the politically tough vote [raising the nation's debt limit] on the last day before Congress adjourns for a weeklong St. Patrick's Day recess." [10] If the Senate failed to enact this "must pass" measure, the Senate would likely have had to remain in session until it did pass the legislation, scrambling the senators' travel and other recess plans.

Stalemates in processing legislation can also be a campaign issue as the majority party blames the minority for obstructing the chamber's business. The majority leader, for example, could schedule several votes on a motion to proceed to a bill, knowing full well that he lacks the votes to overcome dilatory tactics by the minority. His goal—to put minority members on record as "obstructionists." For their part, minority members would castigate the majority for managing a "do-nothing" Senate.

The political ramifications of scheduling loom large in election years. The majority leader may schedule issues with a small chance of passage, but a large role in rallying the party's electoral supporters and promoting fund-raising efforts. Constitutional amendments to prohibit gay marriage or to ban flag-burning are issues that energize conservative Republicans. When Frist was majority leader, he "purposefully scheduled the vote on the flag-burning amendment to coincide with the July Fourth holiday, heightening the argument of supporters that passing it is a patriotic duty." [11] Senate Democratic leader Harry Reid, Nev., made clear his intention to force the Senate to vote, repeatedly if necessary, on raising the minimum wage. "The wage hike," wrote a journalist, "is part of the Democrats' national platform [in 2006], and one of several domestic priorities they plan to tout heading into November." [12]

The president, too, influences Senate scheduling, especially if his party is in charge and it is an election year. President George W. Bush, for example, urged Majority Leader Frist to schedule rapid action on the White House's executive and judicial branch nominees before the traditional Labor Day kickoff to the November campaign season. "If the Democratic Party believes that it's going to be in the majority next Congress, they may not see a lot of incentive to cooperate," said the White House's chief Senate liaison. "The closer we get to the election, the harder it will be to move these nominations." [13]

Strategic scheduling is also part of deadline or end-game politics. Legislation may be scheduled during the closing weeks of a Congress to maximize political pressure for action. Lawmakers, too, are often willing to wait until the end of a Congress, "believing that he, she, or they will have maximum leverage at the end of the tunnel." [14] Or real or contrived crises can be generated as certain deadlines—the start of the fiscal year or the traditional August recess, for example—approach. The sense of urgency can heighten the pressure and the stakes, so members will act before the clock or calendar runs out.

Unlike House members, all senators have an opportunity to participate in scheduling legislation for floor action. Robert J. Dole, R-Kan., who was majority leader from 1985 to 1987 and 1995 to mid-1996, once reported: "The Senate leadership convened a special meeting this morning for all 100 Senators—81 Senators attended to discuss [the schedule for] wrapping up the year's business before adjournment." [15] Majority Leader Reid, with the concurrence of Minority Leader Mitch McConnell, R-Ky., convened a private meeting of all 100 senators prior to the opening of the 110th Congress (2007–2009) to encourage a positive tone and dialogue that could expedite the conduct of the Senate's business. "We need to foster some different ways to make this place work," said a spokesperson for Reid.[16]

This approach to scheduling reflects both the comity that is usually prevalent in the Senate and the power that every member has under senatorial rules. "One person can tie this place into a knot," said a senator. "And two can do it even more beautifully." [17] Minor or noncontroversial bills are expedited to save time for major and controversial measures. And, as noted, insofar as possible, action on important bills is scheduled to suit the convenience of members and to minimize conflicts with legislative activity taking place off the Senate floor. "The Senate operates largely on the basis of unanimous-consent agreements, comity, courtesy, and understanding," said veteran Senator Byrd. [18]

Classifying Measures

The Senate's system for classifying measures for floor debate is simpler and more informal than the House system. In contrast with the House and its four calendars, the Senate has only two calendars: the Calendar of General Orders and the Executive Calendar. All legislation, major or minor, public or private, is placed on the former; treaties and nominations under the Senate's advice and consent authority are placed on the latter.[19] Within the course of a single day, the Senate may consider measures on both the General Orders and Executive Calendars. It may go from executive session to legislative session before finishing pending items on the Executive Calendar. (The motion to enter or exit an executive session is not debatable; however, the nomination or treaty to be taken up can be filibustered.)

Treaties are referred to the Foreign Relations Committee, and presidential nominations are sent to the appropriate committee of jurisdiction. Unlike nominations or regular legislation, treaties do not die at the end of a Congress. For example, the Genocide Treaty was ratified in 1986, thirty-seven years after being submitted by President Harry S. Truman in 1949, by the required two-thirds vote of the Senate. By contrast, presidential nominations must be acted on in a session or they die, and as Senate Rule XXXI states, they must "again be made to the Senate by the President." Under the Constitution, presidents "shall have Power to fill up all Vacancies that may happen during the Recess of the Senate," a power that gives rise to periodic tension between the Senate and chief executive.

Relatively noncontroversial legislation in the House comes up under suspension of the rules procedure or by unanimous consent. Specific days of the month are designated for consideration of legislation on the Private Calendar. The Senate has no comparable procedures. Formal Senate rules for calling up legislation—both controversial and noncontroversial—are cumbersome and consequently are generally ignored. One of these rules, for

SENATE OF THE UNITED STATES
ONE HUNDRED TENTH CONGRESS

FIRST SESSION { CONVENED JANUARY 4, 2007 } DAYS OF SESSION 4

SECOND SESSION {   }

CALENDAR OF BUSINESS

Wednesday, January 10, 2007

SENATE CONVENES AT 9:30 A.M.

PENDING BUSINESS

S. 1 (ORDER NO. 1)

A bill to provide greater transparency in the legislative process. *(Jan. 9, 2007.)*

(UNANIMOUS CONSENT AGREEMENT ON P. 2)

PREPARED UNDER THE DIRECTION OF NANCY ERICKSON,
SECRETARY OF THE SENATE

By DAVID J. TINSLEY, LEGISLATIVE CLERK

59–015

FIGURE 6-2 Senate *Calendar of Business*

Box 6-2   Setting the Daily Schedule

Mr. REID. Mr. President, the Senate will begin a period of morning business until 1 p.m., with the first hour under the control of the Senator from Oregon, Mr. WYDEN, the second hour under the control of the Republicans, and the final hour equally divided and controlled between the two leaders or their designees, with Senators permitted to speak for up to 10 minutes each.

At 1 p.m., we will resume consideration of the ethics legislation. Cloture was also filed on the substitute amendment and the bill. First-degree amendments need to be filed at the desk by 10:30 this morning, and any second-degree amendments should be filed by 4:30 p.m. today. There will be three votes starting at 5:30 today: the Durbin second-degree amendment regarding earmarks; the DeMint first-degree amendment regarding earmarks, as amended, if amended; and then the cloture vote on Reid amendment No. 4. Members should plan their schedules accordingly and remember that rollcall votes are 15 minutes, with a 5-minute grace period.

We are going to finish this legislation this week. If we finish it Thursday, we will be through Thursday. If the Republican leader agrees, we will finish it Thursday; otherwise we will push on until we finish this legislation. I hope we can do it Thursday or Friday, but if we have to be here over the weekend, we are going to do it. We are going to finish this legislation. If cloture is not invoked, we will make a decision at that time as to what we will do with the legislation. We have made a lot of progress. There are still a lot of amendments out there floating around, and we will have to see what the body wants to do with those. That will be determined tonight with the cloture votes.

SOURCE: *Congressional Record,* January 16, 2007, S529.

---

example, requires a daily calendar call, with measures brought up and debated in the order in which they appear on the calendar. An example of the Senate calendar of business appears in Figure 6-2 on page 195. Were the Senate to follow that rule, it would lose virtually all flexibility in processing its workload.

At the start of each day, the majority leader often presents an overview of the Senate's floor agenda for that day, an example of which is provided in Box 6-2. Similarly, the majority leader, or a designee, announces the program for the next day or subsequent day at the conclusion of the daily session. Periodically, the leader indicates what the legislative agenda looks like for longer periods of time. Senators are kept informed of the legislative program through a variety of means, such as weekly whip notices (issued more frequently as needed by each party) listing the measures likely to be considered during the week. The Senate's whip notices are less detailed than those of the House, because Senate rules limit predictability in scheduling.

NONCONTROVERSIAL BILLS

Practically all noncontroversial measures are called up by use of unanimous consent agreements and enacted without debate.[20] In fact, Senator Byrd has estimated that "easily 98 percent of the business of the Senate is called up by unanimous consent." [21] The leaders and staff aides in both parties check with senators to clear minor or noncontroversial legislation before such measures reach the floor, because a single dissent will hold up floor action until the roadblock is cleared away. Once cleared, minor and noncontroversial bills generally take from several seconds to a few minutes to pass. "Locomotive velocity may develop at this point, as bills come up and pass through with no objection," Byrd has noted.[22] Typically, these measures are considered at the end of the daily Senate session, during the wrapup period (see Box 6-3).

The Senate's small size, flexibility, and tradition of cooperation mean that the majority and minority leaders frequently can schedule noncontroversial legislation on a daily basis. Through informal floor discussions or colloquies, each examines the calendar to be sure that noncontroversial bills have been cleared by senators interested in those bills. The measures then are passed quickly by voice vote.

Minor and noncontroversial measures also may reach the Senate floor on a motion by any senator. However, the majority and minority leaders normally try to reach agreement in advance on the floor schedule and are likely to oppose action that will bring bills to the floor without prior clearance from them. The leaders' prerogative of receiving preferential recognition from the presiding officer—first the majority leader, followed by the minority leader—enables them to control the agenda of activities on the floor. As Senator Byrd explained: "A majority leader has enormous power when it comes to the schedule of the Senate, the scheduling of bills and resolutions and the programming of the Senate schedule. The majority leader has the first recognition power and that is a big arrow in his arsenal. . . . Nobody can get recognition before the majority leader." [23] A senator who attempts to bring a measure or matter to the floor without consulting the majority leader in advance may find the proposal subject to a tabling motion. (The motion to table kills the action to which it is directed.)

MAJOR LEGISLATION

Once major Senate bills are reported from committee, the majority leader must consider several questions. First, what measures should be called up? Here the majority leader, after receiving input from numerous sources, such as committee chairs, the minority leader, the White House, and the rank and file, identifies both the must-pass and must-not-pass bills. Second, absent an

Box 6-3 Wrapping Up the Senate's Day

It took just a few minutes for the Senate to act on some 150 nominations and a handful of bills early in the morning of Nov. 21 as work wound down for the session. But getting to that point was a long, long process.

"It can consume a lot of time," said Secretary of the Majority David Schiappa.

Each nomination and measure Majority Leader Bill Frist, R-Tenn., rattled off for final action required hours, even days, of behind the scenes work by the majority and minority cloakrooms. Every senator's office has to be contacted to win agreement. Objections led to negotiations, trades, and promises as Senate leaders and cloakroom staff sort out the bills individually.

Every day when Congress is in session, the majority and minority cloakrooms update the inventory of the legislation awaiting floor action. Such measures are known as "hotlined" bills, and Senate offices learn which ones they are from an actual telephone hotline.

"We may be seeking unanimous consent for the following bills," those calls customarily begin. After that, according to interviews with people involved in the process, the outcome relies on a combination of moxie and modern-day electronics.

Staff assistants e-mail hotline lists to appropriate legislative staff. Staff, in turn, must make hasty evaluations of whether their bosses might have problem with or a strategic reason to try to slow down anything on the list.

Senators' staffs, bill sponsors, and cloakroom personnel then start negotiating. Sometimes, the leadership intervenes. Bills that remain problematic are dropped from the list of measures that can be passed by voice vote—without most senators present—via a unanimous consent request.

The wrapup list typically is dominated by Post Office namings, congratulatory resolutions, and other measure that are noteworthy only in one locality.

"It's not that they are big things," said one Democratic aide, "but they can mean big things back home." Nominations to executive branch boards, judicial posts, commissions and offices can be particularly difficult to hotline.

A case in point was the long list of executive nominations that went through the Senate Nov. 21. The quest of Sen. Harry Reid, D-Nev., to get one of his staffers, Gregory Jaczko, nominated and confirmed to the Nuclear Regulatory Commission began more than a year ago. Reid declared he would block all non-military executive nominations until Jaczko got the seat reserved for a Democrat.

Talks to confirm Jaczko, or to let some other nominations through without his confirmation, were on and off again. Nominations stacked up. It was not until October that a package began to take shape.

The final package was worked out late on Nov. 20 before the senators went home for Thanksgiving. Reid settled for the promise of a two-year Jaczko recess appointment with some strings attached, and the White House saw erased, overnight, its huge bottleneck of unconfirmed nominees.

SOURCE: Adapted from Daphne Retter, "The Road Leading From 'Hotline' to Senate Wrapup Is Not Necessarily a Short Trip," *CQ Today,* November 29, 2004, 3.

emergency or deadline-driven situation, when should the legislation be taken up? In a workload-packed Senate, time is always a factor. "I want to see the votes," said a majority leader. "And I want to see an outline of what the parliamentary situation will be, because time is a consideration around here." [24] Finally, how can legislation be positioned so it can be taken up? Some bills can be considered without sparking any procedural or substantive wrangling. For other measures, substance is at issue. And for yet other legislation, controversy rages over procedure and substance, which is the most difficult scenario for getting a bill called up.

Once the majority leader determines which measure to call up from the legislative calendar, it can take one of two main routes to the floor: through unanimous consent or by motion ("I move to take up S. 1234"). Before these stages are reached, however, the legislation may be subject to the one-day rule, the two-day rule, or to "holds."

One-Day and Two-Day Rules

The one-day rule states that bills and reports must lie over on the calendar for one legislative day before they are eligible for floor consideration. This rule is seldom enforced and commonly is waived by unanimous consent. To speed up action, the majority leader states, "I ask unanimous consent that [these bills] be considered as having been on the calendar 1 legislative day for the purpose of the rules of the Senate." [25] Rarely is an objection heard to the request.

The two-day rule requires that printed committee reports accompanying legislation reported by a committee be available to members for at least two calendar days before those proposals are eligible for floor action. Chapter 7 discusses the difference in the Senate between legislative and calendar days. This rule, too, may be waived by unanimous consent or by joint motion of the majority and minority leaders. However, the Senate usually observes the rule, sometimes to the chagrin of the majority leader, who has primary responsibility for scheduling and moving the Senate's business.

In 1987 two strong-willed Senate leaders—Byrd and Dole—engaged in a classic game of "tit-for-tat" over the two-day rule. That year, the Senate was considering President Ronald Reagan's controversial nomination of Robert H. Bork to the Supreme Court, and Majority Leader Byrd wanted to facilitate floor action on the nominee. He repeatedly asked GOP leader Dole to join him in waiving the two-day rule. "Would the distinguished Republican leader indicate whether or not he is willing to join with me in waiving the 2-day rule?" asked Byrd. "I regret that I am not in a position now to waive the 2-day rule," answered Dole.[26] The discussion surrounding the two-day rule involved jockeying by both parties as they tried to expedite or stretch out debate on the proposed, and ultimately unsuccessful, Bork judgeship.

During the 104th Congress (1995–1997), when Dole was majority leader and Byrd was the Senate's senior Democrat (he had voluntarily relinquished his party leadership role at the start of the 101st Congress), Dole hoped to act quickly on legislation curbing unfunded federal mandates (when the costs of national programs are passed on to state and local governments). To hasten floor action on the unfunded mandates bill, Dole requested the two committees with jurisdiction (Budget and Governmental Affairs) not to submit committee reports with the measure. He did not want the bill delayed by the two-day rule or the Senate rule granting committee members three calendar days to file supplemental, additional, or minority views for inclusion in the report. (Unlike the House, the Senate has no formal rule requiring committee reports to accompany legislation. Senate committees, however, usually file committee reports.) Despite protests from each committee's Democratic members, neither panel issued a formal committee report. Instead, the two GOP committee chairs filed substitute statements in the *Congressional Record*.[27]

Senator Byrd quickly made a floor issue of the speed with which the bill whizzed through committee. "The Senate is not up against a deadline," he said. "We're not up against an adjournment *sine die*." The measure, he argued, needed a thorough examination on the floor. He underscored the importance of formal committee reports, noting, for example, their value "to any court in determining what the legislative intent is with regard to a particular bill." [28] Then for two weeks, Senator Byrd led the Democratic effort to delay action on the GOP proposal. "We have what we know as 'Byrd-lock,' " quipped Majority Leader Dole.[29] After fifty-nine hours of debate on the bill and forty-four roll-call votes, the Senate finally enacted the legislation.[30]

Holds

Holds are an informal custom unique to the Senate. They permit any number of senators—individually or in clusters—to stop (sometimes permanently, sometimes temporarily) floor consideration of legislation or nominations simply by making requests of their party leaders not to take up such matters. Party leaders can move ahead anyway, but then they face the daunting prospect of overcoming various dilatory tactics. Nonetheless, it is ultimately the decision of the majority leader whether to honor a hold and, if so, for how long. Unlike filibusters, which are ostensibly educational and occur in full view of everyone, holds require no public utterance and occur in shrouded circumstances. Sometimes called the "silent filibuster," they are especially effective on limited or special-purpose measures that attract little public or political attention. Must-pass legislation, such as continuing resolutions, will not be killed by holds. Only senators can place holds, but they may do so at the request of House members, lobbyists, or executive branch officials. In some instances, factional leaders place holds on behalf of their senatorial colleagues.[31] Holds may take various forms.

> There are "rolling" holds, a group sport in which one senator after another steps in to keep a measure from coming to the Senate floor. There are also "hostage" holds, where a senator may hold up a nomination, for example, to force concessions on

something else. Then there are what have come to be known as "Mae West" holds: a come-hither message for senators to stop by and work something out.[32]

There are also "political holds." In an election-year, senators in tight races will discover that holds are placed on their bills by opposition party members. The objective of these holds is to prevent senators in competitive races from claiming credit and reaping favorable publicity back home for winning enactment of legislation.

Relatively little is known about holds even among insiders in Washington.[33] No current public record is kept of who places holds, how they are done (often by letter to the party leader), how many holds are placed on any bill, or how long they are honored by the leadership. Senator Byrd has noted that most holds are used so senators "might be assured that they will be informed or contacted so they can be present when the matter is called up, or have an opportunity to offer an amendment." [34] A list of the Democratic and Republican senators who have holds on various measures is kept by the respective leaders of each party, but this information is restricted and closely held. (Some senators have a policy of publicly announcing their holds on legislation or nominations.[35]) To be sure, an advantage of holds for party leaders is that they serve as an "early warning" system, indicating which members or factions have scheduling concerns that could provoke dilatory actions and who needs to be consulted to craft a unanimous consent agreement.

Holds can forestall floor action because they are linked to the Senate's tradition of extended debate and unanimous consent agreements. Party leaders understand that to ignore holds can precipitate objections to unanimous consent requests or filibusters, which require sixty votes to break. Especially during the rush to Senate adjournment, holds can be fatal. "At this stage in the year, you have a finite amount of time and an infinite amount of legislation. Either the hold goes away, changes are made to the legislation or the person with the hold wins," observed a Senate GOP leadership aide.[36] Holds are also used during the end-of-session rush when members are searching for must-pass bills to which they can attach their favorite amendments. For example, one senator placed a hold on the Export Administration Act so he could try to attach his home equity loan amendment to it.[37]

Holds are a more prominent feature of today's Senate because assertive senators recognize the political and policy potential of this extraparliamentary practice. Holds "have come into a form of reverence which was never to be," exclaimed one senator.[38] Periodically, party leaders assert that senators cannot put indefinite or anonymous holds on matters, but the practice still flourishes because senators recognize the tactical benefits.

In 1999, the majority leader and minority leader announced the end of secret holds in a "Dear Colleague" letter (published in the March 3, 1999, *Congressional Record*) sent to all senators. They wrote in part:

[A]ll members wishing to place a hold on any legislation or executive calendar business shall notify the sponsor of the legislation and the committee of jurisdiction of their concerns. Further, written notification should be provided to the respective Leader stating their intentions regarding the bill or nomination.

However, no enforcement procedure was associated with this policy declaration, and the practice of secret holds soon resumed.

Senators Charles Grassley, R-Iowa, and Ron Wyden, D-Ore., have spent a decade trying to end secret holds. In 2006, as part of a lobbying, ethics, and rules reform package (S. 2349), they succeeded in winning adoption of an amendment to the Senate's Standing Orders (directives or regulations that have the force and effect of a formal rule) ending the practice of secret holds. As Senator Lott noted, the amendment requires that the majority and minority leaders "can only recognize a hold that is provided in writing. Moreover, for the hold to be honored, the Senator objecting would have to publish his objection in the *Congressional Record* 3 days after the notice is provided to a leader." [39] However, S. 2349 required enactment into law before the new holds policy could take effect, but the 109th Congress ended before this could occur. The 110th Senate passed a similar provision as part of an ethics and lobbying reform bill (S. 1).

Some senators have expressed concerns with the Grassley-Wyden amendment. For example, Senator Jeff Sessions, R-Ala., asked if senators who want time to examine a bill must tell "their leader on the phone [that] they have a concern with a bill that was offered that night [and would like some time to review the measure], must they quickly run down to his office and hand the leader a piece of paper?" Senator Sessions's fundamental objection is that the amendment "says passing legislation is always preferable to slowing it down . . . no matter how few Senators have studied or even heard of the bill." [40]

Holds encourage bargaining not only among senators but also between the Senate and the executive branch. Senators regularly place holds on diplomatic and other nominations to extract concessions from the State Department and other federal agencies. Hostage holds, as noted earlier, enable senators to gain leverage to achieve other objectives. Upset that the Pentagon had not provided the promised four C-130 cargo planes to the Idaho Air National Guard, Sen. Larry Craig, R-Idaho, placed a hold on the nominations of over 850 air force officers slated for promotion.[41] After extracting a promise from the White House to work with him to resolve the matter, Senator Craig dropped his holds. "These holds served their purpose," he said.[42] Or as Sen. Christopher Dodd, D-Conn., said about holds: "The only way you get compromise sometimes is by stopping the trains and making people listen." [43] Holds have become so common for presidential nominations that a Democratic leader said jokingly that nominees should feel lonely if they're not subjected to a hold. "You know, who's your holder? That seems to be the question of every nominee. It's almost a status symbol among senators. 'I have no holds. I'm going to have to pick out a nominee to get to know him or her a lot better.' It works that way. . . . 'Hello, I'm your holder. Come dance with me.' " [44]

Unanimous Consent Agreements

If the Senate strictly observed every rule, it would become mired in a bog of parliamentary complications. Instead, the chamber expedites its business by unanimously agreeing to waive the rules. Any senator can object to a unanimous consent agreement. As Majority Leader George Mitchell, D-Maine (1989–1995), once said, "I regularly propound unanimous-consent requests on the floor, and . . . when Senators object we hear within seconds—within seconds. Frequently when I am in the middle of a sentence, the phone rings and staff comes running out to say, 'Senator so and so objects.' " [45] GOP and Democratic leaders "hot line" requests for unanimous consent agreements to all senators' offices via special telephone lines. Senators are provided with a specific timeframe in which to object; otherwise, the measure or matter will come to the floor. As Senator Sessions explains:

> What is a hotline? In each Senate office there are three telephones with hotline buttons on them. Most evenings . . . these phones begin to ring. The calls are from the Republican and Democratic leaders to each of their Members, asking consent to pass this or that bill—not consider the bill or have debate on the bill but to pass it. Those calls will normally give a deadline. . . . If the staff miss the hotline, or do not know about it or were not around, the Senator is deemed to have consented to the passage of some bill. . . . [46]

Unanimous consent agreements (UCAs) are often the product of intensive and extensive negotiations, with drafts of agreements (even letters between the two party leaders) exchanged on and off the floor among concerned senators; once an accord is reached among the key actors, each side will try to sell the UCA to their other colleagues. In the 109th Congress, Majority Leader Frist and Minority Leader Reid negotiated for nearly a year trying to work out an accord to permit the Senate to vote on a controversial but bipartisan House-passed stem-cell bill providing federal funding for research beyond that permitted by a 2001 executive order issued by President Bush. Many conservative senators opposed action on the legislation, viewing stem-cell research as akin to abortion; supporters urged action on the research bill because of its potential to produce cures for diseases such as Alzheimer's. (President Reagan died of the disease in 2004, and his wife, Nancy, is a strong advocate of stem-cell research.) Under an artful UCA negotiated by the two sides, a package of three stem-cell bills (the House-passed measure and two others) would be brought to the floor for a combined twelve-hour debate equally divided between the two sides. No amendments would be permitted to any of the bills, and each must pass by sixty or more votes (obviating the threat of any filibuster). As Minority Leader Reid, asked Majority Leader Frist, "[I]f any one of these three bills or all of them receive 60 votes, they would be passed." Frist responded: "That is correct. Each of these bills will have a 60-vote threshold." [47] The UCA further provided that the Senate would not consider any amendment or bill relating to stem-cell research during the remainder of the 109th Congress.

UCAs also have a political dimension, as reflected in this accord. The stem-cell UCA was a "win-win" for both parties. From a Republican perspective, despite the initial reluctance of many GOP senators to go along with the accord, they recognized that Democrats would offer stem-cell research amendments at every opportunity and force vulnerable Republicans in an election year to cast votes on an issue supported, according to polls, by the general public. And with three bills to be voted upon, many Republicans who opposed destroying life in any form could vote for a bill sponsored by Senator Rick Santorum, R-Pa.(defeated for reelection in November 2006), "that promotes stem-cell research methods that don't destroy embryos." [48] From a Democratic perspective, proponents are likely to win Senate passage of a bill that expands federal funding for stem-cell research plus Senate Democrats "are convinced that a [promised—which was kept] presidential veto of stem-cell research legislation would provide their candidates with an effective wedge issue to exploit in the mid-term elections this fall." [49] (A stem cell bill was adopted on January 9, 2007, as part of Speaker Pelosi's "100-hour " agenda. Its Senate fate is unclear.)

The Senate, in brief, is fundamentally a unanimous consent institution. Every day the Senate is in session, there are scores of routine and complex consent requests. As one senator stated:

> [T]he way the Senate conducts its business hour after hour, day after day, week after week, and year after year, is Senators voluntarily waive the rights which they possess under the rules. I would guess in the course of a typical week we probably enter into anywhere from 10 to 200 unanimous consent agreements, literally, where Senators by unanimous consent, with 100 Senators agreeing to yield some right that they may have—the right to debate, to offer amendments, the right to do this, that or the other thing—waive their rights so that the body may proceed in a way that seems expeditious.[50]

Once accepted, UCAs are as binding on the Senate as any standing rule and may be set aside or modified only by unanimous consent, as underscored by this consequential example. In October 1999 the Senate agreed to a UCA that set a final date for a vote on the Comprehensive Nuclear Test Ban Treaty, a top priority of President Clinton. However, the administration quickly realized that it lacked the required two-thirds vote for approval and wanted to put off the vote. Intensive negotiations then began on how to gracefully avoid a showdown on the floor. But, as Connecticut senator Joseph I. Lieberman pointed out, "the interesting procedural trick is that you need unanimous consent" to postpone the vote.[51] In the end, several conservative GOP senators refused to accept any change in the UCA, and the treaty went down to defeat. The vote "marked the first time an arms control agreement has been rejected by the Senate and only the sixth time in history that senators rejected any treaty." [52]

Overview

Two general types of unanimous consent permeate Senate operations: simple and complex. Senators can use both types to set aside the rules, precedents, and orders of the Senate. A single objection ("I object") blocks a unanimous consent request. The two types share a general purpose: to do things on the floor that could not be done without unanimous consent. However, the complex form has large procedural and policy implications.

Simple UCAs. Simple unanimous consent requests are made from the floor by any senator; these almost always deal with routine business or noncontroversial actions. For example, senators regularly ask and receive permission for staff members to be present on the floor during a debate ("I ask unanimous consent that my legislative fellow, Jane Doe, be granted floor privileges during consideration of the bill S. 1234"). Simple unanimous consent requests also may be submitted to rescind quorum calls, add senators as cosponsors of bills, insert material in the *Congressional Record,* or dispense with the reading of amendments. From its beginning, the Senate provided a conducive environment for simple unanimous consent. Its small size, few rules, and informality encouraged the rise of this practice. Several of the Senate's early rules even incorporated unanimous consent provisions to speed the Senate's routine business. For example, a Senate rule adopted on April 16, 1789, stated: "Every bill shall receive three readings to its being passed; and the President [of the Senate] shall give notice at each, whether it be first, second, or third; which readings shall be on three different days, unless the Senate unanimously directs otherwise."

Complex UCAs. Complex unanimous consent agreements establish a tailor-made procedure for handling virtually anything considered on the Senate floor: bills, joint resolutions, simple resolutions, concurrent resolutions, amendments, nominations, conference reports, and treaties. Fundamentally, the Senate operates much differently with them than without them. As two Senate parliamentarians wrote: "Whereas the Senate Rules permit virtually unlimited debate, and very few restrictions on the right to offer amendments, these agreements usually limit time for debate and the right of Senators to offer amendments." [53] In effect, UCAs are a form of voluntary cloture, as Table 6-2 shows. Senators generally accept the debate and amendment restrictions common to most UCAs largely for two overlapping reasons: they facilitate the execution of the Senate's workload, and they serve the interests of individual senators because they make floor scheduling more predictable. In truth, so many variations of complex agreements exist today that they cannot be distinguished adequately.

UCAs are based on trust. Majority leaders request and receive unanimous consent to modify UCAs if any senator believes he or she was misinformed or ill-informed about its terms. As Majority Leader Mitchell said on one occasion:

The agreement was reached in good faith, but I am now advised that due to a misunderstanding and an inadvertent error, a Senator's right to make a point of order was not protected and included in the agreement. That was an honest mistake. And since becoming majority leader, I have taken the position that whenever an agreement is reached that includes a provision placing a Senator at a disadvantage as a result of an inadvertent error or mistake, either by a Senator or staff, that the disadvantage should be removed and the agreement modified to reflect the circumstances which should have existed when the agreement was adopted.[54]

Senator John Kerry, D-Mass., underscored the comity that suffuses these accords at a time when he might have won quick Senate approval of a unanimous consent request: "Mr. President, I am going to be asking unanimous consent to proceed forward on the bill, but I am not going to do that until someone is here from the other side. And I know they are going to object. . . ."[55]

UCAs are proposed orally—usually by the majority leader—and often after protracted negotiations among other party and committee leaders and key senators.[56] Once agreed to, they are formally recorded in the *Congressional Record,* the daily *Calendar of Business,* and the *Senate Journal.* Such agreements may establish the order in which measures will be taken up, pinpoint when measures will reach the floor, and set the rules for debate, including time limitations and, frequently, a requirement that all amendments be relevant to the bill under consideration. For example, a UCA could specify that the amendment offered by Senator A will have a time limit of twenty minutes equally divided between the two opposing sides or that the amendment cosponsored by Senators B and C will have a time limit of thirty minutes equally divided and controlled in the usual form—that is, between the mover of the amendment and an opponent.

TABLE 6-2 Purposes and Features of a Complex Unanimous Consent Agreement

Broad Purposes	General Features
Impose time limits on debate	Is a negotiated contract accepted by all senators
Expedite scheduling the Senate's workload	Can be changed only by another unanimous consent agreement
Establish predictability and permit flexibility	Is comprehensive or partial in character
	Limits debate on measures and any motions related thereto
	Structures the amendment process
	May require the relevancy of amendments
	Waives points of order

Commonly, party leaders are able to negotiate only partial, or incremental, unanimous consent agreements (covering parts but not the entire bill) before they call up the bill for floor action. Many piecemeal UCAs—limiting debate on specific amendments or deciding when to call up a measure—are hammered out on the floor. Party leaders and floor managers take what they can get when they can get it and work from there to more embracing unanimous consent agreements. It is "so hard to get these agreements," said one majority leader. "I find it is somewhat better to do them a little bit at a time." [57] Or as a congressional scholar wrote: "A dozen or more complex agreements are no longer uncommon for complicated contentious measures." [58]

The primary objective of UCAs is to limit the time needed to dispose of controversial issues in an institution noted for unlimited debate. These agreements, therefore, expedite action on legislation and structure floor deliberation. Numerous precedents have evolved over time to govern UCAs. Typically, agreements impose time limitations on every debatable—and thus delaying—motion, including amendments and final passage, points of order, or appeals from the rulings of the presiding officer. These agreements, however, may allow an unlimited number of amendments to be offered, thereby permitting what Sen. Ted Stevens, R-Alaska, once dubbed a "time agreement filibuster."

A UCA could ban or restrict the number of amendments or place time limits on them, preventing a time agreement filibuster. Thus, depending on what the circumstances warrant, party leaders can craft highly detailed, complex, and creative UCAs to accommodate the diverse procedural contingencies that might arise on the floor. Their fundamental problem is winning consent from senators reluctant to waive any of their procedural prerogatives. As Senator Byrd once said: "The leader is the prisoner of Senators, and always has been. Any Senator can object to time agreements, they can make it difficult for every other Senator." [59]

Complex UCAs usually specify which senators from opposing sides of the issue will control the time for debate on the bill and all amendments. Common, too, is the requirement that amendments be relevant. Senate rules do permit nongermane floor amendments, but UCAs often prohibit them to prevent extraneous issues from being taken up. Some agreements may also set the date and time for the vote on final passage of the measure. In an institution noted for procedural flexibility and sparseness, as compared with the House, UCAs underscore the Senate's recognition that it needs to voluntarily impose additional rules on itself to expedite its business.

Complex UCAs generally impose limitations on two of the most significant prerogatives associated with being a member of the Senate: the right of unlimited debate and the right to offer an unlimited number of floor amendments, even if they are nonrelevant. The irony of UCAs is that, on the one hand, if they are accepted by everyone, the Senate can do almost anything it wants (one exception, for example, is that UCAs cannot waive the constitutional requirement that veto overrides occur by recorded vote). On the other hand, if even one senator objects, then the Senate has difficulty accomplishing anything.

In today's Senate, whose paramount contextual features are perhaps individualism and partisanship, party leaders have to work harder to negotiate unanimous consent agreements that accommodate the partisan and individual interests of senators. Party leaders understand that the business that comes before the Senate attracts varying degrees of interest and support from lawmakers. This situation creates opportunities for bargaining when fashioning unanimous consent agreements. Senators may make it clear to party leaders that their consent to a UCA hinges on whether they receive expeditious floor action on another measure or nomination.

Senate Leadership and UCAs

The majority leader generally has an important scheduling ally in the minority leader. In contrast to the House, where scheduling is the sole prerogative of the majority leadership, Senate scheduling traditionally involves the leaders of both parties. The Senate system derives not merely from equity but also from necessity, because Senate rules confer on each individual member formidable power to frustrate the legislative process, including the right to object to any unanimous consent request. The majority and minority leaders constantly consult with one another and with their top aides, other senators, executive officials, lobbyists, and key staff members on legislative scheduling.

Since the post–World War II period, all party leaders have relied extensively on unanimous consent agreements to process the Senate's workload. During the majority leadership of Lyndon B. Johnson (1955–1961), these agreements were often comprehensive in scope, identifying, for example, when a measure was to be taken up, when it was to be voted on for final passage, and everything in between. Two subsequent majority leaders—Democrats Mike Mansfield of Montana, who held the post longer than any other senator (1961–1977), and Robert Byrd (1977–1981; 1987–1989)—were largely responsible for refining and extending the use of unanimous consent agreements. During their tenure, UCAs became more complicated and governed floor action on a larger number of measures.

The personal style of other majority leaders and the political context in which they served (the size of the majority party, for example, or whether their party occupied the White House) also influenced how they employed unanimous consent agreements. For example, Howard H. Baker Jr., R-Tenn., majority leader from 1981 to 1985, brought measures to the floor without first obtaining comprehensive agreements. With the Senate and White House in GOP hands, the Democrats were reluctant to enter into broad agreements restricting their floor options because they had little idea what amendments might surface. Thus narrower agreements were often negotiated on the floor, typically regulating the consideration of a particular amendment or a series of amendments. Today, in a period of rampant individualism and partisanship, UCAs tend to be piecemeal, such as establishing debate limits on specific amendments.

Reaching Agreement

The Senate's tradition of individual and minority rights means that strategic considerations often permeate the use and shape of unanimous consent agreements. Their use as action-forcing devices, as well as for partisan gain, is highlighted by these examples.

UCAs as Action-Forcing Devices. Two weeks prior to the scheduled mid-August 1986 recess of the Senate, Majority Leader Robert Dole circulated a unanimous consent agreement outlining how he planned to juggle floor action on four major measures: a Defense Department authorization bill, a debt ceiling extension measure, economic sanctions against South Africa, and aid to the contras (a paramilitary group) in Central America. The controversy between the parties involved the last two bills. Broad bipartisan support existed for economic sanctions against South Africa because of its policy of apartheid (racial separation), with Democrats urging a final vote by Friday, August 15. Aid to the contras, a priority of the Reagan administration, attracted only a bare majority of the Senate and almost all from GOP ranks.

After lengthy negotiations with Minority Leader Byrd and other senators, a unanimous consent agreement was reached that took Majority Leader Dole nearly an hour to read and that consumed three pages of the *Congressional Record*.[60] In fact, the agreement was "so complicated that senators admitted they could not understand it even after two or three readings." [61] Strategically, Dole's UCA forged an interdependent link between the two bills.

The UCA required the Senate to consider the contra aid package before South Africa sanctions. At Dole's insistence, a key clause had been added to the UCA. As Dole explained the provision, "unless cloture is invoked on both items, meaning South Africa and Contra aid, then this agreement is null and void, with the proviso . . . that as much of the August recess, as necessary, be null and void in order to complete action" on both proposals.[62] Not only did Dole threaten to delay the Senate's long-awaited August recess if these two issues were not resolved, but he also effectively choked off any Democratic incentive to filibuster the contra aid package. Furthermore, the agreement headed off dilatory action by senatorial opponents of South Africa sanctions.

On August 13 the Senate invoked cloture on both measures, thus ensuring a final vote on each bill. Under the UCA, a cloture vote was to be taken first on contra aid. It failed on a 59–40 vote (sixty votes are needed). The UCA then required a cloture vote on sanctions against South Africa. Despite the Reagan administration's opposition to sanctions, cloture was overwhelmingly approved 89–11. Then another cloture attempt occurred on contra aid, because the UCA explicitly required cloture to be invoked on both measures. On the second attempt, cloture was invoked (62–37).

Partisan Overlay to UCAs. Both parties and individual senators assess the political and policy costs and benefits of going along with a unanimous consent agreement. Position taking, electoral advantage, media coverage, and partisan advantage are among the many factors that influence Senate acceptance of these compacts. The controversy associated with a measure may have little or no bearing on when or whether an accord is reached.

In the aftermath of President Clinton's impeachment trial and subsequent acquittal by the Senate, Majority Leader Trent Lott wanted to accelerate action on popular issues and refocus public attention on legislative accomplishments. Therefore, Lott called up a measure—waiving certain federal educational requirements and popularly referred to as "ed-flex"—that enjoyed broad bipartisan support among senators and the nation's governors. The bill easily passed the Senate on March 11, 1999, by a 98–1 vote. However, when the ed-flex measure had been called up two weeks earlier, it had immediately bogged down in partisan and procedural wrangling over the ground rules for debating and amending the legislation.

"It's a bill we can get a [time limitation] agreement on and pass," declared Majority Leader Lott.[63] No UCA was forthcoming, however. Lott wanted the Senate to pass the modest educational measure quickly. Democrats, however, wanted to showcase the differences between the parties on education, especially with the 2000 elections as the backdrop, and offered various amendments advocated by President Clinton, such as reducing class size by hiring 100,000 more teachers. Minority Leader Daschle said to Lott, "Look. We will agree to these five or six amendments; we will agree to time limits and up-or-down votes of these five or six amendments; and then let's move on." [64] The last thing Lott wanted was to permit a high-profile debate of Democratic initiatives when Republicans hoped to claim education as one of their top priorities. "What they need to do is back off from all their amendments," declared Lott. "We set the agenda." [65]

Both sides were at a standoff. Republicans did not want to vote on the Democratic amendments. Yet they also realized Democrats had the votes to prevent final action on the popular bill. To determine if he could move the bill toward final passage, Lott employed a number of parliamentary maneuvers, such as filing cloture (hoping to invoke a germaneness requirement for amendments) and filling the amendment tree (preventing Democrats from offering their amendments).

In the end, the two sides reached a unanimous consent agreement that served their respective purposes. Republicans achieved a final vote on the bill, and they defeated the Democratic amendments on party-line votes. Politically, they were able to take credit for acting on an agenda issue that voters rated highly. Thus passage of the legislation helped Republicans to recast their public image from the party that wanted to abolish the Department of Education to the party with a strong commitment to education. The immediate GOP cost before an agreement was reached was two weeks of gridlock and bitter partisanship.

Benefits rather than costs largely accrued to Democrats for rejecting attempts by Lott to reach an accord that limited their ability to offer amendments. They won media coverage of their educational proposals and gained the opportunity to offer and debate a series of prized amendments. Even though their proposals were rejected, Democrats knew they could always offer them again on another bill. A short-term cost for Democrats was an uptick of sharper partisanship between the two sides.

Majority Leader Frist also made partisan use of unanimous consent agreements. For example, he wanted to call up for immediate consideration a controversial measure that would make it a federal crime if an unborn child died because of violence against the pregnant mother. The majority leader asked unanimous consent that

> at a time to be determined by the majority leader, in consultation with the Democratic leader, the Senate proceed to the immediate consideration of calendar item No. 89, S. 1019, the Unborn Victims of Violence Act, under the following conditions: 2 hours of debate equally divided in the usual form [between a proponent and an opponent]; further, that no amendments be in order and that all points of order be waived; that upon the use or yielding back of time, the bill be read a third time and the Senate proceed to a vote on passage of the measure, with no intervening action or debate.[66]

Senator Reid objected to Frist's request, in part because at least two members on his side wanted to offer amendments to the legislation. Press accounts indicated that Frist knew he had no chance of getting unanimous consent, but nevertheless he made the request to energize pro-life GOP voters and to criticize Democrats. As one account noted, after Reid objected, Frist and several GOP senators "held a news conference to castigate Democratic 'obstructivism.' Frist must have known in advance that he would not get the approval he sought . . . because he announced the news conference the night before." [67] To be sure, leaders of both parties understand the position-taking and publicity potential of UCAs.

In short, scheduling involves numerous considerations. Party leaders must balance their interest in planning the Senate's business on a daily, weekly, and annual basis with (1) the needs of committees, which require concentrated periods of time, particularly early in the session, to process legislation assigned to them; (2) the needs of senators, who prefer some degree of predictability and certainty so they can schedule their time most efficiently; and (3) the needs of their party, which means considering an agenda that facilitates their continued majority status. These various imperatives mean that no matter how carefully Senate leaders plan the legislative agenda—the times and dates measures will be scheduled, and in what order they will be considered on the floor—they still must juggle bills to satisfy senators, take account of external events and political circumstances, and, where possible, influence policy outcomes in the interests of their own party. As Mitchell once said:

> The ability of any Senator to speak without limitations makes it impossible to establish total certainty with respect to scheduling. When there is added to that the different and very demanding schedules of 100 Senators, it is very difficult to organize business in a way that meets the convenience of everybody.[68]

THE TRACK SYSTEM

Another device sometimes used for scheduling purposes is the track system. The track system was instituted in the early 1970s by Majority Leader Mansfield with the concurrence of the minority leadership and other senators. It permits the Senate to have several pieces of legislation pending on the floor simultaneously by designating specific periods during the day when each proposal will be considered. The system is particularly beneficial when many important bills are awaiting floor action or when a protracted floor debate is taking place on a bill.

Majority Whip Alan Cranston, D-Calif., found that with the two-track system the Senate could "continue to work on all other legislation on one 'track' while a filibuster against a particular piece of legislation is . . . in progress on the other 'track.' " [69] Dual tracking aims to facilitate consideration of "must-do" legislation. Majority Leader Frist said on one occasion that he preferred to move to a dual track process "that will divide the chamber's daily sessions between appropriations bills and reauthorizations." [70] Or, as an acting Democratic leader announced:

> Madam President, we are trying something in the Senate that we have tried on a number of other occasions. . . . We are going to do two bills at one time. It is dual tracking. We are going to take up the Interior Appropriations bill in the morning and go until 12 noon on that legislation. At 12 o'clock, we will have an hour of morning business, and then we will go back to the Homeland Security bill. We will do the same thing on Thursday.[71]

Use of the track system is implemented by the majority leader after obtaining the unanimous consent of the Senate. Or the different tracks can be put into place by agreement between the majority leader and the minority leader. At times, the Senate may operate on triple or quadruple tracks.

The use of unanimous consent agreements and the track system impose a measure of discipline on the Senate. Formerly, senators could arrive in the midst of a debate on a banking bill, for example, obtain recognition from the chair, and launch into a lengthy discussion of the wheat harvest prospects. Today, complex agreements and the track system prevent that from happening. Now, senators generally know what measure will be considered on a specific day and at what time, when they are scheduled to speak on that bill, and how long they will have the floor.

SCHEDULING PROCEDURES COMPARED

The Senate has nothing that compares with the scheduling function of the House Rules Committee.[72] That panel regulates the flow of major bills to the floor, specifies the time for general debate, stipulates whether amendments can be offered, and decides if points of order are to be waived. The legislative route in the House is clearly marked by firm rules and precedents, but that is not so in the Senate. "Rules are never observed in this body," a president pro

TABLE 6-3 Comparison of House Special Rule and Senate Unanimous Consent Agreement

House Special Rule	Senate Unanimous Consent Agreement
Specifies time for general debate	May specify time for debating the bill and amendments offered to the bill
Permits or prohibits amendments	Often restricts the offering of nonrelevant amendments
Formulated by Rules Committee in public session	Formulated by party leaders informally in private sessions; also on the Senate floor
Approved by majority vote of the House	Agreed to by unanimous consent of senators
Adoption generally results in immediate floor action on the bill	Adoption often aimed toward prospective floor action
Covers many aspects of floor procedure	Geared primarily to debate restrictions on amendments and other debatable motions
Does not specify date and exact time for vote on final passage	May set date and exact time for vote on final passage
Effect is to waive House rules	Effect is to waive Senate rules

tempore observed long ago in a bit of an overstatement. "They are only made to be broken. We are a law unto ourselves, and it is entirely immaterial in my judgment whether we have a code of rules or not." [73]

Nonetheless, UCAs and the special rules drafted by the Rules Committee are similar in several respects as Table 6-3 shows. Each waives the rules of the respective chamber to permit timely consideration of important measures and amendments. Each must be approved by the members—in the Senate by unanimous consent of all senators and in the House by majority vote of the representatives. Each effectively sets the conditions for debate on the legislation in question and on all proposed amendments. And special rules and UCAs are formulated with the involvement of party leaders, although such participation in the House is generally limited to the majority party. The House majority leadership usually plays a significant part only for rules on crucial or controversial measures.

Among the more important differences between special rules and UCAs are that rules are considered in public session by a standing committee, whereas UCAs are often negotiated privately by senators and staff aides.

Measures given a rule in the House are commonly taken up almost immediately, but UCAs generally involve prospective action on bills.

The amendment process in each house also makes for important differences. Rules from the Rules Committee may limit the number of permissible amendments or prohibit them altogether. Senate UCAs, except those prohibiting nonrelevant amendments, do not usually limit or forbid floor amendments. Senate practices regard an amendment as relevant—even when it is not relevant to a bill—if it is specifically enumerated in the unanimous consent agreement.

Finally, a special House rule specifies almost every significant floor procedure that will affect consideration of the bill. Complex agreements in the Senate focus on two points in particular: (1) setting limits on the debate time to be allowed for amendments, motions, points of order, and appeals from the rulings of the chair; and (2) structuring the amendment process. In general, procedural experimentation is easier to accomplish in the smaller Senate than in the 435-member House.

NOTES

1. Adam Graham-Silverman, "Senators Leave Piles of Work to Take the Pulse Back Home," *CQ Today,* October 6, 2003, 6.
2. Mark Preston, "Lott Wants Five-Day Workweek," *Roll Call,* May 11, 2000, 1.
3. *Congressional Record,* December 9, 1987, S17474.
4. Cameron Joseph, "Senate Democrats Plan More Legislative Workdays," *The Hill,* December 5, 2006, 6.
5. *Congressional Record,* June 4, 1997, S5277.
6. *CongressDaily* (*National Journal*), July 11, 2003, 6.
7. *Congressional Record,* July 26, 1989, S8870.
8. Shailagh Murray, "On Daschle's Agenda: Getting the Senate to Show Up," *Wall Street Journal,* April 12, 2002, A4.
9. Helen Dewar, "Senate Battle on Child Health Care Symbolizes Kennedy-Lott Power Struggle," *Washington Post,* May 23, 1997, A9.
10. Greta Wodele, "Partisan Rhetoric Rises As Senate Nears Debt Limit Vote," National Journal's *CongressDailyPM,* March 10, 2006, 4.
11. John Stanton, "Frist Plans Another Base Week," *Roll Call,* June 22, 2006, 27.
12. Erin Billings, "Reid Threatens Member COLA," *Roll Call,* June 28, 2006, 1, 30.
13. Erin Billings, "Bush Puts Focus On Nominees," *Roll Call,* May 30, 2006, 17.
14. Norman Ornstein, "Let the End Games Begin," *Roll Call,* September 12, 1994, A23.
15. *Congressional Record,* November 17, 1989, S15948.
16. Charles Babington, "Senators to Gather in Closed Meeting," *Washington Post,* December 9, 2006, A3.
17. *New York Times,* May 21, 1987, B10.
18. *Congressional Record,* March 21, 1980, S2789. Senator Byrd, who wrote a multivolume Senate history, is widely regarded as the premier authority on the chamber's rules and precedents.
19. Each calendar is printed separately. There are also separate executive and legislative *Journals.* The General Orders Calendar is found in the Senate's *Calendar of*

Business, which is printed each day the Senate is in session. Measures on the calendar are assigned a calendar order number. The Senate's *Executive Calendar* appears whenever there is executive business.

20. *Congressional Record,* January 26, 1973, 2301. According to Senate rules, "Any rule may be suspended without advance notice by unanimous consent of the Senate."

21. *Congressional Record,* August 5, 1987, S11293.

22. *Congressional Record,* April 8, 1981, S3618.

23. *Congressional Record,* January 4, 1995, S39.

24. *CQ Daily Monitor,* June 10, 1996, 5.

25. *Congressional Record,* December 10, 1982, S14345.

26. *Congressional Record,* October 14, 1987, S14197.

27. *Congressional Record,* January 9, 1995, S646; and *Congressional Record,* January 11, 1995, S783.

28. *Congressional Record,* January 12, 1995, S858–S859.

29. Edwin Chen and Melissa Healy, "Byrd Dogs Republicans with Stall on GOP Proposals," *Los Angeles Times,* January 18, 1995, A5.

30. David Hosansky, "Chipping Away at Opposition, Senate Passes Mandates Bill," *Congressional Quarterly Weekly Report,* January 28, 1995, 276.

31. Lawrence Evans, testimony before the Senate Committee on Rules and Administration, June 17, 2003, 3. Evans is a professor of political science at the College of William and Mary.

32. Helen Dewar, "For Senators, Soul-Searching about the Rules," *Washington Post,* June 23, 2003, A19.

33. Scholarly interest in holds seems to be on the increase. See C. Lawrence Evans, Daniel Lipinski, and Keith Larson, "The Senate Hold: Preliminary Evidence from the Baker Years" (paper presented at the annual meeting of the Midwest Political Science Association, Chicago, April 2003); and the June 17, 2003, testimony of several political scientists and others before the Senate Rules and Administration Committee. The panel was considering a resolution (S. Res. 151) to eliminate secret holds.

34. *Congressional Record,* February 24, 1986, S1512.

35. *Congressional Record,* June 6, 2006, S5486.

36. *CQ's Daily Monitor,* October 4, 1994, 5. For an informative study of holds, see Toby McIntosh, "Senate 'Holds' System Developing as Sophisticated Tactic for Leverage, Delay," *Daily Report for Executives* (No. 165), Bureau of National Affairs, August 26, 1991, C1–C5.

37. *Congress DailyAM* (*National Journal*), October 5, 1994, 5.

38. *Congressional Record,* December 5, 1985, S16916.

39. *Congressional Record,* March 28, 2006, S2458.

40. *Ibid.,* S2455.

41. Eric Schmitt, "Senator Blocks 850 Promotions in the Air Force," *New York Times,* June 9, 2003, A1.

42. Niels Sorrells, "Craig Loosens His Holds, But Hasn't Given Up His Demand for Those Extra Cargo Planes," *CQ Today,* June 24, 2003, 7.

43. Charles Hurt, "Resolution Seeks to End Holds on Bills," *Washington Times,* June 18, 2003, A5.

44. Lawrence Goodrich, "Congressional Journal," *Christian Science Monitor,* November 28, 1997, 4.

45. *Congressional Record,* August 6, 1992, S11692.

46. *Congressional Record,* March 28, 2006, S2454.

47. *Congressional Record,* June 29, 2006, S7170.

48. Sarah Lueck, "Amid Veto Threat, Senate Poised To Weigh Trio of Stem-Cell Bills," *Wall Street Journal,* July 12, 2006, A4.

49. Greta Wodele, "Dems See Political Gain in Stem-Cell Veto," National Journal's *CongressDailyAM,* July 12, 2006, 1.

50. *Congressional Record,* September 25, 1990, S13803.

51. *CQ Daily Monitor,* October 13, 1999, 2.

52. *CQ Daily Monitor,* October 14, 1999, 5.

53. Floyd Riddick and Alan Frumin, *Senate Procedure: Precedents and Practices* (Washington, D.C.: Government Printing Office, 1992), 1311.

54. *Congressional Record,* February 4, 1992, S872.

55. *Congressional Record,* September 19, 2002, S8899.

56. Unlike simple requests, which are formulated orally, complex unanimous consent agreements are formalized in writing and easily reported to senators by means of the *Congressional Record,* the front page of the daily *Calendar of Business,* and in party whip notices.

57. *Congressional Record,* September 13, 1994, S12793.

58. Steven S. Smith, *Call to Order* (Washington, D.C.: Brookings, 1989), 115.

59. *Congressional Record,* June 1, 1989, S5939.

60. *Congressional Record,* August 9, 1986, S10952–S10955.

61. John Felton, "Senate's Climate of Partisanship Yields an Agreement of Unusual Complexity," *Congressional Quarterly Weekly Report,* August 16, 1986, 1878.

62. *Congressional Record,* August 9, 1986, S10952.

63. *CQ Daily Monitor,* March 8, 1999, 5.

64. *Congressional Record,* March 5, 1999, S2359.

65. Sue Kirchhoff and Sumana Chatterjee, "Flood of Democratic Amendments Stalls Senate's Efforts to Pass Bill on Flexibility in Education Aid," *CQ Weekly,* March 6, 1999, 550.

66. *Congressional Record,* July 23, 2003, S9741–S9742.

67. Keith Perine, "Frist Asks for No-Chance Consent Request," *CQ Today,* July 26, 2003, 1876.

68. *Congressional Record,* July 20, 1990, S10183.

69. *Congressional Record,* January 21, 1975, 928.

70. Ethan Wallison, "Frist Plans Dual Track," *Roll Call,* May 1, 2003, 1.

71. *Congressional Record,* September 3, 2002, S8138.

72. The Senate Rules and Administration Committee has jurisdiction over internal Senate matters but is not involved in scheduling bills for floor debate.

73. *Congressional Record,* December 18, 1876, 266.

CHAPTER 7

Senate Floor Procedure

A VISITOR WHO moves from the House gallery to the Senate gallery is struck immediately by the contrast in atmosphere. The Senate chamber is more sedate, it is quieter, and business is conducted at a more relaxed pace. The chamber is smaller and more intimate. Given their higher visibility and fewer number, senators are more easily recognizable than their House counterparts. Typically, only a handful of senators are present on the floor. The remainder are busy in committee meetings or occupied with constituent or other legislative business. All senators, however, generally arrive on the floor quickly in response to buzzers announcing roll-call votes or quorum calls.

The Senate chamber is ringed by an upper level of galleries for the press, visitors, and dignitaries. Figure 7-1 shows a map of the Senate floor with desks arranged in four semicircular tiers. Each of the one hundred senators has an assigned desk, complete with snuffbox and open inkwell. A broad aisle separates the Republicans, sitting on the right (facing the podium), from the Democrats, on the left. Depending on the makeup of the Senate, more seats may be on one side than the other. The Senate has no electronic voting machines; each senator responds aloud as his or her name is reached during a roll call. Both the Senate and the House employ microphones on the floor, but, unlike representatives, each senator has a microphone.

On the raised platform, the constitutional president of the Senate—the vice president of the United States—presides on expected close votes crucial to administration policy. He may vote only to break a tie. (From 2001 through 2006, Vice President Dick Cheney has cast seven tie-breaking votes. The record is held by Vice President John Adams, 1789–1797, who cast 29 tie-breaking votes.)[1] The vice president usually is not present, however.[2] The Constitution provides for a Senate president pro tempore, elected by that body, to preside in the vice president's absence. (Sometimes, the Senate establishes the post of deputy president pro tempore as well.) The president pro tem usually is the most senior senator of the majority party. (In the 110th Congress, Sen. Robert Byrd, D-W.Va., is the president pro tempore.) In practice, each day's session is chaired by several temporary presiding officers—majority-party senators chosen by the president pro tem to serve on a rotating basis for about an hour.

Neither the president pro tem nor the presiding officer is analogous to the Speaker of the House, in part because neither possesses the political resources to exert such wide-ranging influence in the Senate. (One consequence is that it is not unusual for rulings of the presiding officer to be appealed and over-

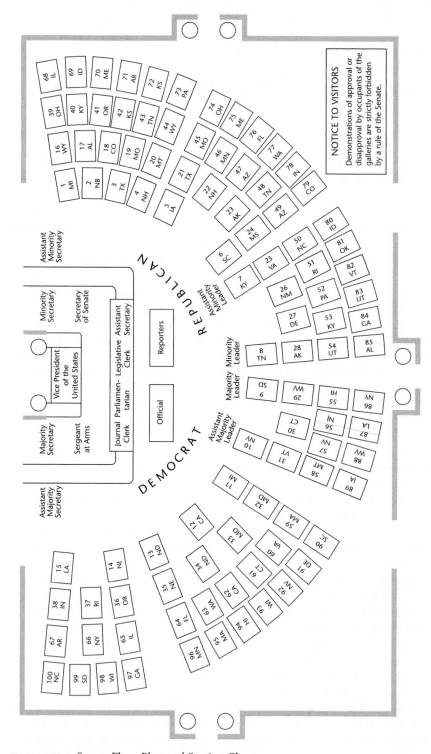

Figure 7-1 Senate Floor Plan and Seating Chart

turned by the Senate; the Speaker's rulings in the House are seldom appealed and virtually never overturned.) The president pro tempore "has never been able to establish his authority as a party leader to the extent of the Majority Leader," said Byrd, the longest serving Senate member in history. (Byrd also served as president pro tem from 1989 to 1995, from June 2001 to January 2003, and since 2007, and as majority leader from 1977 to 1981 and from 1987 to 1989. He was minority leader from 1981 to 1987.) "This is partly the result of the President pro tempore's irregular appointments and uncertain tenure over the years while serving in the absence of the Vice President." [3]

The principal elective leaders of the Senate are to be found at the two front desks on the center aisle, those assigned to the majority and minority leaders. Next to the majority leader and next to the minority leader sit the party whips, second in command in the Senate party hierarchy. These party leaders, or their designees, customarily remain on the floor at all times to protect their party's interests.

The leadership and individual senators are in frequent contact. To a much greater extent than in the House, each member has the power to influence the course of the legislative process on a daily basis. Any senator can disrupt the Senate's consideration of a bill more easily and with more telling effect than any one representative in the House. That this does not occur on a regular basis is a tribute to the operation of the Senate's system of unanimous consent, the skill of party leaders, and the long tradition of trust, accommodation, and reciprocal courtesy among members, which has survived periodic lapses into hard-line partisanship and confrontation.

LEGISLATIVE AND CALENDAR DAYS

The Senate, unlike the House, regularly distinguishes between a calendar day and a legislative day.[4] "Calendar day" is the commonly understood notion of what constitutes a day—the twenty-four-hour period of time. "Legislative day" refers to the period when the Senate convenes after an adjournment and ends when it next adjourns. Recesses and adjournments determine the sequence of legislative days and calendar days. If the Senate adjourns at the end of a daily session, the legislative day ends with that calendar day. If, however, it chooses to recess, the legislative day is carried over to the next calendar day. For example, if the Senate recesses on May 3 and continues that practice for several calendar days, the legislative day remains May 3 even if the calendar day is May 21. However, once the Senate adjourns after a series of recesses, the legislative day and calendar day become the same.

The distinction between the types of days is important because many of the Senate's rules are tied to the legislative day. For example, according to Senate precedents, the "word 'day,' as used in the rules, unless it is specified as a calendar day, is construed to mean a legislative day." [5] The decision to adjourn or recess is made either by unanimous consent (the usual way) or by majority vote (rare) on a motion made by the majority leader. The majority leader's decision to ask for a recess or an adjournment can have some influence on controversial legislation before the Senate (see "morning hour," below). Senate rules prescribe a daily order of business, but it may be followed only when the Senate begins a new legislative day.

DAILY ORDER OF BUSINESS

Under resolutions adopted at the start of each Congress, the Senate generally convenes each day at noon. On the opening day of the 110th Congress, for example, the Senate adopted S. Res. 7, which stated: "*Resolved,* That the hour of daily meeting of the Senate be 12 o'clock meridian unless otherwise ordered." The leadership, by a unanimous consent request or motion, may modify the time on a day-to-day basis to stay abreast of the Senate's workload.

The regular order of business in the Senate after the call to order, as in the House, begins with a prayer followed by the Pledge of Allegiance. Next is leader's time (usually ten minutes each to the majority leader and the minority leader). The majority leader, for example, might state what the Senate is expected to accomplish during that day or make a statement about a substantive matter. If neither leader wants any time, then the Senate typically either permits members who have requested time to make brief statements or resumes consideration of unfinished or new business often under the terms of a unanimous consent agreement.

The Senate, too, must keep and approve a *Journal* of the previous day's activities. The *Journal* usually is "deemed approved to date" by unanimous consent when the Senate adjourns or recesses at the end of each day. Any senator could object to the *Journal*'s approval and propose amendments to it, but this is an exceedingly rare occurrence. (In 1986 the Senate amended its rules to permit a nondebatable motion for the *Journal*'s approval. Previously, reading the *Journal* was sometimes used as a filibustering device.)

At the start of a new legislative day, the first two hours of Senate activity are traditionally called the morning hour—even if this period occurs in the afternoon. (The morning hour is rarely invoked, and recent Senates have not observed it.) Morning business occurs by unanimous consent nearly every day the Senate is in session. Technically, morning business is conducted during the morning hour; it includes the receipt of messages, reports, and communications from the president, the House, and heads of executive branch departments. Bills and resolutions are introduced and referred to committee, committee reports filed, statements inserted in the *Congressional Record,* and brief speeches delivered. As Senator Byrd summarized:

> "Morning business" and the "morning hour" do not mean the same. The morning hour is the first two hours after the Senate convenes following an adjournment. Morning business is that period within the morning hour during which senators may introduce resolutions, bills, petitions, or memorials; committees may report matters, and certain matters come over from the previous day.[6]

Senators may speak during morning business only by unanimous consent, which is why the party leaders usually ask unanimous consent that a period be set aside for the transaction of routine morning business and that senators be allowed to speak therein, often for up to five or more minutes. "[O]ne of the great opportunities that comes with having been elected a Member of the U.S. Senate is to participate . . . in what we call here morning business," said Connecticut senator Joseph I. Lieberman. "I have always seen [it] as the people's forum," he added, "an opportunity to speak on the events of the day, both public and, in some senses, those that are more personal." [7]

The leadership may restrict or change morning business by unanimous consent. (Sometimes, a single calendar day has several morning business periods or an entire day could be consumed by morning business.) Both parties are increasingly using morning business to highlight their partisan agenda and goals. Each party has their communications "war room" and rapid response team to refute partisan attacks.

Noteworthy is that during the morning hour a nondebatable motion to proceed to any item on the calendar also is in order. Rarely is such a motion made during this period. However, if the Senate is in a procedural "hardball" situation, the majority leader may adjourn, rather than recess, the Senate, so he can employ the rarely-used morning hour to call up a measure or matter and obviate at least one filibuster: on the motion to proceed. Even if the majority leader recessed the day before, when the Senate next convened he could adjourn the Senate for one minute, create a new legislative day, and use morning hour to offer the nondebatable motion to take up a measure.

After these preliminaries, the Senate proceeds to unfinished business—legislation pending from a previous day. If there is no unfinished business, the majority leader or that leader's designee receives unanimous consent or offers a motion to take up a new measure that the leadership, after consultation with the minority leader and other interested senators, has scheduled for floor action. This is a critical juncture in the proceedings, for opponents of the bill could begin delaying tactics, such as a filibuster, to prevent it from being considered.

DEBATE IN THE MODERN SENATE

In the early Congresses, the Senate was characterized by protracted debates and great orators: Daniel Webster, John C. Calhoun, and Stephen A. Douglas on slavery, and later by Henry Cabot Lodge and others on the League of Nations. Today, senators are so busy, and the legislative agenda so crowded, that extended give-and-take among numerous senators is the exception rather than the rule. "In this United States Senate it is rare indeed to have one-third of the members present to hear debate," observed a senator. "There is dialogue and debate, but most of it does not take place on the floor under public scrutiny." [8]

Debate still serves to publicize issues, address constituencies, critique executive policies, identify areas of consensus, and influence Senate votes. After one spirited floor session, a senator declared, "I was really undecided on the pending amendment, but [the] Senator so ably presented his case that I will join him" in opposing the amendment.[9] Or as then Senate Minority Leader Harry Reid, Nev., stated after listening to a discussion between two senators: "Mr. President, people wonder if debate helps. This is a perfect example of how. This debate has helped resolve a very contentious issue." [10] However, not all speeches are so persuasive. As another senator said, "There almost never is a mind changed by debate on the floor of the Senate because, for the most part, no one is ever listening." Or senators have already committed themselves before debate begins.

Great debates can capture national attention and mobilize national sentiment on critical issues such as civil rights, terrorism, health care, or Social Security. Debate, too, is used to reshape a party's public image on issues ostensibly owned by the other party or to inoculate a party against campaign attacks. During debate on an education bill, noted a senator, both parties were "rehearsing political attack lines in the event" the education bill failed to pass.[11]

Debate in the modern Senate often consists of prepared speeches perfunctorily read (or inserted in the *Congressional Record* without having been formally delivered before a largely empty chamber).[12] "I am surprised by the lack of deliberation in the World's Greatest Deliberative Body," remarked freshman senator Barack Obama, D-Ill.[13] He further elaborated, "Each of us is speaking to an empty floor and to C-SPAN [the Cable Satellite Public Affairs Network] giving stock speeches." [14]

When intensive debate does occur, it is often among only a handful of senators with special interest in the legislation. To minimize personality clashes, the Senate (like the House) forbids first-person references during debate. "One of the reasons for the rule that a Senator must address another Senator through the Chair and not in the first person," explained Senator Byrd, "is to avoid casting aspersions, and causing acridness in debate and hurt feelings." [15]

Although the Senate is known for its principle of unlimited debate, debate can be restricted on four occasions. First, unanimous consent agreements typically limit debate on, for example, bills, amendments, and various motions. Second, when the Senate invokes cloture (or Rule XXII), debate is limited to a specific number (30) of hours. Third, the motion to table is nondebatable and is often used by floor managers to simultaneously stop debate on and to kill floor amendments. Rarely is a motion to table made on the bill itself, because if the motion were agreed to, it would kill the measure. Fourth, various statutes have debate-limiting features built into them. The Congressional Budget and Impoundment Control Act of 1974, for example, is replete with restrictions on debate, such as a two-hour limit on any amendment to the concurrent budget resolution and a ten-hour limit on the budget conference report.

Unlike the House, where the Speaker's recognition power is discretionary ("For what purpose does the gentlelady rise?"), the Senate presiding officer (addressed as either "Mr. President" or "Madam President") must recognize the first person seeking to speak unless the majority leader, minority leader, or one of the two floor managers is seeking recognition at the same time. Then Senate precedents stipulate that one of the four in the order mentioned has priority. Once a lawmaker is recognized, however, Senate precedents say that that senator may hold the floor for as long as he or she chooses. When senators yield the floor, others may be recognized to speak. The presiding officer may not put the pending measure or matter to a vote if senators are still seeking recognition to speak.

As in the House—even though only a scattering of members are on the floor—a quorum technically is present in the Senate until a member suggests otherwise. Any senator may suggest the absence of a quorum. When this occurs, the presiding officer is obligated to direct the clerk to call the roll of members. In contrast to House practice, the presiding officer may not first count the senators present to determine whether a quorum exists, except during post-cloture proceedings. The calling of the roll is mandatory unless it is dispensed with by unanimous consent.

Quorum calls are commonly employed to give senators time to work out procedural arrangements (positive delay, as opposed to negative delay), such as a unanimous consent agreement, or to give a member scheduled to speak time to reach the floor. (A reading clerk calls the roll of senators very slowly.) "What I would like to do is suggest the absence of a quorum," said a senator, "so that the parties involved here might sit down in the quiet of some room to see exactly how we can get this particular [amendment] to a point where we can vote up or down." [16] Once this is done, further calling of the roll to establish a quorum is dispensed with by unanimous consent. When Lyndon B. Johnson was majority leader (1955–1961), he "would ask for a quorum call and wait, sometimes for close to an hour, while the reading clerk droned slowly through the names. Then, when Johnson was ready for the Senate to resume, he would suspend the calling of the roll." [17] Cumulatively, the Senate spends considerable time on quorum calls—about six weeks of its work year, according to one calculation.[18]

Quorum calls to delay proceedings temporarily are to be distinguished from live quorums. For the latter, a senator insists that at least a majority of the members come to the chamber and answer to their names. It can be a time-consuming process. As one senator observed, "It took almost one hour to round up fifty-one Senators to respond to their names." [19] The two types of quorum calls are distinguished by the different number of bells that ring in members' offices and Senate committee rooms.

If the Senate officially discovers that it lacks a quorum, it has two options: (1) it adjourns (recesses if there is a previous order to that effect), or (2) it votes to instruct the sergeant at arms to request (compel) the attendance of senators—"Mr. President, I move to instruct the Sergeant at Arms to request the attendance of absent Senators."

Television and Debate

In 1986, after years of consideration, the Senate authorized gavel-to-gavel coverage of its floor proceedings, which are carried over C-SPAN. Television has brought about some change in floor debate and activity. Speeches are more numerous, but they are better organized and livelier than before. Senators "are making better speeches," said Senator Byrd. "They are using more gestures and rhetorical flourishes, and it seems to me that overall, the debate has improved from a substantive point of view." [20]

The staff members of senatorial offices regularly monitor the floor debate so they can alert their bosses when issues are being discussed that require their attendance. Senators also watch floor proceedings from their offices, and what they observe may prompt them to go to the floor. "I came here to talk about this amendment," said Senator Reid, because "I watched with interest from my office." He continued: "I was especially impressed with, and was able to watch, the remarks of my colleague." [21] Senators, too, are using more props, graphs, and charts to illustrate their points. Some senators, to attract local media coverage, wait to offer floor amendments until it is prime time back home.

Floor Managers' Role

Floor managers have the major responsibility for guiding legislation to final passage. "I lean on the manager of the bill and the ranking [committee] members to carry the load" on the floor, Senator Byrd once observed.[22] Usually, two floor managers (one from each party from the reporting committee) are assigned per measure. In the case of multiply referred legislation, several majority and minority floor managers may be designated.

Senate floor managers, like their House counterparts, have varied responsibilities. For example, they identify favorable times to schedule their legislation; they negotiate time-limitation agreements on amendments, work to efficiently dispose of them, or develop a manager's package comprised of scores of discrete amendments that can be agreed to by unanimous consent; they may offer amendments to strengthen their bills as well as to counter proposed weakening amendments; they have to respond to any points of order raised against language in the legislation; and they must alert proponents when their support is needed on the floor.

To be sure, strategic calculations are a manager's stock in trade, such as deciding when to offer an amendment at an advantageous time, who to enlist to propose friendly amendments, how to combat unfriendly amendments, or whether to raise a point of order. Points of order can be raised at any time a bill, amendment, or motion is pending before the Senate. The principal exception occurs when the Senate is debating an amendment under a time constraint imposed by a unanimous consent agreement. All time must expire or be yielded back before a point of order can be made.

BILLS CONSIDERED BY UNANIMOUS CONSENT

Unanimous consent agreements (UCA) are crucial to the efficient operation of the legislative process in the Senate. "We aren't bringing [measures] to the floor unless we have [a unanimous consent] agreement," exclaimed a senator. "We could bring child-care legislation to the floor right now, but that would mean two months of fighting. We want to maximize productive time by trying to work out as much as we can in advance [of floor action.]." [23] Box 7-1 shows a typical example of a UCA specifying the bill's number and the terms of its consideration.

BOX 7-1   **Unanimous Consent Agreement**

S. 1042 (Order No. 102)

3.—*Ordered*, That at a time determined by the Majority Leader, with the concurrence of the Democratic Leader, the Senate resume consideration of S. 1042, a bill to authorize appropriations for fiscal year 2006 for military activities of the Department of Defense, for military construction, and for defense activities of the Department of Energy, to prescribe personnel strengths for such fiscal year for the Armed Forces, and for other purposes; provided, that all of the pending amendments be withdrawn and the bill be considered as follows: that only the first degree amendments in order be up to 12 amendments to be offered by each of the two Leaders or their designees; provided further, that the amendments be within the jurisdiction of the Armed Services committee or relevant to the underlying bill; further, that these amendments be subject to second degree amendments which are to be relevant to the amendment to which they are offered.

Ordered further, That the first degree amendments be limited to 1 hour of debate, equally divided in the usual form, with any second degree amendments limited to 30 minutes of debate, equally divided; provided, that the only other amendments in order other than the above listed amendments be the managers' amendments which have been cleared by both managers of the bill.

Ordered further, That there be 2 hours of general debate on the bill divided between the two managers; provided that at the expiration of that time and the disposition of the above amendments, the bill be read a third time and the Senate proceed to a vote on the passage of the bill as amended, if amended, without intervening action or debate. (Oct. 26, 2005.)

SOURCE: Senate of the United States, 109th Congress, *Calendar of Business*, November 2, 2005, 2.

Bipartisan trust is essential to the use of unanimous consent agreements. Occasionally, however, hard feelings can be generated over expectations or interpretations associated with unanimous consent agreements. An especially contentious case involving a major GOP priority occurred soon after Republicans won control of the Congress in the mid-1990s. Many senators expected to vote on February 28, 1995, on final passage of a constitutional amendment to balance the budget (H. J. Res. 1), a major plank in Speaker Newt Gingrich's, R-Ga., Contract with America (ten major proposals all to be considered during the first one hundred days of the 104th House). To the chagrin of opponents, Majority Leader Robert J. Dole, R-Kan., recessed the Senate because he was one vote short of the sixty-seven (or two-thirds) needed to pass a constitutional amendment. "I thought a deal was a deal," complained Minority Leader Tom Daschle, D-S.D.[24]

> The stalling move . . . was technically allowed under the unanimous consent agreement that governed the last several days of the debate. The agreement only promised a final roll call "following the stacked votes" on proposed changes to the amendment on Feb. 28. It did not specify precisely when thereafter the final vote would occur, giving Dole the loophole he needed to claim extra time to search for the 67th vote needed to approve H. J. Res. 1. In addition, a majority leader is traditionally recognized when he calls for the Senate to go into recess.[25]

Dole was unable to find another vote, and the Senate defeated the centerpiece of the GOP's Contract with America. (When the outcome was plain, Senator Dole switched his vote from "yea" to "nay" and entered a motion to reconsider to comply with Senate rules requiring members to be on the prevailing side to be eligible to offer that motion, thus giving the Senate another chance to review and revote on the issue at some time in the future. Dole suggested he would call for another vote if he could round up one more supporter, but he never did.) Although relations between the parties remained tense for some time, the two party leaders of necessity continued to cooperate in crafting unanimous consent agreements.

The complex agreement in Box 7-1, like many others controlling floor action on legislation, reflects several general procedures common to many of these accords. First, the majority leader determines, with the concurrence of the minority leader, when to resume consideration of the defense authorization bill. Second, a limited number (twelve) of relevant amendments are made in order, and each is subject to relevant second-degree amendments. Third, debate limits are imposed on these amendments. Fourth, there are two hours of general debate on the measure, equally divided. Finally, after time has expired and the amendments disposed of, the Senate would proceed to final passage.

Measures governed by UCAs are commonly called up by the majority leader or the majority floor manager. Customarily, the presiding officer recognizes the bill's floor manager, usually the chair of the committee or subcommittee that handled the bill, for a short description of the legislation and its intent. The floor manager is followed by the ranking minority committee or subcommittee member, who presents similarly brief opening remarks. The Senate then is ready to consider and debate amendments to the bill.

THE AMENDING PROCESS

The Senate's amending process provides lawmakers with an opportunity to make changes in the text of a measure or a pending amendment during floor consideration. Although the amending process can be complex, it is subject to certain conditions and principles. These conditions or principles, however, can be waived by unanimous consent of the membership.

Like the House, the Senate distinguishes among types (perfecting or substitute), degrees (first-degree and second-degree), and forms (motions to strike, to insert, or to strike and insert) of amendments. Furthermore, certain factors affect any senator's eligibility to offer floor amendments. One factor is spatial. Are there any limbs (or places) left on the amendment tree? The Senate's volume of precedents, *Senate Procedure: Precedents and Practices*, presents four charts that depict the number of amendments that may be pending at the same time. (The House effectively functions with only one amendment chart.) Which chart (or "amendment tree") is in use on the Senate floor depends on whether the first amendment is a motion to insert (Chart 1); an amendment to strike (Chart 2); an amendment to strike and insert (Chart 3); or a complete substitute—an amendment that replaces the entire text of the pending bill (Chart 4). The simplest tree (Chart 1), used later for illustrative purposes, permits a maximum of three amendments; the most complex tree (Chart 4) allows as many as eleven amendments to be pending simultaneously (a rare occurrence).

Another factor that influences the amending stage is time. Is the amending process regulated by a time-limitation agreement that may specify when or in what order amendments are to be offered and limits debate on each one? Still another factor is contextual. For example, are there formal (the imposition of cloture, for example) or informal (the floor managers want to limit amendments to their bill) circumstances that impinge on the amending process?

Unlike the House, the Senate has neither a Committee of the Whole nor a five-minute rule for debating amendments. The Senate has no closed rules. Any measure is open to virtually an unlimited number of amendments unless a unanimous consent agreement specifies otherwise. In the 108th Congress (2003–2005), nearly 400 amendments were filed to an energy bill. Worth noting is that senators may "file" (handed for printing to a Senate clerk) as many amendments as they want, but they must be called up, or "pending," to be considered in the Senate. The Senate must dispose of all pending amendments, but not those filed but never called up for floor consideration. A recent trend is that hundreds of amendments are often filed on major bills. A knowledgeable congressional journalist explains why.

> Senators and their staffs have become quite adept at stymieing major bills by raising—or threatening to raise—scores or even hundreds of amendments. Senators can

use this little-noticed tool to jam the legislative gears without ever resorting to the musty and old-fashioned filibuster.[26]

Senators also file "placeholder" amendments ("Byrd relevant," for example), which gives them the right to call up their amendments.

Senators, unlike House members in the Committee of the Whole, can modify their own amendments without the need for unanimous consent or the majority approval of the chamber. A senator, for example, might propose an amendment that the floor manager will support if the language is discretionary, not mandatory. The senator can make the change on his or her own authority and facilitate the amendment's chances of being adopted by the Senate. These modifications are permissible until the Senate takes some "action" on the amendment, such as agreeing to take a vote on it or arranging a unanimous consent agreement limiting debate time. Senators sometimes quickly ask for action on their amendments because, even though they lose the right to modify them, they gain the right to offer amendments to their own amendments should the need arise.

Senators must be recognized by the presiding officer before they can offer amendments. Officially reported committee amendments automatically take precedence over those offered by other members from the floor. Committee amendments are subject to further amendment from the floor.

Senators can propose amendments at any time to any section of a bill. This approach differs from the more orderly routine followed by the House, where the rules specify that each part of a measure be considered in sequential order, usually section by section. Senate custom gives individual senators greater leeway in offering and amending legislation. This flexibility means that a senator can eventually force virtually any issue to the floor through amendments and displace the best-laid agenda of any majority leader.

To avoid having senators offer their favorite bill as an amendment to other measures or amendments, a majority leader may promise the lawmaker a specific time when the Senate will consider and vote on the legislation. Amendments must be read by the Senate clerk, but this usually is dispensed with by unanimous consent unless an attempt is being made to delay the bill. Opposed to a bill, a senator said he planned to offer continuous and very long second-degree amendments to the bill and require that each be read in full. "It was a good old-fashioned filibuster," remarked a Senate aide.[27] (For several House-Senate differences in the amending process, see Table 7-1.)

Principle of Precedence

An important concept that shapes the Senate's amending process is precedence. The basic idea is that something, such as a motion, of lower priority cannot displace something of higher priority, but something of higher priority can be offered while something of lower priority is pending. Fundamentally, the principles of precedence determine (1) the number of amendments that may be pending simultaneously and (2) the order in which those amend-

TABLE 7-1 Selected Bicameral Differences in the Amendment Process

House	Senate
Measures read for amendment section by section or title by title	Measures open to amendment at any point, unless a unanimous consent agreement states otherwise
Strict germaneness rule	No general germaneness rule
Amendment rights of members are commonly limited by the Rules Committee	Unlimited freedom for senators to offer amendments, unless unanimous consent agreement stipulates otherwise
Third-degree amendments are prohibited	Third-degree amendments are prohibited, but they can still be offered by unanimous consent
Five-minute rule for discussing amendments	No debate limit for amendments unless imposed by a unanimous consent agreement
Points of order against amendments must be raised after an amendment is read but before debate on it has begun	Points of order against amendments can often be raised at any time
Representatives have no right, in the Committee of the Whole, to modify or withdraw amendments on their own authority	Senators have the right to modify or withdraw their amendments unless action (such as a call for a vote on the amendment) has been taken on it by the Senate

ments will be voted upon. To be sure, amendment theory does not always comport with the realities or practicalities of floor decision making. For example, despite the prohibition against third-degree amendments, third-degrees might be made in order by unanimous consent. Further, the Senate might have dozens of amendments pending simultaneously on the floor. This situation occurs because senators ask and receive unanimous consent to set aside the pending amendments so they can offer theirs.

Two principles of precedence merit review, because they provide useful insight into amendment procedure. The first principle: a first-degree amendment has precedence over a second-degree amendment (an amendment to the first-degree). The second principle: a perfecting amendment takes precedence over a substitute amendment. These principles determine which type of amendment (perfecting or substitute) may be offered when others are pending and the order in which those amendments are voted on. A perfecting amendment is one that alters language, either to the bill or to a pending amendment, but does not seek to substitute new text for the entirety of the pending proposal. Perfecting amendments (which are always motions to strike, to insert, or to strike and insert) have precedence—or priority—over substitutes (always a motion to strike and insert). Thus, if Senator A offers a perfecting amendment to a bill (a first-degree amendment to insert) and Senator B then proposes a second-degree perfecting amendment to it, no other amendments are in order until the second-degree proposal is disposed of. And if the latter is adopted, other second-degree amendments—perfecting or substitute—may be offered until there are no unamended parts to alter.

Alternatively, as depicted in Figure 7-2, Senator B may offer a second-degree substitute for Senator A's amendment to add something to the bill. Then Senator C, under the Senate's principles of precedence, can propose a second-degree perfecting amendment to Senator A's amendment, which would be voted upon before the substitute. The order of offering amendments is the inverse of the order of voting. Thus, the last offered amendment is the first to be voted on.

Lawmakers often calculate where they would like to be on the amendment tree depending in part on whether they want the first or last vote. Knowing that the first amendment is likely to be the target of many amendments, a senator may draft his amendment as second-degree perfecting so it will be voted on first. If a senator believes he has the votes to fend off any attempts at change, he might opt to offer his idea as a first-degree amendment. Predicting the optimal place on the amendment tree can be difficult, because much will depend on broader political dynamics and the kinds of ongoing substantive changes that amendments typically undergo on the floor.

The concept of filling the amendment tree has two meanings. First, as illustrated by the actions of Senator C in Figure 7-2, every available branch of the tree is filled according to the chart in play. Senators, as a result, cannot offer further amendments until a limb comes open. Second, as illustrated by the actions of Senators A and B in the first example, even though a branch of the tree is open, the principles of precedence prevent senators from offering a motion of lower precedence (the second-degree substitute) to a motion of higher precedence (the second-degree perfecting).

Strategic Uses of Amendments

Timing, strategy, lobbying, patience, and skillful drafting are important parts of the amending process. Floor managers and party leaders contemplate a number of questions during the amending phase: Do I want the first vote? Do I want to protect my amendment from further amendments? Do I want to stop further amendments entirely? Prospects for amendments are influenced by these and other considerations, such as filling the amendment tree, the second-degree strategy, the poison-pill approach, or November amendments.

Filling the Amendment Tree. With a Republican majority in the Senate, a well-known congressional journal declared 1999 to be the year of the amendment tree. When Democrats were in the majority, they also did the same thing—but less frequently, they said. (No systematic studies identify the extent of tree building in recent years.) When in the minority, Senate Democrats

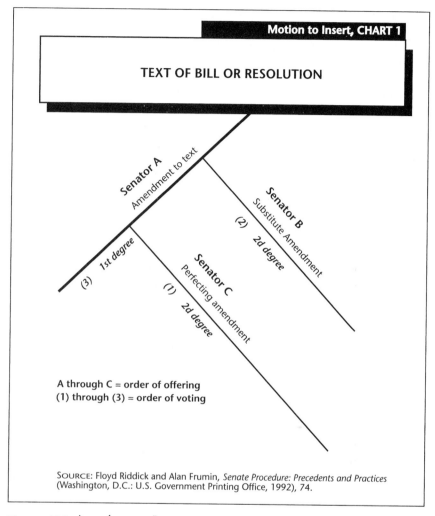

FIGURE 7-2 Amendment to Insert

are on the lookout for openings to offer their policy priorities via floor amendments. "Keep in mind," said the Democratic leader, "we have so few opportunities to talk about our agenda if we can't talk about them in the form of amendments to bills." [28] The majority leader has different goals in managing the Senate. He wants to move the Senate's business without having to contend with nonrelevant minority amendments, and he needs to protect majority senators from having to cast politically troublesome votes.

Although any senator can fill the amendment tree, the majority leader has special advantages if he or she chooses to use this parliamentary tactic. The majority leader is able to fill the tree easily because Senate precedents grant the majority leader preferential recognition. Thus, despite other precedents stating that senators lose the floor when they propose an amendment, the majority leader is able to offer amendment after amendment until the tree is filled. (The ultimate tree is achieved when the majority leader also fills a separate tree on the motion to recommit, or commit, a bill to committee with instructions. In the House, this is a preferential motion for the minority party. In the Senate, however, the motion is higher on the precedence ladder than motions to amend. Thus, the majority leader may fill the tree on a bill and then immediately on the motion to recommit the measure to close off every possibility for minority party amendments.) As a frustrated Democratic senator stated when Majority Leader Bill Frist, R-Tenn., filled the tree on a top GOP priority:

> I checked with the Parliamentarian about the procedural status we are in this morning. I am informed this is the status: We have S. 2062, which is this bill to reform class action [legal] procedures. There is an amendment offered to that by Senator Frist, a perfecting amendment [to insert]. There is a second-degree perfecting amendment offered to that. There is a motion to commit that has been made by Senator Frist. [The amendment tree for a motion to commit is identical to the chart in Figure 7-2.] There is a Frist perfecting amendment to the motion to commit, and there is a Frist second-degree perfecting amendment to the first-degree perfecting amendment to the motion to commit. So the obvious question I put to the Parliamentarian is, what is there that is in order for us to offer at this time for the Senate to consider? The answer is, nothing. Nothing is in order. The tree is full . . . and nothing can be offered.[29]

Filling the tree is a controversial tactic that arouses the anger and frustration of senators, especially those in the minority party. Therefore, it is not an everyday occurrence, but one that is used to achieve different purposes, such as forcing votes on issues or protecting a bill from divisive amendments that might fracture support for the legislation. Often, its primary purpose is to prevent the minority party from offering controversial nonrelevant amendments that can attract public attention away from the majority's priorities.

Second-Degree Strategy. The second-degree strategy is relatively easy to employ by any senator, but especially the majority leader because of that leader's priority of recognition. The idea is that every time a senator offers a first-degree amendment, another senator comes after to propose a second-degree amendment that may prevent an up or down vote on the first-offered amendment. Recall that under the principles of precedence, second-degree amendments are voted on before first-degree amendments, and, if adopted, they may replace or wipe out the first-degree proposition. Second-degree amendments are employed for various political reasons, such as fending off unwanted propositions or providing political cover to senators.

Senators understand that second-degree amendments, if adopted, can undermine the intent or purpose of the first-degree proposal. To counter this tactic, according to a Senate procedural expert, minority lawmakers since the mid-1990s began to insist that second-degree amendments be transformed into two first-degree amendments so senators could get a "clean" vote on each of their first-degree proposals.[30] Senators often call this approach "side-by-side" amendments.[31] Even if both first-degrees are adopted and they contradict each other, no Senate rule or precedent prohibits inconsistent amendments. These kinds of conflicts are typically resolved in conference with the other chamber.

Poison-Pill Approach. One strategy of a bill's opponents is to load down the legislation with controversial amendments, possibly sparking a filibuster and jeopardizing Senate passage. "Overweight the plan, sabotage it with an unrealistic amendment," and that will ensure defeat of the legislation, noted a senator.[32] Another senator said about a bill he opposed, "If this amendment worsens it a little more, then I'm for it." [33] A third senator explained that the way you kill a bill is with "nongermane amendments that are called killer amendments or poison pills, because they are political amendments one side or the other does not want." [34] But as in the House, senators also employ amendments as "sweeteners" to entice colleagues to vote for their legislation.

November Amendments. Senators turn up the political heat on colleagues as the November elections get closer. A senator pointed out that amendments were being offered to one measure "with only one and only one purpose in mind. Let us be realistic. [This] is an opportunity for Senators on either side of the aisle, whether it be Democrats or Republicans, to develop ammunition to be used in some 30-second spot ad in the next political campaign. These votes are not about substance. They are strictly about politics, positioning, window dressing, and so forth." [35] The reverse approach is to work to avoid troublesome votes. A Democratic minority leader complained that the majority leader was protecting Republicans who had close November election contests from having to cast votes on issues that might cost them support back home. "They don't want to have votes on anything but naming airports," declared the minority leader. The majority leader's spokesman replied: "The Democrats are just frustrated because we aren't voting on the things they want to vote on. Welcome to the minority." [36] Both parties allow senators in tight election contests to offer popular amendments that could win them votes back home.

Voting on Amendments

The Senate has three types of voting: voice, division (standing), and roll call. Voice and division voting are similar to House procedures, but the Senate has nothing comparable to the electronic voting procedures of the House. But the system of buzzers that summons senators to the floor for a vote is much like that of the House.

During a roll call, members respond "yea" or "nay" as their names are called alphabetically. The Senate establishes the length of time for roll-call votes at the start of each Congress. When the 110th Congress convened on January 4, 2007, the Senate agreed by unanimous consent

[t]hat for the duration of the 110th Congress, there be a limitation of 15 minutes each upon any roll call vote, with the warning signal to be sounded at the midway

point, beginning at the last 7 1/2 minutes, and when roll call votes are of 10-minute duration, the warning signal be sounded at the beginning of the last 7 1/2 minutes.

When votes are grouped back to back, referred to as stacking, the second and succeeding votes often occur, by unanimous consent, at ten-minute intervals. Prior to each vote in a stacked sequence, each side customarily is allowed at least one minute to explain what the issue is about.[37]

Party leaders and floor managers make every effort to ensure that their supporters are on the floor when needed for a vote. "My experience convinces me," commented Senator Byrd, that voting "is the most critical step in the legislative process. . . . [The leaders and the floor managers must] have the right members at the right place and at the right time." [38] As President Lyndon Johnson told advocates pressing for legislation from Congress: "[Y]ou can get anything you want if you've got the votes. How many votes have you got?" [39]

Recorded votes in the Senate usually can be obtained easily; only a sufficient second—one-fifth of the senators present—is needed, with a minimum of eleven as required by the Constitution. If the minimum number is not on the floor at the time the request is made, a senator can summon other colleagues through a quorum call, try to get their support, and then renew the request for a roll-call vote. As Byrd explained: "If any Senator wants a roll-call vote around here, he will ultimately get it. If he does not get it at first, he will put in a quorum and he will not let us call off the quorum. So we have to have a live quorum or give him the yeas and nays." [40] Most roll calls occur on amendments.

Casting Procedural Votes. On controversial amendments, members often maneuver for procedural, instead of substantive, votes. A vote to table (kill) amendments or other motions is a classic ploy to avoid being recorded directly on politically sensitive policy issues. Senator Byrd has explained the difference:

> A motion to table is a procedural motion. It obfuscates the issue, and it makes possible an explanation by a Senator to his constituents, if he wishes to do so, that his vote was not on the merits of the issue. He can claim that he might have voted this way or he might have voted that way, if the Senate had voted up or down on the issue itself. But on a procedural motion, he can state he voted to table the amendment, and he can assign any number of reasons therefor, one of which would be that he did so in order that the Senate would get on with its work or about its business.[41]

Therefore, if a procedural vote can be arranged to kill or delay a controversial bill, it is likely to win the support of senators who may prefer to duck the substantive issue. Moreover, senators generally support the party leadership on procedural votes. As one senator has pointed out, on a procedural vote, members "traditionally stick with the leadership." [42]

Part of members' consideration in casting procedural or substantive votes involves the role of such votes in political campaigns. Votes are not used simply to make decisions or as trading material; they also are used by interest group organizations, who select issues of concern to them to characterize legislators as heroes or zeroes, depending on how members voted on the groups' legislative priorities.

Votes are also used to test sentiment for or against amendments or legislation. A key test vote might occur on a motion to table (kill) an amendment or to take up a bill. A lopsided vote for an amendment might provide the momentum required to get it through the House. Sometimes unanimous consent agreements impose a sixty-vote requirement for the adoption of two competing amendments—a "parliamentary convenience recognizing that both sides could have used procedural tactics that would have required the other party to muster 60 votes." [43]

Like the House, the Senate permits vote pairing, either live or dead pairs. In a live pair, one senator is present on the floor during the vote. The practice is for the senator to cast a vote, "yea" or "nay," then withdraw it and announce, "I have a pair with the senator from [naming the state]. If he were present and voting, he would vote ["yea" or "nay"]. If I were at liberty to vote, I would vote ["yea" or "nay"]." In a dead pair, both senators are absent from the floor. Their positions are published after each roll call in the *Congressional Record*. Live and dead pairs are not tabulated on roll-call votes, but a live pair can affect the outcome of a vote.

Explained Senator Byrd:

> The arranging of pairs has been decisive from time to time on very close votes, because it is possible to pair off enough present Senators to affect the outcome of the vote and perhaps make a difference of 1 or 2 votes which, had the Senators present not been paired, would have decided the issue opposite to the outcome that resulted.[44]

Senators generally will not agree to give a live pair except on the condition that the outcome is not changed by virtue of the pair given.[45]

Final Action on a Bill

"When no Senator seeks recognition," Senator Byrd explained, "the Chair automatically puts the question of adoption of amendments and passage of bills." [46] Unlike the House, which has procedures for bringing measures to a final vote, so long as any senator wishes to be recognized to discuss a debatable proposition, a vote on final passage cannot occur. Typically, once the amending process is completed the Senate proceeds to a vote on final passage, unless a UCA has been made setting a later date and time for the final vote. The floor manager announces that no further amendments are pending. He or she then requests a third, and final, reading of the bill. The presiding officer orders the bill engrossed—put in the precise form in which it emerged from the Senate's amending process—and read a third time (the title of the bill only), a procedure that takes only a few seconds. Then the question is put on final passage of the measure.

The final vote is not over until the chair announces the outcome. Senate rules prohibit "any Senator from voting after the Chair has announced the decision," Senator Byrd pointed out. Senate rules provide "that the Chair cannot even entertain a unanimous consent request to suspend this rule." [47] Senators, like House members, may change their vote during the regular fifteen-minute voting period, which is a minimum and not the maximum time allowed. For example, during an unusually lengthy Senate roll call dozens of senators switched their votes and defeated a proposal offered by a senator. "I just want to announce that Dr. Cary's in his office for everyone whose arm is out of socket," exclaimed the senator.[48] (Dr. Freeman Cary was the Senate physician.)

After the result of the final vote on the bill has been announced, one more parliamentary step is required before Senate action is complete. This step is available only to the side that prevailed on the final vote. If the bill is passed, a senator who voted for the bill, or who did not vote, makes a motion to reconsider the vote. On a voice or standing vote, any senator can offer the motion. (The motion is in order that day or the next two days of session. Sometimes the majority leader, per the earlier Dole example, will "enter" a motion to reconsider which means that he can determine when, or if, he may try at some future date during that Congress to trigger a revote on the measure or matter.) Immediately after the motion to reconsider is offered, another proponent of the bill moves to table it. By this procedural device Senate rules protect the bill from further consideration. Rarely does the motion to table fail. This procedure also is used after votes on amendments. The House procedure is basically identical, except for the idea of "entering" the motion to reconsider.

BILLS WITHOUT UNANIMOUS CONSENT

Sometimes party leaders are unable to achieve unanimous consent agreements. This may happen for a variety of reasons: intense opposition to the bill by certain senators, a general desire for unrestricted debate and amendment, commitments by some senators to protect the interests of absent colleagues, or personal pique of some senators against party leaders. Passage of legislation then becomes a much more difficult task. Debate will be extensive and amendments will be numerous. Operating under the Senate's rules, this can be extremely time-consuming. Moreover, if one or more senators are intensely opposed to a bill, the well-known device of the filibuster may be threatened (like holds, this is another version of the silent filibuster) or actually used.[49] In the days leading up to scheduled recesses or at the end of legislative sessions, the threat or use of filibusters is especially effective.

Determining when extended debate becomes a filibuster can be difficult, because a senator does not make a motion to filibuster a bill. Extended debate may occur because the issue warrants lengthy discussion. Extended debate also may occur because senators intend to stall action on measures. How to determine senators' intent during debates is often not an easy task. Senator Byrd once said, "I will be able to perceive one, because I know one when

I see it." [50] There are a lot of senators, he added, "who wouldn't know a filibuster if they met one on the way home . . . or if they met it in the middle of the road." [51]

Long viewed as the tool of last resort, today the threat of a filibuster is part of the Senate's daily life. Lengthy or around-the-clock filibusters are largely a thing of the past. In the contemporary Senate, as a former Senate Parliamentarian noted, "there is very little distinction between a filibuster and a threat to filibuster. Any credible threat to filibuster is treated as if it were a filibuster because the Majority Leader, who has limited time in which to work, must regard it as such. Thus, the filibuster is largely silent, invisible, and relatively painless to the minority." [52] Or, as a senator put it, "you don't have to talk to filibuster." [53]

Filibuster threats send signals to the majority leadership that sixty votes (to invoke cloture) may be needed to pass legislation. The Senate, unlike the House, is a supermajoritarian institution, because sixty votes—three-fifths of the membership—are commonly required to enact major and controversial legislation. The political reality often is, as a majority leader observed, that "everything in this Senate needs 60 votes." [54] Another senator said: "It isn't good enough to have the majority. You've got to have 60 votes." [55] Little surprise that many commentators call it the "sixty-vote Senate." The filibuster (real or threatened) is a source of leverage for any senator. "The power to block the other person's bill gives you the power to influence the content," noted Sen. Thad Cochran, R-Miss.[56]

The Filibuster

Generally characterized in the public mind as a nonstop speech, a filibuster in the fullest sense employs every parliamentary maneuver and dilatory motion to delay, modify, or defeat legislation. Asked for filibustering pointers by a colleague, one senator said: "If it takes unanimous consent, object. If not, you make a little speech, suggest the absence of a quorum, then . . . use parliamentary procedures[,]. . . motions to adjourn, motions to recess." He added: "You have to have the floor protected 100 percent of the time." [57]

More has been written about extended debate in the Senate than about any other congressional procedure. Hollywood even glamorized the filibuster in the 1939 movie *Mr. Smith Goes to Washington*, starring Jimmy Stewart. The filibuster permeates virtually all senatorial decision making. Measures might not be reported from committee or scheduled for floor action because senators are threatening a filibuster. "In many instances, it's the threat of a filibuster that keeps a bill from coming up," observed Senator Byrd.[58]

The filibuster has long been part of the Senate, but unrestricted debate aroused little concern during much of the nineteenth century. The number of senators was small, the workload was limited, and lengthy deliberations could be accommodated more easily. Since Rule XXII (cloture) was adopted in 1917, the number of filibusters has varied over time. Scholars have identified three distinct filibuster periods.

The first lasts from roughly 1917 to 1937, in which the number of filibusters per Congress averages about 4.1. That period is followed by a quiet period between 1937 and 1968, where the mean number of filibusters is 2.1. In the 1970s, however, filibustering reaches new levels, before mushrooming in the 1980s and 1990s. Indeed, over the past twelve [89th to 101st] congresses, the number of filibusters has averaged 17.6.[59]

Defenders of the filibuster say it is needed to prevent bad bills from becoming law, protect minority rights against majority steamrollers, ensure thorough analysis of legislation, and dramatize issues for the public. As Senator Byrd put it:

> One of the things that makes the United States Senate the unique upper body that it is is the ability to talk at great length. And there have come times when the protection of a minority is highly beneficial to a nation. Many of the great causes in the history of the world were at first only supported by a minority. And it's been shown time and again that the minority can be right. So this is one of the things that's so important to the liberties of the people. As long as a people have a forum in which members can speak at length, the people's liberties will be safe.[60]

Opponents argue that the filibuster thwarts majority rule, delays or kills legislation, brings the Senate into disrepute, and permits small minorities to extort unwarranted concessions in bills supported by Senate majorities. Exasperated by the blocking actions of a dozen filibustering senators near the close of a session, a majority leader declared in frustration, citing an earlier test vote: "Only in the United States Senate and only in the last few days of a session can 85 Senators vote one way: Yes, for this bill; 12 Senators vote another way: No, against the bill—and the no's prevail." [61] Senator Byron Dorgan, D-N.D., said on another occasion: "The only thing it's easy to do in the Senate is slow things down. The Senate is 100 human brake pads." [62]

These pro and con arguments highlight a dilemma: how to strike a balance between the right to debate and the need to decide. There is no easy answer. (Analysts sometimes suggest that the Senate gives too much weight to minority prerogatives while the House overemphasizes majority rule.) What is apparent is that the filibuster is a powerful bargaining device. Even the possibility of its use can force compromises in committee or on the floor. Senators of widely diverse viewpoints have resorted to it from time to time or have threatened to use it in order to influence legislation.

Every measure faces at least two primary filibusters: the first on the motion to take up the legislation and the second on consideration of the bill itself. The 1964 civil rights bill filibuster consumed sixteen days on the motion to take up the measure and fifty-seven days on the legislation itself. Those filibusters were unique in that they marked the first time the Senate had ever voted to end an extended debate on a civil rights bill. (Strom Thurmond set the filibuster record when he was a Democrat by talking for twenty-four hours and eighteen minutes against the 1957 civil rights bill.)

Wider Use of Filibusters. Before the 1970s, conservative senators—often southern Democrats who used extended debate to defeat or delay civil rights measures—were almost the only users of filibusters. Recent decades witnessed an increase in the overall number of filibusters, including those conducted by moderate and liberal senators in each party. The filibuster is a "parliamentary tool available to liberals and conservatives who wish to dramatize issues in the only forum of our national government that provides for thorough analysis and unhurried consideration of proposed public laws." [63]

Furthermore, filibusters (and threats of filibusters) are occurring on issues of great national importance and visibility as well as on a wide range of less momentous topics. Lamented a majority leader:

> Not long ago the filibuster or threat of a filibuster was rarely undertaken in the Senate, being reserved for matters of grave national importance. That is no longer the case. . . . The threat of a filibuster is now a regular event in the Senate, weekly at least, sometimes daily. It is invoked by minorities of as few as one or two Senators and for reasons as trivial as a Senator's travel schedule.[64]

Several factors account for the increase in filibusters. First, new senators (many of whom are former House members socialized by rough partisan politics) prefer to push their own agendas even if the Senate's institutional activities grind to a halt. On occasion, one senator noted, senators are "determined to follow [their] own perspective even to the perversion, the distortion, and the destruction of the [legislative] process." [65]

Second, filibusters have enhanced potency in an institution that is workload-packed and deadline-driven. Insufficient time is available to accommodate the manifold claims on the Senate's agenda. Thus, senators who simply indicate their intention to filibuster can exercise significant leverage. In addition, the tactic of ending filibusters by exhaustion is no longer a realistic option in today's Senate. The time demands on senators are too large for them to wait out the filibusterers. "Electoral demands are quite severe, both in terms of senators' need to spend time in their home states as well as the perpetual drive to raise campaign funds." [66]

Third, the internal incentives (the "get-along, go-along" approach, for example) that fostered deference to seniority and party leaders are gone. Richard F. Fenno Jr., a noted congressional scholar, has studied how the 1950s Senate evolved from a "communitarian" institution, where senators were expected to use extended debate sparingly and only for high-stakes national issues, to today's "individualistic" Senate. He found that with "more openness, more media visibility, more candidate-centered elections," more interest groups, more political obligations, and more staff, Senate newcomers are independent entrepreneurs unwilling to submerge their personal and political objectives "to the norms of any collectivity." [67] Senators have increased incentives for obstructive behavior, such as from specialized groups that may encourage members to launch or threaten filibusters in exchange for campaign funds and support. When Lyndon B. Johnson was majority leader, he exercised tight control over floor proceedings, including use of the filibuster.

> While Johnson went to great lengths to avoid filibusters, once they had begun . . . he tended to regard filibusters as a personal challenge to his stewardship. Instead of making an end run around the combatants . . . he often preferred to break the filibuster by keeping the Senate in session for long hours, even around the clock, and forcing the minority ultimately to give up in exhaustion.[68]

By contrast, contemporary party leaders may accommodate filibustering senators who have meetings to attend back home.

Fourth, partisanship has contributed to gridlock and stalemate in the Senate. According to two scholars, "As the two parties became internally more cohesive and the differences between them grew larger, holding together a party-backed filibuster became significantly easier." [69]

Ending a Filibuster. Besides mistakes that cause filibustering senators to lose the floor, two interrelated and broad methods of ending a filibuster are by informal compromise or by the formal Senate procedure used to terminate debate called cloture.[70] Frequently, cloture cannot be obtained unless compromises are made. Party leaders sometimes try "shuttle diplomacy" between the two sides to avoid full-scale filibusters.[71]

Informal Compromise. The threat of filibusters can encourage policy-making compromises. During a filibuster, senators may meet in the cloakroom—off the Senate floor—or in the offices of the party leaders to conduct negotiations, which can go on day and night. The process may take several days or even weeks, depending on how controversial the bill is. If compromise fails, the odds increase that opponents of the legislation will win the battle and thus sidetrack the bill indefinitely. Alternatively, proponents may invoke cloture.

Cloture. After decades of determined resistance by many senators, the Senate in 1917 adopted Rule XXII, which gave the Senate the formal means—cloture—to end extended debate. Until that time, debate could be terminated only by unanimous consent, an impossibility in the face of a filibuster, or exhaustion. In 1893 Sen. Orville Platt, R-Conn., stated:

> There are just two ways under our rules by which a vote can be obtained. One is by getting unanimous consent—the consent of each Senator—to take a vote at a certain time. Next comes what is sometimes known as the process of "sitting it out," that is for the friends of a bill to remain in continuous session until the opponents of it are so physically exhausted that they can not struggle any longer.[72]

Unanimous consent and exhaustion have been the hardy perennials of Senate procedure.

What finally prompted the Senate to adopt Rule XXII was a filibuster that killed a bill to arm U.S. merchant ships against attacks by German submarines. President Woodrow Wilson strongly criticized the filibuster and called a special session of the Senate, which adopted the cloture rule on March 8, 1917, five weeks before war was declared.

Under Rule XXII a cloture petition signed by sixteen senators first must be filed with the presiding officer (see Box 7-2 and Box 7-3). (A senator who is holding the floor can be interrupted by a colleague so he or she can present the cloture petition. The petition, or cloture motion, must be presented when the bill or amendment to which it is directed is pending before the Senate.) Two days later, and one hour after the Senate convenes, the presiding officer must ascertain (unless waived by unanimous consent) whether a quorum is present. That having been established, the presiding officer is obliged to ask, "Is it the sense of the Senate that the debate shall be brought to a close?" A vote is held immediately. If three-fifths of the entire Senate membership (sixty of one hundred members) vote in favor, cloture is invoked. Thereafter, there is an additional thirty hours of debate with senators permitted to speak for no more than one hour on a first-come, first-served basis. Rule XXII also stipulates that first-degree amendments must be filed by 1:00 p.m. on the day following the filing of the cloture petition; second-degree amendments also must be filed in a timely manner—until one hour prior to the cloture vote. Before 1975, when the current three-fifths rule was adopted, a two-thirds majority of those senators present and voting was required to invoke cloture. (The two-thirds requirement still applies to proposals to amend the Senate's rules.)

No limit has been placed on the number of times cloture can be sought on a single piece of legislation. The record for cloture votes is eight, which occurred during the 100th Congress on a bill to limit campaign expenditures for Senate general election races. Majority Leader Byrd had made the spending-limit measure a priority, but Senate action was stymied by a three-month, GOP-led filibuster. Seven cloture votes were held in 2003 on a controversial federal circuit court nomination, Miguel Estrada, before he withdrew his name from consideration. This nomination and several others sparked unusual partisan acrimony as Senate Democrats used the filibuster to challenge President George W. Bush and Senate Republicans over who would control the ideological balance of power on federal courts.

Today, cloture is often used for purposes unrelated to ending talkathons. (Thus, counting the number of cloture votes is not a good indicator of how many filibusters occur in any year.) It is not unusual for a majority leader to file a cloture motion on a measure (or the motion to proceed) immediately after asking the Senate to consider a certain bill. The majority leader may then bring other matters to the floor, leaving the clotured bill in a state of parliamentary limbo (not subject to debate or amendment) until the Senate votes two days later on whether to invoke Rule XXII. A minority leader railed against this practice. "There is a time and a place for cloture," he said on one occasion, "but that time and place is not as soon as the bill is laid down." [73] On another occasion, he lamented: "I am reminded, again, as we file cloture, that the motion to invoke cloture is a motion to end debate. I am always amused by that phrase, 'end debate.' How do you end debate that you haven't even started?" [74]

Box 7-2   A Cloture Motion

Mr. REID. Mr. President, . . . I send to the desk a cloture motion on the bill.

The PRESIDING OFFICER. The cloture motion having been presented under rule XXII, the Chair directs the clerk to read the motion.

The legislative clerk read as follows:

CLOTURE MOTION

We, the undersigned Senators, in accordance with the provisions of rule XXII of the Standing Rules of the Senate, do hereby move to bring to a close the debate on S. 1 Transparency in the Legislative Process, as amended.

Harry Reid, Dianne Feinstein, Joseph Lieberman, Tom Carper, Ken Salazar, Robert Menendez, Patty Murray, Jon Tester, Jack Reed, Joe Biden, Debbie Stabenow, Daniel K. Akaka, Benjamin L. Cardin, Dick Durbin, Ted Kennedy, Evan Bayh.

SOURCE: *Congressional Record*, January 12, 2007, S503.

There are infrequent occasions when the minority leader will file a cloture petition. This is unusual because it is typically the majority party that is trying to invoke cloture on the dilatory actions of the minority leader and his partisan colleagues. Minority leaders may, however, file a cloture petition to force votes on issues of political and substantive significance. For example, Minority Leader Reid filed cloture on a major immigration reform bill in 2006 to prevent unwanted amendments from undermining the integrity of a bipartisan reform package favored by Democrats and many Republicans, but not Majority Leader Frist.[75] Reid's cloture motion failed to attract sixty votes, but, in the end, the Senate passed immigration reform legislation supported by both Reid and Frist.

In a Senate grown more individualistic and partisan, the majority leader will employ cloture to prevent filibusters or other dilatory actions. But that leader often has another objective in mind: to prevent the minority party from offering their priorities as nonrelevant amendments to the pending bill. If invoked, Rule XXII requires all amendments to be germane to the bill. "For the information of all Senators," said Sen. John W. Warner, R-Va., at the instruction of the majority leader, "a cloture motion was just filed on the [Defense Department] authorization bill in an effort to keep the bill free from extraneous matters."[76] In a Senate closely divided by party, the majority leader is unlikely to attract the required sixty votes, but this may set the stage for continued negotiations between the two sides on how to structure the floor amendment process. Cloture, too, is used to test sentiment for or against a

---

Box 7-3   Ending a Senate Filibuster

Cloture

Day 1 Petition signed by sixteen members.
Day 2 First-degree amendments are to be filed by 1 p.m.
Day 3 Second-degree amendments are to be filed until one hour before the
      cloture vote.

A constitutional three-fifths (or sixty) vote is required to invoke cloture in
the one-hundred-member chamber. A two-thirds vote is required to invoke cloture on proposals to change Senate rules.

Postcloture

- Thirty-hour debate limit with time counted for votes, quorum calls, and
  other matters.
- Amendments must be germane.
- One-hour debate per senator.
- Presiding officer can rule out dilatory motions on his or her own initiative
  without waiting for a point of order.
- The measure on which cloture has been invoked remains the unfinished
  business of the Senate to the exclusion of all other business.

---

measure, expedite action on legislation, permit party position-taking on issues, or, if it is invoked, keep unwanted amendments off the floor.

A marked increase in attempts to invoke cloture has characterized recent
Congresses. For example, the decade 1961–1971 saw 5.2 cloture votes per
Congress,[77] whereas during the 107th Congress (2001–2003) alone, there
were 61 cloture votes. The number of cloture petitions filed on the leader's
motion ("I move to take up S. 1234") to proceed to legislation or nominations has increased as well. From only two cloture motions filed during the
96th Congress (1979–1981), the 1990s regularly saw cloture motions in the
double digits on the leader's motion to bring legislation to the floor. The high-
water mark was thirty-five cloture petitions filed during the 102d Congress
(1991–1993) on the leader's motion to take up measures or matters.

In testimony presented to a congressional joint reorganization committee,
a majority leader highlighted the obstacle course that legislation must complete if opposition to it is strong.

> When a filibuster occurs or is threatened, a cloture motion to terminate debate must
> be filed. The vote on that motion cannot occur until two days after it is filed. So if a
> cloture motion were filed today, Tuesday, the vote on it would occur on Thursday.
> If three-fifths or more vote to invoke cloture, there are still up to thirty hours of de-
> bate on the motion, post-cloture, or effectively two more days. So right now under

Senate rules, cloture could be required up to six separate times on a single bill: on the motion to proceed to the bill, on the committee substitute, on the bill itself, and then . . . three times to get to conference with the House—[on the motions (1) to insist on Senate amendments, or disagree to House amendments, (2) to request a conference with the House, or (3) to authorize the chair to appoint conferees].[78]

Periodically, frustration with dilatory tactics gives rise to attempts to change Rule XXII. For example, Majority Leader Frist's frustration with Democratic attempts to block President Bush's judicial nominations prompted him to introduce a proposal (S. Res. 138) to amend the Senate's cloture rule. My "remedy is narrow, aimed not against the filibuster generally, but against filibusters on nominations," he said. If adopted, the proposal "would have declining cloture requirements of 60, 57, 54, 51, and then a simple majority on successive cloture votes." [79]

Frist also contemplated a parliamentary "nuclear option" to end the partisan stalemate over judicial nominations by forcing their approval by majority vote. Under one version of this parliamentary maneuver, Frist would raise a point of order that further debate on a judicial nominee is dilatory and out of order and a vote on the judicial nominee should occur within a certain number of days or hours. The president of the Senate (Vice President Dick Cheney) would sustain the point of order, thereby setting aside and disregarding the Rule XXII (or sixty-vote) procedure for ending the talkathon. No doubt a Democratic senator would appeal the ruling of the presiding officer, and Frist would then move to table (or kill) the appeal. If the nondebatable tabling motion had been agreed to, the Senate would have set a new precedent for ending judicial filibusters by majority vote.[80] The Frist-led Republicans contended that filibusters impose an unconstitutional supermajority requirement—invoking cloture to end a talkathon—for the confirmation of judges. Judgeships, they say, should be subject to an up-or-down majority vote. Democrats responded that the Constitution authorizes each chamber to "determine the rules of its proceedings," which today means a sixty-vote requirement to end a filibuster under Senate Rule XXII. If cloture is invoked, then senators have a right to confirm judges by majority vote. (Democrats opposed several of Bush's judicial nominees on the ground that they were right-wing extremists; Republicans contended they were in the judicial mainstream.)

Frist and Reid negotiated for months to reconcile their fundamental disagreements over how judicial nominees are to be considered by the Senate. Talks broke off in mid-May 2005 with Frist making it clear that he would pull the nuclear trigger if Democrats filibustered a controversial judicial nominee he planned to call up for the Senate's consideration. (Although GOP Senator Trent Lott, R-Miss., coined the term "nuclear option," Republicans call the parliamentary maneuver the "constitutional option," because the word nuclear implies that something bad was to happen in the Senate.) Senate Democrats promised that if Frist used the nuclear option, the parliamentary fallout would be so severe as to produce gridlock in senatorial decision making except for the most essential measures.

In the end, an ad hoc group of senators—seven Democrats and seven Republicans—came up with a compromise that avoided use of the nuclear, or constitutional, option. This so-called "gang of fourteen" signed a memorandum of understanding on judicial nominations, a key part of which stated that the seven Republicans would not support use of the nuclear option and the seven Democrats would not filibuster judicial nominees except under "extraordinary circumstances." [81] This ambiguous phrase was not defined, but the test for what it means in practice probably depends largely on whether President Bush selects polarizing figures for the federal bench.

Once cloture is invoked, filibusters by amendment are broken, and other delaying tactics have ended, the Senate proceeds to a final vote on the bill under consideration. If obstructionist tactics cannot be stopped, the leadership may withdraw the bill and proceed to other business. While frustrating floor action is relatively easy, Senate rules make it difficult to bottle up measures in committees and prevent them from reaching the floor.

PROCEDURES TO CIRCUMVENT COMMITTEES

Bypassing committees, while not an everyday occurrence in the Senate, is easier to accomplish in that chamber than in the House. House members have access to various procedures for bringing to the floor bills that are blocked in committee, including the discharge petition, the power of extraction by the Rules Committee, and the suspension of the rules procedure. Yet, except for suspension, which generally is used for relatively noncontroversial bills, these procedures are seldom employed and rarely successful.

In the Senate, at least four techniques are available: (1) proposing nonrelevant amendments, also known as riders; (2) placing House-passed and Senate-introduced bills immediately on the Calendar of General Orders; (3) suspending Senate rules; and (4) implementing the discharge procedure. The first two are the most effective. The latter two are rarely used.

Technically, there is yet one other way to bypass a Senate committee: by unanimous consent. The Senate can do almost anything it wants by unanimous consent. However, unanimous consent will not be obtained if a single member—presumably a member of the committee that would be bypassed—objects. (It is common practice for the Senate to discharge measures from committees by unanimous consent—meaning with the committee's permission.)

Nongermane Amendments

Unlike the House, the Senate has never had a rule requiring that amendments be germane to pending legislation. This feature probably ranks just below the filibuster as one of the Senate's most distinctive characteristics. "Amendments may be made," wrote Thomas Jefferson, "so as totally to alter the nature of the proposition." [82] A classic case occurred in 1965 when Sen. Everett McKinley Dirksen, R-Ill. (1951–1969), tried to add a proposal for a constitutional amendment on legislative reapportionment to a joint resolution designating August 6 to September 6 as National American Legion Baseball Month. Dirksen's amendment had been blocked by the Judiciary Committee. An opponent of the proposal called the senator's attempt a "foul ball."

Periodically, the Senate has considered rules changes that would permit it to impose a germaneness requirement on floor amendments. Proponents argue that such a requirement would improve efficiency, expedite the workload, enhance relations with the House (which has a strict germaneness requirement), strengthen committees as centers of policymaking, and promote predictability in scheduling. Opponents contend that the right of senators to offer nonrelevant amendments serves as a safeguard against capricious committee actions, permits any senator to raise important issues, and enables the Senate to respond quickly to new developments. "What is at stake [in the ability of senators to offer nongermane amendments] is the right of a minority—even a tiny minority, even one Senator—to raise an issue," declared one senator.[83]

Germaneness sometimes has been a vexing issue for the Senate. On the one hand, the lack of a general prohibition on extraneous riders permits senators to raise and debate popular and unpopular issues and lessens the opportunity for arbitrary committee action. On the other hand, some senators complain that the practice wastes the Senate's time by permitting contentious debate on matters unrelated to the fundamental purpose of a pending bill.

Senate Prohibitions. Although the Senate does not have a general germaneness rule, the chamber requires germane amendments to pending legislation in four situations:

1. for UCAs containing a requirement that amendments be germane (today, the term *relevant* is employed because it is less restrictive);
2. for amendments to general appropriations bills;
3. when cloture has been invoked; and
4. during consideration of certain measures governed by law, such as reconciliation bills.

When the Senate operates under a germaneness requirement, its tests for determining whether amendments are germane are stricter than those in the House. A Senate report noted that "a legislative amendment is germane if, and only if, it proposes to strike out or to change a number or date, or if its effect would be to restrict the scope of the measure or the powers it grants." [84] A presiding officer once noted, if an "amendment expands the effect of the bill or introduces new subject matter it is not germane." [85] Thus, if a farm bill dealt with five items—barley, wheat, rice, cotton, and soybeans—and a senator sought to amend the measure by adding a sixth item to the list, a germaneness point of order could be made against the amendment. Sense-of-the-Senate (or sense-of-Congress) amendments, which are nonbinding and generally symbolic in intent, and amendments to strike language are considered germane in most circumstances. (In 2000 the Senate agreed that sixty votes are needed to add sense-of-the-Senate amendments to budget resolutions.)

In the mid- to late 1980s, the Senate so narrowed its meaning of what constituted a germane amendment that when the germaneness requirement was in effect it prevented consideration of "policy alternatives that are highly pertinent but nonetheless nongermane because they expand the coverage of the bill or the powers it conveys." [86] The Senate needed a broader term to permit subject-related amendments to be offered to pending measures when they were governed by the germaneness stricture. Therefore, beginning in the mid- to late 1980s, the Senate began to employ the term *relevancy*. The test for relevancy is defined by Senate precedent:

> When relevancy of amendments is required by a unanimous consent agreement, that test is broader than the germaneness test as it is a subject matter test, and amendments that deal with the subject matter of the bill to which this requirement attaches are in order, provided they do not contain any significant matter not dealt with in that bill.[87]

Periodically, the question of the relevancy of amendments provokes sharp controversy on the Senate floor.[88] Sometimes a unanimous consent agreement will stipulate that the two floor managers, rather than the Senate parliamentarian advising the presiding officer, "will be the arbiters of relevancy." [89]

Today, UCAs almost always use "relevant" in describing what kinds of amendments are in order. On occasion, cloture has been invoked—which triggers the stricter germaneness standard—and a UCA has permitted selective relevant amendments to be offered post-cloture. As a recent majority leader noted after cloture had been invoked, "Under an additional consent, relevant trade amendments are in order in addition to the germaneness requirement under rule XXII." [90]

Placing Measures on the Calendar

When bills or joint resolutions are introduced in the Senate or passed by the House and sent to the Senate, they customarily are referred to a committee. According to Senate Rule XIV, all measures, including House-passed bills, must be read twice on different legislative days before they can be referred to committee. If an objection is raised after the first reading, the second reading cannot occur until the next legislative day. After the second reading, the bill or joint resolution is sent to the appropriate committee. However, if an objection to further consideration of the bill is raised at the second reading, the measure is placed directly on the legislative calendar (see Box 7-4). Placing a bill on the calendar gives the leadership the option of calling up the House-passed measure or, if one exists, the Senate committee-reported version.

BOX 7-4   Placing a Measure on the Calendar

March 28, 2006

MEASURE READ THE FIRST TIME—S. 2467

MR. McCONNELL. Mr. President, I understand there is a bill at the desk. I ask for its first reading.

THE PRESIDING OFFICER. The clerk will report.

The assistant legislative clerk read as follows:

A bill (S. 2467) to enhance and improve the trade relations of the United States by trade enforcement efforts and encouraging United States trading partners to adhere to the rules and norms of international trade, and for other purposes.

MR. McCONNELL: I now ask for a second reading and in order to place the bill on the calendar under the provisions of rule XIV, I object to my own request.

THE PRESIDING OFFICER. Objection is heard. The bill will be read for the second time on the next legislative day.

MEASURE PLACED ON THE CALENDAR—S. 2467

MR. SESSIONS. Mr. President, I understand there is a bill at the desk that is due for a second reading.

THE PRESIDING OFFICER. The clerk will report.

The legislative clerk read as follows:

A bill (S. 2467) to enhance and improve the trade relations of the United States by strengthening the United States trade enforcement efforts and encouraging United States trading partners to adhere to the rules and norms of international trade, and for other purposes.

MR. SESSIONS. In order to place the bill on the calendar under the provisions of rule XIV, I object to further proceeding.

THE PRESIDING OFFICER. Objection is heard. The bill will be placed on the calendar.

SOURCE: *Congressional Record,* March 29, 2006, S2543.

Rule XIV has been used increasingly in recent years.[91] Although it is not used for the vast majority of measures, Rule XIV is often invoked on party issues of high priority. The majority leader may employ it to bypass committees because no time is available for lengthy committee review, because some senators fear a bill might get stuck in committee, because the Senate wants to vote quickly on a measure, or because the majority leader wants an issue ready to be called up at his discretion.

For instance, Majority Leader Frist, concerned about the pace of deliberation in the Judiciary Committee on an immigration reform measure, said he would use Rule XIV to place his alternative immigration measure on the legislative calendar. (Instead, he asked and received unanimous consent to place his bill on the calendar.) Frist threatened to bring his bill directly to the floor, bypassing Judiciary, unless the panel reported its version of immigration reform in eleven days.[92] Judiciary met the deadline. Sometimes a majority leader will both introduce a bill and have it referred to committee and also use Rule XIV to place a virtually identical measure on the legislative calendar. In this way, if the committee is unable to act on the bill, the majority leader has it positioned to be called up at his discretion. (House-passed measures are held at the desk when similar Senate bills are pending on the calendar or are expected to be reported shortly out of committee.)

Suspension of the Rules

Senate rules can be suspended, provided there is one day's written notice and the terms of the suspension motion are published in the *Congressional Record*. Suspension motions are primarily used by senators who want to offer policy amendments to general appropriations measures. Policy amendments to appropriations measures are forbidden by Senate rules, but there are various ways they can be made, including the suspension route. For example, Senator Hillary Clinton, D-N.Y., stated in her notice of intent to suspend the rules:

> Mr. President, in accordance with rule V of the Standing Rules of the Senate, I hereby give notice in writing that it is my intention to move to suspend paragraph 4 of rule XVI for the purpose of proposing to the bill, H.R. 2862, the Science, State, Justice, Commerce appropriations bill, the following amendment: [to establish in the legislative branch a Hurricane Katrina Commission].[93]

The objective of the Commission was to study and report on all aspects of the governmental (local, state, and national) response to Hurricane Katrina, which wreaked such devastation on the Gulf Coast. The rules are silent on the number of votes needed to suspend Senate rules. Precedents require two-thirds of those present and voting, a quorum being present, to approve suspensions. The procedure is seldom used and rarely successful largely because it represents a challenge to the Appropriations Committee and the voting requirement to suspend is so high.

Discharge Petition

The formal process to discharge a bill from a committee under Rule XVII has taken place only fourteen times in the history of the Senate. It was last employed successfully in 1964. More recently, in 2003, Majority Leader Frist, seeking to demonstrate his determination to force action on several of President Bush's controversial judicial nominations, introduced several resolutions to discharge these nominees from the Judiciary Committee.[94] His resolutions were placed on the Executive Calendar and received no further action.

The prevailing sentiment in the Senate is that the discharge procedure undercuts the committee system and also that the rules governing its use are cumbersome. The discharge motion can be made by any senator, but only during the morning hour, which has fallen into disuse in today's Senate, and it must remain at the clerk's desk for one legislative day. Party leaders can forestall discharge motions for days or weeks by recessing, thus keeping the Senate in the same legislative day. If debate on the motion is not concluded within the morning hour, the motion is placed on the calendar where it faces the threat of a series of filibusters. A vote to discharge a committee of a bill requires a simple majority vote unless cloture must be invoked to stop a filibuster.

NOTES

1. For Cheney, see Steven Dennis, "Democrats' Procedural Gambit Sends Budget Savings Bill Back to the House," *CQ Today*, December 22, 2005, 6.
2. During his service as vice president, John Adams (1789–1797) "cast 29 tie-breaking votes, more than any of his [forty-five] successors in that position." *Congressional Record*, April 21, 1987, S5204.
3. *Congressional Record*, May 21, 1980, S5674.
4. On November 17, 1982, for the first time since 1793, the House had two legislative days in the same calendar day. It adjourned at 1:19 p.m. (the first legislative day) and then reconvened at 4:00 p.m. (the second legislative day). Sharp partisanship stimulated the Democratic leadership to employ this rare tactic.
5. *Senate Procedure: Precedents and Practices*, 97th Cong., 1st sess., 1982, S. Doc. 97–2, 565.
6. *Congressional Record*, March 26, 1987, S3927.
7. *Congressional Record*, February 27, 1998, S1175.
8. *Congressional Record*, April 16, 1985, S4256.
9. *Congressional Record*, June 9, 1977, 18179.
10. *Congressional Record*, June 21, 2004, S7086.
11. Kenneth Cooper, "Battle May Be Brewing on Hill over Renewal of Education Act," *Washington Post*, May 14, 2000, A10.
12. A Senate rule requires three hours of germane discussion at the beginning of each day's debate on a measure. Called the Pastore Rule after its sponsor, Sen. John O. Pastore, D-R.I. (1950–1976), its purpose is to confine debate to pending business.
13. Kirk Victor, "Reason to Smile," *National Journal*, March 18, 2006, 22.
14. Kathy Kiely, "Fresh Faces in Congress Stress Cooperation," *USA Today*, June 6, 2005, 10A.
15. *Congressional Record*, January 21, 1986, S8.
16. *Congressional Record*, May 21, 1987, S6979.
17. Rowland Evans and Robert Novak, *Lyndon B. Johnson: The Exercise of Power* (New York: New American Library, 1966), 115.
18. Material developed by legislative expert Betsy Palmer, Government and Finance Division, Congressional Research Service.
19. Joseph S. Clark, *Congress: The Sapless Branch* (New York: Harper & Row, 1964), 247–248.

20. *New York Times,* June 8, 1986, E5.
21. *Congressional Record,* September 27, 1993, S12550.
22. *Congressional Record,* October 28, 1977, 5857.
23. Susan Rasky, "With Few Bills Passed or Ready for Action, Congress Seems Sluggish," *New York Times,* May 14, 1989, 24.
24. *Wall Street Journal,* March 2, 1995, A16.
25. *CQ Daily Monitor,* March 2, 1995, 5.
26. Richard Cohen, "Amendment Mania," *National Journal,* November 1, 2003, 3335.
27. John Bresnahan, "Democrats Angered by Senate Maneuvering on FEC," *Roll Call,* August 3, 1998, 3.
28. *CQ Daily Monitor,* February 24, 2000, 2.
29. *Congressional Record,* July 8, 2004, S7785.
30. Martin B. Gold, *Senate Procedure and Practice* (Lanham, Md.: Rowman & Littlefield, 2004), 91–92.
31. *Congressional Record,* June 21, 2004, S7062.
32. *Congressional Record,* November 5, 1985, 30522.
33. *Washington Post,* July 24, 1991, A1.
34. *Congressional Record,* July 8, 2004, S7785.
35. *Congressional Record,* May 20, 1996, S5339.
36. *Congress DailyAM (National Journal),* May 11, 2000, 5.
37. *Congressional Record,* April 1, 1998, S2896.
38. *Congressional Record,* January 26, 1973, 2301.
39. Colbert King, "Democrats Are on the Wrong Battlefield," *Washington Post,* July 23, 2005, A17.
40. *Congressional Record,* December 9, 1987, S17476.
41. *Congressional Record,* September 23, 1975, 29814.
42. *Congressional Record,* June 23, 1987, S8442.
43. Bill Swindell, "Wage Increase Amendments Fail, Setting Stage for Future Fights on the Issue," *CQ Today,* March 8, 2005, 11.
44. *Congressional Record,* April 8, 1981, S6874.
45. *Congressional Record,* April 8, 1981, S3618.
46. *Congressional Record,* July 22, 1983, S10701.
47. *Congressional Record,* October 10, 1985, S13114.
48. *New York Times,* December 21, 1982, D29.
49. The word *filibuster* derives from the Dutch word *Vrijbuiter,* meaning freebooter. Passing into Spanish as *filibustero,* the term was used to describe military adventurers from the United States who in the mid-1800s fomented insurrections against various Latin American governments. For an account of William Walker, filibusterer of the 1850s, see *Smithsonian,* June 1981, 117–128. The first legislative use of the word is said to have occurred in the House in 1853, when a representative accused his opponents of "filibustering against the United States." By 1863 the word *filibuster* had come to mean delaying action on the floor, but the term did not gain wide currency until the 1880s.
50. *Congressional Record,* July 18, 1983, S10216.
51. *Congressional Record,* November 12, 2002, S11034.
52. Robert B. Dove, "Senate Rule XXII: The Good, the Bad, and the Ugly," *Roll Call,* November 13, 2003, 20.
53. *Congressional Record,* July 8, 2004, S7789.

54. *Congressional Record,* July 20, 1995, 19662.
55. Doug Obey, "Alaska," *The Hill,* July 10, 1996, 27.
56. *Washington Post,* February 20, 1994, A13.
57. *New York Times,* December 12, 1982, 4E.
58. *Washington Times,* November 17, 1987, A6.
59. Sarah Binder, Eric Lawrence, and Steven Smith, "Explaining Senate Change: The Rise in Filibustering, 1917–1996" (paper presented at the annual meeting of the Midwest Political Science Association, Chicago, April 10–12, 1997), 3.
60. *CongressDailyAM (National Journal),* November 10, 1993, 1, 7.
61. *Congressional Record,* October 5, 1992, S16577.
62. "Democrats to Forgo Control in Brief Edge," *Washington Times,* November 29, 2000, A4.
63. *Congressional Record,* February 26, 1979, 3232.
64. *Operations of Congress: Testimony of House and Senate Leaders,* hearing before the Joint Committee on the Organization of Congress, 103d Cong., 1st sess., January 26, 1993, 50.
65. *Congressional Record,* September 27, 1984, S12137.
66. Gregory J. Wawro and Eric Schickler, *Filibuster: Obstruction and Lawmaking in the U.S. Senate* (Princeton, N.J.: Princeton University Press, 2006), 260.
67. Richard F. Fenno Jr., "The Senate through the Looking Glass: The Debate over Television," *Legislative Studies Quarterly* (August 1989): 316.
68. *Congressional Record,* March 3, 1986, S1915.
69. Sarah Binder and Steven Smith, *Politics or Principle? Filibustering in the United States Senate* (Washington, D.C.: Brookings, 1997), 15.
70. One example of a mistake that filibustering senators can make with the result that they lose the floor is violation of the two-speech rule, which forbids members from making a third speech on the same question in the same legislative day. For a contentious debate on the two-speech rule, see *Congressional Record,* September 25, 1986, S13687–S13710; and *Washington Post,* October 1, 1986, A17.
71. *Washington Post,* June 11, 1982, A11.
72. *Congressional Record,* September 21, 1893, 1636.
73. *Congressional Record,* July 7, 1998, S7565.
74. *Congressional Record,* March 28, 2000, S1832.
75. *Congressional Record,* April 4, 2006, S2793. For another example of a minority leader filing cloture, see Jessica Kimpell, "Partisanship Prevails in the Senate As Daschle Tries to Force Republicans to Vote," *CQ Weekly,* May 1, 2004, 1001.
76. *Congressional Record,* June 19, 1998, S6666.
77. David Baumann, "The Collapse of the Senate," *National Journal,* June 3, 2000, 1759.
78. *Operations of Congress,* 116.
79. *Congressional Record,* June 27, 2003, S8844.
80. See Martin B. Gold and Dimple Gupta, "The Constitutional Option to Change Senate Rules and Procedures: A Majoritarian Means to Overcome the Filibuster," *Harvard Journal of Law and Public Policy,* Fall 2003, 206–271. Senator Robert C. Byrd refuted claims by Gold and Gupta that Byrd as majority leader established precedents that justify the nuclear option. See *Congressional Record,* March 20, 2005, S3100–S3103.

81. The memorandum is printed in the *Congressional Record*, May 24, 2005, S5830–S5831.
82. *Constitution, Jefferson's Manual, and Rules of the House of Representatives*, 102d Cong., 2d sess., H. Doc. 102–405, 233.
83. *Congressional Record*, February 26, 1986, S1663.
84. Senate Committee on Rules and Administration, *Report on Senate Operations, 1988*, 100th Cong., 2d sess., September 20, 1988, S. Print 100–129, 55.
85. *Congressional Record*, February 9, 1982, S599.
86. *Ibid.*
87. Floyd Riddick and Alan Frumin, *Senate Procedure: Precedents and Practices* (Washington, D.C.: Government Printing Office, 1992), 1362–1363.
88. See, for example, *Congressional Record*, May 21, 2003, S6827–S6828.
89. *Congressional Record*, June 21, 2002, S5882.
90. *Congressional Record*, November 2, 1999, S13632. See Richard Cohen, "Amendment Mania," *National Journal*, November 1, 2003, 3334–3338.
91. C. Lawrence Evans and Walter J. Oleszek, "Message Politics and Senate Procedure," in *The Contentious Senate*, Colton Campbell and Nicol Rae, eds. (Lanham, Md.: Rowman & Littlefield, 2001), 107–127.
92. Jonathan Weisman, "Frist Pushes for Quick Vote on Immigration," *Washington Post*, March 17, 2006, A4.
93. *Congressional Record*, September 8, 2005, S9800.
94. *Congressional Record*, July 7, 2003, S8893.

CHAPTER 8

Resolving House-Senate Differences

BEFORE LEGISLATION can be sent to the president for signature or veto, it must be passed by both houses of Congress in identical form. House- and Senate-passed versions of the same bill frequently differ, sometimes only slightly but often on critical points. But whatever the differences, the two versions must be reconciled by mutual agreement. Whenever possible, this reconciliation is undertaken informally. However, a fair percentage of all bills passed by both chambers require action by a House-Senate conference committee—an ad hoc joint committee composed of members selected by each chamber to resolve differences on a particular bill in disagreement.[1] Of the 465 public laws enacted by the 103d Congress (1993–1995), 13 percent (62) went through conference; for the 107th Congress (2001–2003), of 377 public laws, 9 percent (33) went through conference; and for the 108th Congress (2003–2005), of 410 public laws, 7 percent (36) went to conference.[2] Major and controversial legislation usually requires conference committee action.

Conference committees are called the "third house" of Congress. Here the final version of a bill is written, often by a small number of lawmakers, who sometimes are only majority party members. A senator who taught college government courses underscored the key role of conference committees.

> I used to teach political science classes. . . . You know, I feel guilty. I need to refund tuition to students for those 2 weeks I taught classes on the Congress. I was so off in terms of a lot of the decision making.
>
> I should have focused on the conferences committees as the third House of Congress, because these folks can do any number of different things. And the thing that drives me crazy is you can have a situation where the Senate did not have a provision in the bill, and the conference committee just puts it in the bill. Then it comes back for an up-or-down vote. No opportunity to amend.
>
> Or you can have a situation where the Senate and the House pass bills with provisions in them and the conference takes it out. It is, I think, the least accountable part of decision making in Congress.[3]

OBSCURITY OF THE PROCESS

The conference committee process is older than Congress itself. State legislatures used conference committees before 1789 to reconcile differences between the chambers of their bicameral legislatures. The conference committee system was taken for granted when the first Congress convened, and it has been in use ever since.[4] Nevertheless, for many citizens the conference committee is a little-known or -understood entity compared with the other aspects of the legislative process.

Until the mid-1970s, conference committees almost always met in secret sessions with no published record of their proceedings. The conference committee reports they produced revealed the results of the secret negotiations, but the bargaining and deliberations that led to these results were not formally disclosed.

In one of the most significant reforms of congressional procedure, both chambers in 1975 adopted rules requiring open conference committee meetings unless a majority of the conference members (called conferees or managers) from either chamber voted in public to hold secret sessions. In 1977 the House went a step further, adopting a rule requiring the full House to vote to close a conference. Closure usually occurs on legislation dealing with national security. For example, the head of the House conference delegation will offer the nondebatable motion to close the conference committee "to the public at such times as classified national security information is under consideration." [5]

Conferees still conduct much of their important business in secret, however. As the late Senator Russell B. Long, D-La. (who voluntarily retired at the end of the 99th Congress after 38 years of service) once noted in a statement that holds true today:

> The Senator knows when we started the openness thing we found it more and more difficult to get something agreed to in the conferences, it seemed to take forever. So what did we do? The Senator knows what we did. We would break up into smaller groups and then we would ask our chairman . . . to see if he could not find his opposite number on the House side and discuss this matter and come back and tell us what the chances would be of working out various and sundry possibilities.[6]

Relatively few complaints have been raised about closed sessions. Political commentators and others recognize the value of candid exchanges (away from the glare of special interest groups) in closed meetings. Furthermore, reporters are usually kept well informed of the results of closed conferences. In today's open and video politics era, "secret" does not mean what it used to on Capitol Hill. On occasion, conference negotiating sessions have been televised over the Cable-Satellite Public Affairs Network (C-SPAN). Televising conferences, which is usually the prerogative of the overall conference committee chairman, might even be part of the strategy to influence conference decision making. Televising an energy conference, remarked Senator Larry Craig, R-Idaho, "might help public opinion" to overcome "opposition to domestic oil production in an election year with rising gasoline prices." [7]

The conference committee is one of the most critical points in the legislative process. For several reasons, however, members of Congress may try to avoid this stage and resolve House-Senate differences on legislation without recourse to the conference committee process. First, pressure exists to approve the legislation quickly. Second, one house may be concerned that conferees of the other chamber will try to weaken (or filibuster) the legislation. For example, on a nuclear waste storage bill, the House leadership "decided to go with the Senate version in an attempt to avoid a filibuster threatened by Nevada's [the proposed nuclear waste storage site] senators on any conference report to the legislation." [8] Third, a conference committee could become deadlocked—particularly in the weeks and days before the final adjournment of Congress. Failure of the conferees to reach agreement before the end of a Congress means that the bill dies. Sometimes lawmakers from each chamber may not want to officially create a conference until they get a sense through private negotiations that a compromise can be worked out. In these cases creation of a conference committee "will be more an indication that a deal is done than a forum to find one." [9]

AGREEMENT WITHOUT A CONFERENCE

There are two ways of achieving bicameral agreement—that is, each chamber approves the same bill—without a conference. First, one chamber can adopt verbatim the version of the bill produced by the other. This route is the one taken most frequently in lawmaking, because most of the legislation agreed to is noncontroversial, such as measures to name post office buildings after prominent individuals. However, there are occasions when the "rubber stamp" route is tried on controversial measures. The "rubber stamp" approach may also involve informal consultation before or after passage of the bill by one chamber.

Second, the two houses may send measures back and forth several times, amending each other's amendments, before they agree to identical language on all provisions of the legislation. "This method is frequently used in the closing days of a Congress to save time," wrote a congressional journalist. "Bills may be sent back and forth on an hourly basis until there is a meeting of the minds, or one side backs down, or the two chambers give up in failure." [10] The "ping-pong" approach may also be employed in combination with conference committee negotiations. Table 8-1 presents data on how often different procedures for reaching bicameral agreement were used in selected Congresses.

House and Senate committee staff communicate regularly on legislation of mutual interest. Drafts of measures are exchanged for comment and consistency, companion bills are studied, and strategies are devised to facilitate passage in each chamber. Executive branch officials and pressure groups often participate in these informal strategy sessions. This kind of prior consultation frequently helps clear away obstacles to passage—allowing legislation to be approved by both houses in identical form, thus avoiding the need for a conference.

Consultation may take place after a bill has passed one or both chambers. For example, on the first day of the 104th Congress, the House overwhelmingly passed the landmark Congressional Accountability Act (H.R. 1), ap-

TABLE 8-1 Bicameral Reconciliation of Legislation, 103d (1993–1995), 105th (1997–1999), 106th (1999–2001), 107th (2001–2003), and 108th (2003–2005) Congresses

Reconciliation	103d Congress		105th Congress		106th Congress		107th Congress		108th Congress	
	Number	Percent	Number	Percent	Number	Percent	Number	Percent	Number	Percent
Simple adoption by one chamber of the version sent to it by the other	291	(63)	277	(71)	436	(75)	289	(77)	317	(82)
Amendments between the houses	112	(24)	77	(20)	106	(18)	55	(14)	56	(11)
Conference reports	46	(10)	39	(10)	38	(7)	33	(9)	36	(7)
Both conference reports and amendments between the houses	16	(3)	0	(0)	0	(0)	0	(0)	0	(0)
Public laws (total)	465		393		465		377		410	

SOURCES: 103d Congress: Ilona Nickels, congressional specialist, Government Division, Congressional Research Service, Library of Congress; 105th Congress: Denise S. Feriozzi, Monroe scholar, College of William and Mary; 106th, 107th, and 108th Congresses: Elizabeth Rybicki, expert on congressional conference committees, Congressional Research Service.

plying federal workplace safety and antidiscrimination laws to the legislative branch. When the legislation went to the Senate, members there wanted to make some changes. After consultations with the House sponsors of the legislation, the Senate passed S. 2, its version of the accountability act, and sent that measure to the House. To avoid the need for a conference committee, House Republican leaders decided to take up S. 2 under suspension of the rules, and it was passed by more than the two-thirds vote (390–0) required under that procedure. The House action cleared the legislation for submission to President Bill Clinton, who signed the measure into law.

Limits to Nonconference Tactics

Two points are worth noting about the ping-pong approach. First, a technical limit exists to the number of times measures may be shuffled between the chambers. The third-degree amendment prohibition applies to amendments between the House and Senate. Each chamber gets two shots at amending the amendments of the other body. "In short, after each chamber has passed the same bill for the first time (for example, the House passes a House bill and the Senate passes the House bill with Senate amendments), each chamber may have one opportunity to amend the amendments of the other chamber." [11] Like many legislative procedures, the two-shot principle can be waived, ignored, or overturned. The Consolidated Omnibus Reconciliation Act of 1985, for example, bounced between the chambers a record-setting nine times.

Second, the back-and-forth procedure is usually employed intentionally to avoid conferences and is feasible only when circumstances warrant its use. For example, a House chair may ask the chamber to concur in the Senate amendment to the House amendment to the Senate-passed bill. House approval is "appropriate parliamentary procedure, which allows us to avoid the trouble of a conference when faced with such small [bicameral] differences." [12] The House in this case agreed to the Senate amendment, which cleared the bill for the president. Lack of time also can prevent formation of conference committees and necessitate use of the back-and-forth approach.

PRECONFERENCE CONSIDERATIONS

It is often clear from the outset that controversial measures will end up in conference. Members plan their floor strategy accordingly. They make floor statements that emphasize their unyielding commitment to their own chamber's positions. In advance of a "House-Senate conference," noted one senator, "it is not unusual for the respective [chambers] to stake out positions for themselves and even to utter statements about their absolute intransigence, that sometimes does not always prevail when the conference convenes." [13]

Members frequently add expendable amendments to use as bargaining chips in conference. Such amendments can be traded away for other provisions considered more important. Members who sponsor floor amendments are mindful of the bargaining chip ploy. As one senator remarked:

I have been in this body long enough to beware of the chairman of a committee who says in an enticing voice, "Let me take the amendment to conference," because I think that is frequently the parliamentary equivalent of saying, "Let me take the child into the tower and I will strangle him to death." [14]

With conference committees presumptively open, or at least subject to public review, conferees sometimes must put up a fight for such amendments before dropping them. Conferees understand, too, that some bargaining chips are more influential than others. Before these amendments are dropped, conferees will consider the implications of offending powerful members.

Another preconference tactic is for one chamber to deliberately keep out of its bill something it knows the other chamber wants. During a conference, the House conferees, for example, may give in to the Senate, but only in return for Senate acceptance of something favored by the House. For these reasons, counting the number of times one house appeared to give in to the other is not a good indication of the winners and losers in conference.[15] It is difficult to identify chamber "winners" or "losers," in any case, without knowing the goals and motives of the respective conferees.

House and Senate floor managers also consider whether they want recorded votes on certain amendments when they are debated in their chamber. For example, one senator's strategy on an amendment he opposed was to seek a recorded vote on it "to beat the amendment, and beat it good, burying the issue in the Senate once and for all, and also putting him in a position to tell a Senate-House conference on the bill that the proposal was resoundingly defeated in the Senate." [16] Alternatively, floor managers sometimes prefer not to draw attention to amendments they oppose (or favor)—and thus hope to avoid taking roll-call votes—on the assumption that it will then be easier to drop (or advocate) them in conference.

Members, too, are sensitive to the overall contours of their bill and the margin of support for its passage on the floor. A large vote on passage of legislation in either chamber may generate political pressure on the other house to embrace the measure. "A strong vote for final passage [of this tax cut bill] will certainly strengthen our hand [in conference]," said Senator Max Baucus, D-Mont., "and we did receive a strong vote of 62 Senators." [17]

In an unusual preconference move, then Speaker Hastert directed the chairs of the several committees with jurisdiction over a major immigration reform bill to conduct field hearings around the country to build support for the House's bill, which focused on border security. The legislation also made it a felony for illegal aliens to live in the United States. The Senate's version, backed by President Bush and agreed to after the House passed its bill, also addressed border security, but it included a pathway to citizenship for the estimated 12 million illegal immigrants living in the country. House Republicans lambasted the Senate's bill as providing "amnesty" to illegal aliens. They "decided to focus on strengthening their bargaining position [if and when the two sides meet in conference] through public hearings." [18]

Not to be outdone, the chairman of the Senate Judiciary Committee, the panel with jurisdiction over immigration reform, announced that his committee would also hold field hearings to generate public backing for the Senate's broader and more moderate immigration reform package. The dueling hearings underscore not only the controversial and complex nature of the issue, but also the fractiousness within GOP ranks as House Republicans are pitted against Senate Republicans and President Bush. No conference was convened in the 109th Congress on the Senate- and Bush-favored immigration reform bill.

CONFERENCE COMMITTEE PROCESS

The five major steps in the conference committee process are: (1) requesting a conference by one house and the other chamber agreeing to it, the so-called stage of disagreement; (2) selecting and, as a possibility, instructing conferees; (3) bargaining in conference, including negotiating objectives and procedural issues; (4) filing the conference committee report; and (5) taking final House and Senate action on the conference committee version of the bill.

Requesting a Conference

When the House passes a bill which is then amended by the Senate and returned, the House has several options. It may refuse to take further action, in which case the measure dies; it may approve an entirely new version of the bill and send it to the Senate; it may agree to the Senate's amendments, negating the need for a conference; it may amend the Senate's amendments and return the measure once again to the Senate; or it may request a conference.

Occasionally, the Speaker will refer the Senate amendments, especially if they are nongermane to the House-passed measure, to the standing committee that has jurisdiction over the subject matter of the amendments. More commonly, though, on major legislation a member will ask and receive unanimous consent for the House to disagree to the Senate's amendments and request a conference with the Senate. The Speaker usually recognizes an appropriate committee member to make the unanimous consent request to go to conference on the bill. ("Mr. Speaker, I ask unanimous consent to take from the Speaker's table the bill H.R. 1234 with the Senate amendments thereto, disagree to the amendments of the Senate, and ask for a conference with the Senate.")

If any representative objects to this request, the legislation can get to conference in three other ways. First, the House can suspend its rules (an action that requires a two-thirds vote) by adopting, for example, the following motion: "Mr. Speaker, I move to suspend the rules and take from the Speaker's table the bill H.R. 1234 with the Senate amendments thereto, disagree to the amendments of the Senate, and ask for a conference with the Senate." If the legislation is controversial, this procedure is unlikely to be employed because of its supermajority requirements.

Second, the Rules Committee can report a rule sending a measure to conference. On occasion, the Rules Committee will report a rule that not only specifies how a House measure will be debated and amended but also provides for an automatic Senate hook-up following completion of floor action on the bill. A hook-up provision in a special rule permits a companion Senate-passed measure to be immediately called up and the House-passed version inserted after the Senate's bill number. Technically, the House and Senate have passed the same numbered measure (a requirement if a measure is sent to conference). The practical effect is that conference committee negotiations will involve two versions (the House's and Senate's) of the same numbered bill.

Third, representatives can invoke House Rule XXII to get a measure to conference. This rule permits legislation to reach conference by majority vote of the House if a member of the committee of jurisdiction, typically the chair, is authorized by his or her panel to offer the motion to go to conference. A new House rule adopted at the start of the 109th Congress and continued in the 110th eases committees' use of this procedure. The provision states, "A committee may adopt a rule providing that the chairman be directed to offer a [Rule XXII motion] whenever the chairman considers it appropriate." Then, if a member objects to a unanimous consent request for a conference, the chair will be immediately recognized by the Speaker to offer the Rule XXII motion: "Mr. Speaker, by direction of the Committee on _____, I move to take from the Speaker's table the bill H.R. 1234, with a Senate amendment thereto, disagree to the Senate amendment, and agree to the conference asked by the Senate." This motion is subject to debate under the one-hour rule. (For bills that are referred to several committees, all committees with a primary or initial claim on the legislation, and those that have reported the bill, must agree to the Rule XXII procedure.)

When the situation is reversed and a Senate-passed bill is amended by the House and returned to the Senate, it is "held at the desk and almost always subsequently laid before the Senate by the Presiding Officer upon request or motion of a Senator [usually the manager of the bill]." [19]

The House amendment or amendments may be dealt with in four ways by the Senate: (1) by adopting a motion to refer the amendment(s) to the appropriate standing committee, (2) by further amending the House amendments, (3) by agreeing to the House amendments (thus clearing the bill), or (4) by disagreeing to the House amendments, in which case a conference is requested by motion or unanimous consent.

The usual way for the Senate to get to conference on a House-passed bill is for the majority leader or majority floor manager to ask unanimous consent, or offer a motion, to call up the House measure. (An alternative is for the Senate to call up a House-passed amendment to a Senate-passed measure, disagree to the House amendment, and request a conference with the other body.) Then the majority leader or floor manager would say: "Mr. President, I move to strike all after the enacting clause of H.R. 1234 and insert in lieu thereof the text of the Senate bill, S. 567." After adoption of this motion (virtually always by consent), the Senate would then pass H.R. 1234, as amended. Parliamentarily, the House and Senate have now passed the same bill, but there are two different versions of it. Next, the majority leader will offer this motion: "Mr. President, I move that the Senate insist on its amendments, request a conference with the House on the disagreeing votes thereon, and that the Chair be authorized to appoint conferees." The normal routine for the Senate is to agree to the three-part motion—insist (or disagree), request, and authorize—by unanimous consent. As Robert B. Dove, the former parliamentarian of the Senate, noted: "The three steps are usually bundled into a unanimous consent agreement and done within seconds. But if some senators do not want a conference to occur and if they are determined, they can force three separate cloture votes to close debate, and that takes a lot of time. It basically stops the whole process of going to conference." [20]

In a precedent-making move, GOP senators opposed to sending a campaign finance bill to conference during the waning days of the 103d Congress (1993–1995) launched filibusters against each part of the triple motion. (Senate precedents allow any Senator, solely on demand, to request the division of a question for separate consideration of each part if each is substantively and grammatically distinct.) "In the 210 years in the history of the United States Senate, never—until last week—has there been a series of filibusters on taking a bill to conference," stated Majority Leader George J. Mitchell, D-Maine.[21] With GOP expectations high for recapturing control of the Senate after the November 1994 elections, Republicans wanted to block action on this largely Democratic initiative. They were successful on both counts.

By the early 2000s, given an environment of sharper partisan conflict, what had been precedent-shattering to Majority Leader Mitchell in 1994 became a fairly common occurrence in the Senate. Minority party senators often blocked the Senate from going to conference with the House. The triggering cause was the exclusion of Democrats from conference committee negotiations, even though they had been officially appointed as conferees by the Senate. As Senator Richard Durbin, D-Ill., exclaimed, "I have been appointed to conference committees in the Senate in name only, where my name will be read by the [presiding officer] and only the conference committee of Republicans goes off and meets, adopts a conference report, signs it, and sends it back to the floor without even inviting me to attend a session."[22]

With the two parties at loggerheads, stalemate is often the order of the day. Senate Democrats lambasted the other party for abusing its power and suggested greater use of preconference methods to achieve bicameral agreement on legislation. Republicans countered that Democrats were obstructionists, unwilling to negotiate in good faith with the other body. Republicans also noted that Democratic conferees are invited to participate in conferences if they are constructive negotiators who share the majority's policy goals. On occasion, the majority will play procedural "hard ball" and file, or threaten to file, cloture on the various motions to proceed to conference with the other body. Their objectives are two-fold: to encourage the minority to reach a deal on forming a conference and thus avoid a vote on cloture and, if cloture fails, to blame the minority for stymieing action on an issue of vital importance to the public.

This impasse, like so many in the Senate, is usually resolved on a case-by-case basis when the frustration level rises so high that each side is willing to hammer out a mutually acceptable accord. The minority stops their blocking actions and receives assurances from the majority that their conferees will be full participants in the House-Senate negotiating sessions. (Following the November 2006 elections, the new Democratic Senate majority promised to end the practice of excluding minority party conferees from these bicameral negotiating forums.) "I bet most of you here have never watched a congressional conference committee in session," said Senator Reid to a group of journalists. "We need to do that" with the participation of both Democratic and Republican conferees.[23] Similarly on January 4, 2007, the 110th House adopted new rules stating that every House conferee shall "receive notice of the [conference] meeting and a reasonable opportunity to attend."

Both chambers vote themselves into a state of disagreement before going to conference. Reaching the so-called "stage of disagreement" is a threshold with procedural implications, especially in the House. Simply put, before the stage of disagreement precedence is given to amendments that perfect the legislation; after the stage of disagreement precedence is granted motions that encourage agreement between the two chambers. For example, once the stage of disagreement has been reached, a motion to concur with the other chamber's amendment has priority over a motion already offered to further amend it; the opposite condition applies prior to the stage of disagreement.

Selecting and Instructing Conferees

Selecting Conferees. The selection of conferees is governed in both chambers by rules and precedent. Each time a bill is sent to conference, the Speaker and the presiding officer of the Senate formally appoint the respective conferees. In practice, both chambers usually rely on the chair and ranking minority member of the committee that originally considered and reported the bill to recommend the selections. Sometimes, chairs will suggest delay in naming conferees to signal displeasure with the other body and to apply "leverage on the other body [and encourage it to] cave in on . . . key issues" even before a conference is formally convened.[24] Other factors, too, may slow the appointment of conferees. For example, as a form of hostage politics, senators may block the appointment of conferees on a bill they oppose until conferees are named on a measure they support. Or the Speaker may delay naming conferees, seeking, for example, to first ensure that the soon-to-be-named conferees will include what the Speaker wants in the conference report or to pressure the other body to concede to the House on certain provisions.

The Speaker may also delay in appointing conferees to prevent the minority party from offering repetitive motions to instruct (see below), thus avoiding votes on politically attractive issues that party colleagues would be hard-pressed to vote against. House and Senate leaders may also delay in naming conferees because they need more time to develop their strategy for dealing with significant measures heading to conference. For example, strategic considerations are often critical when time is at a premium and the majority leadership is working to formulate an "end game" that effectively wraps up action on priority business as the first or second session of a Congress comes to a close.

The Speaker and the presiding officer typically appoint conferees from the list given them in advance by the committee leaders, who select members of their own committees. (The Speaker, after the original appointment, also has the authority to remove managers or name additional conferees.) A member of another committee may be appointed when he or she has special knowledge of the subject matter or if the bill is of particular interest to the member's state or district. (Or members who have not formally been named conferees may be invited to attend the bicameral meetings because of their specialized knowledge.) When a bill has been referred to several committees (multiple referral), it is common to have conferees from all the committees that handled it. Party ratios on conference committees generally reflect the party membership in the House and Senate.

House and Senate party leaders get actively involved in naming conferees on issues of fundamental importance. For example, in a virtually unprecedented decision, in 1995 Speaker Newt Gingrich named a Democratic member, Gary A. Condit of California, as a conferee on unfunded mandates legislation. Condit, who ranked tenth in seniority on the committee of jurisdiction (Government Reform), was supporting GOP efforts to inhibit congressional passage of bills that imposed financial costs on state governments. However, he could not persuade either the ranking Democrat on the Government Reform panel or the minority leader to appoint him as a conferee. (Under party rules at the time, the "Democratic Leader shall make recommendations to the Speaker of all Democratic Members who shall serve as conferees.") Speaker Gingrich was amenable to the idea and appointed Condit to one of the designated GOP conferee slots. As a result, the House conference delegation was bipartisan: four Republicans and four Democrats. (Condit belonged to a conservative Democratic group called "The Coalition," whose support Gingrich sought to help pass GOP legislation.)[25]

House rules state that the Speaker shall "appoint no less than a majority [of conferees] who generally supported the House position as determined by the Speaker," those "who are primarily responsible for the legislation," and, to the fullest extent possible, include "the principal proponents of the major provisions of the bill" passed by the House. Clearly, this language grants wide discretion to the Speaker in appointing conferees and allows him the opportunity to "stack" a conference with majority party members who favor his position on the legislation. For example, after the House adopted a major amendment opposed by the Speaker, he chose not to name the GOP authors of the amendment as conferees. Instead, most of the conferees he appointed opposed the amendment; they did, however, support the House position on the overall bill "as determined by the Speaker." Lamented one of the GOP authors of the amendment, "Is that stacking the deck, is that trying to subvert the will of the House, or what?" [26] (Seniority used to be a nearly inviolable criterion in the appointment of conferees, but junior members in both chambers are now selected, as are vulnerable lawmakers whose designation as conferees may boost their reelection prospects.)

Conferee selection in the Senate sometimes arouses controversy over both the number of managers and the ratio of majority to minority members. For example, a major pension reform bill was stalled in getting to conference over these issues. "There is a dispute over whether the conference should have seven Republicans or eight Republicans," exclaimed Democratic leader Harry Reid, Nev. "I need an extra Senator. I need 8 to 6." [27] The GOP leader insisted on a 7 to 5 ratio. Finally, after nearly a three-month delay, a unanimous consent agreement authorized the presiding officer to appoint conferees at a ratio of 9 to 7. As the GOP leader explained:

> We had originally requested 7 to 5. As my colleagues know, the Democratic leader insisted on an 8 to 6 ratio. The 9 to 7 ratio we agreed to allows us to have equal representation from the Finance and HELP Committees. As I repeatedly insisted, it is important we not stack the deck in favor or against either committee. Through mutual agreement, we have reached that objective.[28]

There are occasions when House and Senate party leaders are named as conferees—a sign that they want to direct conference negotiations on high-stakes issue important to each party. The House majority leader often serves on important tax conferences. "The House has a special sense of its constitutional obligation to initiate tax bills," said a majority leader. "We always felt we wanted a strong statement from our leadership, protecting our institution." [29] During the 108th Congress (2003–2005), a conference on a major expansion of Medicare—to provide a prescription drug benefit to the elderly—included the leadership of the Senate (Majority Leader Bill Frist, Tenn., and Minority Leader Tom Daschle, D-S.D.). Both also served on the Senate committee of jurisdiction (Finance). However, as Senate leader Frist explained:

> I could have stayed off the [conference] committee and sat back with Speaker Hastert to help make some of the fundamental decisions. But I wanted to be involved in the process, to fully understand, to listen to the debate on both sides and to be in the best position to help make some of the major decisions that inevitably are going to have to be made.[30]

Speaker Hastert named then Majority Leader Tom DeLay, R-Texas, whom he dubbed his "super conferee," to be a lead negotiator for the House on the Medicare measure. When top majority party leaders of either chamber are appointed conferees, it signals both the importance of the measure and that the negotiating session will be, as one senator declared, a "majority-party driven" conference.[31]

The House, less so the Senate, often appoints both "general" conferees, who are authorized to negotiate all matters in bicameral disagreement, and "limited" conferees, who are responsible for negotiating differences on certain provisions or sections of the legislation. Importantly, one chamber cannot outvote the other by appointing more conferees, because each house votes as a unit, with a majority vote deciding each issue. Each house, in effect, has one vote ("yea" or "nay") to cast. Large conference delegations, especially for the House, are not uncommon. Multiple committee consideration of comprehensive bills that crosscut the jurisdiction of several panels is the driving force behind big conferences. Large conference delegations affect the mechanics of conference decision making. They often divide into smaller groups called subconferences.

The largest conference in congressional history involved the 1981 omnibus budget reconciliation bill. "Over 250 Senators and Congressmen met in 58 [subconferences] to consider nearly 300 issues" in disagreement, noted Senate Majority Leader Howard H. Baker Jr., R-Tenn.[32] The use of subconferences enables bicameral negotiators to proceed on several fronts simultaneously and to expedite what is inherently (because of numbers) a more complex process.

The nature of the issues in disagreement may account most for the length of conferences on megabills, and those issues are likely to be contentious. Large conference delegations invariably require more time to iron out bicameral differences; the diversity of views that need to be harmonized affects the pace of deliberations. Finally, the larger the number of conferees, the easier it is for lawmakers who are not conferees, interest groups, and executive officials to have access to the negotiations. (Many conferences involve multilateral instead of bilateral negotiations, because scores of outside actors and interests can influence conference outcomes.) If large conferences become unwieldy even if they divide into subconferences, they often break down into smaller and smaller groups. This process was followed during a huge savings and loan conference, which embraced nearly one-quarter of the House, including every member of the House [Financial Services] Committee. As one House conferee put it:

> One hundred and two conferees were appointed and no progress was made until the four principals [the House Financial Services and Senate Banking chairmen and ranking minority members] went behind closed doors. And I'm not complaining. If [the House Financial Services chairman] had not reduced the conference from 102 members to four, we would still be there arguing over this bill. He should get an Oscar for his starring role in, "Honey, I shrunk the conference." [33]

Instructing Conferees. After either chamber has agreed to go to conference but before the conferees have officially been named, the House (see Box 8-1 on page 273) or Senate may adopt motions instructing their conferees, for example, to sustain the majority position of the chamber on a particular amendment or provision. A member of the minority party is granted priority in the House to offer the motion to instruct, and only one can be made at this stage.[34] (Instructions are in order before, during, and after a conference.) Senators may offer several successive instruction motions prior to the naming of conferees, which are debatable and, therefore, subject to a filibuster. In each chamber, conferees cannot be instructed to do that which is not within their authority (delete text which both chambers have agreed to, for instance) or, in the case of the House, the motion to instruct may not include argumentative language.

Instructions place additional political and moral pressure on the conferees and may strengthen their position in conference committee bargaining. "We need to give the House conferees some backbone to stand up to the Senate on this issue," declared a House member in support of a motion to instruct conferees.[35] However, instructions adopted by either chamber are not binding. (The practice is more common in the House than the Senate, because it appears unseemly to instruct senators and those motions are mainly symbolic.) As a result, conferees may disregard the instructions, particularly when they feel the need for room to maneuver or compromise. The full House and Senate still have an opportunity to accept or reject the conference committee report on the bill, and a new conference may be requested if either house feels that its conferees have grossly violated their instructions or authority. For example, conferees from both chambers are obligated by rule and precedent to address only the matters in bicameral disagreement and not introduce new matter that has not been considered in either chamber.

During the early 1990s, when Democrats controlled the House, Republicans began to use the instruction motion to bring their issues before the chamber. In 1993 it was used eleven times; the next year, more than double that number. Only one motion to instruct can be offered prior to the appointment of conferees, as noted earlier, and this motion is reserved to the minority. However, if a conference during this era could not reach agreement within twenty calendar days, House rules permitted lawmakers to offer (with one day's notice) an unlimited number of instruction motions. During a 1994 crime conference that ran more than twenty days, for example, Republicans offered "nine motions to instruct conferees on, among other things, provisions regarding 'racial justice,' prison construction, and the death penalty." [36]

Democrats did the same thing when they were in the minority: they offered instruction motions to force votes on their election-year and political priorities.[37] To somewhat constrain this practice, the majority party modified House rules at the start of the 108th Congress (2003–2005). The change retained the twenty-calendar-day period but added ten legislative days to boot. This modification is designed to give the conference committee a chance to enter into serious negotiations before motions to instruct are in order. For example, under the old rule a conference committee might officially convene only a few times before Congress adjourned for the traditional August recess. Once the House returned in early September, multiple motions to instruct would be in order even though conferees hardly had time to meet and greet one another, let alone resolve bicameral disagreements. The addition of ten legislative days ensures that conference committees have two or more weeks to resolve interchamber differences before instruction motions are in order.

To sum up, party and committee leaders often devote considerable time to who is named a conferee and who is passed over. Regularly, lawmakers lobby committee or party leaders to be chosen as conferees, because they are then strategically positioned to advance their substantive and political goals. On bills of great partisan and substantive importance, the top leaders of the House (by custom, the Speaker is not a conferee) or the Senate, including the majority leader, are named conferees.

Bargaining in Conference

Before the conferees officially convene, informal pre-conference negotiations are usually held. These negotiations commonly involve only key House and Senate staff aides but may also include committee members, party leaders, and others. Pre-conference sessions are used, among other things, to differentiate between minor and major matters in disagreement, to identify the administration's position on significant issues, and to try and forge a unified position on important matters before beginning the formal negotiations. These private pre-conference sessions may involve only majority party members and staff aides.

No formal rules, such as quorum or proxy voting requirements, govern internal conference committee bargaining. The only stipulation is that the conferences must meet formally at least once in open session (unless they have taken the appropriate steps to meet in private). The lack of rules is deliberate to foster an informal give-and-take environment conducive to reaching bicameral compromises, especially when the chambers have passed starkly different measures. As a Ways and Means chairman said of trying to meld major bicameral differences on a health bill, "It's akin to mating a Chihuahua with a Great Dane." [38]

A conference chair is selected in an ad hoc fashion, because there are no House or Senate rules that govern the procedure. On recurring measures that go to conference annually, such as appropriations and revenue bills, custom dictates that leadership rotates between the two houses. The chair plays an influential role in the conference process, arranging the time and place of meetings, the agenda of each session, and the order in which disagreements are negotiated. The chair also has charge of the official "papers"—the House and Senate versions of the measure in conference and other relevant communications between the chambers. As House Energy and Commerce Chairman John Dingell, D-Mich., pointed out, "Whoever controls the papers gets to control the final product the conference votes on." [39]

The chair also sets the pace of the bargaining (often meeting in private to hammer out deals), proposes compromises, and recommends tentative agreements. For example, at a major energy conference Senator Pete Domenici, R-N.M., chairman of the conference, indicated he would first start out with the least controversial provisions and then "work up to the more difficult questions, such as ANWR [drilling for oil and gas in the Arctic National Wildlife Refuge] and electricity regulation, trying to build momentum" for an eventual bicameral accord.[40] Or the conference chair, to facilitate bargaining flexibility, may suggest observance of a common negotiating practice: "Nothing is agreed to until everything is agreed to."

On occasion, disputes arise as to which chamber's turn it is to chair. Institutional pride, ego, public attention, and more are factors that give rise to these disputes. The chairmen of the two tax-writing committees are sometimes at odds over who should chair conference committees. For example, one might work to avoid going to conference on a bill of little public visibility because it is his turn to chair the next conference and it is on a major tax bill. The other chairman, however, might add controversial matters to a relatively noncontroversial measure, trying to force a conference so it will be his turn to chair the major tax conference. Indeed, the party leaders of both chambers are "often called upon to help settle disputes between the two chairmen, who regularly jockey for the right to chair conference committees and are rumored to have resorted to a variety of ploys to prevent the other from presiding over high-profile House-Senate negotiations." [41]

Staff members, too, play an important role in conference deliberations. They draft compromise amendments, negotiate agreements, provide advice to members, and prepare the conference reports. Aides played a particularly important role during a complex conference on an omnibus budget reconciliation bill. According to the executive director of the House Budget Committee, "The role of the staff has been not only to explore where there may be areas of agreement, but also to make the deal. How else are you going to get hundreds of issues resolved in a couple of weeks unless you give the staff some kind of license?" [42]

Conference committee bargaining, like bargaining throughout the legislative process, is subject to outside pressure. Even before the sunshine rules of the mid-1970s that required open conference meetings, conferees were lobbied heavily by special-interest groups, executive agency officials, and sometimes even the president, who will invite conferees to the White House for a "pep talk" on what the administration expects from the negotiations. The president or presidential aides "write letters to conferees; . . . administration personnel show up at conference meetings; and the president freely threatens to use his veto unless conferees compromise." [43] Conservative and liberal members in the respective chambers will write letters to the conferees warning that they will not vote for the conference report unless certain provisions are contained in the final package. A bipartisan group of ten nonconferee senators formed a "working group" to monitor "the conference committee negotiating the details of the [Medicare] prescription drug legislation in an effort to ensure [that] a final product reflects the bipartisan backing won by the Senate bill." [44] When many Senate Democrats were excluded from participating in an energy conference, Sen. Ron Wyden, D-Ore., reminded Republican conferees that if minority party views were ignored, floor consideration of the conference report could trigger the "procedural nuclear weapon"—the Senate filibuster.[45]

The party leaders of Congress, as noted earlier, also get directly involved—brokering compromises or urging conferees to meet a certain timetable or objective. Occasions also arise when the real negotiators are not the conferees but the top congressional leaders and administration officials who convene privately to resolve the issues in disagreement. Their decisions are then implemented by the conferees. On many important bills in the 108th and 109th Congresses, "the real [conference] decision-making is done by the Republican leaders of the House and Senate and the Republican committee chairmen, along with the White House." [46]

Bargaining Objectives and Tactics. Three key—and conflicting—objectives underlie the bargaining and informal give-and-take at conference sessions: (1) conferees usually want to sustain the position of their respective chambers on the bill; (2) they want to achieve a result acceptable to a majority of each chamber's conferees; and (3) they want to craft a compromise product that is acceptable to a majority of the membership of both chambers and one that the president will sign. These objectives cannot be upheld consistently. "We caved so quickly to the House side, it was like watching water go over a waterfall," exclaimed Sen. Joseph R. Biden Jr., D-Del., about a conference on an antiterrorism measure.[47]

The conferees may be able to reach compromises quickly on their differences. For example, splitting the difference on bills appropriating funds for federal programs is often relatively painless. As one senator said, if the Senate bill contains a number, "say it is 200, and the House number is 100, if we cannot get together, we would say 'Let's make it 150. Let's split the difference.' " [48] Or logrolling may occur, with House conferees agreeing to certain Senate-passed provisions to gain leverage to win acceptance of House-passed provisions elsewhere in the bill that are strongly supported by members of their own chamber. Offers and counteroffers are part of the often-exhausting conference process.

Conferees also employ other techniques and tactics during the bargaining process. For example, if conferees chair subcommittees, they may convene hearings while the conference is under way to generate outside pressures on conference decision making. Senators may say that they cannot accept a House compromise offer because it would generate a filibuster in the Senate. Similarly, House conferees may say that a Senate offer is unacceptable because it violates House rules. One side may even fight hard for a position on which it plans to yield, so the conferees can tell their parent chamber that they put up a good battle but the other side would not relent.

The bargaining skills of individual conferees can produce favorable results for their chamber's positions. One House staff aide reflected upon the skill of certain conferees during marathon bargaining sessions: "You're talking about a poker game," he said. "There are people with an enormous degree of patience who will just wait and wait and wait until the other side either slips or collapses or falls asleep." [49]

Sometimes, to break a deadlock, the conferees of one chamber will threaten to break off negotiations and return to their chamber for instructions—thereby reinforcing their position when negotiations resume. A House member once described this ploy as follows:

> Last year there was a difference of about $400 million between the House and Senate versions of the foreign aid appropriations [bill]. The chairman of the House delegation in the conference took a very firm position that we had to end up with slightly less than 50 percent of the difference as a matter of prestige. It was the day we [Congress] were to adjourn. We were in conference until about 10:30 p.m., and the Senate [conferees] wouldn't give in. I think the difference between conferees was only five or ten million dollars. The Senate was fighting for its prestige, and our chairman for his. At 10:30 he started to close his book [staff papers prepared for the conference] and he got up saying he would get instructions from the House. All the rest of our [House] conferees did the same. That prospect was too much for the senators. They capitulated.[50]

This example illustrates some of the factors in conference bargaining: the importance of timing and leadership; the influence of certain members on the negotiations; the effect of threats to convene another series of protracted meetings after one side receives instructions; the role that fatigue can play in resolving hotly contested issues; and the political and professional investment that senators and representatives have in upholding the prestige of their respective chamber and committees.

Another Approach Possible for Appropriations Conferences. Most measures sent to conference are not spending measures, and they reach the conference stage in a manner that gives the conferees maximum bargaining flexibility and discretion. One of the chambers takes a bill from the other, strikes out everything after the enacting clause, and inserts a completely new version of the bill. This, as noted in Chapter 7, is called an amendment in the nature of a substitute. In effect, the House and Senate are dealing with only one amendment in disagreement. In such cases, the conference committee can consider the versions of both houses (in effect, two entirely separate bills) and draft a third rendition of the legislation, provided that it is a pertinent modification of either the House or Senate version.

Until the mid-1990s, the appropriations conferences always considered a number of discrete amendments in disagreement. By custom, the House initiates appropriations bills, and the Senate would then adopt separate amendments to the various provisions in the appropriations legislation. As a result, appropriations conferees enjoyed less latitude in arriving at compromises because relating the House provisions to the corresponding Senate amendment (which was numbered for the convenience of everyone) was not difficult. Also, the House-passed bill and Senate amendments dealt with specific amounts of money that are easy to compare.

An advantage enjoyed by the appropriators was that their conferences, unlike those dealing with one amendment in disagreement, could submit a partial conference report to their respective chambers. Everything they agreed on was included in the partial conference report. Amendments on which they still disagreed, either in a technical (such as a rule violation) or true (such as a conflict over policy) sense, were then submitted separately in each chamber without jeopardizing adoption of the partial report. Until relatively recently, then, appropriations conferences took a two-pronged approach to resolving bicameral differences on bills: they agreed first to a partial conference report and then the House and Senate sent amendments back and forth until they reached agreement.

When Republicans won control of Congress in the mid-1990s, their leadership decided to expedite action on these measures. No longer does the Senate adopt discrete, numbered amendments to appropriations bills; instead, it follows the practice of the other committees by striking the entire text of the House-passed bill and replacing it with a complete substitute amendment. The Senate can return at any time to its former way of handling appropriations bills sent to conference, but, to date, that has not occurred.

Procedural Limits on Bargaining

Theory and practice often diverge on whether the formal rules of either chamber inhibit the bargaining discretion of the conferees. Scope and germaneness are two important procedural constraints—points of order can be raised against the conference report if either of these constraints is violated.

Scope. Scope is a complex technical term embedded in the rulebook of each chamber. It essentially means the conferees are not to add new matter, reopen provisions that both chambers agreed to, or exceed the range of the matters in disagreement committed to them—that is, conferees are not to write new law not previously considered and adopted by either body. For example, Senate Rule XXVIII states that conferees "shall not insert in their report matter not committed to them by either House, nor shall they strike from the bill matter agreed to by both Houses." If then the House authorizes $5 million for a program and the Senate authorizes $10 million, precedents state that the agreement must be sought within these high and low figures, which represent the scope of the bicameral disagreement. (Splitting the difference, $7.5 million in this case, is a common compromise device.) However, when words, not numbers, are in disagreement, judging whether a policy provision reworded by the conferees meets scope requirements is usually harder.

Today, violations of scope are quite common. In the House, it is customary that special rules waive all points of order against the conference report and its consideration in the House.[51] Thus no lawmaker can raise a point of

---

Box 8-1   Instruction of Conferees

APPOINTMENT OF CONFEREES ON H.R. 2691,
DEPARTMENT OF THE INTERIOR AND RELATED AGENCIES
APPROPRIATIONS ACT, 2004

MR. TAYLOR of North Carolina. Mr. Speaker, I ask unanimous consent to take from the Speaker's table the bill (H.R. 2691) making appropriations for the Department of the Interior and related agencies for the fiscal year ending September 30, 2004, and for other purposes, with a Senate amendment thereto, disagree to the Senate amendment, and agree to the conference asked by the Senate.

THE SPEAKER pro tempore. Is there objection to the request of the gentleman from North Carolina?

There was no objection.

MOTION TO INSTRUCT CONFEREES OFFERED BY MR. DICKS

MR. DICKS. Mr. Speaker, I offer a motion to instruct conferees.

The Clerk read as follows:

MR. DICKS moves that the managers on the part of the House at the conference on the disagreeing votes of the two Houses on the Senate amendment to the bill H.R. 2691 be instructed to provide an additional $400,000,000 of emergency funding for fiscal year 2003 forest fire suppression costs.

THE SPEAKER pro tempore. Pursuant to clause 7 of rule XXII, the gentleman from Washington (MR. DICKS) and the gentleman from North Carolina (MR. TAYLOR) each will control 30 minutes.

SOURCE: *Congressional Record*, October 1, 2003, H9061.

---

order against a conference report, because it is protected from parliamentary challenge by the waiver rule. In the Senate, a 1996 precedent so completely undermined Rule XXVIII that it later had to be reinstated. On October 3, 1996, when a point of order was made that a conference report violated scope by adding new matter, the Senate presiding officer ruled: "[I]t is the opinion of the Chair that the conference report exceeds the scope, and the point of order is sustained." [52] The majority leader appealed the ruling of the chair, and the Senate voted to reject the chair's decision. In the Senate, precedents established in this authoritative fashion trump formal rules. Thus, Rule XXVIII was rendered a nullity. New lawmaking by Senate conferees became the order of the day, subject only to the willingness of the House to adopt a special waiver rule for the conference report.

"Conferences are marvelous," exclaimed a senator. "They're mystical. They're alchemy. It's absolutely dazzling what you can do." [53] And with a weakened Rule XXVIII, lots of dazzling processes were devised and new provisions were tucked into conference reports. For example, in the fall of 1999 conferees added a huge Labor-Health and Human Services (HHS) appropria-tions bill to a District of Columbia appropriations conference report. Congress was a month late in getting the appropriations bills enacted by the start of the fiscal year, and the majority leaders of each chamber were under pressure to get the spending measures passed to avoid any shutdown of governmental ser-vices. Thus, the $313.6 billion Labor-HHS bill and the $429 million District of Columbia appropriations measure were married. "Out of that marriage of an elephant and ant," said a senator, "we now have before the Senate the confer-ence report on the District of Columbia with the enormous addition of a $313 billion Labor-HHS 'rider.' " [54] Both houses agreed to the conference report.

However, party leaders and many senators soon became concerned that things had gotten out of hand when scores of extraneous matters were added to conference reports. In mid-December 2000, the Senate statutorily restored Rule XXVIII via an amendment offered by Senator Robert C. Byrd, D-W.Va., to an appropriations bill.[55] Violations of "scope" could now be raised as points of order against conference reports containing provisions not in either the House or Senate version of the measure submitted to conference. If the presiding officer sustained the point of order, the conference report would fall.

On January 18, 2007, the Senate in S. 1 (the Legislative Transparency and Accountability Act) again addressed Rule XXVIII by stipulating "that ear-marks added to a conference report that are not considered by the Senate or the House of Representatives are out of scope." Further, all earmarks are to be disclosed in conference reports and join explanatory statements with any senator able to make points of order to remove specific out-of-scope earmarks without "taking down the entire conference report."[56] Items deleted from a conference report on one or more points of order enable the Senate (if S. 1 is enacted into law) to repackage the remaining portions of the conference re-port as an amendment and then seek the House's concurrence on it. Even with the restoration of Rule XXVIII, senators to date have seldom invoked the rule because the result might be rejection of a major conference report that contains matter important to the national interest and to most lawmakers.

Worth noting is that Senate precedents are quite broad for judging whether new and extraneous provisions are included in conference reports. A prece-dent still on the books is that matters not "entirely irrelevant" to the subject matter of the conference report are allowed. This standard is difficult to in-terpret when one chamber passes a bill and the other replaces the entire text of the measure with a complete substitute. In this case the conferees have wider leeway to write a third version of the legislation so long as it is "ger-mane to the provisions of one or the other passed bills." [57]

Germaneness. The Senate is able to add amendments to House-passed measures that are considered nongermane under House rules. For years, House conferees were faced with a take-it-or-leave-it proposition—accept the nongermane Senate amendments or lose the bill in its entirety, including the House-passed provisions, given that conference reports are not open to amendment. Members of the House expressed frustration over this recurring dilemma. The House finally acted against the Senate practice by adopting a 1972 rule change permitting separate votes on the nongermane portions of conference reports. The rule was designed to accommodate the Senate's right to offer nongermane amendments while protecting the procedural prerogatives of the House. Rarely is this House rule invoked.

Any House member may make one or more points of order against a conference report when it is called up for final approval on the ground that it contains nongermane material. The member simply says, "Mr. Speaker, I make a point of order under House Rule XXII that the last section of the conference report contains nongermane material." Typically, special rules are obtained from the Rules Committee to protect the conference report against such points of order. Assume there is no rule, and the Speaker sustains the point of order. The representative who raised the objection on the floor will then move to reject the nongermane conference matter. Forty minutes of debate, equally divided between those who support and those who oppose the motion, are permitted under this procedure, after which the House votes on the motion to reject. If it is adopted, the nongermane material is deleted, and the pending question before the House is disposition of the remaining conference material minus the nongermane portion. Defeat of the motion permits the House to keep the nongermane matter in the conference report.

Filing the Conference Report

When a majority of the conferees from each chamber have reached agreement, they instruct committee staff aides to prepare a conference report, which embodies their negotiated recommendations on the matters in bicameral disagreement. Figure 8-1 provides an example of a conference report. Conference reports must be accompanied by a joint explanatory statement. This statement is prepared by the conferees (and appropriate staff) of both houses so that the explanation of what was decided upon will not be different in the two houses, and thus subject to differing interpretations. The conference report contains statutory language while the joint explanatory statement provides a more readable summary of the conferees' decisions. An appropriate conferee will submit, or file, the conference report for printing to the chamber (usually the House because it initiates revenue and appropriation measures) that requested the conference.

A majority of the conferees from each house—sometimes they are only from the majority party—must sign the report for it to be sent back to the House and Senate. When conferences end, the conferees sometimes scatter quickly, forcing staff members clutching official signature pages to track down managers for both Houses in their offices or in elevators, hallways, or restaurants. The parliamentarians will not accept photocopied signatures or other facsimiles.[58] After the necessary signatures are obtained, the conference committee has concluded its work. (Unlike reports of standing committees of each chamber, conference reports are prohibited by precedent from containing minority or additional viewpoints.)

109TH CONGRESS ⎱
2d Session   ⎰ HOUSE OF REPRESENTATIVES ⎰ REPORT
                                                 109–597

CARL D. PERKINS CAREER AND TECHNICAL EDUCATION
IMPROVEMENT ACT OF 2006

JULY 25, 2006.—Ordered to be printed

Mr. McKEON, from the committee of conference,
submitted the following

CONFERENCE REPORT

[To accompany S. 250]

The committee of conference on the disagreeing votes of the two Houses on the amendments of the House to the bill (S. 250), to amend the Carl D. Perkins Vocational and Technical Education Act of 1998 to improve the Act, having met, after full and free conference, have agreed to recommend and do recommend to their respective Houses as follows:

That the Senate recede from its disagreement to the amendment of the House to the text of the bill and agree to the same with an amendment as follows:

In lieu of the matter proposed to be inserted by the House amendment, insert the following:

SECTION 1. SHORT TITLE; AMENDMENT.

    (a) SHORT TITLE.—*This Act may be cited as the "Carl D. Perkins Career and Technical Education Improvement Act of 2006".*

    (b) AMENDMENT.—*The Carl D. Perkins Vocational and Technical Education Act of 1998 (20 U.S.C. 2301 et seq.) is amended to read as follows:*

"SECTION 1. SHORT TITLE; TABLE OF CONTENTS.

    "(a) SHORT TITLE.—*This Act may be cited as the 'Carl D. Perkins Career and Technical Education Act of 2006'.*

    "(b) TABLE OF CONTENTS.—*The table of contents for this Act is as follows:*

"Sec. 1. Short title; table of contents.
"Sec. 2. Purpose.
"Sec. 3. Definitions.
"Sec. 4. Transition provisions.
"Sec. 5. Privacy.
"Sec. 6. Limitation.
"Sec. 7. Special rule.

49–006

FIGURE 8-1 Conference Report

Sometimes the official filing of conference reports is delayed for strategic reasons, such as the need to make changes to pick up votes or to encourage lawmakers to support another measure. During the 109th Congress, House GOP leaders delayed the filing of a highway conference report, because they were uncertain if they had the votes to pass the Central America Free Trade Agreement (CAFTA). The highway conference report was replete with projects for many lawmakers and the GOP leadership implied to its members that their position on CAFTA could affect the fate of their highway projects. As House GOP Whip Blunt explained: "[I]t's certainly not beyond the realm of possibility that members come and say, 'Gee, how am I doing with my projects in the highway bill?' And we're probably not beyond saying, we'll check and see how you're doing" on CAFTA.[59] Both measures passed the House.

Party leaders can stir sharp controversy if they add or delete material after a conference committee has officially concluded its work. This type of action seldom occurs. However, a conference committee on a defense appropriations bill had new matter added after the negotiators had signed and issued the bicameral accord and announced it to the public. Technically, the conference was over. No further changes were permitted to be made to the defense conference report unless the conference committee was reconvened for that purpose. As David Obey, Wis., the ranking Democrat on the House Appropriations Committee, exclaimed:

> [A]fter the conference was finished at 6 p.m., Senator Frist marched over to the House side of the Capitol about 4 hours later and insisted that over 40 pages of legislation, which I have in my hand, 40 pages of legislation that had never been seen by conferees, be attached to the bill. The Speaker joined him in that assistance so that, without a vote of the conferees, that legislation was unilaterally and arrogantly inserted into the bill after the conference was over in a blatantly abusive power play by two of the most powerful men in Congress.[60]

To prevent this from happening again, the House on January 4, 2007, adopted new rules stating that conference reports are "inviolate to change" unless all the House conferees have a chance to reconsider their decisions. In addition, it is not in order for the House to consider a conference report whose substantive content does not reflect the decisions of the conferees on all the differences between the two chambers.[61]

Conference reports must be published in the *Congressional Record* before they are brought before the House or Senate for final action. House rules require a three-day layover for conference reports, which must be available to all members for reading at least two hours prior to floor consideration. Senate rules state that conference reports must be available on each senator's desk before they can be taken up on the floor. In each chamber, these rules can be set aside, usually by a rule from the House Rules Committee and by unanimous consent in the Senate.

Final Floor Action on Conference Reports

Once the conference report is agreed to and filed with the House and Senate, it must be acted on by both chambers before it is cleared for the president. Customarily, the chamber that requests a conference acts last on the conference report, but only if the papers are in its possession. The papers, as mentioned earlier, are the official documents, such as the bill as originally passed by one chamber and the amendments added to it by the other chamber. Normally, the papers are held by the chamber that agreed to go to conference; that house then would be the first to consider the conference report. However, the papers may be transferred to the other chamber by agreement of the conference committee or one house may simply walk out with them.

Policy outcomes sometimes are influenced by which chamber acts first or last on the conference report. For example, the chairman of the committee that reported legislation creating the Department of Education got the House in 1979 to ask for a conference with the Senate. He wanted the House to act last on the conference report so that the parliamentary options available to the bill's opponents—who were more numerous in the House—would be limited.

The first chamber to act on a conference report has three options: adopt, reject, or recommit (return it to the conferees for further deliberation). When the first chamber to act adopts the conference report, however, this automatically dissolves the conference committee, and the other chamber is faced with a "yes" or "no" vote on the report. The chairman's strategy worked in the case of the Department of Education bill. After intense lobbying by the White House and various education groups, the House agreed to the conference report establishing the new department.

Conference reports are privileged and may be brought up at almost any time the House and Senate are in session, subject to each chamber's requirement for the availability of conference reports and typically with the prior approval of the leadership. The senior majority and minority conferees from each house's delegation normally act as the floor managers of the conference version. Both chambers require conference reports to be accepted or rejected in their entirety; they are not open to amendment. However, conference reports can be changed via adoption by both chambers of a concurrent resolution authorizing either the Clerk of the House or the Secretary of the Senate to correct language in a conference report during the enrollment process (see below). Another option is to enact a separate bill to change the text and intent of a conference report.

In the Senate, conference reports are usually brought up by unanimous consent at a time agreed to by the party leaders and floor managers, as shown in Box 8-2. Because conference reports are privileged, if any senator objects to the unanimous consent request the majority leader (or a proponent) can offer a nondebatable motion to take up the conference report: "Mr. President, I move to proceed to the conference report to accompany S. 1234." The conference report itself, however, can be filibustered. (Commonly, conference reports are debated under a time-limitation agreement.) Furthermore, it used

---

Box 8-2   Calling Up a Conference Report: Unanimous Consent Agreement

CONFERENCE REPORT TO ACCOMPANY H.R. 4939

1.—Ordered, That on Wednesday, June 14, 2006, upon the conclusion of Morning Business, the Senate resume consideration of the conference report to accompany H.R. 4939, an act making emergency supplemental appropriations for the fiscal year ending September 30, 2006, and for other purposes; provided that there be 25 minutes for debate under the control of the Senator from Mississippi (Mr. Cochran) and 75 minutes of debate under the control of the Senator from West Virginia (Mr. Byrd) to be allocated as follows:

Reid—10 minutes
Landrieu—20 minutes
Durbin—15 minutes
Dayton—10 minutes
Harkin—15 minutes
Akaka—5 minutes

Ordered further, That upon the use of yielding back of time, the conference report be set aside; provided further, that at 10:00 a.m. on Thursday, June 15, 2006, the Senate proceed to vote on the adoption of the conference report to accompany H.R. 4939, without intervening action or debate. *(June 13, 2006.)*

SOURCE: Senate of the United States, 109th Congress, *Calendar of Business,* June 14, 2006, 2.

---

to be the case that before the Senate took action on the motion to take up the conference report, any senator could demand that it be read in full. This requirement was eliminated, however, in mid-December 2000, at the same time the Senate reinstated the scope provision of Rule XXVIII.

In the House, there are three main routes to the floor for conference reports, which because of their privileged character can be called up at almost any time. Most conference reports are considered under the one-hour rule, with the time divided equally between the majority and minority floor managers. In 1985 the House changed its rules to permit one-third of the time to be assigned to a member who opposes the bicameral accord if both the GOP and Democratic floor managers support it. Suspension of the rules is sometimes used to bring conference reports to the floor, but this is not a preferred procedure because it involves a severe requirement: a two-thirds instead of majority vote for adoption. It is usual practice for a rule to be obtained from the Rules Committee, an example of which can be seen in Box 8-3. Conference managers seek a rule when they want to waive the three-day layover requirement (either to meet deadlines or exploit favorable political circumstances) or to prevent points of order against the conference report for violations of scope or germaneness. Conference reports are seldom rejected. As one congressional attorney explained:

> [The] chief reason conference reports pass is the basic rule that such reports must be adopted or rejected as a whole. . . . Thus, the question for Members is not how they feel about any particular provision, but how they feel about the bill as a whole, and they can always justify a vote for a conference report on the ground that they accepted the distasteful parts only to save the good ones.[62]

Outright rejection of a conference report kills the bill and may require a repetition of the entire legislative process. This becomes particularly significant in the weeks immediately before the final adjournment of a Congress, when members face the choice of accepting the bill as is; recommitting it to a conference committee, in all probability jeopardizing final approval; or killing the bill, knowing no time is left to move a revised bill through Congress.

Box 8-3   Calling Up a Conference Report by Special Rule

WAIVING POINT OF ORDER AGAINST CONFERENCE REPORT ON H.R. 2863, DEPARTMENT OF DEFENSE APPROPRIATIONS ACT, 2006

MR. COLE OF OKLAHOMA. Mr. Speaker, by direction of the Committee on Rules, I call up House Resolution 639 and ask for its immediate consideration.

The Clerk read the resolution, as follows:
H. RES. 639
Resolved, That upon adoption of this resolution it shall be in order to consider the conference report to accompany the bill (H.R. 2863) making appropriations for the Department of Defense for the fiscal year ending September 30, 2006, and for other purposes. All points of order against the conference report and against its consideration are waived. The conference report shall be considered as read.

THE SPEAKER pro tempore (Mr. Boozman). The gentleman from Oklahoma (Mr. Cole) is recognized for 1 hour.
MR. COLE OF OKLAHOMA. Mr. Speaker, for the purpose of debate only, I yield the customary 30 minutes to the gentlewoman from New York (Ms. Slaughter) pending which I yield myself such time as I may consume. During consideration of this resolution, all time yielded is for the purpose of debate only.
Mr. Speaker, the rule waives all points of order against the conference report and against consideration and provides that the conference report shall be considered as read.

SOURCE: *Congressional Record,* December 18, 2005, H12225.

Once both houses approve the conference report, the papers are delivered to the house that originated the measure. A copy of the bill as finally agreed to by Congress is prepared by an enrolling clerk. The enrolled bill is signed by the Speaker and presiding officer of the Senate, or by other authorized officers, and sent to the president. In a first-time-ever enrollment ceremony, Speaker Hastert and Senate president pro tempore Strom Thurmond, R-S.C., electronically signed a year 2000 (Y2K) liability bill and sent it via e-mail to the president. "For the first time in history Congress is sending an electronically signed bill to the president," declared the Senate majority leader.[63] Congress also transmitted a signed paper version of the measure to the White House. These little-used "bill signing" ceremonies are also organized by the Speaker and Senate majority leader, if both are of the same party, to showcase partisan colleagues facing tough reelection fights.[64]

Although most enrolled bills are sent quickly to the White House, sometimes there are delays of a few days or weeks in getting them there. A measure's length and complexity might slow its processing by the enrolling clerks, or the delay might be intentional. For example, to eliminate a bill as a campaign issue and to free the president from electoral pressures, its transmittal can be timed by party leaders so the chief executive has until after Election Day to decide whether to sign or veto (or pocket veto, if Congress has adjourned) the measure.[65]

PRESIDENTIAL APPROVAL OR VETO

Under the Constitution (Article I, Section 7), the president has a qualified veto power. The president's options are four. First, the president can sign measures into law. Second, the president can disapprove of legislative acts, subject to the ability of Congress during its two-year life to override the vetoes by a two-thirds vote, a quorum being present, of each house. Once an enrolled bill is sent to the White House, the president has ten days, excluding Sundays, to sign or veto it. Third, if no action is taken within the ten-day period and Congress is in session, the bill automatically becomes law without the president's signature. Fourth, if Congress adjourns *sine die* (that is, ending the second session) before the ten-day period is up, therefore preventing the return of a bill, and the president does not sign the measure, the legislation dies as a "pocket veto." Unlike a regular veto, Congress has no opportunity to override a pocket veto. Periodically, controversies erupt between Congress and the White House when presidents try to pocket veto measures when Congress is in recess.

Woodrow Wilson wrote that the president, in using the veto power, "acts not as the executive but as a third branch of the legislature." [66] The president can use the veto, or the threat of a veto, to advance legislative and political goals. Often, the threat of a veto is itself enough to persuade Congress to change its legislative course, because attracting the two-thirds vote required in each house to override presidential vetoes is difficult. Periodically, the administration will submit Statements of Administration Policy to Congress highlighting, for example, the president's problems with certain legislation. One senator vividly described the president's power when he told the Senate why a conference committee agreed to a specific compromise: "There is another fundamental reason we did it—that is because we faced the veto, that great, big monster of a veto." [67]

Presidents use their veto power because they consider a measure to be unconstitutional, believe it encroaches on the chief executive's powers and duties, or hold that it represents ill-advised policies. When President Richard Nixon vetoed the 1973 War Powers Resolution (which Congress subsequently enacted by overriding his veto), he cited all three factors as the basis of his action. Vetoing bills because they cost too much is another favorite rationale of presidents.

Chief executives may issue "signing statements" to accompany a piece of legislation they have signed into law. Signing statements have been used by presidents at least since the time of Andrew Jackson, but George W. Bush, according to many analysts and scholars, has employed them more frequently than any previous president to reassert and strengthen executive power. Even though the Constitution states that the president is obligated "to take care that the laws be faithfully executed," President Bush, since taking office in 2001, has issued "signing statements on more than 750 new laws, declaring that he has the power to set aside the laws when they conflict with his legal interpretation. The federal government is instructed to follow the statements when it enforces the laws." [68] To be sure, Congress is paying close attention to the implications of signing statements as challenges to its legislative authority.[69]

Presidents contemplate how vetoes can be employed to advance their electoral and policy agendas, especially when their party does not control Congress. As national elections approach, for example, presidents will use the veto against an opposition Congress to show how their policies differ from the other party's and thus highlight their fundamental beliefs to the electorate. Conversely, an opposition Congress will send measures to the White House that it expects the president to veto. This strategy could be called the politics of differentiation or contrast politics.

When the president vetoes a measure, the Constitution provides that "he shall return it with his Objections to that House in which it shall have originated" and that chamber shall "proceed to reconsider it." This means that some action must be taken, but not necessarily a veto override vote. Neither chamber is under any obligation to schedule an override attempt. Party leaders may realize they have no chance to override and may not even attempt it. Because of popular support for the president's action, or for other reasons, the political environment may not be conducive to a successful override. Thus, a motion may be made to refer the message to committee rather than risk a loss on override. If an override attempt fails in one chamber, the process ends and the bill dies. If it succeeds, the measure is sent to the other chamber, where a second successful override vote makes it law. The Constitution requires roll call votes on override attempts.

Whether signed by the president, allowed to become law without the president's signature, or passed over a veto, the bill becomes a public law and is sent to the National Archives and Records Administration for deposit and publication in *Statutes at Large*, an annual volume that compiles all bills that have become law. (Figure 8-2 shows an example of a public law.)

---

119 STAT. 4   PUBLIC LAW 109–2—FEB. 18, 2005

Public Law 109–2
109th Congress
An Act

Feb. 18, 2005   To amend the procedures that apply to consideration of interstate class actions
[S. 5]   to assure fairer outcomes for class members and defendants, and for other purposes.

Class Action   *Be it enacted by the Senate and House of Representatives of*
Fairness Act of   *the United States of America in Congress assembled,*
2005.
28 USC 1 note.   **SECTION 1. SHORT TITLE; REFERENCE; TABLE OF CONTENTS.**

(a) SHORT TITLE.—This Act may be cited as the "Class Action Fairness Act of 2005".

(b) REFERENCE.—Whenever in this Act reference is made to an amendment to, or repeal of, a section or other provision, the reference shall be considered to be made to a section or other provision of title 28, United States Code.

(c) TABLE OF CONTENTS.—The table of contents for this Act is as follows:

Sec. 1. Short title; reference; table of contents.
Sec. 2. Findings and purposes.
Sec. 3. Consumer class action bill of rights and improved procedures for interstate class actions.
Sec. 4. Federal district court jurisdiction for interstate class actions.
Sec. 5. Removal of interstate class actions to Federal district court.
Sec. 6. Report on class action settlements.
Sec. 7. Enactment of Judicial Conference recommendations.
Sec. 8. Rulemaking authority of Supreme Court and Judicial Conference.
Sec. 9. Effective date.

28 USC 1711   **SEC. 2. FINDINGS AND PURPOSES.**
note.
(a) FINDINGS.—Congress finds the following:

(1) Class action lawsuits are an important and valuable part of the legal system when they permit the fair and efficient resolution of legitimate claims of numerous parties by allowing the claims to be aggregated into a single action against a defendant that has allegedly caused harm.

(2) Over the past decade, there have been abuses of the class action device that have—

(A) harmed class members with legitimate claims and defendants that have acted responsibly;

(B) adversely affected interstate commerce; and

(C) undermined public respect for our judicial system.

(3) Class members often receive little or no benefit from class actions, and are sometimes harmed, such as where—

(A) counsel are awarded large fees, while leaving class members with coupons or other awards of little or no value;

(B) unjustified awards are made to certain plaintiffs at the expense of other class members; and

---

FIGURE 8-2 Public Law

A question rarely heard on Capitol Hill was raised during the 109th Congress—Is it a law? At issue was whether the Deficit Reduction Act of 2005 was unconstitutionally signed into law (P.L. 109–171). Federal court challenges are underway to address this issue. Briefly, on December 19, 2005, the House narrowly adopted (212–206) the conference report on the deficit measure (S. 1932). The Senate considered the conference report for three days, but on December 21, several budget points of order were successfully raised against the conference report, which led to its rejection. The Senate repassed S. 1932 with an amendment (the conference report minus the offending items) with Vice President Richard Cheney casting the tie-breaking vote.

However, a Senate clerk made an error (changing 13 months to 36 months as the length of time Medicare recipients could lease certain health-care equipment) in the process of transmitting S. 1932, as amended, to the House. Although informed of the error, House GOP leaders chose not to correct the error, perhaps because that would require another vote in the closely divided Senate. Thus, on February 1, 2006, the House enacted S. 1932 with the 36-month mistake in it. Because the Senate originated the bill, it was returned to that chamber where a Senate clerk corrected the error, changing 36 to 13 in the enrollment process. Speaker Hastert and President pro tempore Ted Stevens signed official documents certifying that S. 1932 had passed both the House and Senate. They forwarded the bill to the White House. On February 8, 2006, President Bush signed S. 1932 into law. To sum up: Because the text of S. 1932 that passed the Senate is different from the text of S. 1932 that passed the House—mindful that a corrected version of S. 1932 was certified as passing both chambers and then signed into law by the president—is this measure a constitutionally enacted statute? With legal and legislative battles under way, the resolution of this issue at this juncture remains unclear.[70]

NOTES

1. Ada G. McCown, *The Congressional Conference Committee* (New York: Columbia University Press, 1927), 12. See also Gilbert Steiner, *The Congressional Conference Committee, Seventieth to Eightieth Congresses* (Urbana: University of Illinois Press, 1951); David J. Vogler, *The Third House: Conference Committees in the United States Congress* (Evanston, Ill.: Northwestern University Press, 1971); and Lawrence Longley and Walter J. Oleszek, *Bicameral Politics: Conference Committees in Congress* (New Haven, Conn.: Yale University Press, 1989).

2. Information for the 103d Congress was compiled by Ilona Nickels, congressional specialist, Government Division, Congressional Research Service (CRS), Library of Congress. The data for the 107th and 108th Congresses were provided by Elizabeth Rybicki, a congressional specialist in the Government and Finance Division, Congressional Research Service, who is an expert on conference committees.

3. *Congressional Record,* July 8, 1998, S7650.

4. Roy Swanstrom, *The United States Senate, 1787–1801,* 99th Cong., 1st sess., 1985, S. Doc. 99–19, 232.

5. *Congressional Record,* September 13, 1999, H8129.

6. *Congressional Record,* February 20, 1986, S1463.

7. Dave Boyer, "GOP Considers TV for Energy Hearings," *The Washington Times,* April 26, 2002, A4.

8. *CQ Daily Monitor,* March 20, 2000, 3.

9. Gary Andres, "A Deal or No Deal," *The Washington Times,* June 8, 2006, A19.

10. Richard Cohen, *National Journal,* July 28, 2001, 2396.

11. Senate Committee on Rules and Administration, *Congressional Handbook,* U.S. Senate ed. (Washington, D.C.: Government Printing Office, 1994), III-30.

12. *Congressional Record,* March 21, 1974, 7589. See also *Congressional Record,* April 10, 1974, 10569.

13. *Congressional Record,* December 20, 1982, S15757.

14. Richard F. Fenno Jr., *The Power of the Purse* (Boston: Little, Brown, 1966), 610.

15. John Ferejohn, "Who Wins in Conference Committee?" *Journal of Politics* (November 1975): 1033–1046; and Walter J. Oleszek, "House-Senate Relationships: Comity and Conflict," *The Annals* (January 1974): 80–81.

16. Elizabeth Drew, *Senator* (New York: Simon and Schuster, 1979), 174.

17. *Congressional Record,* May 23, 2001, S5527.

18. Janet Hook and Peter Wallsten, "Border Battle Now a GOP Turf War," *Los Angeles Times,* June 22, 2006 (online edition).

19. *Enactment of a Law,* 97th Cong., 2d sess., 1992, S. Doc. 97–20, 24.

20. Carl Hulse and Robert Pear, "Feeling Left Out on Major Bills, Democrats Turn to Stalling Others," *New York Times,* May 3, 2004, A18.

21. Ceci Connolly, "Legislation Goes Overboard as Legislators Eye the Exits," *Congressional Quarterly Weekly Report,* October 1, 1994, 2755.

22. *Congressional Record,* May 16, 2000, S3991.

23. *Congressional Record,* November 13, 2006, S10846.

24. *Congressional Record,* July 18, 1985, H5937.

25. *Washington Times,* February 14, 1995, A11.

26. Mary Agnes Carey, "Hastert's Choice of Conferees Diminishes Prospects for Survival of House's Managed Care Bill," *CQ Weekly,* November 6, 1999, 2657.

27. *Congressional Record,* March 2, 2006, S1600.

28. *Congressional Record,* March 3, 2006, S1755.

29. Alan K. Ota, "With DeLay Setting a Partisan Tone, House Stands Firm on Child Credit," *CQ Weekly,* June 21, 2003, 1531.

30. John Cochran, "Management by Objective: How Frist Deals in 51–49 Senate," *CQ Weekly,* August 30, 2003, 2063.

31. Jonathan Allen and John Cochran, "The Might of the Right," *CQ Weekly,* November 8, 2003, 2762.

32. *Congressional Record,* July 29, 1981, S8711.

33. *Congressional Record,* August 3, 1989, H5003.

34. For an example of a majority party member offering an unusual instruction motion, see *Congressional Record,* November 8, 2001, H7945.

35. *Congressional Record,* June 23, 1983, H4435.

36. *CQ Daily Monitor,* August 8, 1994, 3.

37. In 2003, for example, Democrats offered numerous motions to instruct, urging House conferees to provide a child tax credit to families earning between $10,000 and $26,000. A goal of Democrats was to make Republicans appear insensitive to the needs of low-income working families.

38. Robert Pear, "Negotiators Stall on Patients' Rights Bill," *New York Times*, May 26, 2000, A15.

39. Jackie Koszczuk, "After Half a Century, He's Still Got a To-Do List," *CQ Weekly*, February 20, 2006, 475.

40. Samuel Goldreich, "Domenici, Tauzin Say They Will Write Energy Bill," *CQ Today*, September 12, 2003, 6.

41. Emily Pierce, "Tax Conference Getting 'Parental Supervision,'" *Roll Call*, May 22, 2003, 26.

42. *New York Times*, July 23, 1981, A19. See also Michael J. Malbin, *Unelected Representatives: Congressional Staff and the Future of Representative Government* (New York: Basic Books, 1980), chap. 5.

43. Ted Siff and Alan Weil, *Ruling Congress* (New York: Grossman, 1975), 184.

44. Julie Rovner, "Senators Form 'Working Group' to Watch Medicare Negotiations," *CongressDailyAM*, August 1, 2003, 7.

45. Joseph Anselmo, "GOP Leaders Take a Short Time-Out in Final Push on Omnibus Energy Bill," *CQ Today*, October 2, 2003, 5.

46. David S. Broder, "A Distaff Defense of Kids," *Washington Post*, June 6, 2003, A27.

47. Laurie Kellman, "Senators Lament Cutting Anti-Terror Bill Features," *Washington Times*, April 17, 1996, A6.

48. *Congressional Record*, August 1, 1984, S9605.

49. *CQ's Congressional Insight*, October 19, 1990, 1.

50. Quoted in Charles L. Clapp, *The Congressman* (Washington, D.C.: Brookings, 1962), 249.

51. For a rare point of order against a conference report for violating scope, see *Congressional Record*, November 14, 2002, H8824.

52. *Congressional Record*, October 3, 1996, S12231.

53. Marc Lacey, "Senate Panel Opts to Split Bill on Immigration," *Los Angeles Times*, March 15, 1996, A8.

54. *Congressional Record*, November 1, 1999, S13597–S13598.

55. *Congressional Record*, December 15, 2000, S11856.

56. *Congressional Record*, January 18, 2007, S741.

57. Floyd M. Riddick and Alan S. Frumin, *Senate Procedure: Precedents and Practices* (Washington, D.C.: Government Printing Office, 1992), 463.

58. Martin Gold, Michael Hugo, Hyde Murray, Peter Robinson, and A. L. "Pete" Singleton, *The Book on Congress* (Washington, D.C.: Big Eagle Publishing, 1992), 343.

59. Martin Vaughan and Susan Davis, "With Extra Time and Bush's Help, CAFTA Squeaks Through," National Journal's *CongressDailyPM*, July 28, 2005, 2.

60. *Congressional Record*, December 22, 2005, H13181.

61. *Congressional Record*, January 4, 2007, H27.

62. Charles Tiefer, *Congressional Practice and Procedure* (New York: Greenwood Press, 1989), 818.

63. Matthew Rarey, "Congress Breaks into Cyberspace with Electronically Signed Bill," *Washington Times*, July 16, 1999, A3.

64. Erin Billings and John Stanton, "Leaders Boost Profiles of Senate's Endangered," *Roll Call*, March 2, 2006, 22.

65. See, for example, John H. Cushman Jr., "Congress Lets President Delay His Tax Bill Veto," *New York Times*, October 23, 1992, A14.

66. Woodrow Wilson, *Congressional Government* (Boston: Houghton Mifflin, 1885), 52. Wilson wrote (p. 260) that the "president is no greater than his prerogative of veto makes him; he is, in other words, powerful rather as a branch of the legislature than as the titular head of the Executive."

67. *Congressional Record*, December 20, 1982, S15678.

68. Charlie Savage, "Bush Challenges Hundreds of Laws; President Cites Powers of His Office," *Boston Globe*, April 30, 2006, A1.

69. Phillip J. Cooper, "George W. Bush, Edgar Allen Poe, and the Use and Abuse of Presidential Signing Statements," *Presidential Studies Quarterly*, September 2005, 515–532. See Jennifer Yachnin, "Democrats Guard Legislative Power," *Roll Call*, June 7, 2006, 1.

70. Several informative discussions of this issue include: *Congressional Record*, March 30, 2006, E474–E476; Stephen Dinan, "Democrats Cry Foul Over Clerical Error in Bill," *The Washington Times*, February 11, 2006, A2; Jonathan Weisman, "Spending Measure Not a Law, Suit Says," *Washington Post*, March 22, 2006, A4; and T. R. Goldman, "Loose Language in Deficit Act Elicits Lawsuit," *Legal Times*, April 3, 2006, 1.

CHAPTER 9

Legislative Oversight

"WE ARE GOING TO PROVIDE the time for committees to do oversight of the executive department and of the way the people's money is being spent and the effectiveness of the policy implementation of the president," exclaimed House Majority Leader Steny Hoyer, D-Md., at the start of the new Democratically controlled 110th Congress.[1] Prior to the Democratic takeover of the GOP-controlled Congress, there was considerable talk by many journalists, pundits, and even some Republicans that Congress had largely abdicated its "checks and balance" responsibility. "[W]e've delegated so much authority to the executive branch of the government, and we ought to devote more time to oversight than we do," said Sen. Charles Grassley, R-Iowa, chairman (2001–2007) of the Finance Committee.[2]

To be sure, there was not a collapse of oversight across the board. A number of House and Senate committee chairs, such as Grassley, conducted extensive oversight of various programs and agencies. For example, the House Judiciary chair held sixty-eight oversight hearings on strengthening immigration laws and fifty-six oversight hearings on the USA Patriot Act.[3] The collapse theme expressed by various lawmakers, analysts, and journalists was directed at the lack of meaningful, thorough, and systematic investigations of many crucial issues, such as administrative dysfunctions at the Department of Homeland Security; fraud in Iraq's reconstruction, including contractors charging $45 to $50 for a case of Coca-Cola; and the "Breathtaking Waste and Fraud in Hurricane [Katrina] Aid," a front-page headline in the June 27, 2006, *New York Times*. Critics of Congress's supervisory role suggested that it was following another dictionary meaning of oversight—"failure to notice" executive branch activities embarrassing to the White House.

If important functions of legislative oversight are to promote accountability in government and to raise and ask the tough questions of public officials and others that may help them fix mistakes or prevent their good decisions from going bad, then Congress's monitoring role is perhaps more important today than ever before. Since the terrorist attacks of September 11, 2001, there has been a large expansion of the federal government with the creation of the mammoth Department of Homeland Security, the enlargement of federal police powers under the USA Patriot Act, large military and intelligence expenditures for the global war on terrorism, a major overhaul of the intelligence community, the reconstruction of Iraq and Afghanistan, and the rebuilding of the Gulf Coast in the aftermath of Hurricane Katrina.

Many Democrats have an affirmative view of government and many Republicans advocate small government. Today's reality suggests that while the size and scope of government remain a perennial issue for the two parties, perhaps more important to the general public is to have a competent, efficient, and cost-effective government that can generate the right set of policies to meet today's many challenges (the terrorist threat, the clash between security versus liberty, the spread of dangerous diseases that know no borders, mass migration, etc.).

Congressional oversight is the continuing review by the House and Senate, especially through their committee structures, of how effectively the executive branch is carrying out congressional mandates. It implies some form of "supervision," "watchfulness," or "review" of executive actions and activities. Only by investigating how a statute is being administered can Congress discover deficiencies in the original statute and make necessary adjustments and refinements.

Laws passed by Congress are often general guidelines and sometimes their wording is deliberately vague or convoluted. Implementation of these laws commonly requires the executive agencies to draft administrative regulations and agency officials to undertake day-to-day program management. A key goal of legislative oversight is to hold executive officials accountable for their implementation of delegated authority. As one senator put it: "I believe that oversight is one of the Congress's most important constitutional responsibilities. We must do more than write laws and decide policies. It is also our responsibility to perform the oversight necessary to insure that the administration enforces those laws as Congress intended." [4]

Congress's "watchdog" role is crucial for other reasons. Oversight shines the spotlight of public attention on many significant issues, allowing the American people to make informed judgments about executive performance, policy success or failure, and the conduct of officeholders who serve in the federal government. "The informing function of Congress," wrote Woodrow Wilson in his classic 1885 study of the legislative branch, "should be preferred even to its legislative function." He added:

> Unless Congress have and use every means of acquainting itself with the acts and dispositions of the administrative agents of the government, the country must be helpless to learn how it is being served; and unless Congress both scrutinize these things and sift them by every form of discussion, the country must remain in embarrassing, crippling ignorance of the very affairs which it is most important it should understand and direct. [5]

Another fundamental goal of oversight is to protect Congress's policy-making role and its place in our constitutional separation of powers system as the "first branch" of government. The huge growth of the executive establishment—the "fourth branch of government"—has produced a policy-making rival to Congress. Administrators do more than simply "faithfully execute" our laws according to the intent (which may be vague) of Congress. Federal agencies are filled with knowledgeable career and noncareer experts who, among other things, write rules and regulations that have the force of law; formulate policy initiatives for the White House and Congress; interpret statutes in ways that may expand their discretionary authority or, conversely, undercut legislative intent; and shape policy development by Congress, in part by "selling" their ideas to lawmakers and committees via hearings, agency reports, and other means.

It is this function of oversight—reviewing and investigating the executive branch, along with its informing function—that is under challenge as Congress faces a president in George W. Bush who has an expansive view of executive authority. Many of the president's claims of unilateral power—for example, his authorization of the National Security Agency's program to eavesdrop on the domestic telephone calls of suspected terrorists, overriding the purposes of the 1978 Foreign Intelligence Surveillance Act—stem from the president's assertive interpretation of his constitutional commander-in-chief role in prosecuting the global war on terror.

OVERSIGHT: AN OVERVIEW

Congress's oversight roles are both to take stock of national governmental responsibilities and to ensure, as the Constitution states, that "the laws are faithfully executed" by the president and federal administrators. Oversight has been part of the principal functions of the legislative branch since the nation's beginning. Congress's power of the purse, its authority to pass laws that create programs and agencies, its power of impeachment and confirmation, and its right to investigate executive branch activities are among the explicit and implicit oversight functions rooted in the Constitution. The framers, according to historian Arthur M. Schlesinger Jr., believed the review function did not require specific mention in the Constitution. "[I]t was not considered necessary to make an explicit grant of such authority," wrote Schlesinger. "The power to make laws implied the power to see whether they were faithfully executed." [6]

Congress formalized its legislative oversight function in the Legislative Reorganization Act of 1946. That act required congressional committees to exercise "continuous watchfulness" of the agencies under their jurisdictions and implicitly divided oversight functions into three areas:

1. Authorizing committees (such as Agriculture, Armed Services, and Commerce) were required to review federal programs and agencies under their jurisdictions and to propose legislation to remedy deficiencies they uncovered.
2. Fiscal oversight was assigned to the Appropriations Committees of each chamber, which were to scrutinize agency spending.
3. Wide-ranging investigative responsibility was assigned to the House Oversight and Government Reform Committee and the Senate Homeland Security and Governmental Affairs Committee to probe for inefficiency, waste, and corruption in the federal government. To some degree, all committees perform each type of oversight.

Each of the three overlapping types of oversight—legislative, fiscal, and investigative—aims to fulfill the basic goals or purposes of oversight, such as clarifying statutory intent; evaluating program administration and performance; eliminating waste, fraud, abuse, and red tape; reviewing whether programs have outlived their usefulness; ensuring that programs and agencies are administered in a cost-effective and economical manner; and correcting executive abuses of authority.

Congress has also enacted other laws that strengthen its oversight capacities. These laws establish mechanisms, procedures, or entities within the executive branch that provide Congress with oversight-related information and assessments of administrative activities. They include statutes that address, for example, paperwork reduction, the preparation of regular financial statements by individual departments and agencies, and the purchase of the most cost-effective information technology.

The Government Performance and Results Act of 1993 (GPRA or the Results Act) aims to promote more cost-effective federal spending by requiring agencies to set strategic goals (for example, a statement of their basic missions and the resources required to achieve those objectives) and to prepare annual performance plans and annual performance reports, which are submitted to Congress and the president. A fundamental purpose of the GPRA is to hold agencies accountable for the implementation of their performance goals. It assists Congress in determining agency budgets and which programs are effective and which are ineffective by providing credible information on agency performance or nonperformance. The GPRA may also help to reduce unnecessary duplication and overlap among federal agencies that implement similar policy areas. As a House majority leader noted as he held up a pizza box: "If this were a cheese pizza, it would be inspected by the [Food and Drug Administration]. If it were a pepperoni pizza, it would be inspected by the [U.S. Department of Agriculture]. . . . We definitely have a great deal of duplication here." [7] (The Bush administration has recommended that Congress create a bipartisan Results Commission to identify duplicative and unnecessary programs.)

The Congressional Review Act of 1996 enables Congress to review and disapprove agency rules and regulations. The act provides for expedited procedures if a lawmaker introduces a joint resolution of disapproval. Under the act, Congress has sixty legislative days to exercise a regulatory veto power; otherwise, the rules will go into effect. However, the law has been little used by Congress to block agency rules. For example, since the law went into effect only one rule has been rejected (an ergonomics rule in 2001) despite nearly 42,000 rules that have become effective.[8] Various structural and interpretive flaws, such as "whether a disapproval resolution may be directed at part of a rule," account for its limited use.[9] Members also acknowledge that the law contains a fatal flaw: The president can veto the joint resolution of disapproval, which Congress is unlikely to override. Still, the law is available to either chamber to express its views about agency rulemaking. Congress, too, can employ its spending power to stipulate that no funds shall be used by federal entities to implement unwanted rules or regulations. (Outside groups can also bring suit in federal court to block what they consider to be illegally promulgated rules.)

In 2006, President Bush signed into law the Federal Funding Accountability and Transparency Act, informally called the "Google your government" law because it requires the Office of Management and Budget by 2008 "to provide a user-friendly, searchable database" of nearly $1 trillion in federal grants and contracts.[10] The potential inherent in the law is that it could enable any interested citizen or watchdog group to monitor federal spending, thereby providing greater transparency and accountability to the government's funding decisions. Many "citizen auditors" would no doubt make their evaluation of federal expenditures known to congressional lawmakers and committees.

Formalizing Oversight

The House and Senate have always had authority to investigate programs and agencies of the executive branch. The first congressional investigation in American history, in 1792, delved into the conduct of the government in the wars against the Indians. One of the broadest investigations was an 1861 inquiry into the conduct of the Civil War. Other notable probes have included investigations into the Crédit Mobilier scandal in 1872–1873, the "Money Trust" in 1912, the Teapot Dome scandal in 1923, stock exchange operations in 1932–1934, and defense spending during World War II. In the mid-1980s, a House and Senate select committee jointly investigated the Iran-contra affair, which involved covert and deceptive operations by the National Security Council and others during the Reagan administration. The hearings were televised nationally. More recently, House and Senate panels have conducted inquiries into the *Columbia* space shuttle disaster and the George W. Bush administration's management of the Iraq insurgency.

The 1946 reorganization act stated Congress's intention to exercise its investigative authority primarily through standing committees rather than by means of specially created investigating committees. (In 1995 the House amended its rules to grant explicit authority to the Speaker to appoint "special ad hoc oversight committees for the purpose of reviewing specific matters within the jurisdiction of two or more standing committees.") The 1946 act provided for continuous review of programs instead of sporadic hearings whenever errors, malfeasance, or injustices surfaced. The continuous watchfulness precept of the act implied that Congress would henceforth participate actively in administrative decision making, in line with the observation that "administration of a statute is, properly speaking, an extension of the legislative process." [11]

During the 1970s, both houses amended their rules to grant additional oversight authority to the standing committees. The Legislative Reorganization Act of 1970 rephrased in more explicit language the oversight duties of the committees and required most House and Senate panels to issue biennial reports on their oversight activities. The House Committee Reform Amendments of 1974 assigned special oversight responsibilities to several standing committees. The Senate adopted the same approach, called comprehensive policy oversight, when it adopted the Committee System Reorganization Amendments of 1977. Both special oversight and comprehensive policy oversight are akin to the broad review authority granted the House Oversight and Government Reform Committee and the Senate Homeland Security and Governmental Affairs Committee.

Explained Sen. Adlai E. Stevenson III, D-Ill. (1970–1981), floor manager during Senate debate on the 1977 change:

> Standing committees are directed and permitted to undertake investigations and make recommendations in broad policy areas—for example, nutrition, aging, environmental protection, or consumer affairs—even though they lack legislative jurisdiction over some aspects of the subject. Such oversight authority involves subjects that generally cut across the jurisdictions of several committees. Presently, no single committee has a comprehensive overview of these policy areas. [This rule change] corrects that. It assigns certain committees the right to undertake comprehensive review of broad policy issues.[12]

Rules Governing Oversight

Other notable changes were made in House and Senate rules regarding oversight. For example, the House directed its committees to create oversight subcommittees, undertake futures research and forecasting, and review the impact of tax expenditures (credits, incentives, and the like) on matters that fall within their respective jurisdictions.[13] The Senate required each standing committee to include regulatory impact statements in committee reports accompanying the legislation it sends to the floor. One of these statements, for example, might evaluate the amount of additional paperwork that would result from enactment of a proposed bill.

Passage of the 1974 Congressional Budget and Impoundment Control Act, another notable change, strengthened Congress's review capabilities by directing the Government Accountability Office (GAO)—a legislative support agency of Congress—to assist House and Senate committees in program evaluation and in the development of "methods for assessing and reporting actual program performance."

In 1995 the House adopted a new rule requiring all standing committees to prepare by February 15 of the first session of each Congress a comprehensive oversight plan. The objective was "to ensure that committees make a more concerted, coordinated and conscientious effort to develop meaningful oversight plans at the beginning of each Congress and to follow through on their implementation, with a view to examining the full range of laws under their jurisdiction over a period of five Congresses."[14] Four years later, in a move designed to encourage more monitoring of administrative performance, the House amended its rules to permit committees to have a sixth sub-committee (under House rules, most standing committees are limited to five subcommittees) if it is an oversight subcommittee. When the 109th Congress began, the House adopted another rule "directing committees to review matters within their jurisdiction to ferret out duplicative government programs as part of their oversight planning at the beginning of each Congress." [15]

Congress requires these additional oversight devices because it faces an executive establishment of massive size and diffuse direction. As a scholar wrote: "[W]e should not deceive ourselves into thinking that the Federal Government of the future will be a shrinking violet, retreating to the modest proportions it had in George Washington's or Grover Cleveland's time." [16] Although many lawmakers and presidents regularly call for less government, they also recognize that numerous voters support a large number of the government's specific roles—and may even welcome their selective expansion—in ensuring clean air and water, a strong national defense, quality health care, law enforcement, and safety from terrorist attacks.

In carrying out its oversight responsibilities, Congress must be able to choose from a variety of techniques to hold agencies accountable, so that if one technique proves to be ineffective, committees and members can employ others singly or in combination.

TECHNIQUES OF OVERSIGHT

The objectives of oversight vary from committee to committee. The focus may be on promoting administrative efficiency and economy in government; protecting and supporting favored policies and programs; airing an administration's failures and wrongdoing or its achievements; publicizing a particular member's or a committee's goals; reasserting congressional authority vis-à-vis the executive branch; assuaging the interests of pressure groups; or generating favorable publicity for programs.

Needless to say, the press and media play a large and often controversial role (publicizing information that the government prefers to keep secret, for example) in investigating and reporting on governmental activities. The House even passed a resolution condemning the news media for publicizing a secret governmental program monitoring bank transactions of potential terrorist suspects.[17] Still, it is worth recalling a statement made by former Supreme Court Justice Potter Stewart: "In the absence of governmental checks and balances present in other areas of national life, the only effective restraint upon executive policy and power in the area of national defense and international affairs may lie in an enlightened citizenry. . . .Without an informed and free press, there cannot be an enlightened people." [18]

Hearings and Investigations

The traditional method of exercising congressional oversight is through committee hearings and investigations into executive branch operations. Legislators need to know how effectively federal programs are working and how well agency officials are responding to committee directives. And they want to know the scope and intensity of public support for government programs to assess the need for legislative changes.

For more than two hundred years, Congress has conducted investigations of varying types with varying results. Along the way, there have been abuses and excesses, successes and accomplishments. Although no explicit provision in the Constitution authorizes Congress to conduct investigations, the Supreme Court has decided in several cases that the investigative function is essential to the legislative function. In *Watkins v. United States* (1957), for example, the Court declared that the "power of the Congress to conduct investigations is inherent in the legislative process. That power is broad. It encompasses inquiries concerning the administration of existing laws as well as proposed or possibly needed statutes." The Supreme Court has also made clear that the investigative power is not unlimited, and Congress has no authority, for example, "to expose for the sake of exposure." Congress, too, has established procedures (for example, the right of witnesses before investigative hearings to be accompanied by their own counsel) to ensure that individuals are treated fairly when they testify before committees.

The success or failure of investigating panels hinges on the skill of their committee leaders, the degree of bipartisan cooperation among members, and good preparatory work by competent staff. Surprise and luck are also factors. As Sen. Daniel K. Inouye, D-Hawaii, the only veteran of both the Watergate and Iran-contra investigating committees, noted:

> I happened to be [at a hearing on Watergate] . . . and the question was asked by one of the Republican staffers [Fred Thompson, minority counsel and later a GOP senator from Tennessee] to one of the lesser witnesses [former Nixon White House aide Alexander P. Butterfield]. Thompson asked, "Mr. Butterfield, are you aware of any listening devices in the Oval Office of the President?" Butterfield responded, "I was aware of listening devices, yes sir." [19]

The rest, said Senator Inouye, was history.

Although excessive use of hearings and investigations can bog down governmental processes, judicious use of such tools helps to maintain a more responsive bureaucracy while supplying Congress with information needed to formulate new legislation and to inform the public.[20] Committee members and committee staffs may conduct oversight hearings around the country (field hearings) to observe first-hand public programs in operation and to take testimony from citizens and local officials.

Legislative Veto

In 1932 Congress began to include provisions in statutes that, while delegating authority to the executive branch, reserved to Congress the right to approve or disapprove executive actions based on that authority within a specified time period. This procedure, known as the legislative veto and

---

Box 9-1 A Committee Veto

For the appropriation account "Transportation Administrative Service Center," no assessments may be levied against any program, budget activity, subactivity or project funded by this statute "unless notice of such assessments and the basis therefor are presented to the House and Senate Committees on Appropriations and are approved by such Committees." Department of Transportation and Related Agencies Appropriations Act 2001, 114 Stat. 1356A-2 (2000).

SOURCE: Cited in *Congressional Oversight Manual*, Congressional Research Service, January 3, 2007, 95.

---

mentioned earlier with respect to the Congressional Review Act, allows one or both chambers, by majority vote, to veto certain executive branch initiatives, decisions, and regulations. In a similar maneuver, Congress sometimes authorizes committees—the committee veto—to approve, or disapprove, executive actions (see Box 9-1).

The legislative veto was an attractive oversight technique because, even though Congress seldom exercised its veto prerogative to overturn agency decisions, committees and members felt the practice kept federal administrators sensitive and responsive to congressional interests. It was employed in legislation dealing with both domestic and international issues. The legislative veto also served executive branch purposes by permitting agencies to make binding decisions without going through the lengthy lawmaking process.

On June 23, 1983, however, the Supreme Court declared in a historic decision, *Immigration and Naturalization Service v. Chadha*, that the legislative veto was unconstitutional. In a 7-2 vote, the Court majority said the device violated the separation of powers, the principle of bicameralism, and the presentation clause of the Constitution (legislation passed by both chambers must be presented to the president for a signature or veto). The decision, wrote Justice Byron R. White in a dissent, "strikes down in one fell swoop provisions in more laws enacted by Congress than the court has cumulatively invalidated in its entire history."

Despite the *Chadha* ruling, Congress still employs legislative and committee vetoes. As scholar Louis Fisher pointed out:

In response to the Court's ruling, Congress repealed some legislative vetoes and replaced them with joint resolutions, which satisfy the [Supreme Court's] ruling because joint resolutions must pass both Houses and be presented to the President. However, Congress has also continued to enact legislative vetoes to handle certain situations. From June 23, 1983 to the end of the [107th Congress, hundreds of legislative vetoes of generally the committee-veto variety] have been enacted into law.[21]

Indeed, Congress and the executive branch have adapted to the post-*Chadha* era largely through informal accommodations and statutory adjustments. On the one hand, executive agencies want discretion and flexibility in running their programs; on the other hand, Congress is generally unwilling to grant open-ended authority to executive entities. The legislative and committee vetoes remain important review devices, because both branches recognize their value.

Authorizing Process as Oversight

Not only does Congress have the authority to create or abolish executive agencies and transfer functions between or among them, but it also can enact "statutes authorizing the activities of the departments, prescribing their internal organization and regulating their procedures and work methods." [22] The authorization process is an important oversight tool. As a House member observed during debate on a bill to require annual congressional authorization of the Federal Communications Commission (FCC):

> Our subcommittee hearings disclosed that the FCC needs direction, needs guidance, needs legislation, and needs leadership from us in helping to establish program priorities. Regular oversight through the reauthorization process, as all of us know in Congress, is necessary, and nothing brings everybody's attention to spending more forthrightly than when we go through the reauthorization process.[23]

Significant issues are often raised during the authorization process. Lawmakers may ask such questions as: Can an agency be made smaller? If a program or agency did not exist, would it be created today? Should functions that overlap several agencies be merged or consolidated? What fundamental changes need to be made in how various agencies operate? In an era of outsourcing jobs, what and whose federal jobs should be cut?

The authorizing process, however, is often not exercised effectively as an oversight tool. Many programs and agencies fail to be reauthorized for years, yet they still continue to operate because appropriators provide funding for them. For example, Congress did not reauthorize the Department of Justice from 1980 until 2002; the Toxic Substances Control Act has not been reauthorized since 1983. While lawmakers give many reasons for failing to reauthorize federal programs or entities (conflict between the chambers and branches or too little time, for example), the consequence is "increasingly poor congressional oversight over federal programs." [24]

Today's Congress is, however, paying special attention to the Department of Homeland Security (DHS) because of its important mission and the fact that its establishment constituted the largest governmental reorganization in the nation's history. The House even created a new standing Committee on Homeland Security at the start of the 109th Congress with important authorizing and oversight responsibility for DHS. However, various accounts indicate that the department is hobbled by "start-up" problems, such as disorganization and turf battles (trying to meld the different "cultures" of the twenty-two entities merged to form the department).[25] Moreover, the lack of readiness in responding effectively to Hurricane Katrina revealed the inadequacies of DHS and its component unit, the Federal Emergency Management Agency (FEMA).[26] In addition to the human tragedy, that event "produced one of the most extraordinary displays of scams, schemes and stupefying bureaucratic bungles in modern history, costing taxpayers up to $2 billion." [27]

Appropriations Process as Oversight

Congress probably exercises its most effective oversight of agencies and programs through the appropriations process. By cutting off or reducing funds, Congress can abolish agencies or curtail programs. By increasing funds, it can build up neglected program areas. In either case, it has formidable power to shape ongoing public policies. The power is exercised mainly by the House and Senate Appropriations Committees, particularly through their powerful subcommittees, whose broad budgetary recommendations are only infrequently changed by the full committee or by the House and Senate. The House Appropriations Committee also has a separate survey and investigations staff (made up mostly of former FBI, CIA, GAO, and other professionals) that often reviews spending by the defense and intelligence community.[28] Their reports are not made public.

The Appropriations Committees define the precise purpose for which money may be spent, they adjust funding levels, and they often attach provisos prohibiting expenditures for certain purposes. The appropriations process as an oversight technique, notes congressional budget expert Allen Schick, is comparable to a Janus-like weapon: "The stick of spending reductions in case agencies cannot satisfactorily defend their budget requests and past performance, and the carrot of more money if agencies produce convincing success stories or the promise of future results." [29] The appropriations process is a potent tool for requiring federal officials to justify the continued existence of their programs and agencies and to comply with the appropriators' directives.

For example, in 2004, the House Appropriations Subcommittee on Homeland Security stated in its report on the DHS appropriations bill that the "Coast Guard is directed to submit quarterly reports to the [Appropriations] Committee on its actions with respect to this plan [to properly maintain its vessels and aircraft]." Lack of compliance with this directive produced a different outcome the next year. The panel stated that it was "extremely frustrated in the Coast Guard's apparent disregard for Congressional direction and has reduced funding for headquarters directorates" by $5 million. . . . The Committee cannot adequately oversee Coast Guard programs when the agency fails to answer basic questions or fails to provide timely and complete information." [30]

Members also add amendments to appropriations measures, or the bills may include spending limitations when reported from committee, that restrict or prohibit agencies from carrying out certain functions. For example,

Sen. Tom Harkin, D-Iowa, offered an amendment, approved by the Senate, that stated that none of the funds provided to the Department of Labor by an appropriations bill "shall be used to promulgate or implement any regulation" redefining worker eligibility for overtime pay.[31] "These amendments," wrote two GOP senators, "are an important way for Congress to save taxpayers from wasted agency spending, and they enjoy a long-standing precedent because of their use by Republican and Democratic Congresses alike to rein in the excesses of Republican and Democratic administrations." [32]

Inspectors General

Congress has created statutory offices of inspectors general (IGs) in nearly sixty major federal agencies and departments. The IGs are located in every cabinet department and major agency, including the Central Intelligence Agency (CIA). Granted wide latitude and independence by the Inspectors General Act of 1978, as amended in 1988, these officials conduct investigations and audits of their agencies to improve efficiency, end waste and fraud, and discourage mismanagement. Collectively, the IG offices "employ 11,400 auditors, investigators, inspectors and other professionals." [33] The IGs keep Congress fully and currently informed about federal activities, problems, and program performance through the issuance of periodic reports. As the IG of the Department of Health and Human Services said about her job, "I believe that a successful IG must . . . be willing to go beyond just the traditional after-the-fact investigations and audits. Instead, the IG should . . . not just detect, but also prevent fraud and abuse." [34] There are occasions, too, when IGs feel the "wrath of government bosses or their supporters in Congress after investigations cited agencies for poor performance, excessive spending, or wasted money." [35]

Lawmakers like the idea of having an independent office of inspector general located within an agency performing a watchdog role for Congress. The House, in the wake of internal bank and post office scandals, created its own Office of Inspector General in 1992; the position was filled the next year. One function of the House's IG is to conduct audits of the chamber's financial activities. (The House periodically may contract with a major accounting firm to conduct a comprehensive auditing review of its spending practices.)

Nonstatutory, Informal Controls

Congress also is able to influence federal administrators using various informal means. Executive officials, conscious of Congress's power over the purse strings, are attuned to the nuances of congressional language in hearings, floor debate, committee reports, and conference reports. For example, in committee reports the verbs *expect, urge, recommend, desire,* and *feel* display in roughly descending order how obligatory a committee comment or viewpoint is intended to be.[36] If federal administrators believe congressional directives to be unwise, they are more likely to ask for informal consultation with members and committee staff than to seek new laws. In fact, executive officials are routinely in frequent contact with committee members and staff. Analyzing the House Appropriations Committee's relationship with the federal bureaucracy, one scholar wrote:

> [There] is a continuing and sometimes almost daily pattern of contacts between the Committee on Appropriations and the executive branch. When Congress is not in session, communication continues by telephone or even, on occasion, by visits to the homes of members of the committee. If the full story were ever known, the record probably would disclose a complex network of relationships between members of the Committee on Appropriations and its staff and officials, particularly budget officers, in the executive branch.[37]

Such informal contacts enable committees to exercise policy influence in areas in which statutory methods might be inappropriate or ineffective. Informal methods of program review are probably the most prevalent techniques of oversight.

Members sometimes urge their colleagues, administrative agencies, and the courts to exercise caution in interpreting committee reports, floor debate, and other nonstatutory devices as expressions of the intent of Congress. Abner J. Mikva, one of the few public officials to have served in all three national branches of government (as a House member, federal judge, and President Bill Clinton's White House counsel), recounted a story about the pitfalls of interpreting a bill's legislative history:

> I remember when [Rep. Morris K.] Mo Udall (D-Ariz., 1961–1991) was managing the strip-mining bill, and there had been all sorts of problems getting it through. They'd put together a very delicate coalition of support. One problem was whether the states or the feds would run the program. One member got up and asked, "Isn't it a fact that under this bill the states will continue to exercise sovereignty over strip mining?" And Mo replied, "You're absolutely right." A little later someone else got up and asked, "Now is it clear that the Federal Government will have the final say on strip mining?" And Mo replied, "You're absolutely right." Later, in the cloakroom, I said, "Mo, they can't both be right." And Mo said, "You're absolutely right."[38]

Interpreting statutory intent is a hot issue at the Supreme Court because legal phraseology is often ambiguous. Justice Antonin Scalia advocates that judges, in clarifying statutory language, reject committee hearings, reports, or floor debate (congressional history), which can be conflicting and have not been voted on. Instead, they should focus on the exact legal language and the statutory text in which it is embedded (the plain-meaning principle). Justice Stephen G. Breyer, by contrast, recommends use of congressional history in statutory interpretation so judges can better understand the goals and objectives of the legislation signed into law.[39] "It is dangerous," says Breyer, "to rely exclusively upon the literal meaning of a statute's words."[40]

Government Accountability Office Audits and Reports

The Government Accountability Office (GAO), created by the Budget and Accounting Act of 1921, is known as Congress's watchdog. One of its primary functions is to conduct financial and management audits. For example, in 2005, GAO "reported that 19 of 24 Federal agencies . . . could not fully explain how they had spent taxpayer money appropriated by Congress."[41] GAO also conducts reviews of executive agencies and programs at the request of committees and members of Congress to ensure that public funds are properly spent. In addition, it conducts field investigations of administrative activities, prescribes accounting standards for the executive branch, prepares policy analyses, and provides legal opinions on government actions and activities. Prior to the start of the 110th Congress (2007–2009), GAO sent top party and committee leaders a list of suggested oversight areas in need of review and categorized them according to near-term targets for oversight (government contracting, for example); programs in need of fundamental reform (immigration, as an example); and twenty-first century governance issues (transparency of executive operations, for instance).

The GAO, which has a staff of about 3,300, submits hundreds of reports to Congress annually on ways to root out waste and fraud in government programs and to promote program performance. For example, the GAO produces important reports on government programs and activities that are "high risk"—one such report is titled "GAO's 2005 High-Risk Update." GAO studies frequently lead to the introduction of legislation, congressional hearings, or cost-saving administrative changes. The head of the GAO, the comptroller general, is appointed for a single fifteen-year term by the president, subject to the advice and consent of the Senate. The GAO works only for Congress.

Reporting Requirements

Numerous laws require executive agencies to submit periodic reports to Congress and its committees. As one scholar explained:

> Reporting requirements are provisions in law requiring the executive branch to submit specified information to Congress or committees of Congress. Their basic purpose is to provide data and analysis Congress needs to oversee the implementation of legislation and foreign policy by the executive branch.[42]

Some reports are of minimal value because they are couched in broad language that reveals little about program implementation; others may be more specific. Some reports address large policy issues; others, the narrow interests of a small number of lawmakers. (One way to resolve problems in the legislative process, such as mobilizing support from lawmakers who are uncertain about the worth of a program or activity, is to ask an agency for a report.) Generally, however, the report requirement encourages self-evaluation by the executive branch and promotes agency accountability to Congress. For example, when Congress became exasperated with Pentagon delays in implementing a major reorganization of defense offices, it directed the secretary of the army "to report every 30 days to Congress on what he [was] doing to put the legislation into place."[43] Thus, reports can "drive a reluctant bureaucracy to comply with laws it would otherwise ignore."[44]

Periodically, Congress and the executive branch recommend the elimination of certain reports (currently there are about five thousand reports submitted to Congress).[45] Sometimes the impulse to eliminate reports reflects legislative and executive concern about micromanagement of executive affairs by legislative committees. The ever-present tension, even distrust, that suffuses legislative-executive relations explains to a large degree why Congress gets involved in managerial details and demands reports from federal entities. "We wrote an extraordinary amount of detail into the Clean Air Act," said one House member, "because we didn't trust the Environmental Protection Agency . . . with too much discretion."[46] The concern about reporting requirements involves weighing Congress's need for information to conduct evaluations of agencies and programs against the imposition of burdensome, costly, or irrelevant obligations on executive entities.

Ad Hoc Groups

Numerous formal and informal groups and caucuses of Senate and House members focus on specific issues and programs and monitor executive branch activities. For example, the Congressional Automotive Caucus works with appropriate government agencies to resolve issues associated with the automobile industry. The Senate Democratic Policy Committee established an "Oversight and Accountability Project." In the minority, Democrats or Republicans lack the ability to hold hearings, conduct investigations, or subpoena witnesses. As a result, the Democratic or GOP Policy Committees may conduct informal hearings on issues that, in their estimation, receive little scrutiny by the opposition-controlled standing committees.[47]

Outside organizations also provide Congress with information on inadequacies in federal programs and other problems with the bureaucracy and exert pressure for more ambitious oversight. For example, private watchdog groups, such as Citizens Against Government Waste, the Project on Government Oversight, and Taxpayers for Common Sense, regularly identify federal projects that, in their judgment, are a waste of taxpayers' dollars. Think tanks such as the Brookings Institution and the Heritage Foundation periodically study public policy issues and advise members of Congress and others on how well federal agencies and programs are working. More broadly, Congress receives much free advice from all kinds of groups on how to cut back the size of government and, alternatively, how to make federal programs and departments work more effectively. Groups also point out which national activities might be candidates for expansion.

Bloggers are also involved in government oversight. With advances in technology, citizens have the capacity to get involved—and get others engaged—in investigating governmental activities and spending decisions, including spending for congressional earmarks. The use of the Internet by amateur investigators is "probably the biggest expansion of government oversight that we'll ever have," declared the head of a watchdog group (Citizens Against Government Waste).[48]

Senate Confirmation Process

High-ranking public officials are chosen by the president "by and with the Advice and Consent of the Senate," in accord with the Constitution. In general, the Senate gives presidents wide latitude in selecting cabinet members, but it closely scrutinizes judicial and diplomatic appointments as well as nominees to regulatory boards and commissions. Increasingly in recent years, Senate committees are probing the qualifications, independence, and policy predilections of presidential nominees, seeking information on everything from physical health to financial assets. As one commentator noted:

> These days, if you want to run for office [or] accept a position of public trust, everything is relevant. Your moral, medical, legal and financial background, even your college records, become the subject of public scrutiny. In the old days, the scrutiny was done in private, and certain transgressions could be considered irrelevant.[49]

Today, frustration with the confirmation process is running high. "The nomination system is a national disgrace," wrote one scholar of the presidential appointment process.[50] Nominees often complain about lengthy delays that can turn the process into an ordeal and the rough treatment some of them receive from senators and outside groups. However, as Sen. Robert C. Byrd, D-W.Va., pointed out, if the Senate "rushes through a nomination without adequate investigation, it is accused of 'consent without advice' or 'half rubber, half stamp.' "[51]

Nomination hearings establish a public record of the policy views of nominees, on which appointed officials can be called to account at a later time. "We all ask questions at confirmation hearings, hoping to obtain answers that affect actions," observed Sen. Carl Levin, D-Mich.[52] Committees, too, may take nominees already in the executive branch to task for the way their agencies have addressed management problems. For example, when the nominee for deputy director for management at the Office of Management and Budget (OMB) appeared before the Senate Homeland Security and Governmental Affairs Committee, the chair criticized OMB's efforts to improve agency performance and pointed out that federal agencies "have not addressed half of the 'high-risk' programs identified by congressional auditors as vulnerable to waste, fraud, and abuse." [53] Committees may also extract pledges from nominees that they will testify at hearings when requested to do so, with the not-so-subtle threat that otherwise the appointee's name will not be sent to the full Senate for action.

Program Evaluation

Program evaluation is an approach to oversight that uses social science and management methodology, such as surveys, cost-benefit analyses, and efficiency studies, to assess the effectiveness of ongoing programs. It is a special type of oversight that has been specifically included in many agency appropriations bills since the late 1960s and in the 1974 Congressional Budget and

Impoundment Control Act. The studies often are carried out by the GAO and by the executive agencies themselves.[54]

Despite the multiplicity of methods to evaluate programs, members of Congress sometimes disagree about how to measure performance. Several factors frequently account for their divergent perspectives. For one thing, they may not agree on the objectives of certain programs. Public laws often are the products of conflicts and compromises, and when those compromises are translated into legislative language, ambiguity about program goals may be the result. Many policies have competing objectives or produce unintended results. In addition, no agreement may have been reached about criteria—quantitative or qualitative—for determining program success or failure. Finally, even if decision makers agree on objectives and criteria, they may interpret the assessments differently. Members and committees who support particular programs are unlikely to view with favor evaluations that recommend repeal or revision of those programs.

Casework

Each senator's and representative's office handles thousands of requests each year from constituents seeking help in dealing with executive agencies. The requests range from inquiries about lost Social Security checks or delayed pension payments to disaster relief assistance and complicated tax appeals to the Internal Revenue Service. "Constituents perceive casework in nonpolitical terms," wrote two scholars. "They *expect* their representatives to provide [this service]." [55] As a House member wrote:

> Last year, one of my constituents, a 63-year-old man who requires kidney dialysis, discovered that he would no longer be receiving Medicare because the Social Security Administration thought he was dead. Like residents of Southern Indiana who have problems dealing with the federal bureaucracy, this man contacted my district office and asked for help. Without difficulty, he convinced my staff that he was indeed alive, and we in turn convinced the Social Security Administration to resume sending him benefits.[56]

Most congressional offices employ specialists, called case workers, to process these types of petitions. Yet, depending on the importance or complexity of a case, the members themselves may contact federal officials, bring up the matter in committee, or discuss the case on the floor. Casework has the positive effect of bringing quirks in the administrative machinery to members' attention. And solutions to an individual constituent's problems can suggest legislative remedies on a broader scale.

Studies by Supporting Agencies

In addition to the GAO, Congress receives support from the Congressional Research Service and the Congressional Budget Office. Each prepares (or contracts for) reports or studies to assist committees and members in reviewing federal agency activities, expenditures, and performance. Their analyses can spark legislation to correct administrative shortcomings.

Resolutions of Inquiry

House members may introduce a privileged simple resolution, called a resolution of inquiry, which requests the president or the head of an executive department to furnish specific factual information and documentation to the House about the administration of a particular federal program. (A resolution of inquiry enjoys its privileged status only if it asks for facts and not opinion from the executive branch. There is no exact Senate counterpart to these resolutions.) A House member explained some objectives of a resolution of inquiry: "It is a vehicle to provide information to Congress, to foster cooperation between the executive and legislative branches, and to encourage auditing of how taxpayers' dollars are spent." [57] House precedents state that the "effectiveness of such a resolution derives from comity between the branches of government rather than from any element of compulsion." [58]

House rules stipulate that if the resolution of inquiry is not reported by a committee within fourteen legislative days of its introduction, any lawmaker can offer a privileged motion to discharge the committee of the resolution. However, if a committee reports the resolution, either favorably or unfavorably, the House is under no obligation to take up the measure. A resolution brought to the floor is debatable under the one-hour rule. The resolution can be tabled, or killed.[59]

With a Republican in the White House, Democratic members of the House have introduced dozens of resolutions of inquiry on often "hot button" topics, such as the contracts awarded relating to Hurricane Katrina recovery, the treatment of prisoners in Iraq, Guantanamo Bay, and Afghanistan, or the public disclosure of Valerie Plame as a CIA operative, a violation of federal law. Most of these resolutions have been turned down and not brought up in the House. However, in a surprise to the Bush administration, Judiciary Chairman James Sensenbrenner, R-Wis., became upset with Attorney General Alberto Gonzales for frustrating his panel's ability to oversee the Department of Justice. "How can we discharge our oversight if, every time we ask a pointed question, we're told the [NSA's domestic surveillance program] is classified? I think that . . . is stonewalling." [60] Sensenbrenner voted for the resolution of inquiry introduced by Rep. Robert Wexler, D-Fla., "to send a message to the administration and Justice Department" to turn over documents related to the NSA's collection of numerous telephone records.[61] The House took no action on the resolution.

Oversight by Individual Members

Some members conduct their own personal reviews of agency activities and develop ways to publicize what they believe to be examples of governmental waste and inefficiency. Sen. William Proxmire, D-Wis. (1957–1989), periodically bestowed a "Golden Fleece Award" on agencies that, in his estimation, were wastefully spending tax dollars.[62] Rep. Berkley W. Bedell, D-Iowa (1975–1987), utilized another technique: "One of the practices I have is to make unannounced visits to the executive branch of the Government. I simply select an agency at random, open a door, walk in, and start asking questions of the people who work in that office." [63] Senator Charles Grassley, R-Iowa, has also tried the personal approach. He "marched into the Department of Health and Human Services headquarters . . . asserting his congressional right to receive" the information he requested.[64]

On occasion, individual members will conduct ad hoc field oversight hearings. These sessions usually permit constituents to testify about their problems with federal agencies. They usually garner favorable publicity for the legislator, too.

From his perch as ranking minority member on the House Government Reform Committee, Henry Waxman, D-Calif., played an important role in monitoring the activities of the George W. Bush administration. As one news account noted:

> One day he's prodding Vice President [Richard B.] Cheney to reveal the identities of nongovernmental officials who helped the White House craft its energy policy. The next day he's bestowing a 'golden jackpot' award on the administration for loosening arsenic level standards for public drinking water. . . . [H]is staff released a report on abuses in nursing homes that led the "CBS Evening News" that day.[65]

When Waxman became chair of the panel following the November 2006 elections, a magazine article had this headline: "The Scariest Guy in Town, With Subpoena Power Henry Waxman Could Be the Republicans' Worst Nightmare." [66] Waxman has also employed a rarely used law dubbed the "Seven Member Rule," which states that upon the request of seven members of the House Oversight and Government Reform Committee or five members of the Senate Homeland Security and Governmental Affairs Committee, "an executive agency . . . shall submit any information requested of it relating to any matter within the jurisdiction of the committee." [67]

IMPEACHMENT

The ultimate check on the executive and judicial branch is the removal power, and it is vested exclusively in Congress. Article II, Section 4, of the Constitution states: "The President, Vice President, and all Civil Officers of the United States, shall be removed from office on Impeachment for, and Conviction of, Treason, Bribery, or other high Crimes and misdemeanors." The House has the authority to impeach an official by majority vote. (Impeachment, in effect, is the formal lodging of charges against an official.) House trial managers then prosecute the case before the Senate, where a two-thirds vote is required for conviction. In the history of the United States, the House has impeached seventeen persons—two presidents, one Supreme Court justice, one senator, one cabinet officer, and twelve federal judges. Of those, the Senate convicted seven judges, who were removed from office.

The House impeached President Andrew Johnson in 1868, after Radical Republicans in the House charged that he had violated the Tenure of Office Act by dismissing the secretary of war. The Senate acquitted Johnson by a single vote. President Richard Nixon resigned in 1974, after the House Judiciary Committee voted articles of impeachment; he faced probable impeachment and conviction. In December 1998 President Bill Clinton became the first elected president to be impeached by the House (Johnson was not elected; he became president when Abraham Lincoln was assassinated.) The charges against Clinton were perjury and obstruction of justice. Two months later, the Senate voted acquittal on both of these articles of impeachment.

OVERSIGHT TRENDS AND INCENTIVES

Legislators and scholars often complain that congressional oversight is irregular and shallow. Several scholars suggest that over time there has been greater legislative interest in the process.[68] As one specialist of congressional oversight explained:

> There are no authoritative, comprehensive statistics on the amount of oversight or even the number of specialized investigations throughout the history of Congress. This absence is, in part, because scholars have disagreed as to what constitutes oversight and, therefore, how it should be measured. Nonetheless, some statistics . . . are available. . . . [T]hese data tend to show that Congress has increased its oversight activity over history, particularly over the past three decades.[69]

Oversight attracts interest because a fundamental topic of public debate is the appropriate role of the national government. As one senator put it: "The two most important questions policymakers must ask themselves are, 'What should government be doing?' and 'At what level of government should it be done?' " People may react negatively to big government in the abstract, but voters want more rather than less government in many areas, especially safety and security in the aftermath of the September 11, 2001, attacks. Lawmakers, too, typically defend government programs supported by their constituents.

Among other factors that often contribute to heightened interest in oversight are the following:

- public dissatisfaction with and concern about government waste, fraud, program performance, and escalating expenditures;
- congressional assertiveness and distrust of the executive branch in the wake of such events as the Vietnam War, Watergate, the Iran-contra affair, the insurgency in Iraq, and revelations of abuses and intelligence failures by agencies such as the CIA, Federal Bureau of Investigation (FBI), and IRS;

- the influx of representatives and senators who are skeptical about the national government's ability to resolve public problems;
- the proliferation of federal programs and regulations that touch the lives of practically every citizen, and citizens, who, in turn, inform their elected officials about problems they are encountering with federal agencies;
- the proliferation of interest groups and trade associations that pressure Congress to examine government actions that affect their special interests;
- the availability of staff resources and procedural tools, which permits the new breed of aggressive legislators to scrutinize federal activities; and
- aggressive investigative reporting into executive activities by the print and broadcast media.

The sharp increase in the fiscal deficit after the September 11, 2001, attacks—a function of factors such as tax cuts, spending increases for homeland security, and the war against terrorism—compelled members and committees to scrutinize program activities and expenditures. Hard choices confronted lawmakers, such as: "Shall Washington reconstruct Iraqi schools and hospitals . . . or America's?" [70] With no extra money, House and Senate GOP leaders targeted government waste and federal fat as one way to find additional monies (or offsets) for programs they favored while still maintaining limits on spending. Electorally, making fraud, waste, and abuse a top GOP priority is appealing to voters who favor a smaller government. Democrats contend that Republicans often cut the wrong programs and that they want to curb spending to make room in the budget for big tax cuts for the wealthy.

Divided government (one party in control of the White House; the other in control of Congress), which is what the electorate got following the November 2006 elections, provides another incentive for oversight. Opposition lawmakers, for example, monitor and supervise agency activities, and, at the same time, they are on the lookout for ways to politically bash the administration. The Clinton White House complained about the oversight activities of House Republicans. "It seems a pattern has developed where [they] are requesting information not so they can evaluate the effectiveness of the government's performance," stated a White House spokesman, "but so that they can use [requests for information] to thwart those who might be carrying out the laws as they've been properly passed by Congress." House Republicans refuted that charge.

By comparison, under unified government President George W. Bush did not face the deluge of subpoenas and investigative hearings faced by the Clinton administration.[71] Representative Tom Davis, R-Va., the chairman of the Government Reform Committee, observed that "Republican Congresses tend to overinvestigate Democratic administrations and underinvestigate their own." [72] Or as Rep. Ray LaHood, R-Ill., put it: "Our party controls the levers of government. We're not about to go out and look beneath a bunch of rocks to try and cause heartburn. Unless they really screw up, we're not going to go after them." [73] In the judgment of Rep. Christopher Shays, R-Conn., "We ended up functioning like a parliament, not a Congress. We confused wanting a joint agenda with not doing oversight." [74]

Electoral and political incentives may encourage members to oversee the bureaucracy. The opportunity to receive favorable publicity back home is a potential electoral bonus for lawmakers. Committee and subcommittee chairs "seek a high pay off—in attention from the press and other agencies—when selecting federal programs to be their oversight targets." [75]

LACK OF CONSENSUS ON OVERSIGHT

Despite the importance of Congress's oversight functions, many members and commentators still fault congressional efforts in this area. As GOP senator Craig Thomas of Wyoming said:

> Congressional oversight is something that, unfortunately, we probably don't do as much as we should. That is what committee meetings are for. That is what audits are for. When you pass a law and say here is where we want to go, then you have to say: How are we getting there? We don't do that well.[76]

Several factors help to account for this general perception, although those who are the targets of oversight—executive branch officials—no doubt prefer to be left alone. First, no clear consensus has emerged on how to measure oversight, quantitatively or qualitatively. As a result, members' anxiety about Congress's ability to review the massive federal establishment remains high. Quantitatively, no one knows how much oversight Congress is doing. However, undercounting characterizes statistical analyses of oversight no matter what definition of that activity is employed. Part of the problem is that legislative review is a ubiquitous activity carried out by many entities: committees, members' offices, legislative support agencies, and committee and personal staff aides. Almost any committee hearing, for example, even ones ostensibly devoted to formulating new legislation, might pay considerable attention to reviewing past policy implementation. Qualitatively, little agreement exists among members on the criteria that can be used to evaluate effective oversight.

Second, some legislators favor oversight objectives that appear impossible to meet. They would like to see Congress conduct comprehensive reviews of the entire executive establishment. But then they find Congress's selective and unsystematic oversight approach generally unsatisfactory even when there is more of it. As some see it, oversight is too often a guerrilla foray rather than the continual watchfulness contemplated by the 1946 Legislative Reorganization Act. "It requires a blunder of major proportions, a calamity that is poorly addressed, before you get oversight," remarked a political scientist.[77] In general, Congress conducts dual types of oversight: "fire-alarm" and "police-patrol." The former occurs when outside events or public interest trigger agency reviews; it is episodic and reactive in character. The latter is proactive and involves deliberate House and Senate committee decisions to oversee on a regular basis federal activities under their jurisdiction.[78]

Third, some committees and individual members believe they have minimal impact on the bureaucracy. Exclaimed Rep. Jim Wright, D-Texas (1955–1989), who served as Speaker from 1987 to 1989:

> Fighting the red tape and the overregulation of bureaucratic rulemaking and guideline writing are among the most frustrating things any of us have had to do in Congress—it is almost like trying to fight a pillow. You can hit it—knock it over in the corner—and it just lies there and regroups. You feel sometimes as though you are trying to wrestle an octopus. No sooner do you get a hammerlock on one of his tentacles than the other seven are strangling you.[79]

To some members of Congress, the best way to handle this problem is to eliminate or downsize agencies or programs. (President Bush and various lawmakers support formation of a "sunset" commission. Sunset mandates the periodic review of programs and agencies; they would terminate automatically unless reauthorized by law.)

Fourth, oversight may produce more questions than answers. Congress finds it easier "to highlight what's going wrong and to blame it on someone," declared a senator, "than to try to determine what to do about it." [80] And even with more oversight, agency problems can remain uncorrected absent sustained and determined follow-through by the relevant congressional committee.

Fifth, Congress seeks to shape executive actions to its own objectives, not simply to conduct or commission neutral evaluation studies of departmental activities. Oversight is part of the legislative-executive tug-of-war that characterizes the U.S. separation of powers system. According to one commentator:

> The key issue for Congress is not administrative performance but its ability to influence agency actions. Congress is interested in performance, but it expresses this interest by seeking dominion over agencies. The distribution of political power between the legislative and executive branches, not simply [or even mainly] the quality of programs, is at stake.[81]

A fragmented and assertive Congress is sometimes frustrated by its inability to control and coordinate a fragmented and sophisticated bureaucracy. For example, occasionally Congress confronts the issue of whom to hold accountable for program performance when a contractor workforce is carrying out the bulk of a department's activities under the supervision of federal employees. Indeed, the Department of Energy relies on contractors for "almost everything it does. More than 90 percent of its budget is paid to 100,000 outside workers." [82] More broadly, thousands of nonfederal employees—defense contractors, state and local officials, or university administrators—are increasingly carrying out activities once performed by civil servants. As a result, it is harder for Congress to hold accountable those who administer policies or deliver services.

Another development that has the potential to weaken congressional oversight is lockbox government. Federal officials are looking for ways to avoid the constraints of the congressional appropriations process by encouraging the passage of laws that give them a guaranteed funding stream for a specific activity. For example, federal oil and gas royalties flow into the Land and Conservation Fund to be spent on congressionally designated environmental programs. A consequence of removing agencies and programs from the regular appropriations process is that it robs "legislators of an opportunity to hold agency officials accountable for policy decisions. If functions are spun off to private organizations, oversight could be weakened further." [83]

Despite Congress's general interest in oversight, other considerations limit effective performance. For one thing, legislators still have too little time to devote to their myriad tasks, including oversight. Huge investments of time, energy, and staff assistance are required to ferret out administrative inadequacies. The term *lawmaker* suggests where most House and Senate members prefer to spend much of their time. As former Speaker Newt Gingrich, R-Ga., pointed out:

> This is the city [Washington, D.C.] which spends almost all of its energy trying to make the right decisions and almost none of its energy focusing on how to improve implementing the right decisions. And without implementation, the best ideas in the world simply don't occur.[84]

Some members are reluctant to support massive investigations that may reveal only that a program is working fairly well—a determination that does not attract much constituent attention or media coverage. "Effective oversight is, of necessity, time-consuming and tedious," said a Republican senator. "To do it right, you have to hear an endless stream of witnesses, review numerous records, and at the end of it you may find an agency was doing everything right. It is much more fun to create a new program." [85]

Many members, however, accept that much of their effort in this area is unglamorous. Moreover, the review process is sometimes inhibited by the alliances that develop among committees, agencies, and clientele groups. Examples of these subgovernments or "iron triangles," as the alliances are called, are the axis of the House and Senate Veterans' Affairs Committees, the Department of Veterans Affairs, and the veterans groups, and the combine of the congressional Agriculture Committees, the Department of Agriculture, and the various farm groups. Each component of such an alliance is usually supportive of the other. In such cases, committees find it harder to review agency programs critically absent a countervailing view of them.

Some policy areas are also harder for Congress to oversee. Intelligence and national security issues are prime examples. Congress must conduct most of its intelligence oversight in secret, and the lawmakers who serve on the intelligence committees are subject to an array of restrictions that inhibit the disclosure of sensitive material even to their colleagues, let alone the media or others. Intelligence is also a highly complex and technically substantive area.

There is defense intelligence, tactical intelligence, strategic intelligence, and so on that requires years of study and analysis. However, members of each chamber's intelligence panels are subject to tenure limits to reduce the chances that lawmakers will be co-opted by the intelligence community.[86]

Finally, some members and scholars say that Congress lacks enough electoral, political, and institutional incentives for oversight. As a result, some legislators are "insufficiently dissatisfied with their oversight behavior to feel a strong enough stimulus to alter existing patterns." [87] Lawmakers are also mindful that hard-hitting oversight could offend various groups and constituents, which could cost them votes in the next election.

In short, Congress will decide how it can best pursue its oversight responsibility. Much will depend on the context of the times, the willingness of lawmakers to watch and analyze executive branch activities, and Congress's relationship with the executive branch. This relationship may range from cooperative to confrontational, but it is fundamental to Congress's job that it ensure that executive policies reflect the values of the American people, anticipate long-range trends, and meet the challenges of a changed world.

NOTES

1. Gail Russell Chaddock, "New Congress to Toughen Oversight," *Christian Science Monitor,* December 21, 2006, 2.
2. Geoff Earle, "Dems Did Oversight Better, Says Grassley," *The Hill,* May 13, 2004, 2.
3. *Congressional Record,* September 21, 2006, H6864–H6865 (immigration) and *Congressional Record,* February 1, 2006, H61–H62 (the Patriot Act).
4. *Congressional Record,* June 21, 1983, S8822. For several studies on oversight, see Morris S. Ogul, *Congress Oversees the Bureaucracy* (Pittsburgh: University of Pittsburgh Press, 1976). Professor Ogul's book contains a lengthy bibliography on oversight. See also Frederick Kaiser, "Congressional Oversight of the Presidency," *The Annals* (September 1988): 7589; Christopher Foreman, *Signals from the Hill: Congressional Oversight and Social Regulation* (New Haven, Conn.: Yale University Press, 1988); and Joel Aberbach, *Keeping a Watchful Eye: The Politics of Congressional Oversight* (Washington, D.C.: Brookings, 1990).
5. Woodrow Wilson, *Congressional Government* (Boston: Houghton Mifflin, 1885), 303.
6. Arthur M. Schlesinger Jr. and Roger Burns, eds., *Congress Investigates: A Documented History, 1792–1974,* vol. 1 (New York: Chelsea House, 1975), xix.
7. Jennifer Kabbany, "Armey Targets Waste in Federal Agencies," *Washington Times,* February 12, 1999, A6.
8. Morton Rosenberg, *Congressional Review of Agency Rulemaking: An Update and Assessment of the Congressional Review Act After Ten Years,* CRS Report, RL30116, March 29, 2006, 1.
9. Morton Rosenberg, "Whatever Happened to Congressional Review of Agency Rulemaking? A Brief Overview, Assessment, and Proposal for Reform," *Administrative Law Review* (fall 1999): 1060.

10. Bill Myers, " 'Google your government' Database Bill Signed Into Law," *Washington Examiner*, September 29, 2006, 17.

11. David B. Truman, *The Governmental Process* (New York: Knopf, 1953), 439. The continuous watchfulness provision was retitled legislative "review" in the Legislative Reorganization Act of 1970.

12. *Congressional Record*, February 1, 1977, S2897.

13. Michael J. Malbin, *Unelected Representatives* (New York: Basic Books, 1979). See Chapter 6 for an analysis of a House oversight subcommittee in action.

14. *Congressional Record*, January 4, 1995, H35.

15. *Congressional Record*, January 4, 2005, H13.

16. *Workshop on Congressional Oversight and Investigations*, 96th Cong., 1st sess., 1979, H. Doc. 96–217, 198.

17. Charles Babington, "House GOP Chastises Media," *Washington Post*, June 30, 2006, A25.

18. Quoted in Daniel Schorr, "The Government's Current War With the Free Press," *Christian Science Monitor*, July 7, 2006, 9.

19. *Washington Post*, March 17, 1994, A15.

20. Congressional requests for executive agency information may be blocked by executive privilege. See Bernard Schwartz, "Executive Privilege and Congressional Investigatory Power," *California Law Review* (March 1959): 350; Raoul Berger, *Executive Privilege: A Constitutional Myth* (Cambridge, Mass.: Harvard University Press, 1974); *U.S. v. Nixon*, 418 U.S. 683 (1974); and "Symposium: *United States v. Nixon*," *UCLA Law Review* (October 1974): 140.

21. Information supplied by Louis Fisher, noted specialist on the separation of powers, Law Library, Library of Congress. See Louis Fisher, "The Legislative Veto Invalidation: It Survives," *Law and Contemporary Problems* (autumn 1993): 273–292.

22. Joseph P. Harris, *Congressional Control of Administration* (Washington, D.C.: Brookings, 1964), 284.

23. Quoted in Louis Fisher, "Annual Authorizations: Durable Roadblocks to Biennial Budgeting," *Public Budgeting and Finance* (spring 1983): 38.

24. David Baumann, "Government on Autopilot," *National Journal*, March 13, 1999, 689.

25. John Mintz, "Government's Hobbled Giant," *Washington Post*, September 7, 2003, A1.

26. Tim Stark, "Revisiting Homeland Security," *CQ Weekly*, June 26, 2006, 1772–1779.

27. Eric Lipton, "'Breathtaking' Waste and Fraud in Hurricane Aid," *New York Times*, June 27, 2006, A1.

28. In October 2006, Appropriations Chair Jerry Lewis, R-Calif., dismissed most of the S & I staff. See Steven T. Dennis, "House Appropriations Dismisses 60 Investigators," *CQ Today*, October 19, 2006, online version. However, it is expected that in 2007, David Obey, Wis., the Democratic chair of the Appropriations Committee, will reconstitute the S & I team.

29. *Workshop on Congressional Oversight and Investigations*, 199.

30. "Department of Homeland Security Appropriations Bill, 2005," House Report 108–541, June 15, 2004, 60; and "Department of Homeland Security Appropriations Bill, 2006," House Report 10–979, May 13, 2005, 58.

31. *Congressional Record*, September 5, 2003, S11136; Helen Dewar, "Senate Blocks Overtime Revamp," *Washington Post*, September 11, 2003, A1.

32. Slade Gorton and Larry Craig, "Congress's Call to Accounting," *Washington Post*, July 27, 1998, A23.

33. Christopher Lee, "Into the Oversight Void Step the Inspectors General," *Washington Post*, January 12, 2006, A19.

34. *The Inspectors General Act: 20 Years Later*, hearings before the Senate Committee on Governmental Affairs, 105th Cong., 2d sess., September 9, 1998, S. Hrg. 105737, 4. See K. Daniel Glover, "In the Belly of the Beast," *National Journal*, November 1, 2003, 3350–3352.

35. Larry Margasak, "Gov't Watchdogs Under Attack from Bosses," *Los Angeles Times*, December 27, 2006, (online edition).

36. Michael Kirst, *Government without Passing Laws* (Chapel Hill: University of North Carolina Press, 1969), 37. See also William Rhode, *Committee Clearance of Administrative Decisions* (East Lansing: Michigan State University Press, 1959).

37. Holbert N. Carroll, *The House of Representatives and Foreign Affairs*, rev. ed. (Boston: Little, Brown, 1966), 172. A good example of nonstatutory controls involves the reprogramming of funds within executive accounts. Reprogramming refers to the expenditure of funds for purposes not originally intended when Congress approved the department's budget. Agencies secure approval for reprogramming from the appropriate House and Senate committees.

38. *New York Times*, May 12, 1983, B8. See also *New York Times*, October 22, 1982, A16.

39. See, for example, Robert A. Katzmann, "Justice Breyer: A Rival for Scalia on the Hill's Intent," *Roll Call*, May 30, 1994, 5, 15. See also Cornell Clayton, "Separate Branches Separate Politics: Judicial Enforcement of Congressional Intent," *Political Science Quarterly* (winter 1994–1995): 843–872; *Interbranch Relations*, hearings before the Joint Committee on the Organization of Congress, 103d Cong., 1 sess., June 29, 1993.

40. Jonathan Kaplan, "High Court to Congress: Say What You Mean," *The Hill*, February 5, 2003, 21.

41. *Congressional Record*, June 27, 2006, H4675.

42. Ellen C. Collier, "Foreign Policy by Reporting Requirement," *Washington Quarterly* (winter 1988): 75.

43. *New York Times*, December 31, 1987, A20.

44. Guy Gugliotta, "Reporting on a Practice that's Ripe for Reform," *Washington Post*, February 11, 1997, A19.

45. See *Reports To Be Made To Congress*, House Document 108–188, 108th Congress, 2d Session, December 20, 2004.

46. Phillip Davis, "After Losing Pollution Battle, White House Seizes Victory," *Congressional Quarterly Weekly Report*, May 23, 1992, 1440. See also Pamela Fessler, "Complaints Are Stacking Up as Hill Piles on Reports," *Congressional Quarterly Weekly Report*, September 7, 1991, 2562–2566.

47. John Stanton, "Democrats Put Money On New Oversight Plan," *Roll Call*, January 25, 2006, 19.

48. Richard Wolf, " 'Blogosphere' Spurs Governmental Oversight," *USA Today*, September 12, 2006, 4A.

49. George Archibald, "Panel Ties Funding to Ridge Testimony," *Washington Times,* March 22, 2002, A1.
50. G. Calvin McKenzie, "Hung Out to Dry," *Washington Post,* April 1, 2001, B5.
51. *Congressional Record,* July 29, 1987, S21504.
52. *New York Times,* April 14, 1983, B10.
53. Stephen Barr, "OMB Nominee Gets Earful at Confirmation Hearing," *Washington Post,* September 16, 1999, A11.
54. See, for example, Robert T. Nakamura and Frank Smallwood, *The Politics of Policy Implementation* (New York: St. Martin's Press, 1980); George C. Edwards III, *Implementing Public Policy* (Washington, D.C.: CQ Press, 1980); and *Program Evaluation: Improving the Flow of Information to the Congress,* General Accounting Office Report, GAO/PEMD-95–1, January 1995, 84.
55. John R. Johannes and John C. McAdams, "Entrepreneurs or Agent: Congressmen and the Distribution of Casework, 1977–1978," *Western Political Quarterly* (September 1987): 549.
56. Lee H. Hamilton, "Constituent Service and Representation," *New Bureaucrat* (summer 1992): 12.
57. *Congressional Record,* July 14, 1988, E2397.
58. Richard S. Beth, *Resolutions of Inquiry in the House of Representatives: A Brief Description,* Congressional Research Service Report 87–365, April 22, 1987, 2.
59. See Louis Fisher, "House Resolutions of Inquiry," CRS Report, May 12, 2003.
60. Quoted in "Judiciary," National Journal's *CongressDailyPM,* April 6, 2006, 13.
61. Michael Posner, "Judiciary Votes To Seek NSA Surveillance Documents," *National Journal's CongressDailyPM,* June 21, 2006, 8.
62. See *Christian Science Monitor,* August 5, 1982, 1.
63. *Congressional Record,* June 8, 1983, H3737.
64. Marc Kaufman, "Senator's HHS Trip for Antibiotic Data Yields Only Ire," *Washington Post,* June 15, 2006, A10.
65. Juliet Eilperin, "Focus Falls on a Reluctant Warrior," *Washington Post,* August 16, 2001, A23.
66. Karen Tumulty, *Time,* December 4, 2006, 47.
67. Ben Pershing, "Waxman Invokes Arcane Rule in Suit," *Roll Call,* March 25, 2002, 3.
68. See especially Aberbach, *Keeping a Watchful Eye.*
69. *History of the United States House of Representatives, 1789–1994,* H. Doc. 103324 (Washington, D.C.: Government Printing Office, 1994), 262. Frederick Kaiser, specialist, Congressional Research Service, Library of Congress, wrote this study's chapter on oversight.
70. David Firestone, "Dizzying Dive to Red Ink Poses Stark Choices for Washington," *New York Times,* September 14, 2003, A1.
71. See Susan Page, "Bush Unscathed by Investigations: Here's Why," *USA Today,* August 13, 2003, 1A.
72. Dana Milbank, "Bush's Fumbles Spur New Talk of Oversight on Hill," *Washington Post,* December 18, 2005, A7.
73. David Nather, "Congress as Watchdog: Asleep on the Job?" *CQ Weekly,* May 22, 2004, 1190.
74. Ronald Brownstein, "Treating Oversight as an Afterthought Has Its Costs," *Los Angeles Times,* November 19, 2006 (online edition).

75. Richard Cohen, "King of Oversight," *Government Executive,* September 1988, 17.
76. *Congressional Record,* June 12, 2000, S4945.
77. Robin Toner, "For Republicans, a Swelling Tide of Trouble," *New York Times,* September 29, 2005, A21.
78. Matthew D. McCubbins and Thomas Schwartz, "Congressional Oversight Overlooked: Police Patrols versus Fire Alarms," *American Journal of Political Science* (February 1984): 165–179.
79. *Workshop on Congressional Oversight and Investigations,* 5.
80. *Ibid.,* 144.
81. Allen Schick, "Politics through Law: Congressional Limitations on Executive Discretion," in *Both Ends of the Avenue,* ed. Anthony King (Washington, D.C.: American Enterprise Institute for Public Policy Research, 1983), 166.
82. Joel Brinkley, "Energy Dept. Contractors Due for More Scrutiny," *New York Times,* November 24, 2002, 21.
83. Alasdair Roberts, "Lockbox Government," *Government Executive,* May 2000, 28.
84. Tichakorn Hill, "Gingrich: Government's Problem Is 'Gotcha' Culture," *Federal Times,* July 18, 2005, 12.
85. *Congress Speaks: A Survey of the 100th Congress* (Washington, D.C.: Center for Responsive Politics, 1988), 163.
86. See Frank Smist, *Congress Oversees the United States Intelligence Community, 1947–1994,* 2d ed. (Knoxville, Tenn.: University of Tennessee Press, 1994) and Mark Lowenthal, *Intelligence: From Secrets to Policy,* 2d ed. (Washington, DC: CQ Press, 2003).
87. Morris S. Ogul, "Congressional Oversight: Structures and Incentives," in *Congress Reconsidered,* 2d ed., ed. Lawrence C. Dodd and Bruce I. Oppenheimer (Washington, D.C.: CQ Press, 1981), 330.

CHAPTER 10

A Dynamic Process

A NYONE WHO views lawmaking in Congress as a precise, neat process of drafting, debating, and approving legislation overlooks the dynamic forces at work on Capitol Hill. It is not a static institution, in part because of the constant influx of new members who bring fresh views, ideas, and perspectives to the lawmaking process. Thus, "the reality of passing legislation on Capitol Hill," observed Sen. Richard Durbin, D-Ill., "deals a lot with people. If you don't understand the people and the power they have, you're not likely to succeed." [1]

For better or worse, the interests, pressures, perceptions, and prejudices of members of Congress change quickly, a result in part of the election cycle, but also of other conditions and influences. The demands made by the presidency and the courts, international events, lobbying groups, and media disclosures are some of the ever-present forces that affect lawmaking. Congress is an institution in which procedures reflect and, in turn, perpetuate the messiness, openness, pragmatism, compromise, and deliberateness so characteristic of much American policymaking. As a House chairman said: "Legislation is like a chess game more than anything else. It is a seemingly endless series of moves, until ultimately somebody prevails through exhaustion, or brilliance, or because of overwhelming public sentiment for their side." [2] Sen. Orrin Hatch, R-Utah, provided this explanation of why certain ideas become law and others do not.

> Bills become law generally for one of three reasons. First, a member makes the bill a top priority and is willing to expend the time and effort to build sufficient support to guarantee its passage. Second, a large group of constituents in multiple jurisdictions make passing a bill more politically attractive than doing nothing. Third, Congress is forced to respond to an event so tragic or compelling that the event itself overwhelms all possible criticism. [3]

At every stage of the legislative process a winning coalition must be formed to carry a policy recommendation up the next rung of the legislative ladder; otherwise, its progress is jeopardized. Along that way, that coalition changes as the forces that mold it change. Meanwhile, while some coalitions are forming to advance legislation, others may be forming to tear it down. If opponents fail in one session of Congress, they always can come back in the next to try again. In the judgment of Sen. Alan K. Simpson, R-Wyo. (1979–1997), "In politics there are no right answers, only a continuing flow of compromises between groups resulting in a changing, cloudy, and ambiguous series of public decisions where appetite and ambition compete openly with knowledge and wisdom." [4]

Despite its built-in—and frequently beneficial—inefficiencies, Congress's policymaking role is firmly grounded in the Constitution. But the preeminent place envisioned for Congress by the drafters of the Constitution has been modified by the growth in executive power that characterized the twentieth century and, so far, the early twenty-first century. President George W. Bush has been especially aggressive in claiming executive authority (warrantless wiretaps and reinterpreting laws via signing statements are examples) in part, as Senator Chuck Hagel, R-Neb., said, because "Congress has essentially been complicit in letting him do it. The key is that Bush ha[d] a Republican Congress [for most of his two terms]; of course if it was a Clinton presidency we'd be holding hearings." [5] Whether the elective branches are united or divided in terms of party control, the basic point is that with assertive presidents "Congress must constantly stand guard for increased encroachment by the President on the basic powers of the House and Senate because of the danger that these powers can be absorbed or redistributed to the advantage of the chief executive." [6] Still, the constitutional separation of powers has preserved for Congress an independent role that distinguishes it from legislative bodies in most other democracies.

The mechanics of legislating influence the policymaking process. Procedural details and nuances have a crucial policy impact, and understanding why certain policies are adopted and others are not is impossible without an appreciation of the rules governing the process. Substance, in short, can be shaped through procedure. The Senate's tradition of lengthy debate is "a wonderful tool to . . . expose legislation to more careful consideration," said a Senate Democratic leader. "You hold many of these pieces of legislation up to the light of day and share the concerns you have with the American public, and that exposure is extremely powerful." [7]

Congress's informal procedures and practices are often as important as its formal rules. For example, neither chamber needed rules changes to permit lawmaking through megabills. They emerged from a variety of governing challenges (issue complexity, fiscal deficits, jurisdictional strife, and the like) that compounded the difficulties of lawmaking—and augmented the authority of party leaders—and from legislative-executive conflicts. As a legislative scholar noted: "Leaders gain power with omnibus bills and, because they assemble omnibus bills, are afforded the opportunity to advance party agenda items." He added that omnibus legislating "also helps Congress by veto-proofing items the president opposes. Legislation that is headed to a veto stands a better chance in an omnibus bill alongside main items the president supports." [8] Rank-and-file lawmakers sometimes lament the use of megabills, even though they may vote for them, because they usually have little time to learn the content of these massive bills.

Moreover, no rules changes mandated that legislators must play both the inside game (maneuvering behind the scenes at multiple lawmaking stages to pick up support for legislation) and the outside game (generating public support) to push controversial measures through the House and Senate. "Being a good legislator means you have to do both," remarked a House leader. "If you are going to pass important legislation, you have to both deal with Members and put together coalitions in the country." [9]

The rules of the game are as important in illuminating the outcomes of the legislative process as they are in comprehending who wins at any competition—the presidential nominating system, for example. The electoral strategy of a presidential candidate in the general campaign cannot be fully appreciated without understanding the electoral college or the techniques of raising campaign funds. Similarly, one cannot comprehend the behavior of members of Congress as participants in policy formation without knowledge of the formal and informal rules and procedures under which they operate.

Congressional rules and practices have an effect on policy outcomes. For example, according to one Senate rule, an extraordinary majority of the Senate is required to invoke cloture. Therefore, in the Senate a well-organized minority can block passage of legislation desired by a majority—such as in the 1950s and 1960s when civil rights legislation was repeatedly delayed by the opponents' use of the filibuster. Final policy outcomes also are influenced by special rules from the House Rules Committee, which may limit or prevent amendments from being offered on the floor by minority party members.

However, the rules themselves may change in response to events or policy goals. Some rules are modified or ignored, while new ones come out of struggles over a particular problem. The mixed results and unanticipated consequences that attend some procedural revisions can even disgruntle members who originally supported rules changes. For example, simplifying the complexities of the budget process, which today can require members to vote over and over on the same issue as they consider authorization, appropriation, budget, or tax measures, is no easy task when 535 lawmakers want a say in how and what fiscal decisions are made.

An ostensibly procedural decision also can be used to mask a policy objective. When members vote to table a bill, procedurally it appears as if they are merely postponing consideration of it. But such a procedure usually sidetracks the legislation permanently, while allowing members to say they did not take a position on the measure.

Important, too, are the differences in the way the two chambers operate. Each chamber functions under rules and procedures that reflect its basic constitutional design. A close examination of the differences as well as the similarities between the two bodies is indispensable to an accurate understanding of how Congress functions. Unlike those of the House, said Sen. Robert C. Byrd, D-W.Va., the rules in the Senate favor the minority: "They were meant to favor the minority to prevent the majority from running over the minority. That is why there is a Senate. That is why this Senate ought to remain a Senate and not become a second House of Representatives." [10]

The most significant and enduring feature of the rules is that they usually require bills to pass through a labyrinth of decision points before they can become law. Generally, passing legislation is more difficult than defeating it. To move their bills through the multiple decision points, each a potential roadblock, members of Congress must engage in a constant cycle of coalition building, using various bargaining techniques. The shifting coalitions combine, dissolve, and recombine in response to the widely varying issues and needs of members. Unlike in the past, when a few barons dominated legislative policy making, today's Congress operates in an environment in which scores of members have some—and often significant—bargaining power.

Coalition building is possible primarily for two reasons. First, members of Congress, who represent diverse constituencies, are not equally concerned about every item on the legislative agenda. Second, members pursue many objectives other than the enactment of legislation. They may seek reelection, election to higher office, appointment to prestigious committees, or personal conveniences such as additional staff or office space. These conditions create numerous opportunities for coalition building through three major types of bargaining—logrolling, compromise, and the distribution of nonlegislative favors (primarily by the congressional leadership).

Another factor determining whether a series of majority coalitions can be built is the extent to which members are in general agreement that a law is required or inevitable on a particular subject. Members may have widely divergent views on the solution to the problem, but they usually will work to compromise their differences when dealing with must-pass legislation.

Time influences the entire congressional process. As the two-year cycle of a Congress runs its course, every procedural device that can be employed has a policy consequence—either delaying or speeding up the processing of legislation. Frequently, as the countdown to final adjournment occurs, the bargaining process shifts into high gear. Bills that have been deadlocked for months are moved along swiftly as logrolling and compromises save bills in which members have a vested interest. Deadlines and threatened or actual procedural and policy crises frequently activate the lawmaking process. There, "the sharpness of the ideological, political, and partisan divisions [in contemporary Congresses] means that most controversial areas come down to end games; every major player is willing to wait, believing that he, she, or they will have maximum leverage at the end of the tunnel." [11] Stalled legislation dies if not enacted before Congress's final adjournment.

During the past dozen years, Congress has undergone significant transformations. Some of the changes resulted from the 1995 GOP takeover of Congress after Republicans had been the House minority for forty years; other changes have been under way for some time or have recently assumed greater significance. Together, they have influenced the character of Congress's procedural and policy politics. Among these developments are the following.

Centralization of Authority in the Speakership. Recent Speakers of the House, such as Jim Wright, D-Texas (1987–1989) and Thomas S. Foley, D-

Wash. (1989–1995), had an impressive array of formal and informal powers that strengthened their hand in the lawmaking process. None, however, compares with authority exercised by Speaker Newt Gingrich, R-Ga. (1995–1999), in the House and in the larger political system. Strongly supported by party colleagues, especially junior Republicans, Gingrich took command of the House in the mid-1990s as few leaders before him. Not only did he set the nation's agenda when he assumed the Speakership, functioning as the House's chief executive officer and relying on Majority Leader Dick Armey of Texas to be the chief operating officer on the House floor, but he also bypassed the custom of seniority to handpick loyalists to chair committees crucial to the success of the Republican agenda. As one congressional journalist noted about Gingrich's first 100 days in office, "The notion of a House that's balkanized into legislative fiefdoms ... has become antiquated. Instead, the House is driven by a Speaker who wields extraordinary power and by rank-and-file Members who are intent on proving to a skeptical public that they can change how Washington works." [12]

In an unprecedented event and path-breaking expansion of the bully pulpit role long associated with presidents, Speaker Gingrich requested and received free, prime-viewing television time to address the nation after House action on the GOP's governing agenda, called the Contract with America.[13] But congressional history demonstrates that centralized authority is not a permanent condition in either chamber; instead, the forces of centralization versus decentralization are constantly in play, and they regularly adjust and reconfigure in response to new conditions and circumstances. And so later, at the end of the 105th Congress (1997–1999), Gingrich left the House, in large measure because he had lost the support of many GOP colleagues.

His successor, J. Dennis Hastert, R-Ill., (1999–2007) operated somewhat differently than Gingrich in his leadership post. Not only did he prefer a lower public profile than that favored by Gingrich, but he also stressed more consultation with the Republican rank and file. Hastert consolidated power in a trio of top GOP leaders—himself (as Speaker), the majority leader (first Tom DeLay, Tex., and later John Boehner, Ohio) and the majority whip (Roy Blunt, Mo.). The three were able to move "top agenda items while wielding a historically small margin of control in a remarkably polarized House." [14] However, Hastert still exercised significant top-down command of the House and his party. Like Gingrich, Hastert was not reluctant to bypass standing committees, utilize task forces, select party loyalists as conferees, impose sanctions against uncooperative chairs or partisan colleagues, instruct committee chairs to deal with certain bills, restrict the role of minority party members, or construct majorities exclusively from within GOP ranks.

It is still too early to know at this juncture how Speaker Nancy Pelosi, D-Calif., (2007–) will manage the House. On the one hand, she has made it plain that she expects to be "Speaker of the House," and not "Speaker of the Democratic Party." However, early signs also indicate that her leadership style will be "closer to that of Gingrich and his GOP leadership successors"—a top-down, centralized approach—than to the consultative model of earlier Democratic Speakers, such as Thomas "Tip" O'Neill, Mass. (1977–1987), and Thomas Foley, Wash. "At every turn," wrote a congressional journalist, "Pelosi has exercised command-and-control," whether it be in crafting the Democrats' "100-hour agenda," orchestrating opening-day procedural changes to the House rulebook, indicating her preference for Rep. Henry Waxman, Calif., to be the Democrats' leader on oversight rather than Rep. John Dingell, Mich., or stifling talk of impeaching President Bush by Judiciary Chairman John Conyers, Mich.[15]

The heightened partisanship in the House and Senate motivates leaders in both chambers—majority and minority—to encourage, and often get, party loyalty on various key votes. "Procedure is always a party vote," emphasized a House GOP leader.[16] And failure to toe the line carries some political risks. "The truth is, if you don't always vote with [the GOP] leadership," said Rep. Jeff Flake, R-Ariz., "you'll often get a primary challenge from somebody who will walk in lockstep with them." [17] The persuasive powers and the assistance top party leaders can provide promote support for leadership decisions. Probably more compelling is the argument made by majority leaders to their partisans that if they are to maintain control, they must stick together and do whatever it takes politically and procedurally to retain their status. Similarly, when the chambers are narrowly divided, minority leaders urge their members to follow the leadership's playbook because it will lead to majority control. "Without unity, we really can't make ourselves heard," noted a Senate minority leader. "When you have multi-voices, you have no voice." [18]

Procedural-Policy Choreography. Both congressional parties in each chamber regularly employ a mix of political strategies to win outside support for their fundamental procedural and policy priorities. They have theme teams, message boards, and scores of party sessions to coordinate and transmit a clear and coherent message to the public. They also hire consultants to assist them in devising effective communications or "message" strategies and employing words as political weapons. For example, congressional Republicans substitute the words "death tax" for the estate tax and contend that "cut and run" is the Iraq policy of Democrats. In reply, Democrats taunt Republicans with phrases like the "debt tax" they impose on American families because of escalating deficits and their strategy of "stay the course" in Iraq. A key objective of such efforts is to frame the national debate in a way that mobilizes public support behind GOP or Democratic congressional objectives and that rebuts attacks by opponents. Both congressional parties employ field hearings, interactive Web sites, rallies, focus groups, on-line petitions, blogs, podcasts, cable TV, polls and surveys, town meetings, Spanish language Web sites, news conferences, talk radio appearances, Internet outlets, newspaper articles, media events, bus tours, and more with the primary objective of winning public support for their causes and candidates.

Making major policy innovations today usually requires combining various external campaigning techniques with internal procedural coordination (for example, who should offer amendments, when, how, and should they be agreed to, modified, or killed). The objective of these efforts is to build extra political pressure to pass priority legislation. Another dimension of the inside-outside game is to hold or win power by trying to keep the other party on the defensive by portraying its members, for example, as "tax-and-spend" Democrats or "tax-cut-and-borrow" Republicans. Thus, the distinction between campaigning and governing is blurred or sometimes obliterated in the House or Senate. Parties in both chambers regularly use the floor to spotlight their priorities and to activate outside supporters. As Sen. Robert F. Bennett, R-Utah, said: "The Senate has become a campaign platform." A similar claim can be made about some measures taken up in the House: they can be characterized, remarked Rep. David Obey, D-Wis., as "institutional press releases aimed far more at sending political messages than they are at solving problems." [19]

Congress and the Information Age. Congress is wired to a high-tech world that enables members, party leaders, and constituents to communicate politically to shape the legislative process. Technology has had and will continue to have a major impact on Congress, including on the campaign trail (Internet fund-raising or the micro-targeting of electoral messages). Three points illustrate the case. First, the agenda of Congress has been transformed because of developments in technology, telecommunications, and other aspects of the information age. Issues of electronic commerce, Internet security, privacy, nanotechnology, copyright, or secrecy increasingly occupy the attention of lawmakers.

Second, electronic advocacy has added a plebiscitary quality to congressional policy making. Today, many citizens and interest groups make their preferences known almost instantaneously to lawmakers. Bloggers, for example, successfully influenced policymaking in the Senate when they helped to overcome opposition to an earmark reform amendment and to a bill allowing citizens to use the Internet to monitor federal spending.[20] Similarly, lawmakers reach out to constituents via their office or committee Web sites. An important issue for Congress is how to achieve an effective balance between representative government (where policy usually proceeds slowly) and electronic democracy (where fast action is often the objective).

Third, the strategy for moving legislation, as noted earlier, is as much technological—television, radio, the Internet, blogs, and so on—as it is political or procedural. Lawmakers understand the importance of the technological in framing issues, molding public opinion, and generating grassroots support to achieve policy initiatives on Capitol Hill. Technology, too, is one of many factors that influence how legislators make decisions. "[W]e're in the Information Age and we're making decisions in so many different areas that it's a huge help," said Rep. Kevin Brady, R-Texas. "[F]rom a policy standpoint, [computer technology is] very productive for me and it's a very productive way to learn." [21]

Ad Hoc Lawmaking. Today, ad hoc lawmaking is a growth industry on Capitol Hill. At least two different tracks are available for the consideration of legislation. On the first track are measures that follow traditional textbook lawmaking—introduction of a bill, referral to committee, hearings and markup, floor deliberation and conference action, and presidential consideration. On the second track are the priority measures of each party as well as run-of-the-mill measures that get caught up in partisan battles and may become hostages to larger concerns. In these cases, ad hoc lawmaking is often the name of the game. Members find new uses for old rules, employ innovative devices, or bypass traditional procedures and processes altogether to achieve their political and policy objectives. In a hard-to-govern era because of factors such as sharper partisanship, razor-thin congressional majorities, and fiscal deficits, new and unexpected procedural twists to lawmaking are to be expected.

The politics of procedure is different today than in earlier periods. Then, procedural issues were basically an insider's game, driven largely by various tactical considerations (logrolls or compromises, for example) associated with forging winning coalitions. Today, the process of building coalitions on major party and institutional priorities is inseparable from larger, outside political forces (the power of interest groups, the intensity of media coverage, and so on) that influence how Congress operates. The result is a lawmaking process that is more free-flowing and less predictable than in the past.

Resurgence of Sharp Partisanship. Parties have always been important in the modern Congress. Among other things, they organize the House and Senate and advocate substantive agendas. Partisanship is important and useful because it identifies the principles and ideals that orient each party. Former House Majority Leader Tom DeLay, R-Tex., (2003–Sept. 2005), strongly defended a zero-sum (one side wins and the other loses) style of partisanship in his farewell speech to the House. He stated: "For all its faults, it is partisanship based on core principles that clarifies our debates, that prevents one party from straying too far from the mainstream, and that constantly refreshes our politics with new ideas and new leaders." [22] To Republicans, DeLay was a masterful, persuasive, and results-oriented leader; to Democrats, he was a bully who "trampled on legislative traditions in the House and fostered an environment of loose ethical standards that resulted in the growing corruption scandals on Capitol Hill." [23]

Recent Congresses have witnessed heightened political rancor between the parties. Opponents are sometimes viewed as political enemies and compromise and cooperation between the parties on their top priorities are often frowned upon. "Congress has always been a partisan place," said the dean of the House, fifty-year veteran John Dingell, D-Mich., "but never has the atmosphere been as negative and divisive as it is today." [24] Various scholars have highlighted the reasons for this development, such as changes in the constituency bases of the two parties. Democrats have become more liberal and Republicans have become more conservative, placing each party's priority agenda squarely at odds with the other party's. Added to this mix is the ongoing struggle between Democrats and Republicans to win the electoral battle for long-term control of the House and Senate.[25]

Although bitter partisanship in the 1990s and early 2000s was more evident in the "majority rule" House than in the Senate, it is surfacing more frequently in that chamber, even with its reputation for comity and greater reciprocity among its smaller membership. "When I came to the Senate in 1959," said Senator Byrd, "there was partisanship. Everett Dirksen was a partisan. Mike Mansfield was a partisan. But they were not bitter partisans. We didn't have the negativism, the bitter partisanship that we have seen rule the Senate ... and it is getting worse." [26] The breakdown of civility in an environment of partisan polarization compounds the difficulties faced by each chamber in producing legislation. When procedural rules are used solely for dilatory or message purposes, sometimes blocking legislation to influence election outcomes (running against a "do-nothing" Congress, for example), it becomes that much harder for lawmakers to work together in a collegial manner.

Worth noting is that the majority leaders of the 110th Congress—Speaker Pelosi and Senate Majority Leader Harry Reid—have underscored their commitment to run their respective institutions in an open, fair, and collegial manner, restoring the civility that has sometimes been missing in many legislative proceedings. Both leaders, for example, vowed "to conduct full and open conference committees," with no House or Senate conferee excluded from participation because of their partisan affiliation.[27] Of course, if Republicans focus on proposing politically charged amendments designed, for example, to fracture the narrow Democratic majority, then majority leaders will take steps to curb those practices. GOP amendments "which are designed solely for the purposes of creating a 30-second ad," said House Majority Leader Steny Hoyer, Md., are likely to be rejected. "We are not going to be foolish or stupid," he added.[28]

The Return of Deficits. In 2001 the Congressional Budget Office (CBO) projected a surplus of $5.6 trillion over ten years. Today, CBO projects a ten-year deficit of over $2 trillion, stemming largely from tax cuts, entitlement expenditures, the war against terrorists, and homeland security requirements. The deficit projections, combined with a national debt today of about $9 trillion, raise important questions for which there are no easy answers. For example, should Congress revamp its budgeting process so that it can, for example, enact the must-pass appropriations bills on time and strengthen its tools of fiscal discipline? Absent effective congressional budgetary procedures, it is likely that any president's threatened or actual use of the veto will enhance his ability to shape Congress's tax and spending decisions.

Another issue concerns the impending retirement of the "baby boom" generation, some eighty million people. How will Congress be able to pay for the retirement (Social Security) and health needs (Medicare and Medicaid) of this large group of retirees while also funding competing priorities, such as education or homeland security? Governing means making choices, and some of the proposals confronting lawmakers are politically and substantively difficult, such as raising the retirement age or rationing health care. President George W. Bush expressed his belief that a growing economy would eventually resolve the deficit issue, but others disagreed with that view. Optimists hope that current deficit projections are just as wrong as those predicted for most of the 1990s, when the end of that decade saw the arrival of huge, unexpected surpluses.

The Continuity of Congress. After the September 11, 2001, attacks Congress faced an issue that it rarely had to confront in the past: its own survival in the event of a catastrophic attack on the legislative branch that kills or incapacitates most lawmakers. Scores of complex issues are raised by a calamity that could prevent the House or Senate from functioning. Only two will be mentioned to highlight the complicated issues that surround preserving representative government in the event of a catastrophe.

A major issue that confronts the House more than the Senate is how to quickly replace House members when a large number are killed or incapacitated in a terrorist attack. Under the Seventeenth Amendment of the Constitution, senators who are killed can be quickly replaced by gubernatorial appointment. The House is another story, however. Constitutionally, the only method employed to fill House vacancies is special elections, which typically occur 90–120 days after a legislator's death, retirement, or resignation. The Constitution makes no provision for repopulating the House if scores of lawmakers are killed or disabled, a situation that calls into question the institution's ability to function when there are numerous vacancies and many areas of the country lack representation. In 2005, the president signed a law (P.L. 109–55) that called on the states with vacant House seats to hold expedited (within forty-nine days) special elections in the event of extraordinary circumstances. Many lawmakers oppose this idea, and argue that the Constitution should be amended to authorize the appointment of temporary House members in the event of a calamity that causes mass vacancies (twenty-five percent or more of the House membership is dead or incapacitated, for example).

Another concern is the establishment of a quorum in the House. Under the Constitution, "a majority of each [chamber] shall constitute a quorum to do Business." However, under precedents stated in the House rulebook this has been interpreted to mean "that after the House is once organized the quorum consists of a majority of those Members chosen, sworn, and living whose membership has not been terminated by resignation or action of the House." Thus if only five House members were chosen, sworn, and alive after a tragic event, a vote of 3–2 would be sufficient to make crucial policy and political decisions, such as the selection of a new Speaker, even from the minority party. The question, then, is whether decisions made by a handful of lawmakers would be viewed as legitimate by the country.[29]

A related issue is if catastrophic circumstances left scores of lawmakers incapacitated and unable to carry out their legislative duties. How would the House or Senate function a request for a quorum call or a recorded vote revealed fewer than 218 representatives or 51 senators in attendance? To deal with this issue the House adopted a "provisional quorum" rule on the opening day of the 109th and 110th Congresses. It states that after a series of quorum calls (totaling seventy-two hours) reveal the House's inability to establish a quorum, the number of lawmakers who are present will then constitute a provisional quorum for the House to conduct business.[30]

And so the dynamic interplay between policymaking and the rules continues. Precedents and practices are revised or abandoned and new ones established, often with great difficulty, in response to changing needs and pressures. "We always learn in this organization, even though we may think the rules are fixed and firm," stated a senator, "how the fertility of the minds of the Members manages to find ways to expand those rules."[31] Or as Senator Byrd pointed out, the "Senate doesn't operate under the rules it operated under when I came here and that existed up until a few years ago."[32]

Congress's dynamism is ensured by the regular infusion of new members, changing events and conditions, and the fluctuating expectations of citizens. If Congress reduces or increases its lawmaking activity, it usually is not by accident but as a reaction to members' perceptions of what their constituents and the country want. For its part, the nation expects Congress to use its considerable powers and policymaking procedures to help resolve, or at least allay, the pressing issues facing the country.

NOTES

1. Iian Gaff and Mary Lynn Jones, "Lessons About Congress Not Taught in School," *The Hill*, August 7, 2002, 13.
2. *Washington Post*, June 26, 1983, A14.
3. Orrin Hatch, *Square Peg: Confessions of a Citizen Senator* (New York: Basic Books, 2002), 70.
4. *Congressional Record*, May 20, 1987, S6798.
5. Elizabeth Drew, "Power Grab," *The New York Review of Books*, June 22, 2006, 10.
6. Robert V. Remini, *The House: The History of the House of Representatives* (Washington, D.C.: Smithsonian Books, 2006), 467.
7. *New York Times*, April 9, 1995, 18.
8. Glen S. Kurtz, "Omnibus Legislating: An Institutional Reaction to the Rise of New Issues," in *Policy Dynamics*, ed. Frank Baumgartner and Bryan Jones (Chicago: University of Chicago Press, 2002), 212, 225.
9. Richard Cohen, "Taking Advantage of Tax Reform Means Different Strokes for Different Folks," *National Journal*, June 22, 1985, 1459.
10. *Congressional Record*, February 23, 1988, S1124.
11. Norman Ornstein, "Let the End Games Begin," *Roll Call*, September 12, 1994, A23.
12. Richard Cohen, "The Transformers," *National Journal*, March 4, 1995, 528–529.
13. *New York Times*, April 8, 1995, 1.
14. Ben Pershing, "Smith Spars with Leaders," *Roll Call*, March 26, 2003, 13.
15. Richard Cohen, "Fill in the Blanks," *National Journal*, December 16, 2006, 22–23.

16. David Rogers and Jeannie Cummings, "Democrats Aim to Stir Public as Impeachment Nears," *Wall Street Journal,* December 14, 1998, A20.
17. Jonathan Kaplan, "Sometimes, Hammer Acts As Whip," *The Hill,* December 15, 2004, 4.
18. Eliza Newlin Carney, "Running Interference," *National Journal,* November 22, 1997, 2362.
19. The quote by Senator Bennett, *CQ Daily Monitor,* May 23, 2000, 3; and Representative Obey, *Congressional Record,* June 18, 1999, H4643.
20. Robert Bluey, "How Bloggers Took on Harry Reid and Won on Earmark Reform," *The Examiner,* January 18, 2007, 18.
21. George Archibald, "Technology Lets Lawmakers Remain Connected," *Washington Times,* September 12, 1999, C-10. See James A. Thurber and Colton Campbell, eds., *Congress and the Internet* (Upper Saddle River, N.J.: Prentice Hall, 2003).
22. *Congressional Record,* June 8, 2006, H3549.
23. Carl Hulse, "Defiant to the End, DeLay Pats Himself on the Back and Bids the House a Torrid Goodbye," *New York Times,* June 9, 2006, A23.
24. Rep. John Dingell, "Dingell's Own Half Century," *Roll Call,* June 16, 2005, 23.
25. See, for example, David W. Rohde, *Parties and Leaders in the Postreform House* (Chicago: University of Chicago Press, 1991).
26. *Los Angeles Times,* January 30, 1995, A12.
27. Carl Hulse, "With Promises of a Better-Run Congress, Democrats Take On Political Risks," *New York Times,* December 27, 2006, A23.
28. *Ibid.*
29. For a good treatment of these types of issues, see *Preserving Our Institutions: The Continuity of Congress,* The First Report of the Continuity of Government Commission, May 2003. The commission is a joint project of the American Enterprise Institute and the Brookings Institution.
30. John Bryan Williams, "How to Survive a Terrorist Attack: The Constitution's Majority Quorum Requirement and the Continuity of Congress," *William and Mary Law Review,* vol. 48 (2006), 1025–1090.
31. *Congressional Record,* February 26, 1988, S1521.
32. *Congressional Record,* July 26, 2000, S7614.

Glossary of Congressional Terms

act The term for legislation once it has passed both houses of Congress and has been signed by the president or has been passed over the president's veto, thus becoming law. Also used in parliamentary terminology for a bill that has been passed by one house and engrossed. (See **engrossed bill, law.**)

adjournment *sine die* Adjournment without definitely fixing a day for reconvening; literally "adjournment without a day." Usually connotes the final adjournment of a session of Congress. A session can continue until noon, January 3, of the following year, when, under the Twentieth Amendment to the Constitution, it automatically terminates. Both houses must agree to a concurrent resolution for either house to adjourn for more than three days.

adjournment to a day certain Adjournment under a motion or resolution that fixes the next time of meeting. Under the Constitution, neither house can adjourn for more than three days without the concurrence of the other. A session of Congress is not ended by adjournment to a day certain.

amendment A proposal of a member of Congress to alter the language, provisions, or stipulations in a bill or in another amendment. An amendment is usually printed, debated, and voted on in the same manner as a bill.

amendment in the nature of a substitute An amendment that seeks to replace the entire text of a bill. Passage of this type of amendment strikes out everything after the enacting clause and inserts a new version of the bill. A substitute amendment proposes to replace the entire text of a pending amendment.

appeal A member's challenge of a ruling or decision made by the presiding officer of the chamber. In the Senate, the senator appeals to members of the chamber to override the decision. If carried by a majority vote, the appeal nullifies the chair's ruling. In the House, the decision of the Speaker traditionally has been final; seldom are appeals made to the members to reverse the Speaker's stand. To appeal a ruling is considered an attack on the Speaker.

appropriations bill A bill that gives legal authority to spend or obligate money from the Treasury. The Constitution disallows money to be drawn from the Treasury "but in Consequence of Appropriations made by Law."

An appropriations bill usually provides the monies approved by authorization bills, but not necessarily the full amount permissible under the authorization measures. By congressional custom, an appropriations bill originates in the House, and it is not supposed to be considered by the full House or Senate until the related authorization measure is enacted. Appropriations bills are either general or one of two specialized types. (See **continuing resolution, supplemental appropriations bill.**)

authorization bill Basic, substantive legislation that establishes or continues the legal operation of a federal program or agency, either indefinitely or for a specific period of time, or which sanctions a particular type of obligation or expenditure. An authorization normally is a prerequisite for an appropriation or other kind of budget authority. Under the rules of both the House and Senate, the appropriation for a program or agency may not be considered until its authorization has been considered. An authorization also may limit the amount of budget authority to be provided or may authorize the appropriation of "such sums as may be necessary."

bills Most legislative proposals before Congress are in the form of bills and are designated by H.R. in the House of Representatives or S. in the Senate, according to the house in which they originate, and by a number assigned in the order in which they are introduced during the two-year period of a congressional term. Public bills deal with general questions and become public laws if approved by Congress and signed by the president. Private bills deal with individual matters such as claims against the government, immigration and naturalization cases, and land titles, and they become private laws if approved and signed. (See also **concurrent resolution, joint resolution, resolution.**)

bills introduced In both the House and the Senate, any number of members may join in introducing a single bill or resolution. The first member listed is the sponsor of the bill, and all members' names following the sponsor's are the bill's cosponsors. Many bills are committee bills and are introduced under the name of the chair of the committee or subcommittee. All appropriations bills fall into this category. A committee frequently holds hearings on related bills and may agree to one of them or to an entirely new bill. When introduced, a bill is referred to the committee or committees that have jurisdiction over the subject of the bill. Under the standing rules of the House and Senate, bills are referred by the Speaker in the House and by the presiding officer in the Senate. In practice, the House and Senate parliamentarians act for these officials and refer the vast majority of bills. (See also **clean bill, report.**)

budget authority Authority to enter into obligations that will result in immediate or future outlays involving federal funds. The basic forms of budget authority are appropriations, contract authority, and borrowing authority. Budget authority may be classified by (1) the period of availability (one-year, multiple-year, or without a time limitation), (2) the timing of congressional action (current or permanent), or (3) the manner of determining the amount available (definite or indefinite).

calendar An agenda or list of business awaiting possible action by each chamber. The House uses four legislative calendars. (See **Discharge Calendar, House Calendar, Private Calendar, and Union Calendar.**)

In the Senate, all legislative matters reported from committee go on one calendar. They are listed in the order in which committees report them, or the Senate places them on the calendar, but they may be called up out of order by the majority leader, either by obtaining unanimous consent of the Senate or by a motion to call up a bill. The Senate uses one nonlegislative calendar; it is devoted to treaties and nominations. (See **Executive Calendar.**)

Calendar Wednesday   On Wednesdays in the House, committees may be called in the order in which they appear in Rule XV of the House, for the purpose of bringing up any bills from either the House Calendar or the Union Calendar, except bills that are privileged. General debate is limited to two hours. Bills called up from the Union Calendar are considered in the Committee of the Whole. Calendar Wednesday is not observed during the last two weeks of a session and may be dispensed with at other times by a two-thirds vote. This procedure is rarely used and routinely is dispensed with by unanimous consent.

clean bill   Frequently after a committee has finished a major revision of a bill, one of the committee members, usually the chair, will assemble the changes and what is left of the original bill into a new measure and introduce it as a clean bill. The revised measure, which is given a new number, is then referred back to the committee, which reports it to the floor for consideration. This procedure often is a timesaver, because committee-recommended changes in a clean bill do not have to be considered and voted on by the chamber. Reporting a clean House bill also protects committee amendments that might be subject to points of order on germaneness.

cloture   The formal procedure by which a filibuster can be ended in the Senate. A motion for cloture can apply to any measure before the Senate, including a proposal to change the chamber's rules. The signatures of sixteen senators are needed for introduction of a cloture motion, and to end a filibuster the cloture motion must be approved by three-fifths of the entire Senate membership (sixty if there are no vacancies). However, to end a filibuster against a proposal to amend the standing rules of the Senate, a two-thirds vote of senators present and voting is required. The cloture request is put to a roll call vote one hour after the Senate meets on the second day after introduction of the motion. If approved, cloture limits each senator to one hour of debate. The bill or amendment in question comes to a final vote after thirty hours of consideration (including debate time and the time it takes to conduct roll calls, quorum calls, and other procedural motions). (See **filibuster.**)

committee   An entity of the House or Senate that prepares legislation for action by the parent chamber or makes investigations as directed by the parent chamber. Most standing committees are divided into subcommittees, which study legislation, hold hearings, and report bills, with or without amendments, to the full committee. Only the full committee, not a subcommittee, can report legislation to the House or Senate.

Committee of the Whole   The working title of what is formally the Committee of the Whole House on the state of the Union. Its membership is composed of all House members sitting as a committee. Any one hundred members who are present on the floor of the chamber constitute a quorum of the committee. Usually, any legislation must have passed through the regular legislative committee or the Appropriations Committee and must have been placed on the calendar before it can be heard by the Committee of the Whole. Technically, the Committee of the Whole considers only bills directly or indirectly appropriating money, authorizing appropriations, or involving taxes or charges on the public. Because the Committee of the Whole need number only one hundred representatives, a quorum is more readily attained, and legislative business is expedited. Before 1971, members' positions were not individually recorded on votes taken in the Committee of the Whole.

When the full House resolves itself into the Committee of the Whole, it supplants the Speaker with a chair. It then debates a measure and possibly proposes amendments, with votes on amendments as needed. When the committee completes its work on a measure, it dissolves itself by rising. The Speaker returns, and the chair of the Committee of the Whole reports to the House that the committee's work has been completed. At this time members may demand a roll call vote on any first-degree amendment adopted in the Committee of the Whole.

concurrent resolution   A concurrent resolution, designated H. Con. Res. or S. Con. Res., must be adopted by both houses, but it is not sent to the president for a signature and therefore does not have the force of law. A concurrent resolution, for example, is used to fix the time for adjournment of a Congress. It also is used as a vehicle for expressing the sense of Congress on various foreign policy and domestic issues, and it serves as a vehicle for coordinated decisions on the federal budget under the 1974 Congressional Budget and Impoundment Control Act. (See also **bills, joint resolution, resolution.**)

conference   A meeting between representatives of the House and the Senate to reconcile differences when the chambers pass dissimilar versions of the same bill. Members of the conference committee are appointed formally by the Speaker and the presiding officer of the Senate and are called managers, or conferees, for their respective chambers.

A majority of the managers for each house must reach agreement on the provisions of the bill (usually a compromise between the versions of the two chambers) before it can be considered by either chamber in the form of a conference report. When the conference report goes to the floor, it cannot be amended, and, if it is not approved by both chambers, the bill may go back to conference or a new conference may be convened. Informal practices largely govern bargaining in conference committees.

Bills that are passed by both houses with only minor differences need not be sent to conference. Either chamber may concur in the other's amendments, completing action on the legislation. Sometimes leaders of the committees of jurisdiction work out an informal compromise instead of having a formal conference.

continuing resolution   A joint resolution drafted by Congress that continues appropriations for specific ongoing activities of a government department or departments when a fiscal year begins and Congress has not yet enacted all of the regular appropriations bills for that year. The continuing resolution usually specifies a maximum rate at which the agency may incur obligations. This usually is based on the rate for the previous year, the president's budget request, or an appropriations bill for that year passed by either or both houses of Congress, but not cleared.

discharge a committee   Occasionally, attempts are made to relieve a committee from jurisdiction over a measure before it. This is attempted more often in the House than in the Senate, and the procedure rarely is successful.

In the House, if a committee does not report a bill within thirty days after the measure is referred to it, any member may file a discharge motion. Once offered, the motion is treated as a petition needing the signatures of 218 members (a majority of the House). After the required signatures have been obtained, there is a delay of seven days. Thereafter, on the second and fourth Mondays of each month, except during the last six days of a session, any member who has signed the petition must be recognized, if he or she so desires, to move that the committee be discharged. Debate on the motion to discharge is limited to twenty minutes, and, if the motion is carried, consideration of the bill becomes a matter of high privilege.

If a resolution to consider a bill is held up in the Rules Committee for more than seven legislative days, any member may enter a motion to discharge the committee. The motion is handled like any other discharge petition in the House. (For Senate procedure, see **discharge resolution.**)

Discharge Calendar   The House calendar to which motions to discharge committees are referred when they have the required number of signatures (218) and are awaiting floor action.

discharge petition   (See **discharge a committee.**)

discharge resolution   In the Senate, a special motion that any senator may introduce to relieve a committee from consideration of a bill before it. The resolution can be called up for Senate approval or disapproval in the same manner as any other Senate business. (For House procedure, see **discharge a committee.**)

division vote   (See **standing vote.**)

enacting clause   Key phrase in bills beginning "Be it enacted by the Senate and House of Representatives. . . ." A successful motion to strike it from legislation kills the measure.

engrossed bill   The final copy of a bill as passed by one chamber, with the text as amended by floor action and certified by the clerk of the House or the secretary of the Senate.

enrolled bill   The final copy of a bill that has been passed in identical form by both chambers. It is certified by an officer of the house of origin (clerk of the House or secretary of the Senate) and then sent on for the signatures of the House Speaker, the Senate president pro tempore, and the president of the United States. An enrolled bill is printed on parchment.

Executive Calendar This is a nonlegislative calendar in the Senate on which treaties and nominations are listed after being reported from committee.

filibuster A time-delaying tactic associated with the Senate and used by a minority in an effort to prevent a vote on a bill or amendment that probably would pass if voted on directly. The most common method is to take advantage of the Senate's rules permitting unlimited debate, but other forms of parliamentary maneuvering may be used. The stricter rules used by the House make filibusters more difficult, but delaying tactics are employed occasionally through various procedural devices allowed by House rules, such as motions to adjourn. (See **cloture.**)

five-minute rule A debate-limiting rule of the House that is invoked when the House sits as the Committee of the Whole. Under the rule, a member offering an amendment is allowed to speak five minutes in favor, and an opponent of the amendment is allowed to speak five minutes in opposition. Debate is then closed. In practice, amendments regularly are debated more than ten minutes, with members gaining the floor by offering pro forma amendments or obtaining unanimous consent to speak longer than five minutes. (See **strike out the last word.**)

germane Pertaining to the subject matter of the legislation at hand. House amendments must be germane to the bill being considered. The Senate requires that amendments be germane when they are proposed to general appropriations bills, bills being considered once cloture has been adopted, or, frequently, when proceeding under a unanimous consent agreement placing a time limit on consideration of a bill. The 1974 budget act also requires that amendments to concurrent budget resolutions be germane. In the House, floor debate must be germane, and the first three hours of debate each day in the Senate must be germane to the pending business.

House Calendar A listing for action by the House of public bills that do not directly or indirectly appropriate money or raise revenue.

joint resolution A joint resolution, designated H.J. Res. or S.J. Res., requires the approval of both houses and the signature of the president, just as a bill does, and has the force of law if approved. No practical difference exists between a bill and a joint resolution.

A joint resolution generally is used to deal with a limited matter such as a single appropriation. Joint resolutions also are used to propose amendments to the Constitution. They must pass both chambers in identical form but do not require a presidential signature; they become a part of the Constitution when three-fourths of the states have ratified them.

law An act of Congress that has been signed by the president or passed over the president's veto by Congress. Public bills, when signed, become public laws and are cited by the letters P.L. and a hyphenated number. The two digits before the hyphen correspond to the Congress, and the one or more digits after the hyphen refer to the numerical sequence in which the bills were signed by the president during that Congress. Private bills, when signed, become private laws.

legislative day The day extending from the time either house meets after an adjournment until the time it next adjourns. Because the House normally adjourns from day to day, legislative days and calendar days usually coincide. But in the Senate, a legislative day may, and frequently does, extend over several calendar days. (See **recess.**)

marking up a bill Going through the contents of a piece of legislation in committee or subcommittee, considering its provisions in large and small portions, acting on amendments to provisions and proposed revisions to the language, inserting new sections and phraseology, and so on. If the bill is extensively amended, the committee's version may be introduced as a separate bill, with a new number, before being considered by the full House or Senate. (See **clean bill.**)

motion In the House or Senate chamber, a request by a member to institute any one of a wide array of parliamentary actions. A member moves for a certain procedure, the consideration of a measure or amendment, and so on. The precedence of motions, and whether they are debatable, is set forth in the House and Senate manuals.

one-minute speeches Addresses by House members at the beginning of a legislative day. The speeches may cover any subject but are limited to one minute's duration.

override a veto If the president disapproves a bill and sends it back to Congress with his objections, Congress may try to override his veto and enact the bill into law. Neither house is required to attempt to override a veto. The override of a veto requires a recorded vote with a two-thirds majority in each chamber. The question put to each house is: "Shall the bill pass, the objections of the president to the contrary notwithstanding?" (See also **pocket veto, veto.**)

pair A voluntary arrangement between two lawmakers, usually on opposite sides of an issue. If passage of the measure requires a two-thirds majority vote, a pair would require two members favoring the action to one opposed to it. The names of lawmakers pairing on a given vote and their stands, if known, are printed in the *Congressional Record.*

pocket veto The act of the president in withholding approval of a bill after Congress has adjourned. When Congress is in session, a bill becomes law without the president's signature if the president does not act on it within ten days, excluding Sundays, of receiving it. But if Congress adjourns *sine die* within that ten-day period, the bill will die even if the president does not formally veto it. (See also **veto.**)

point of order An objection raised by a member that the chamber is departing from rules governing its conduct of business. The objector cites the rule violated, and the chair sustains the objection if correctly made. The correct order is restored by the chair suspending proceedings of the chamber, until the House or Senate conforms to the prescribed order of business.

president of the Senate   Under the Constitution, the vice president of the United States presides over the Senate. In the vice president's absence, the president pro tempore, or a senator designated by the president pro tempore, presides over the chamber.

president pro tempore   The chief officer of the Senate in the absence of the vice president; literally, but loosely, "president for a time." The president pro tempore, a constitutionally recognized position, is elected by the full membership of the Senate. The recent practice has been to choose the senator of the majority party with the longest period of continuous service.

previous question   A motion for the previous question, when carried, has the effect of cutting off all debate, preventing the offering of further amendments, and forcing a vote on the pending matter. In the House, the previous question is not permitted in the Committee of the Whole. The motion for the previous question is a debate-limiting device and is not in order in the Senate.

Private Calendar   In the House, private bills dealing with individual matters such as claims against the government, immigration, and land titles are put on this calendar. The Private Calendar must be called on the first Tuesday of each month; the Speaker may call it on the third Tuesday of each month as well.

privilege   Privilege relates to the rights of members of Congress and to the relative priority of the motions and actions they may make in their respective chambers. The two are distinct. Privileged questions deal with legislative business. Questions of privilege concern members themselves.

privileged questions   The order in which bills, motions, and other legislative measures are considered by Congress is governed by strict priorities. A motion to table, for example, is more privileged than a motion to recommit. Thus a motion to recommit can be superseded by a motion to table, and a vote would be forced on the latter motion only. A motion to adjourn, however, takes precedence over a tabling motion and is therefore considered of the highest privilege. (See also **questions of privilege.**)

pro forma amendment   (See **strike out the last word.**)

questions of privilege   These are matters affecting members of Congress individually or collectively. Matters affecting the rights, safety, dignity, and integrity of proceedings of the House or Senate as a whole are questions of privilege in both chambers.

Questions involving individual members are called questions of personal privilege. A member rising to ask a question of personal privilege is given precedence over almost all other proceedings. An annotation in the House rules points out that the privilege is derived chiefly from the Constitution, which gives a member a conditional immunity from arrest and an unconditional freedom to speak in the House. (See also **privileged questions.**)

quorum   The number of members whose presence is necessary for the transaction of business. In the Senate and House, it is a majority of the membership: 51 in the Senate and 218 in the House. A quorum is one hundred in the Committee of the Whole. If the absence of a quorum is disclosed in either chamber, the Constitution authorizes a smaller number "to compel the Attendance of absent Members, in such Manner . . . as each House may provide."

readings of bills Traditional parliamentary procedure requires bills to be read three times before they are passed. This custom is of little modern significance. Normally a bill is considered to have its first reading when it is introduced and printed, by title, in the *Congressional Record*. In the House, its second reading comes when floor consideration begins. (This is the most likely point at which a reading of the bill does take place, if there is any.) The second reading in the Senate is supposed to occur on the legislative day after the measure is introduced, but before it is referred to committee. The third reading (again, by title) takes place when floor action has been completed on amendments.

recess Distinguished from adjournment in that a recess does not end a legislative day and therefore does not interrupt unfinished business. The rules in each house set forth certain matters to be taken up and disposed of at the beginning of each legislative day. The House usually adjourns from day to day. The Senate often recesses, thus meeting on the same legislative day for several calendar days or even weeks at a time.

recognition The Speaker of the House has an unchallengeable right of recognition. The presiding officer of the Senate must recognize the first person that he or she sees who is seeking recognition with priority always granted to the Majority Leader.

recommit to committee A motion, made on the floor after a bill has been debated, to return it to the committee that reported it. If approved, recommittal usually is a death blow to the bill. In the House, a motion to recommit can be made only by a member opposed to the bill, and, in recognizing a member to make the motion, the Speaker gives preference to members of the minority party over majority party members.

A motion to recommit may include instructions to the committee to report the bill again with specific amendments or by a certain date. Or the instructions may direct that a particular study be made, with no definite deadline for further action. If the recommittal motion includes instructions to "report the bill back forthwith" and the motion is adopted, floor action on the bill continues; the committee does not actually reconsider the bill.

reconsider a vote A motion to reconsider the vote by which an action was taken has, until it is disposed of, the effect of putting the action in abeyance. In the Senate, the motion can be made only by a member who voted on the prevailing side of the original question or by a member who did not vote at all. In the House, it can be made only by a member on the prevailing side.

A common practice in the Senate after close votes on an issue is a motion to reconsider, followed by a motion to table the motion to reconsider. On this motion to table, senators usually vote as they voted on the original question, which allows the motion to table to prevail, assuming there are no switches. The matter then is finally closed and further motions to reconsider are not entertained. In the House, as a routine precaution, a motion to reconsider usually is made every time a measure is passed. Such a motion almost always is tabled immediately, thus eliminating the possibility of future reconsideration, except by unanimous consent. Motions to reconsider must be entered in the Senate within the next two days of session after the original vote has been taken. In the House they must be entered either on the same day or on the next succeeding day the House is in session.

recorded vote   A vote on which each member's stand is individually made known. In the Senate, this is accomplished through a roll call of the entire membership, to which each senator on the floor must answer "yea," "nay," or, if he or she does not wish to vote, "present." Since January 1973, the House has used an electronic voting system for recorded votes, including yea-and-nay votes formerly taken by roll calls. A recorded vote is commonly obtained on questions in the House via a request for the constitutional yeas and nays (one-fifth of those present), on the demand of one-fifth (forty-four members) of a quorum, or one-fourth (twenty-five members) of a quorum in the Committee of the Whole. (See **yeas and nays.**)

report   Both a verb and a noun as a congressional term. A committee that has been examining a bill referred to it by the parent chamber reports, or votes out, its findings and recommendations to the chamber when it completes consideration. This process is called reporting a bill.

A report is the document setting forth the committee's explanation of its action. Senate and House reports are numbered separately and are designated S. Rept. or H. Rept. When a committee report is not unanimous, the dissenting committee members may file a statement of their views, called minority views and referred to as a minority report. Members in disagreement with some provisions of a bill may file additional or supplementary views. Sometimes, a bill is reported without a committee recommendation. Adverse reports occasionally are submitted by legislative committees. When a committee is opposed to a bill, it usually fails to report the measure at all. Some laws require that committee reports, favorable or adverse, be made.

resolution   A simple resolution, designated H. Res. or S. Res., deals with matters entirely within the prerogatives of one house or the other. It requires neither passage by the other chamber nor approval by the president, and it does not have the force of law. Many resolutions deal with the rules or procedures of one house. They also are used to express the sentiments of a single house, such as condolences to the family of a deceased member, or to comment on foreign policy or executive business. A simple resolution is the vehicle for a rule from the House Rules Committee. (See also **concurrent resolution, joint resolution, rules.**)

rider   An amendment, usually not germane, that its sponsor hopes to get through more easily by including it in other, often "must pass," legislation. Riders become law if the bills embodying them are enacted. Amendments providing legislative directives in appropriations bills are examples of riders, though technically legislation is banned from appropriations bills. The House, unlike the Senate, has a strict germaneness rule. Thus riders often are Senate devices to get legislation enacted quickly or to bypass lengthy House consideration and, possibly, opposition.

rules   The term has two specific congressional meanings. A rule may be a standing order governing the conduct of House or Senate business and listed among the permanent rules of either chamber. The rules deal with matters such as the duties of officers, the order of business, admission to the floor, parliamentary procedures on handling amendments and voting, and jurisdictions of committees.

   In the House, a rule also may be a resolution reported by the Rules Committee to govern the handling of a particular bill on the floor. The committee may report a rule, also called a special order, in the form of a simple resolution. If the resolution is adopted by the House, the temporary rule becomes as valid as any standing rule and lapses only after action has been completed on the measure to which it pertains. A rule sets the time limit on general debate. It also may waive points of order against provisions of the bill in question, such as nongermane language, or against certain amendments intended to be proposed to the bill from the floor. It may even forbid all amendments or all amendments except those proposed by the legislative committee that handled the bill. In this instance, it is known as a closed or gag rule as opposed to an open rule, which puts no limitation on floor amendments, thereby leaving the bill completely open to alteration by the adoption of germane amendments.

Speaker   The presiding officer of the House of Representatives and the overall leader of the majority party in the chamber. The Speaker is selected by the caucus of the majority party's members and is formally elected by the full House at the beginning of each new Congress.

standing committee   (See **committee.**)

standing vote   A nonrecorded vote used in both the House and the Senate. (A standing vote also is called a division vote.) Members in favor of a proposal stand and are counted by the presiding officer. Then members opposed stand and are counted. There is no record of how individual members voted.

strike out the last (or requisite number of) word   A motion whereby a House member is entitled to speak for five minutes on an amendment then being debated by the chamber. A member gains recognition from the chair by moving to strike out the last word of the amendment or section of the bill under consideration. The motion is pro forma, requires no vote, and does not change the amendment being debated.

substitute   A discrete amendment that replaces the entire text of a pending amendment. Passage of a substitute amendment effectively kills the original amendment by supplanting it. The substitute also may be amended. (See also **amendment in the nature of a substitute.**)

supplemental appropriations bill   Legislation appropriating funds after the regular annual appropriations bill for a federal department or agency has been enacted. A supplemental appropriation provides additional budget authority beyond original estimates for programs or activities, including new programs authorized after the enactment of the regular appropriations act. (See also **appropriations bill.**)

suspend the rules   Often a time-saving procedure for passing bills in the House. The wording of the motion, which may be made by any member recognized by the Speaker, is: "I move to suspend the rules and pass the bill. . . ." A favorable vote by two-thirds of those present is required for passage. Debate is limited to forty minutes and no amendments from the floor are permitted. If a two-thirds favorable vote is not attained, the bill may be considered later under regular procedures. The suspension procedure is in order every Monday, Tuesday, and Wednesday and is intended to be reserved for noncontroversial bills.

table a bill   A motion to lay on the table is not debatable in either house, and usually it is used to achieve final, adverse disposition of a matter. Tabling motions on amendments are effective debate-ending devices in the Senate.

unanimous consent   Proceedings of the House or Senate and action on legislation often take place upon the unanimous consent of the chamber, whether or not a rule of the chamber is being violated. Unanimous consent is employed to expedite floor action, especially in the Senate, and frequently is used for both substantive and routine matters. For example, senators may request the unanimous consent of the Senate to have specified members of their staff present on the floor during debate on an amendment.

unanimous consent agreement   A device used in the Senate to expedite legislation. Much of the Senate's legislative business, dealing with both minor and controversial issues, is conducted through unanimous consent or unanimous consent agreements. On major legislation, such agreements often are printed and transmitted to all senators in advance of floor debate. Once agreed to, they are binding on all members unless the Senate, by unanimous consent, agrees to modify them. An agreement may list the order in which various bills are to be considered, specify the length of time bills and amendments are to be debated and when they are to be voted on, and, frequently, require that all amendments introduced be relevant to the bill under consideration. In this regard, unanimous consent agreements are the Senate's version of rules issued by the House Rules Committee for bills pending in the House. (See **rules.**)

Union Calendar   Bills that directly or indirectly appropriate money or raise revenue are placed on this calendar of the House according to the date they are reported from committee.

veto   Disapproval by the president of a bill or joint resolution (other than one proposing an amendment to the Constitution). When Congress is in session, the president must veto a bill within ten days, excluding Sundays, of receiving it; otherwise, the bill becomes law without the president's signature. When the president vetoes a bill, it must be returned to the house of origin with a message stating the president's objections. (See also **override a veto, pocket veto.**)

voice vote   In either the House or Senate, members answer "aye" or "no" in chorus, and the presiding officer decides the result. The term also is used loosely to indicate action by unanimous consent or without objection.

yeas and nays   The Constitution requires that yea-and-nay votes be taken and recorded when requested by one-fifth of the members present. In the House, the Speaker determines whether one-fifth of the members present requested a vote. In the Senate, practice requires only eleven members (one-fifth of 51). The Constitution requires the yeas and nays on a veto override attempt. (See **recorded vote.**)

Selected Bibliography

Chapter 1. Congress and Lawmaking

Arnold, R. Douglas. *The Logic of Congressional Action*. New Haven, Conn.: Yale University Press, 1990.

Bacon, Donald C., Roger H. Davidson, and Morton Keller, eds. *The Encyclopedia of the United States Congress*. 4 vols. New York: Simon & Schuster, 1995.

Binder, Sarah A. *Minority Rights, Majority Rule: Partisanship and the Development of Congress*. New York: Cambridge University Press, 1997.

Gross, Bertram M. *The Legislative Struggle*. New York: McGraw-Hill, 1953.

Lee, Frances E., and Bruce I. Oppenheimer. *Sizing Up the Senate: The Unequal Consequences of Equal Representation*. Chicago: University of Chicago Press, 1999.

Luce, Robert. *Legislative Procedures*. Boston: Houghton Mifflin, 1922.

———. *Legislative Assemblies*. Boston: Houghton Mifflin, 1924.

———. *Legislative Principles*. Boston: Houghton Mifflin, 1930.

———. *Legislative Problems*. Boston: Houghton Mifflin, 1935.

Quirk, Paul J. and Sarah A. Binder, eds. *The Legislative Branch*. New York: Oxford University Press, 2005.

Schneider, Judy and Michael L. Koempel. *Congressional Deskbook, 2005–2007*. Alexandria, Va.:The Capitol.Net, Inc., 2005.

Silbey, Joel H., ed. *Encyclopedia of the American Legislative System*. 3 vols. New York: Charles Scribner's Sons, 1994.

Tiefer, Charles. *Congressional Practice and Procedure: A Reference, Research, and Legislative Guide*. New York: Greenwood Press, 1989.

Chapter 2. The Congressional Budget Process

Fenno, Richard F., Jr. *The Power of the Purse*. Boston: Little, Brown, 1966.

Munson, Richard. *The Cardinals of Capitol Hill*. New York: Grove Press, 1993.

Palazzolo, Daniel J. *Done Deal? The Politics of the 1997 Budget Agreement*. Chatham, N.J.: Chatham House, 1999.

Rubin, Irene S. *Balancing the Federal Budget*. New York: Chatham House, 2003.

Schick, Allen. *Congress and Money*. Washington, D.C.: Urban Institute Press, 1980.

———. *The Capacity to Budget*. Washington, D.C.: Urban Institute Press, 1990.

———. *The Federal Budget: Politics, Policy, Process*. Revised edition. Washington, D.C.: Brookings Institution Press, 2000.

Strahan, Randall. *New Ways and Means: Reform and Change in a Congressional Committee*. Chapel Hill: University of North Carolina Press, 1990.

Wildavsky, Aaron. *The Politics of the Budgetary Process*. 4th ed. Boston: Little, Brown, 1984.

Wilmerding, Lucius. *The Spending Power*. New Haven, Conn.: Yale University Press, 1943.

Chapter 3. Preliminary Legislative Action

Cooper, Joseph. *The Origins of the Standing Committees and the Development of the Modern House.* Rice University Monograph in Political Science, vol. 56, no. 3, Summer 1970.

Davidson, Roger H., and Walter J. Oleszek. *Congress against Itself.* Bloomington: Indiana University Press, 1977.

Deering, Christopher J., and Steven S. Smith. *Committees in Congress.* 3d ed. Washington, D.C.: CQ Press, 1997.

Evans, C. Lawrence. *Leadership in Committee.* Ann Arbor: University of Michigan Press, 1991.

Fenno, Richard F., Jr. *Congressmen in Committees.* Boston: Little, Brown, 1973.

Frisch, Scott, and Sean Q. Kelly. *Committee Assignment Politics in the U.S. House of Representatives.* Norman: University of Oklahoma Press, 2006.

King, David C. *Turf Wars: How Congressional Committees Claim Jurisdiction.* Chicago: University of Chicago Press, 1997.

Krehbiel, Keith. *Information and Legislative Organization.* Ann Arbor: University of Michigan Press, 1991.

Maltzman, Forrest. *Competing Principals: Committees, Parties, and the Organization of Congress.* Ann Arbor: University of Michigan Press, 1997.

Wilson, Woodrow. *Congressional Government.* Boston: Houghton Mifflin, 1885.

Chapter 4. Scheduling Legislation in the House

Cooper, Joseph, and David W. Brady. "Institutional Context and Leadership Style: The House from Cannon to Rayburn." *American Political Science Review,* June 1981, pp. 411–425.

Cox, Gary W., and Matthew D. McCubbins. *Legislative Leviathan: Party Government in the House.* Berkeley: University of California Press, 1993.

———. *Setting the Agenda: Responsible Party Government in the House of Representatives.* New York: Cambridge University Press, 2005.

Hardeman, D. B., and Donald C. Bacon. *Rayburn.* Austin: Texas Monthly Press, 1987.

"A History of the Committee on Rules." Committee Print, 97th Cong., 2d sess. Washington, D.C.: Government Printing Office, 1983.

Peters, Ronald M., Jr. *The American Speakership.* 2d ed. Baltimore, Md.: Johns Hopkins University Press, 1997.

Rae, Nicol, and Colton C. Campbell. *New Majority or Old Minority? The Impact of Republicans on Congress.* Lanham, Md.: Rowan and Littlefield Publishers, 1999.

Rohde, David. *Parties and Leaders in the Postreform House.* Chicago: University of Chicago Press, 1991.

Chapter 5. House Floor Procedure

Alexander, DeAlva Stanwood. *History and Procedure of the House of Representatives.* Boston: Houghton Mifflin, 1916.

Bach, Stanley, and Steven S. Smith. *Managing Uncertainty in the House of Representatives: Adaptation and Innovation in Special Rules.* Washington, D.C.: Brookings Institution Press, 1988.

Damon, Richard E. "The Standing Rules of the U.S. House of Representatives." Ph.D. dissertation, Columbia University, 1971.

Froman, Lewis A. *The Congressional Process: Strategies, Rules, and Procedures.* Boston: Little, Brown, 1967.

Harlow, Ralph V. *The History of Legislative Methods in the Period before 1825.* New Haven, Conn.: Yale University Press, 1917.

MacNeil, Neil. *Forge of Democracy: The House of Representatives.* New York: David McKay, 1963.

Polsby, Nelson W. "The Institutionalization of the House of Representatives." *American Political Science Review,* March 1968, pp. 144–168.

Sinclair, Barbara. *Legislators, Leaders, and Lawmaking: The U.S. House of Representatives in the Postreform Era.* Baltimore: Johns Hopkins University Press, 1995.

Smith, Steven S. *Call to Order: Floor Politics in the House and Senate.* Washington, D.C.: Brookings Institution Press, 1989.

Chapter 6. Scheduling Legislation in the Senate

Clark, Joseph S. *The Senate Establishment.* New York: Hill & Wang, 1963.

Ehrenhalt, Alan. "Special Report: The Individualist Senate." *Congressional Quarterly Weekly Report,* September 4, 1982, pp. 2175–2182.

Fenno, Richard F., Jr. *Learning to Legislate: The Senate Education of Arlen Specter.* Washington, D.C.: CQ Press, 1991.

Harris, Fred R. *Deadlock or Decision: The U.S. Senate and the Rise of National Politics.* New York: Oxford University Press, 1993.

Hibbing, John R., ed. *The Changing World of the U.S. Senate.* Berkeley, Calif.: IGS Press, 1990.

Rudman, Warren. *Combat: Twelve Years in the U.S. Senate.* New York: Random House, 1996.

Chapter 7. Senate Floor Procedure

Binder, Sarah A., and Steven S. Smith. *Politics or Principle? Filibustering in the United States Senate.* Washington, D.C.: Brookings Institution Press, 1997.

Burdette, Franklin L. *Filibustering in the Senate.* Princeton, N.J.: Princeton University Press, 1940.

Caro, Robert A. *Master of the Senate.* New York: Alfred A. Knopf, 2002.

Evans, Rowland, and Robert Novak. *Lyndon B. Johnson: The Exercise of Power.* New York: New American Library, 1966.

Gold, Martin B. *Senate Procedure and Practice.* Lanham, Md.: Rowman & Littlefield, 2004.

Harris, Joseph P. *The Advice and Consent of the Senate.* Berkeley: University of California Press, 1953.

Matthews, Donald. *U.S. Senators and Their World.* Chapel Hill: University of North Carolina Press, 1960.

Mucciaroni, Gary, and Paul Quirk. *Deliberative Choices: Debating Public Policy in Congress.* Chicago: University of Chicago Press, 2006.

Shuman, Howard E. "Senate Rules and the Civil Rights Bill: A Case Study." *American Political Science Review,* December 1957, pp. 955–975.

Sinclair, Barbara. *The Transformation of the U.S. Senate*. Baltimore: Johns Hopkins University Press, 1989.

Chapter 8. Resolving House-Senate Differences

Fenno, Richard F., Jr. *The United States Senate: A Bicameral Perspective*. Washington, D.C.: American Enterprise Institute for Public Policy Research, 1982.

Longley, Lawrence D., and Walter J. Oleszek. *Bicameral Politics: Conference Committees in Congress*. New Haven, Conn.: Yale University Press, 1989.

McCown, Ada C. *The Congressional Conference Committee*. New York: Columbia University Press, 1927.

Pressman, Jeffrey L. *House vs. Senate: Conflict in the Appropriations Process*. New Haven, Conn.: Yale University Press, 1966.

Steiner, Gilbert. *The Congressional Conference Committee, Seventieth to Eightieth Congresses*. Urbana: University of Illinois Press, 1951.

Vogler, David J. *The Third House: Conference Committees in the U.S. Congress*. Evanston, Ill.: Northwestern University Press, 1971.

Chapter 9. Legislative Oversight

Aberbach, Joel D. *Keeping a Watchful Eye: The Politics of Congressional Oversight*. Washington, D.C.: Brookings Institution Press, 1990.

Bond, Jon R., and Richard Fleisher, eds. *Polarized Politics: Congress and the President in a Partisan Era*. Washington, D.C.: CQ Press, 2000.

Fisher, Louis. *Constitutional Conflicts between Congress and the President*. 4th ed., revised. Lawrence: University of Kansas Press, 1997.

Foreman, Christopher H. *Signals from the Hill: Congressional Oversight and the Challenge of Social Regulation*. New Haven, Conn.: Yale University Press, 1988.

Gilmour, Robert S., and Alexis A. Halley, eds. *Who Makes Public Policy: The Struggle for Control between Congress and the Executive*. Chatham, N.J.: Chatham House, 1994.

Harris, Joseph P. *Congressional Control of Administration*. Washington, D.C.: Brookings Institution Press, 1964.

Light, Paul C. *Monitoring Government: Inspectors General and the Search for Accountability*. Washington, D.C.: Brookings Institution, 1993.

Ogul, Morris S. *Congress Oversees the Bureaucracy*. Pittsburgh, Pa.: University of Pittsburgh Press, 1976.

West, William F. *Controlling the Bureaucracy*. Armonk, N.Y.: M. E. Sharp, 1995.

Chapter 10. A Dynamic Process

Bailey, Stephen K. *Congress Makes a Law*. New York: Columbia University Press, 1950.

Binder, Sarah A. *Stalemate: Causes and Consequences of Legislative Gridlock*. Washington, D.C.: Brookings Institution Press, 2003.

Casey, Chris. *The Hill on the Net: Congress Enters the Information Age*. Chestnut Hill, Mass.: Academic Press Inc., 1996.

Davidson, Roger H., ed. *The Postreform Congress*. New York: St. Martin's Press, 1992.

Evans, C. Lawrence, and Walter J. Oleszek. *Congress under Fire: Reform Politics and the Republican Majority.* Boston: Houghton Mifflin, 1997.

Hibbing, John R., and Elizabeth Thiess-Morse. *Congress as Public Enemy.* New York: Cambridge University Press, 1995.

Jones, Charles O. "A Way of Life and Law." *American Political Science Review,* March 1995, pp. 1–9.

Krehbiel, Keith. *Pivotal Politics: A Theory of Lawmaking.* Chicago: University of Chicago Press, 1998.

Mann, Thomas E., and Norman J. Ornstein. *The Broken Branch.* New York: Oxford University Press, 2005.

Redman, Eric. *The Dance of Legislation.* New York: Simon & Schuster, 1973.

Remini, Robert V. *The House: The History of the House of Representatives.* New York: HarperCollins, 2006.

Schickler, Eric. *Disjointed Pluralism: Institutional Innovation and the Development of the U.S. Congress.* Princeton, N.J.: Princeton University Press.

Sinclair, Barbara. *Unorthodox Lawmaking.* 2d ed. Washington, D.C.: CQ Press, 2000.

Sundquist, James L. *The Decline and Resurgence of Congress.* Washington, D.C.: Brookings Institution, 1981.

Wirls, Daniel and Stephen Wirls. *The Invention of the United States Senate.* Baltimore: The Johns Hopkins University Press, 2004.

Wolfensberger, Donald R. *Congress and the People: Deliberative Democracy on Trial.* Washington, D.C.: Woodrow Wilson Center Press, 2000.

Zelizer, Julian E., ed. *The American Congress.* Boston: Houghton Mifflin Co., 2004.

Internet Sources

Architect of the Capitol (http://www.aoc.gov)

C-SPAN (http://www.c-span.org)

CNN(http://www.cnn.com)

Clerk of the House (http://www.clerk.house.gov)

Congressional Budget Office (http://www.cbo.gov)

Congressional Quarterly (http://www.cq.com)

Government Accountability Office (http://www.gao.gov)

Government Printing Office (http://www.gpoaccess.gov)

The Hill (http://www.hillnews.com)

House of Representatives (http://www.house.gov)

Library of Congress (http://www.thomas.loc.gov)

National Journal (http://www.nationaljournal.com)

Roll Call (http://www.rollcall.com)

Senate (http://www.senate.gov)

Washington Post (http://www.washingtonpost.com)

White House (http://www.whitehouse.gov)

Index